SCAPEGOAT

GENERAL PERCIVAL
OF SINGAPORE

'The Meeting of General Yamashita and General Percival.' *Miyamoto Saburo.*

SCAPEGOAT

GENERAL PERCIVAL
OF SINGAPORE

———

CLIFFORD KINVIG

BRASSEY'S
London • Washington

Also from Brassey's:

MCGEOCH
The Princely Sailor: Mountbatten of Burma

WILLIAMSON
A Most Diplomatic General
The Life of Lord Robertson of Oakridge

HILL/FOLCHER
Marching to Captivity
The War Diaries of a French Peasant 1939–45

FARNDALE
The Years of Defeat – Europe and North Africa 1939–41
(History of the Royal Regiment of Artillery, Volume 5)

———————

First English Edition 1996

UK editorial offices: Brassey's, 33 John Street, London, WC1N 2AT
UK orders: Marston Book Services, PO Box 269, Abingdon, OX14 4SD

North American orders: Brassey's Inc., PO Box 960,
Herndon, VA 22070, USA

Clifford Kinvig has asserted his moral right to be identified as the author of this work.

Library of Congress Cataloging in Publication Data
available

British Library Cataloguing in Publication Data
A catalogue record for this book is available from the British Library

ISBN 1 85753 171 X Hardcover

Typeset by M Rules
Printed in Great Britain by Redwood Books Ltd, Trowbridge

CONTENTS

LIST OF MAPS

LIST OF PLATES

ACKNOWLEDGEMENTS

During his unusual and eventful military career General Percival's papers grew to considerable proportions. In later life they were gathered in great piles in the study of his house in Ware. But there was promise of even more. Conscious of his age and mortality the General had on several occasions said to his son, 'If anything should happen to me, the key to the safe is in my dressing gown pocket.' After the General's death the pockets of the dressing gown were duly examined, but no key could be found. A protracted and fruitless search followed and ultimately a specialist lock-smith had to be called before the safe finally yielded up its treasures – no documents, but a Luger pistol and a primed hand grenade! My access to the General's papers has therefore presented no technical difficulties, but I am nevertheless very grateful to Brigadier A J MacG Percival OBE for so readily giving me unfettered use of those in his possession and of his father's official military papers in the custody of the Imperial War Museum.

Among the many individuals who have been kind enough to share with me their personal reminiscences, documentary records or historical insights concerning General Percival and his times, I should like to thank particularly Professor P H G Allen, Mr P Allwood, Mr J B Bradley, Lieutenant Colonel D C Brown, Mr A K Butterworth, Major General J H Cubbon, Professor A Danchev, Brigadier M D K Dauncey, Colonel P S W Dean, Mr P Elphick, Ms S J Flower, Brigadier A L Fowler, Sheriff Principal G S Gimson, General Sir Charles Harington, Mr R Kandler, Group Captain A N MacGregor, Dr J N Miksic, Colonel Shigemi Mizobe, Mr G S Patterson, Mr H L Payne, Air Commodore H A Probert, Brigadier B L Rigby, Lieutenant Colonel J D Sainsbury and Mr W P Winston.

I am pleased to acknowledge the generous assistance I have received from the staff of several libraries and archives and would like to thank especially Roderick Suddaby, Keeper of Documents and the staff of the Department of Documents, Imperial War Museum; Kate O'Brien, Military Archivist Liddell Hart Centre for Military Archives, King's College London; Tim Ward, Librarian and the staff of the Prince Consort's Library Aldershot; Pamela Bendall, Librarian, Staff College Library Camberley; Peter Boyden and the archival staff of the National Army

Museum; Nigel Lutt of the County Record Office, Bedford; and Rusty Maclean, Librarian and Archivist, Rugby School. The staff of the Bingham Library in Cirencester have also been most helpful in accessing books from beyond their local collection.

I am grateful to the following for permission to quote from unpublished material to which they hold the copyright or private papers in their care: the Controller HMSO for Crown Copyright material in the Public Record Office; the Department of Documents Imperial War Museum; the Trustees of the Liddell Hart Centre for Military Archives; King's College London; the National Army Museum; Rhodes House Library, Oxford; and the Military Secretary, Ministry of Defence (Army). The reproductions of Miyamoto Saburo's paintings appear by permission of Miyamoto Mineko. 'The Meeting of General Yamashita and General Percival' is from the collection of the National Museum of Modern Art, Tokyo.

Finally, my thanks are due to my wife who has borne my preoccupation with General Percival's activities with patience and good humour. Of course, neither she, nor any of the many others who have smoothed the path to the preparation of this study bear any responsibility for the views expressed or judgements reached within it.

Clifford Kinvig   Perrott's Brook, 1996

1

BEGINNINGS

It is 30 January 1965 and St Paul's Cathedral is filled to capacity. The representatives of a grateful nation are gathered to pay a final tribute to one of Britain's greatest sons, the embodiment of the nation's determination and fighting spirit in the Second World War. It is the state funeral of Sir Winston Churchill. Among the congregation, in an unremarkable position towards the rear of the north aisle, there stands a bemedalled, grey-haired old gentleman, tall, if a little stooped, and somewhat weightier than during the active years of his military career, when he cut a lanky, angular figure. He is 78 years old and nearing the end of a busy life himself. In little more than a year's time friends and old comrades will be attending his London memorial service. What thoughts are crossing his mind, one wonders, as he considers the life of the great man whom the leading figures of the world have gathered to salute? His admiration for the nation's war leader is unbounded. Perhaps he muses at the way his own career has been linked, at several vital junctures, with Churchill's. Certainly, his loyal service in support of Churchill's policies had played a significant part in his personal rise to modest eminence, just as it assuredly determined his fall, attended by widespread criticism, and his quiet retirement to relative obscurity, on the pension of his substantive rank of major general, without the knighthood to which his erstwhile lieutenant general's command would customarily have entitled him. His name is Arthur Percival.

General Percival's is one of those reputations forever tarnished by the events of a few short weeks. In May 1941 he flew off to Singapore as the newly promoted GOC Malaya with a reputation as one of the ablest of Britain's younger generals. On 15 February 1942 he surrendered the defeated Army of Malaya Command to Japanese General Yamashita, and led it into three and a half years of captivity after one of the most disastrous campaigns in British history. Like Gamelin over a few days in 1940, and Eden in a few weeks in 1956, Percival over 70 days in 1941–42 was laid low by events. His fall was all the greater because it was the much vaunted and apparently impregnable 'fortress' of Singapore which he surrendered.

The Malayan campaign in which Percival was defeated was not one of those magnificent disasters which live in the memory because of the collective heroism with which the participants challenged their fate – like the

1

Charge of the Light Brigade, the first day of the Battle of the Somme, or even the retreat and evacuation from Dunkirk. The campaign did have many acts of individual and group bravery, but what lives in the memory is less these shining episodes than the uncomfortable fact that the Army of Malaya surrendered to a numerically inferior force and that of those who became *hors de combat* during the campaign, the overwhelming majority were prisoners, not killed and wounded. When the British Official History of the war came to be written, the shocking fate of the thousands of prisoners of war from Malaya merited only ten pages of description in the five volumes of *The War Against Japan*. If General Slim led a forgotten Army, Percival's became an Army in purdah.

The fall of Malaya and Singapore was, moreover, an unredeemed disaster. Elsewhere, General Slim was able to atone for having conducted the longest retreat in British history by later driving the Japanese from Burma; Montgomery achieved exculpation from his division's part in the retreat to Dunkirk by recapturing the seaport in 1944; MacArthur was able to make a triumphant return to the Philippines. But for General Percival and his men there was no such redemption. Singapore was never reconquered, though in 1944 Churchill regarded its recapture as the supreme British objective in the whole of the Indian and Far Eastern theatres.[1] Instead, Malaya and Singapore were quietly reoccupied in early September 1945, while Percival and the emaciated men of his Army of Malaya (though alas not all who had become prisoner) were making their way home to families they had not seen for four years.

The most resonant description of the Singapore tragedy was provided by Churchill himself who stigmatised it as 'the worst disaster and largest capitulation in British history'. He promised an enquiry into its causes, but none was ever held. Much of the blame quickly settled, in the way of these things, on the man on the spot, General Percival. His fellow force commanders, Admiral Sir Tom Phillips and Air Vice Marshal Pulford, had suffered even speedier and more spectacular defeats, but sadly they did not survive the campaign. Their deaths brought a kind of absolution. Yet it was partly their rapid reverses which left the field open, as it were, for Percival's own. None of the other senior commanders in Singapore, Brooke Popham, Wavell and Pownall, were more than transient figures on the scene. The mild-mannered Percival who occupied the stage throughout became an easy scapegoat. He scarcely looked the part of a resolute commander, lacking the suave and handsome confidence of Alexander, the jutting-jawed determination of Slim or even the beady-eyed and pocket-sized presence of Montgomery. Percival became the fall-guy. His appearance, his style of generalship, the mistakes he undoubtedly made during the campaign, these became the reasons for the defeat rather than the minuscule accompaniment they truly were, of a strategic reverse whose causes dated back to the flawed conception upon which the construction of the Singapore Naval Base was predicated, fatally compounded by the Far Eastern policy of Prime Minister Churchill. It was all too easy for those for whom Singapore's defence was at best a blind spot ('I ought to have been told, and I ought to have asked', confessed Churchill), at worst a strategic misjudgement of the gravest proportions, to allow the blame to be taken by the dutiful and unassuming Percival.

***

The military career of Lieutenant General Arthur Percival spans almost exactly the two World Wars of this century. He volunteered for the Army a few hours after the expiry of Britain's ultimatum to Germany at midnight on 4 August 1914 and finally retired from the Service 32 years later on 31 August 1946 when the surrender of Japan was less than a year old. The years which his military service encompassed saw a profound transformation of the British Army in practically every dimension in which it is possible to evaluate it. Percival witnessed at first hand its dramatic expansion from the modest, if much admired, all-regular British Expeditionary Force (BEF) of seven divisions which took the field alongside the troops of France and Belgium that fateful August, into a mass army, the largest and most complex single organisation the British nation ever created. It absorbed seven and three-quarter millions of her men before the guns finally fell silent. He served throughout that war and then through the years of social, economic and political turmoil which followed the Versailles settlement, years of military stagnation and retrenchment in the main, and the ensuing short period of frenetic military expansion, development and reorganisation which preceded the Second World War.

In the second conflict Percival's combat experience was brief, intense and unique. In April 1941, after a series of important but bewilderingly brief appointments, he was passed the poisoned chalice of the command in Malaya and, as the conventional post-war wisdom had it, subsequently presided over the disastrous 70-day campaign which lost Britain her richest colony and culminated in the fall of that jewel in the east – Singapore. Following his release from Japanese imprisonment, Percival served on only long enough to put his military affairs in order and complete his long-delayed despatch before passing quietly from the national military scene unhonoured, the scapegoat for the tragedy which had befallen the British cause in Malaya.

The changes which Percival had witnessed in the Great War were largely quantitative: in the main the decisive battles were won and lost with weapons of a kind which already existed when the war began, though mammoth quantities of them had to be provided before the outcome could be determined. The demand for manpower was, if anything, even more exigent. The Second World War was different. Its outcome was profoundly affected, and in the case of the war against Japan, considerably hastened, by technological developments which occurred during its course. The extent of this transformation during the career of a single officer was indeed remarkable. When Percival first put on uniform the belief was still widespread that the cavalry was 'queen of the battlefield'. As the BEF shaped up for its first clash with the German Army, the commander of its 2nd Cavalry Brigade promised an immediate recommendation for a DSO to the first officer to kill a German with the new pattern cavalry sword.[2] Thirty-one years later it was a weapon of almost unearthly character which hastened Percival's release from incarceration and probably saved his life: the atomic bombs dropped on Hiroshima and Nagasaki. War technology had finally leap-frogged the battlefield and hundreds of thousands of undefeated Japanese soldiers were forced to renounce their most feared characteristic, the fight to the death, to give up their prisoners and surrender without struggle.

Despite the profundity of these changes, the human factor remained a critical determinant in both conflicts. Whatever the state of the technological confrontation, morale was still a vital ingredient and generalship a supremely important factor. The campaign which lies at the heart of this book, the Malayan campaign, was in many ways a test to destruction of Percival's generalship, for virtually every other factor contributing to success had been put into the opposing scale of the military balance. It remains for the reader to determine whether the test was in any sense a fair one. The results were certainly dramatic for Percival. After a military career which had brought him virtually every award which courage, ability and determination could acquire, and a rise through the ranks which had been quite dramatic by contemporary standards, his fall from power and esteem was rapid and almost total. During his years as a prisoner of the Japanese, in Parliament, the Press and numerous books and articles, the finger was being pointed in Percival's direction in the search for responsibility for the Singapore disaster. He had, after all, been hustled out of Malaya extraordinarily rapidly and had given up the fortress after the briefest of fights and with the most recent reinforcements scarcely committed. Was he not therefore responsible?

★★★

There was little about the Percival family to suggest that it might one day boast a general. The family had no tradition of military service of the kind which determined the futures of not a few boys of his background in the last years of Victoria's reign. Alfred Reginald Percival, the future general's father, came from a well-known Northamptonshire family, while his mother Edith belonged to one which was active in the Lancashire cotton industry. At the time when Gladstone became Prime Minister for the fourth and final time, the couple were just settling in at Aspenden in east Hertfordshire where Alfred Percival had secured the position of agent for the prosperous and valuable Hamels Park estate. He was to hold the post for a remarkable 50 years.

The couple had two sons, Neville, the elder by ten months, and Arthur, born on Boxing Day 1887. Having that particular year of birth and being so close in age, the boys were known as the 'Jubilee twins'. It was the Indian summer of Britain's imperial prosperity and the two boys enjoyed the country life of a comfortable middle class family. Alfred Percival was a great countryman, an excellent shot and an able sportsman – talents and inclinations which he passed on to his sons in varying degree. It was a close and loving family, though Alfred was a stern disciplinarian who saw to it that his sons grew up with a clear idea of right and wrong and a keen sense of filial duty and obedience.

At school Arthur Percival seems to have lived a little in the shadow of his brother whom he, understandably as the younger boy, trailed somewhat in academic subjects – an inferiority which insensitive schoolmasters were never loath to point out. Arthur was generally painstaking and industrious, but at times a dreamy scholar; the world outside the classroom had so many competing attractions. After some years at Bengeo School, a private Hertford establishment, in 1901 the two boys went off to Rugby, the famous public school noted for its house system, its emphasis on sport and on the development of individual responsibility among its charges. The boys were entered on the classical side of the school and joined School House, one of the two original boarding foundations. Bengeo had provided a sound foundation for Arthur's work at Rugby but it has to be said that he, like many a general officer before and since, was not a great scholar. The classical tradition was still very strong and the educational process was regarded by many not as an awakening and developmental experience, but as a necessary if bitter-tasting mental medicine. The cry, 'It doesn't matter what you teach them so long as they don't like it', was not always uttered in jest. Arthur struggled manfully with his Latin and Greek unseens and composition, but not generally to much effect: 'not a good classic' was one master's verdict. The headmaster noted that he had 'stuck to his work most gallantly', very much like a commanding officer reporting on a young subaltern's tour in the academic trenches. However, it was ultimately all to good purpose. Arthur left Rugby with a sound if undistinguished Higher Certificate which could have secured him a university place if he had chosen one.

Outside the classroom Percival minor was also something of a late developer. He played most games to a reasonable standard. It is said that while at Rugby he scrummed down with Rupert Brooke who was a direct contemporary. If he ever did it must have been in a scratch side for he never played in the School XV, while Rupert Brooke's strong game was cricket. In fact Arthur did not excel at sport while at Rugby, though he was already showing great promise as a cross-country runner and some ability in racquet sports, besides developing well as a batsman. It was in the Cadet Corps, the Rifle Corps at Rugby, that he showed most promise. Rugby's Army connections were strong; it provided a regular entry into Sandhurst via its 'Army Class' which prepared aspirants for the entrance examination. The Rifle Corps was well supported. Rugby had one of the six largest public school contingents in the country with over 200 boys mustering as rifle cadets. In the Corps as in the classroom, Arthur generally marched a pace behind his brother Neville; indeed he took over the running of the School House cadet section from his brother during his final year at school. He had paraded with the Corps when the combined schools' contingents were reviewed by the Duke of Connaught, and held the rank of junior colour sergeant when he paraded the School House section for inspection by Lord Roberts. Arthur's duties included the keeping of the sub-unit's record, his first experience of military staff work. The firm, regular handwriting which was later to characterise his military papers was already evident in this early example, as was the clearly expressed opinion – the School House section had not done well on the recent tactical exercise as it had been issued with a badly drawn map! But when Arthur left Rugby in 1906 he put things military behind him. He took a position in the City, in the offices of Naylor, Benzon and Company, one of the 40 or so London firms of iron ore dealers trading to support the still massive British iron and steel industry. Indeed, Arthur might have spent his entire working life commuting daily to his office in Abchurch Lane, a short walk from Cannon Street Station, but for the outbreak of the Great War.

2

THE INNS OF COURT OTC

'*He realised at once that men of the world (as most of these early recruits were) would be wasting their time if trained on the rigid barrack-square methods employed at Sandhurst. It was not his object to turn out batches of excellent private soldiers, but men capable of taking their places at once as platoon commanders.*'

Views of the CO Inns of Court OTC

No sooner was Britain officially at war than Arthur Percival decided to enlist. On the day when Lord Kitchener, at the summit of the military hierarchy, was making a reluctant transition from the position of British Agent in Egypt to Secretary of State for War, in a London which he little knew and among statesmen whose political ways were unfamiliar to him, Percival was beginning a similar personal odyssey at the other end of the military hierarchy. This time it was an escape from the metropolis. The 27-year-old Percival was exchanging his rather humdrum office life in the City of London for the position of private soldier in the Inns of Court Regiment of the Officer Training Corps (OTC). The unusual position of this regiment within the larger OTC was little known outside London, scarcely common knowledge within it and not even widely appreciated in the War Office itself. Its contribution to the war effort was nevertheless immense.

There had been a long and distinguished association between what later became the Inns of Court and the defence of the realm dating from the time that the Knights Templar of England first established themselves in the area of Chancery Lane in the Twelfth Century. In 1584 a regiment of volunteers formed from members of the Inns of Court was embodied to meet the national danger posed by the Spanish Armada, developing the tradition by which the local lawyers would re-form their dormant corps whenever danger loomed and then promptly disband it and return to their legal duties when the national emergency had passed. The Inns of Court Regiment was formally embodied as a volunteer unit in 1859 and 40 years later sent a contingent to the Boer War among the famous City Imperial Volunteers. By this time the unique character of the unit had become well established: its ranks, both officers and men, were filled by those drawn from the same social and often the same professional class. It was quite normal for men who enlisted as private soldiers to rise progressively through the ranks to become officers and even occasionally to command the regiment itself. The Eton-educated Viscount Hailsham, for example, later Secretary of State for War and Colonel of the Inns of Court Regiment, had been a mere private in its ranks in 1900 when he was a 28-year-old lawyer.[1] So Arthur Percival was in good company. It was this singular unit's value as a recruiting and training ground for officers which led to its formal recognition as part of the larger OTC which Haldane established in 1908 during his remarkable military reform programme. The Inns of Court OTC has a second claim to singularity: true to its volunteer tradition, and unlike the main school and university elements of the OTC, it was also a unit of the Territorial Force, another of Haldane's introductions.

On Sunday 2 August 1914 the Inns of Court OTC had just started its annual camp under canvas at Perham Down on Salisbury Plain. So tense had the international situation become that the commanding officer, Lieutenant Colonel Errington, had been warned by his brigadier that the training might well be cancelled and the Territorial Force put on a war footing. The camp was alive with rumours. Shortly before midnight on the Sunday evening the message finally came through that the camp was cancelled and by 5.30am on what was already promising to be a beautifully sunny August Bank Holiday Monday the unit had returned to London by train and was marching back to base through the deserted streets of the still sleeping city. Once arrived at their Lincoln's Inn headquarters the territorials quickly dispersed for a much-needed breakfast, the First Avenue Hotel (later a building of the ever expanding War Office) being the favourite venue.

The OTC headquarters occupied No 10 Stone Buildings, one of a row of elegant Georgian buildings built of mellow honey-coloured stone set in a quiet backwater on the fringes of the City of London, sandwiched between the bustle of High Holborn and Fleet Street. The character, much of the historical tradition and many of the staff of the unit were drawn from the Inns of Court themselves and particularly from Lincoln's Inn whose manicured lawns and quiet borders lay to the rear of Stone Buildings. Expecting that the order for the embodiment of the Territorial Force would not long be delayed, Errington had dismissed his men with the caution that they should be ready to rejoin at any moment. However, it has to be admitted that the full embodiment of the unit that Monday morning would have added little to the strength of the Territorial Force charged with the home defence of Britain; although the unit had an establishment of 424, it was seriously below strength.

Throughout the day Errington waited impatiently for the rush of recruits which he hoped the growing imminence of war would bring; but his expectations were not met. It was, after all, the last day of a glorious bank holiday week-end. Only six doughty souls presented themselves for enlistment. Convinced that the public at large needed reminding of his regiment's existence, Errington drafted a letter of exhortation to the London newspapers, an act typical of the many independent local initiatives which would do so much to swell recruitment in the coming months, and of course very characteristic of the Territorials. The following day the order for the embodiment of the 14 divisions of the Territorial Force was issued and though it was still some days before Kitchener's piercing eye and stabbing finger were to challenge the national conscience from countless billboards, the flood of recruits began. Two hundred and thirteen presented themselves at Stone Buildings over the next two days, 106 of them, including Arthur Percival, on the first day of the war. By an odd chance Percival was the 1000th recruit to have joined the Inns of Court OTC since it had first become part of the Territorial Force in 1908.[2]

One can but speculate as to Arthur's particular motives for being so quick off the mark, though his impulsions were no doubt shared by many who came forward the instant the threat of war became reality. The golden summer of 1914 has since passed into legend and Arthur may well have spent his sultry office days, and particularly that Bank Holiday week-end, wondering whether he really wanted to spend the rest of his working life commuting to his city office. He had many friends in public service and numerous old Rugbeians of his acquaintance were already regular Army officers, Henry Pownall, George Giffard and John Marshall-Cornwall (all subsequently generals) prominent among them. He frequently sat with Army officers at School House old boys dinners and, of course, he had been prominent in the school's Cadet Corps himself. Though there was no tradition of military service in his family, he would have sensed much less of a gap between himself and those in uniform than many who stepped forward that day. If these had been his thoughts then the international situation which developed over that climactic week-end must surely have ended his doubts and impelled him to action. First had come the peremptory German demand for passage through Belgian territory in anticipation of France's 'hostile attack', then King Albert's courageous refusal, next the roars of supportive applause in Parliament which greeted Lord Grey's account of the threat to Belgium and his reminder of Britain's 'obligations of honour and interest as regards the Belgian treaty'; finally had come the German invasion itself and the British ultimatum demanding a withdrawal. This expired at midnight on the 4th – thereafter Britain was at war.

Percival resolved, with countless others, that Germany was clearly the aggressor and that the British now had to 'show the Boche what they could do'. Besides, he might have mused anxiously, the war could well last only a matter of months and any delay might deny him the chance to be involved in epoch-making action. It could also be a lot of fun. But a sense of duty was no doubt paramount in Percival's mind. All that parents and school (especially school) had taught Arthur and those like him about loyalty, honour, chivalry and sportsmanship impelled them to go to the recruiting centres. These sentiments, scarcely the most fashionable in the 1990s, were part of the standard social training in the public schools of the time, but by no means restricted to them. They formed regular fare in *The Boys' Own Paper* and numerous other mass circulation weeklies which were eagerly devoured by the newly literate generation of working-class youths. Adventure series with public school settings were routinely featured in them, depicting schoolboy heroes protecting their weak chums against the over-mighty and 'teaching bullies a lesson'. Unsurprisingly therefore, many young men now considered military service a compelling duty. In the Charterhouse school debate in summer 1914, the motion, 'That this house is in favour of compulsory military service' had been carried by 113 votes to 6. The principal opposition speaker was the nonconformist Robert Graves; but within two days of the declaration of war he too had decided to enlist.[3] During the first eight months of the war 411 of his fellow Carthusians had taken commissions and 79 had enlisted in the ranks.[4] Percival's Rugby School had contributed 291 to the total of new officers by March 1915.

He spent Tuesday, when the last pieces in the international diplomatic impasse were being set against each other, securing permission to leave his firm for the duration of the war and tidying up his business affairs. Wednesday, the first day of Britain's war, brought a premonitory change in the weather. After what Siegfried Sassoon, another early volunteer, remembered as 'the spellbound serenity of its hot blue skies', the first rain of the late summer was now falling. Arthur Percival took the short walk down the wet and shining pavements of Cannon Street and Fleet Street to the drill hall of the OTC at Stone Buildings where a long queue was already forming. It was composed largely of young men who, like him, worked in the City offices nearby and who were now eager to sign on because, as one of the others in the queue that day later declared, 'it seemed the only thing to do at the time'.

Once Percival had completed the preliminaries of enlistment he became, unlike the school and university OTC members, a genuine embodied Territorial. He now started to receive pay and allowances as a private soldier and to undergo the hurriedly arranged programme of training put together by Major Hay and Lieutenant Mathews whom Errington had put in charge of the recruits. Both officers were themselves products of the regiment's unique system. Hay had started as a private in 1897, working his way to a commission by the turn of the century and gaining his majority in 1908. Mathews had similarly served in the ranks, rising to colour sergeant. He was subsequently commissioned and had later moved into the Territorial Force Reserve. He had only rejoined the unit on the Monday before Percival presented himself for enlistment.

In August 1914 the Inns of Court OTC was organised into four infantry companies and a cavalry squadron. Percival was allocated to 'A' Company and with it began his short and hectic recruit training. In the meantime, more volunteers were crowding in. By 6 August the unit was already well over establishment and had a 'waiting list' (a technical term of no real significance since all the volunteers began to be trained right away) of over 230, of whom about 30 per cent had previous military service of some kind. Fortunately many old and tried members of the Corps were also flocking back to Stone Buildings and offering to help with the training. Among them were a famous Bisley shot who helped with the musketry, and Pelham Warner, later famous for his cricket writing, who took charge of the additional staff. By Percival's third day in the ranks the training routine was in full swing. Each morning the 'Corps', as Errington invariably called it, paraded on the 'lawn' (a provisional term, for despite the centuries of care given to it, with such sudden and vigorous use it remained grassy for only a short while longer) north of Lincoln's Inn under the gimlet eye of Regimental Sergeant Major (RSM) Burns. The men were inspected by Colonel Errington and then moved off to train separately as subunits until 4pm. With growing awareness of the national emergency, training continued throughout the week-end when map-reading and compass work were taught.

The facilities of 10 Stone Buildings were plainly inadequate for the huge influx of recruits and the Corps' activities soon spilled over into all the available open spaces nearby. The squadron and the companies drilled and took their musketry practice in Lincoln's Inn gardens and the Temple Gardens beside the Embankment, while the 'waiting list' trained at Gray's Inn. In wet weather the Corps had to use all the Court Halls and the benchers of Lincoln's Inn also placed at its disposal as many sets of chambers as were needed. Such was the response to the emergency. These facilities were welcome not only for the practical benefits they conferred but also for morale. By associating the Corps with the historic buildings which lay around it, they helped to build a common pride among its members and the first swelling of that mysterious *esprit de corps* which developed among those who passed through this remarkable unit, never itself taking the field of battle but whose officer product found a place in most regiments of the line.

A third distinctive feature of the OTC and one which made it eminently suitable for recruits of mature years like Arthur Percival, was its training philosophy and general ethos. Since 1908 it had been training men to be officers and dealing with older entrants aged 25–35, developing considerable experience along the way; just in time, as it transpired, for the national crisis. It had rejected, as the commanding officer pointed out, 'the Sandhurst system of putting boys under the harrow, so as to enable the good seed to be sown in their future regiments'. Such a process was 'unthinkable when dealing with older men with considerable knowledge of the world, and whose critical faculties were developed'. Furthermore, with the period of training likely to be short, 'to spend it on the barrack square would be an absurdity'.[5] At 10 Stone Buildings the purely technical and professional aspects of the training were subsumed within a larger process which concentrated on developing the moral qualities and character of the potential officers and on fostering *esprit de corps* by every possible means. It was a concept quite advanced for its time; the contemporary Sandhust and Woolwich had no comparable programme for developing leadership.[6] Of course the process was greatly helped by the fact that the other rank training staff were, socially and by education, from much the same background as their trainees and were often their personal friends. But for all that, discipline was strict and obedience to all orders was instant.

Percival's training unit, like virtually every other in the rapidly expanding Army training machine, had many material deficiencies. It had no stock of uniforms, practically no transport and its equipment was the old Slade-Wallace pattern which was so old that it often had to be held together with string. However the unit did possess one priceless commodity – rifles, 800 of them (400 issued in error but whose return to the ordnance depot was resisted), together with 100 carbines, an old Maxim gun and boundless enthusiasm for its task of training officers to play their part in the nation's struggle.

To vary the work and improve the training, the squadron and the companies were soon going out on certain days of the week to manoeuvre on Wimbledon and Richmond Commons. Before the end of the month Errington had gained permission to use the more convenient Regent's Park after closing time and organised a useful if somewhat confusing night exercise there, to the bizarre accompaniment, one trainee noted, of 'grotesque sounds emanating at intervals from the zoo'. An anglophile American gentleman, Mr Hunt, kindly placed his car at the OTC's disposal so that Errington was able to visit his subunits at their scattered locations at ease and in some comfort.

Being so near to both the War Office and Parliament, the activity at the Inns of Court OTC received much high level attention and support. When Percival had been in training for little more than a week, the unit was paid an unexpected visit by the 76-year-old Field Marshall Sir Evelyn Wood VC, who said a few words to the recruits. A couple of days later Lord Haldane himself, architect of the radical Army reforms and now Lord Chancellor, came over to see the companies at work and address them. In his high clear voice he told Percival and his fellow aspirant officers that an expeditionary force had already landed in France to meet 'the common enemy' and wished each of the cadets Godspeed in whatever the future might hold in store. The following Saturday an eminent defence expert, Dr Maguire, visited Stone Buildings and lectured the trainees on the developing international crisis. This was all a far cry from the rather dull business of iron ore trading in a City office in a side street beside Cannon Street station. Favoured by such distinguished interest as well as much local popular support, Percival and his fellows could have been excused for believing that they and their OTC were something rather special. These were exciting days indeed and he was beginning to enjoy it.

On the day he assumed the responsibilities of Secretary of State for War, Lord Kitchener had received Parliament's authorisation for an additional 500,000 men to be recruited to the Army. Very soon afterwards the appeal had gone out for the first tranche of 100,000 men to present themselves for enlistment. An immediate problem was finding sufficient officers to train and lead them. Haldane's OTC had scarcely produced the reservoir of military leaders that was now required. By mid-1912, although 18,000 cadets had passed through the school and university detachments of the OTC, only 283 had taken commissions in the Special Reserve designed to provide a pool of semi-trained reinforcements.[7] Kitchener had anticipated the problem to some extent by requiring the infantry battalions of the BEF to leave behind at the depots three officers each as a nucleus for the new battalions. He also detained in the UK the 500 officers who were on home leave from the Indian Army. 'We are in a tight place and I am sure you will give me every possible assistance', he cabled their Commander-in-Chief on 6 August, adding, 'We want officers badly. Let me know privately if you can spare any from British battalions.'[8] Plans were also made for a drastic shortening of the courses at Sandhurst and Woolwich and a great expansion of their throughput of cadets. Although at this early stage in the war no one had any idea of the horrific attrition rate among young officers which the BEF and its follow-up formations would sustain, Kitchener was one of the few military men who were convinced that the war would be a long affair. The requirement of officers for his New Armies was easy to calculate, but these emergency measures were not producing enough, or sufficiently quickly. In these circumstances untrained but mature and experienced men like Arthur Percival were a godsend.

Four days later an appeal was published in the London papers for 2,000 men to volunteer as junior officers to serve with the regular Army until the war was concluded. The request was for former members of the university OTCs, undergraduates and other men 'of good education' to come forward. Colonel Errington viewed this new departure with some consternation and immediately set off for the War Office to ask why his OTC had not been applied to. The explanation was, he discovered, that 'our existence had been overlooked'.[9] A surprising error in the circumstances which perhaps reflected a little of Kitchener's known antipathy to the Territorial Force, shared at this stage, it must be said, by much of the Regular Army. Whatever the case, Errington was assured that his nominations would now have priority. His irritation somewhat assuaged, he returned to Stone Buildings.

The officer selection system of 1914 was, by comparison with the rather daunting three and a half day affair introduced during the Second World War and adapted from the German model, simple, straightforward and speedy. At this early stage in the conflict the officer corps still relied heavily and rather rigidly on its traditional sources of supply – the peerage, the gentry, traditional military families and, to a lesser extent, the clergy and the professions. A public school education was a virtual prerequisite and even then the list of schools was somewhat restricted. Whilst candidates for entry to Sandhurst and Woolwich sat a competitive (and wholly academic) examination for which many public schools, including Rugby, established an 'Army class' specifically to prepare them, the selection procedure for temporary war-time commissions was rudimentary in the extreme. Providing candidates met Kitchener's OTC or 'good education' criteria, little more was required. By September 1914, the commanding officers of the New Army battalions could select their own candidates and the men who raised what became known as the 'Pals Battalions' were also given considerable freedom to make their own choices. Errington's visit to the War Office had now clarified the position concerning his own selections and it was hoped that War Office approval would not be long delayed.

The Inns of Court selection system was simple and workmanlike. The job was done by a selection committee of two or three senior officers or nominated public figures. Its recommendations were confirmed by an interview with the OC Depot. The criteria observed by the committee were obvious enough. At interview they looked for evidence of the aspirant's personality, examined his educational pedigree and then sought, as the OC Depot rather ponderously put it, evidence that the volunteer had, 'sufficient social position to justify the candidate being trained for a role in which he would be called upon to play the part of one in authority from whom both precept and example would be required'. Evidence of leadership qualities was sought from such factors as proficiency in outdoor sports, experience in the colonies or of the world beyond school. It was a rough and ready system, but entirely adequate, for while the responsibilities of young officers in the Great War had a life-and-death importance, they were not technically complex or difficult. Courage, confidence and a basic professional competence took the young subaltern a long way in a military society still rigidly stratified and in which his right to lead was not generally questioned. Though the training period in these early war days at Stone Buildings was short and hectic, it did give the staff a more measured opportunity to confirm their selections. A few trainees fell at this second hurdle though the great majority came through and acquitted themselves particularly well in the test of war itself.

On all the selection criteria Arthur Percival scored well. He was older and more mature than most with considerable experience of the world of work from his years in the City. He had gained his Higher School Certificate at a public school of the first rank where team games were held in high regard and which had a thriving OTC in which he had reached the cadet rank of colour sergeant. He played individual and team sports to a high standard and excelled at cross-country running, which the Army regarded as a prime training activity. He was also a member of the Youngsbury Rifle Club and had qualified as a skilled shot. Percival was quickly involved in the bustle of the Inns of Court training in the certain knowledge that a commission would soon come his way.

On the matter of the granting of commissions the War Office soon proved as good as its word: two batches of commissions, albeit only in the Special Reserve but totalling 150, had been received by the end of August. On 3rd September Colonel Errington was asked if his Corps could supply officers for Kitchener's New Armies whose first tranche of 100,000 men, popularly known as 'K1', was then being formed into the First New Army. The need for officers was particularly urgent, the War Office declared, since there was also a serious shortage of capable NCOs. These latter continued to be a scarce commodity until the potential of the new recruits could be assessed and developed by training. Ian Hay's 'Junior Sub' explained it more bluntly: 'We are very short of subalterns at present. (We are equally short of NCOs; but you can always take a man out of the ranks and christen him a sergeant, whereas there is no available source of Second Lieutenants save capricious Whitehall).'[10] Errington would have approved of the adjective but nevertheless responded instantly to the War Office request and promised 100 officers almost at once. He selected 111 from among his trainees, Arthur Percival being one, and explained the War Office's request to them. As members of the Territorial Force they were currently committed to home service only, but they all volunteered for active service in K1 despite the novelty of the formations they were joining and the condition of service within them which were, in Errington's words, 'altogether vague'. No sooner had Percival volunteered than he received orders to move. He was to report to Headley Training Camp, Epsom before being allocated to one of the new 'Service' battalions, as the Kitchener Army units were called. By 12 September he was a commissioned officer and ten days later he was posted to 7th (Service) Battalion The Bedfordshire Regiment, then forming at Mandora Barracks, Aldershot.

3

IN KITCHENER'S ARMY

'Anyhow we are Kitchener's Army, and we are sure it will be alright. Just send us to Flanders and see if it ain't. We're Kitchener's Army and we don't care if it snows ink.'

Donald Hankey, A Student in Arms

The mechanisms by which aspirant officers, responding to Kitchener's appeal, found their way into particular regiments in the autumn of 1914 were many and varied. Qualifications, influence, determination and luck all played a part. Sheer persistence had resulted in the over-age Clement Atlee finally managing to enlist in the Inns of Court Regiment. He soon found himself gazetted to the 6th South Lancashire Regiment, despite being very much a Londoner, solely because its commanding officer was the relative of one of his students and had 'asked' for him.[1] For the more tentative Robert Graves, holidaying that summer at Harlech in north Wales, it was the helpful action of the secretary of the local golf club in ringing up the adjutant of the nearest regimental depot at Wrexham which saw the young poet become a subaltern in the Royal Welch Fusiliers.[2] Harold Macmillan ended up in the Grenadier Guards by using the influence of his mother and some university friends to get him an interview with the regimental lieutenant colonel.[3] Sir Tom Bridges took an ex-Imperial Light Horseman into his cavalry regiment although he must have been a good 15 years over the age limit, largely it seems because 'he was an immense size, beyond all regimental clothing, and his chest was a blaze of ribbons from every war in Africa'.[4] Aspirants less well connected or without proven valour were often reduced to advertising themselves in *The Times* whose front page (restricted to small 'ads' rather than world news for the first 180 years of its existence) carried many announcements such as the following:

Accountant cashier, 33, married, desires paymaster's commission.
To commanding officers: sergeant Yeomanry (late Stock Exchange) seeks commission, preferably Transport Officer, Infantry.[5]

Old school and social connections were very powerful levers. The commanding officer of 3rd Royal West Kents was an old Rugbeian and had a strong preference for those from his old school and from Marlborough. These were so well represented among his officers by the winter of 1914 as to be able to field a complete rugby side against the rest. Sporting links could sometimes produce remarkably informal arrangements. An old cricketing chum offered the future Sir David Kelly a commission in the 6th Leicesters and 'one for any friend he liked to bring'.[6]

Neither his sporting prowess nor his years at Rugby saw Arthur Percival join either the Leicestershires or the Royal West Kents. His gazetting to the Bedfordshire Regiment was rather more logical. His county of birth, Hertfordshire, was represented in the Army's order of battle only by a Territorial Force regiment. Arthur had volunteered for the New Army. Although the territorials of Hertfordshire were to have the distinction of being among the first of their kind to be sent to France to reinforce the BEF in November 1914, the county raised no Kitchener Army units. Many sons of Hertfordshire were recruited to the Bedfords during the war; indeed so close was the wartime relationship between the two counties that they finally became a single regiment, popularly the 'Beds and Herts', by royal warrant, in 1919. Soldiering alongside those with familiar accents, from nearby towns and with the same local loyalties is a powerful cohesive factor in war and formed the basis of the British regimental system. Arthur Percival was well content to find himself in the Bedfords, the regiment of the county which bordered his own.

The Bedfordshire Regiment had been raised in 1688 and during the first 23 years of its existence it had seen more fighting than any other single battalion in the Army. Its failure to have acquired by 1914 the cachet enjoyed by more junior regiments owes much to its history in the intervening two centuries. During the Napoleonic Wars when battle honours were first awarded, the Bedfords missed out since they spent most of their time in the West Indies and Latin America. They missed similar distinctions during the Crimean War when they were once again on imperial service in the Caribbean. By the 1880s they were unique among the regiments of the line in being without the distinction of a single battle honour. In the wicked humour of the barrack room they gained the nickname of 'The Peacemakers', despite having unacknowledged service in nine wars. The label remained, even when their earlier campaigns were formally recognised and they began to make a formidable name for themselves in France and Flanders. It became an increasingly inappropriate perception of a regiment which fielded 21 battalions of one sort or another during the Great War and whose regular and service battalions served with great distinction.

Despite this unfortunate piece of folklore Kitchener's call for volunteers was answered with alacrity and enthusiasm throughout the towns and villages of Bedfordshire. The 1st Battalion had been in France since 16

August and in action since the 23rd, one of the battalions of 'old contemptibles', while the 2nd would soon be home from South Africa to reinforce the BEF. Meanwhile the young men of Bedford were flocking to support them. Two new units, 6th and 7th (Service) Battalions, were quickly raised. The Bedfords' Special Reserve battalion provided an immediate draft of about 200 men which gave 6th Bedfords a head start. Within three weeks or so this number had been swelled by volunteers to roughly 2,000, many more than required for a single battalion, so about half were split off to form the 7th.

When Arthur Percival joined 7th Bedfords he found the men still sharing Mandora Barracks with their comrades of the 6th and in that state of enthusiastic disorganisation which characterised most units of the New Armies in those early days. Although the unit was inspected by the King and Lord Kitchener within a week of Percival's arrival, it was four weeks before A Company, to which he was allocated, acquired a company commander, an aged and frail-looking ex-captain. The battalion's first commanding officer, a Lieutenant Colonel Martin, soon left to command a brigade. This speedy elevation, together with the similar rapid departure of his successor, was eloquent of Kitchener's difficulty in finding sufficient officers of the right quality to head up his new battalions and brigades. Some posts were filled, as noted earlier, by officers held back from the BEF or from their units in India. The regular majors commanding the regimental depots provided some more. The remainder came from a variety of sources and were frequently officers pulled out of retirement – 'dug-outs' as they were commonly known. In his desperate search for experienced men Kitchener even resorted to the marginally legal and scarcely ethical expedient of requiring post offices to notify the Adjutant General of all those men receiving letters addressed to 'Colonel', 'Major' and so on. The War Office then sent the gentlemen concerned an invitation to volunteer which it was difficult for them to refuse. The First New Army benefited most from the limited pool of regulars and those recently retired. The Second New Army, in which 7th Bedfords found themselves, was formed on 11 September. It, and the formations which followed, had to rely increasingly on 'dug-outs' and other less orthodox sources of supply – or else they went without. The problem was compounded by the lamentable battlefield 'wastage rate' of young officers, who remained a scarce commodity throughout the war. In the division to which 7th Bedfords initially belonged, scarcely any of the battalions possessed more than four of their establishment of 31 officers when they were formed.

In these circumstances it is not surprising that Percival's advancement was rapid and his new life a very busy one. In late September, before he had been in uniform for two months, he had completed a musketry course and become the battalion musketry officer. He had moved, with the delicate-looking Captain Dew, into very agreeable accommodation in

Woolmer Lodge, a substantial and pleasant country house in Liphook. In December he received his promotion to lieutenant and, in addition to his skill-at-arms duties, which he much enjoyed, was pursuing another of his enthusiasms in training the battalion cross-country team for the Aldershot championships. 'Getting ready to chase the Germans' was the *Sporting Life*'s caption for its photograph of the event, in which the Bedfords did quite well, coming seventh out of the 40 battalion teams competing.

If training was very enjoyable for a relatively young, active, if inexperienced officer like Percival for whom the military life was a new experience, the task of command was a difficult one for the many older officers whose active soldiering had been spent in vastly different circumstances. Those who had the experience and the enthusiasm often lacked the stamina and mental flexibility to cope with the novel circumstances into which they had been, often rather unceremoniously, pitchforked. Weapons, tactics and organisation had, for many commanding officers, undergone fundamental changes since they were last on campaign. A battalion of totally inexperienced and rather unruly citizen soldiers drawn from all classes and employments, rather than the more or less predictable all-regular force, was a culture shock in itself. The shortage of weapons, equipment, experienced junior officers and reliable NCOs produced additional stresses for commanders which not all of them were able to bear. A settled organisation would have helped, but in the hand-to-mouth existence of the New Armies this was not immediately available. 7th Bedfords were at first attached as 'Army troops' to 15th Scottish Division, the senior formation of the Second New Army. Being surrounded by the kilted recruits of 14 highland regiments all speaking an incomprehensible version of the supposedly common language was a further trial for the southerners whether raw or experienced. By November Percival's unit had moved from Aldershot to billets in Liphook, then in January they were on the move again to a camp in Hazlemere and Arthur moved to fresh lodgings with a retired major and his wife.

In February 1915 another change of particular significance occurred. On the 24th the battalion left Hazlemere for Colchester on transfer to 54 Brigade. This Brigade was one of three which made up 18th (Eastern) Division, formed largely of regiments from the Home Counties and East Anglia amongst whom the Bedfords felt much more at home. Of greater import was the fact that 18th Division was commanded by Major General Ivor Maxse, a brilliant trainer of men and one of the foremost soldiers of his generation. Maxse had returned from France where he had been commanding the 1st Guards Brigade to take over the new Kitchener's Army formation. It was not long before the skill, enthusiasm and sheer professionalism of this gifted soldier were impressing themselves on the consciousness of the newest joined subaltern in what was to become a distinguished fighting division. Percival was to remain with the Bedfords, 54

Brigade and 18th Division throughout the war, though his immediate superiors were to come and go constantly. Captain Dew soon retired owing to ill health and was replaced by a Captain Henderson. In February Percival gained his captaincy and became second-in-command of A Company. In the same month he led the battalion cross-country team again, taking it to first place in the Colchester garrison race. 'With an officer of the standard of Captain Percival to pull them along', wrote the *Sporting Life*, 'they would give the Bedfords a big race in the forthcoming championship event.' A 7th Bedfords NCO was the individual winner and Percival was the first officer home. This Saturday victory caused quite a stir; the Bedfords had moved to Colchester only two days previously. They were already being dubbed 'The Shining Seventh' and were a fine example, one newspaper noted, of 'this cooperation of officers and men in sport [which is] a splendid thing, and its far reaching effect will, in due time, be appreciated at its proper worth'. This judgement has a rather dated ring, but bespeaks the extent to which Kitchener's citizen soldiers were bringing change to a rather rigid institution.

Ill health soon saw the departure of the Bedfords' second commanding officer, a 'dug-out' ex-major named Pickard Cambridge, and his successor, Colonel Allenby, stayed less than two months. He was followed by Lieutenant Colonel G D Price, who stayed. He supervised the battalion's training, took it to France and commanded it at the front with considerable distinction. He was not untypical of the men brought in to take over battalions of Kitchener's new force. Forty-seven years of age when he joined the Bedfords (which was not his own regiment), Price's operational experience was limited to minor campaigns in West Africa. When war broke out he had been commanding nothing more portentous than a desk in London as a Recruiting Officer (Class II). Promoted to lieutenant colonel in June 1915, he grew quickly into the post, taking 7th Bedfords through their final months in the UK and their first 15 on active service, including a particularly distinguished performance on the Somme.

In Colchester General Maxse quickly set about turning his division of enthusiastic volunteers into an effective fighting force. From the outset he showed none of the antipathy to the unmilitary and at times querulous citizen soldiers which many regular officers initially displayed, and which some were to exhibit for the duration. He saw the New Armies as first-class raw material and quickly appreciated the excellent physical and moral qualities of the subaltern officers as well as the standard of the rank and file which he averred was 'undoubtedly higher than that of the men we recruited to the old Army'. This was an encouraging attitude to display to such enthusiastic newcomers as Percival. Maxse soon managed to acquire a 32-square-mile stretch of training area outside Colchester and from then on the training of sections and platoons on the barrack square (the customary practice in other formations) was forbidden in the division.

Every subaltern was required to take his platoon onto the training area for all their exercises. Each battalion was allocated a different area daily and no company went on the same ground twice within a fortnight. With subalterns permanently engaged in training their men, which is what Maxse demanded, progress was naturally much more rapid than in the old Army and in some other formations of the New. This was achieved despite the shortage of virtually every item of military equipment. There were only 100 service rifles available in each of Maxse's battalions, but even so he ensured that the whole division had completed its first musketry course by the start of April 1915.[7]

The necessary preliminary to the route marches at Colchester was the order, 'Men without boots to the right, men with worn-out trousers to the left'; but when they were all kitted out properly the results were impressive. The distance covered on the marches was seldom less than 10 miles a day, which scarcely taxed the very fit and long-striding Arthur Percival, and the training culminated in a week's 'trek' through Suffolk in which 62 miles were covered in the last 48 hours with all ranks carrying full marching order.[8] The supporting artillery brigades were afflicted by similar shortages. They drilled with wooden guns and shells, 'Six men, marching in half sections, with a red flag, represented a gun team, and six men with a white flag pretended to be a wagon team.'[9] Despite the fact that the machine gun was already dominating the Western Front battlefield, Maxse noted testily that, 'there is not one machine gun in the whole division'. In such straitened circumstances he made his training aims basic, realistic and attainable. 'By May 1915', he wrote in his training notes, 'we shall have attained three things, a. discipline b. physical fitness c. musketry efficiency.'[10] These qualities were to take the Bedfords a long way.

In May 1915, as part of its work-up for the almost mystical 'Front', which some impatient citizen-soldiers despaired of ever seeing, 18th Division moved to the Salisbury Plain training area. Five Kitchener New Armies had now been formed, each of six divisions of about 20,000 men apiece. Six hundred thousand eager young men, concentrated in these packets of 20,000 were now cramming the encampments scattered throughout the country. Existing barracks had long since overflowed and new wooden huts and tented camps spread their serried ranks across the sun-scorched countryside, straining local amenities to the limit and transforming the face of the rural landscape. There was to be some slight relief when the first of the new divisions began to move across to France in mid-May, but the concentration of the remaining formations in predominantly rural areas must have been traumatic for the bemused locals who, however patriotic, found the even tenor of their bucolic ways radically disturbed by the hordes of erstwhile town-dwellers who now threatened to swamp them.

18th Division was based at Codford where the two small adjoining villages of Codford St Peter and Codford St Mary could scarcely have mustered 700 souls between them. The gentle valleys of the area were now scarred by the regular rows of new hutments produced under the Quartermaster General's emergency accommodation scheme. The summer lanes were alive with the tramp of marching feet and the unfamiliar accents of East Anglia and London. The villages were altered beyond recognition with 'horrid booths and shanties, where tobacco, hosiery, and a thousand odds and ends can be bought at increased cost, for the owner of the property has asked £1 a week in rent for a glorified cupboard which now constitutes a shop'.[11] But it was all in a good cause and, as the modern Ministry of Defence might have put it, remarkably cost-effective. In the Regular Army of 1915 it took about 11 months to produce a well-trained soldier. On the fields of Colchester and Codford, Maxse had trained his division in about eight, despite shortages of virtually every commodity except the recruits themselves. He was reasonably satisfied with the product. 'I am convinced', his training notes recorded, 'that the sections and platoons . . . will be better trained for fighting than is generally expected.[12] By early June, 7th Bedfords had gained the commanding officer who was to take them to war; in the same month Arthur Percival was given command of A Company. For these officers the test of Maxse's judgement was not long to be deferred.

4

THE TASTE OF WAR

'I looked over and saw lines upon lines of infantry get up and calmly walk across to the German trenches in face of a heavy M.G. and shrapnel fire.'

Captain Percival on the advance of 7th Bedfords,
30 June 1916

On 25 July 1915, 7th Bedfords, now at their full war establishment of 820 men and 31 officers, left the UK for 'service abroad', as the battalion's war diary obscurely put it. They sailed from Folkestone aboard SS *Onward* across an English Channel whose sea lanes were secured and vigorously patrolled by the Home Flotilla, for the submarine war was now in full spate, and soon arrived at Boulogne. A night train took them north to Flesselles and from there they marched north to billets in Talmas, a tiny hamlet about 15 miles behind the main trench line. Arthur Percival's A Company had now become one small cell in the gigantic and still expanding organism into which the lean and all-professional BEF of August 1914 had so rapidly mutated. The Bedfords were quickly absorbed into the elaborate administrative and training machine which fitted new battalions for combat on the Western Front. Their work-up resumed in the more realistic environment of the battle zone, with the customary activities of route marches, inspections and musketry now being ominously supplemented by respirator drill and chlorine gas training and later by digging-in, rapid marching and bayonet fighting. There were also special lectures for Percival and his fellow officers given by the Adjutant.

By mid-August the battalions of 18th Division were adjudged ready for their first experience of the front-line trenches and a direct taste of war as it had now developed in northern France and Flanders, the historic cockpit of Europe. The move to the war theatre had already imbued the new units with a fresh earnestness and expectancy. They picketed their local roads enthusiastically for spies, took the nightly 'stand-to' particularly seriously and some men even slept with their arms through their rifle slings although they were still some miles from the nearest German. The move to the Ribemont sector trenches brought a fresh round of precautions: with the idea of concealing themselves from the enemy some 'marched a long way bent almost double, each man keeping touch by grasping the bayonet of the man behind'.[1] The order to extinguish ciga- rettes was given miles from the front although the men would later puff stoically in the front-line trenches themselves.

Percival was taken on his first tour of inspection of the Ribemont trench system on 21 August and soon afterwards his A Company, and B Company commanded by Arthur's firm friend from their Inns of Court days, Wilfred Bull, were sent into part of the line held by the 8th Argylls and 5th Seaforths for their induction into the tactics of trench warfare and the routine of life in the line. It was a fairly safe sector, 'except for one spot', the A Company commander noted, 'where our line is only 10 yards from the Germans'. The trenches themselves were in excellent order, the result of an enormous amount of labour. He noted that 'some of the dugouts have got beds in and they have all got tables and chairs or benches and are quite comfortable'. But that did not make them safe. Within a couple of days they had already cowered under an artillery bar- rage and Percival's company had suffered its first casualty. There was a palpable sense of relief the following morning when C and D Companies arrived to take their places 'under instruction'. In early September the Bedfords were put into the line with a stretch of their own, taking over from the East Surreys. They were now proper 'front-line troops' with their individual section to defend, their particular stretch of no-man's-land to dominate and the enemy trench system to observe and raid.

Percival's men remained in the Ribemont/Fricourt sector until the new year, steadily accustoming themselves to the reality of living half their lives below ground level; for this is what it amounted to, generally eight to ten days in the trenches, then relief by another battalion of 54th Brigade, and a similar period in the rest camp. At this stage in the war the Fricourt sec- tor was a quiet area; no local offensives were undertaken, no attacks were put in by the Germans. The trenches were nevertheless dangerous places in which to spend the long, uncomfortable days. German snipers were always active, machine guns and artillery constantly threatened. Then there were the aerial torpedoes which the Germans threw over most nights. These were 'rather alarming and make a fearful noise when they explode', Percival noted in a letter home, 'but don't seem to do much damage unless they actually land in a trench. You generally have time to see them coming and can bolt into a dug-out'.[2] Patrols had still to go out regularly to test the enemy's defences, gather information or snatch pris- oners. On his third night in the line one of Percival's patrols returned with three men wounded and the following day the Bedfords had their first fatality. Their initial spell in the line had been a long one – 18 days. When they were finally relieved they had lost 10 men killed and eight wounded; five of the casualties were from A Company. And so the autumn and winter wore on with this tedious but dangerous pattern being endlessly repeated: a week or two in the trenches and then the same period out of them, with the chance at last of a decent night's sleep in a dry hut, a bath and a really hot meal.

The Bedfords were fortunate enough to spend Christmas in the rest camp where they enjoyed a battalion football tournament and a special Christmas dinner; but they were back in the trenches for New Year's Eve and their next spell of duty. In the first flush of enthusiasm for joining Kitchener's Army many Bedfords, in common with perhaps the majority of the citizen soldiers, had fondly believed that it would be a case of 'Bash the Hun and home by Christmas'. But Christmas had now come and gone and they had all seen the trench deadlock at first hand. With the turn of the year it was abundantly clear to Percival that victory would not be easily gained, that any major offensive would require massive resources of men and armament, with success only being bought at considerable cost. The last four months of 1915 had been 18th Division's first spell in the line and also its quietest months at the front of the entire war. Nevertheless they cost General Maxse's formation 1,247 casualties. How much more costly an offensive would be they were all later to discover.

'A trench', Ian Hay's 'junior sub' remarks sagely, 'is that most interesting of human devices, a compromise. It is neither satisfactory as a domicile nor efficient as a weapon of offence.'[3] Such was certainly Percival's experience in his front-line domicile during the six months he spent in the Fricourt/Ribemont sector, where the Bedfords' trenches proved to be more overrun with rats than any they were subsequently to occupy. The ways of this intelligent rodent became well known in the battalion. During their first spell in the trenches Percival had complained that he had not dealt with any Germans at all. 'The only bag I have made is one rat which I slew with my stick in fine style', he recorded. In the long spells of relative inactivity it became an unofficial duty of the orderly officer of the day to kill as many rats as he could find. The best drive in the Bedfords, one of 70, went to the keen-eyed Captain Percival. Other light relief in the early days came as a result of the understandable caution and suspicion of the new battalion, such as when one of their first patrols discovered the entrance to 'a German subterranean passage', which on closer examination proved to be nothing more than the long discarded top of a beer barrel.[4]

These were the less serious moments in an otherwise arduous and enervating form of warfare. A particular anxiety was the inadequacy of the British artillery support: guns there were aplenty but ammunition was in short supply and a disconcerting proportion of it proved to be faulty. Enemy bombardments often drew a feeble response and the Bedfords frequently recorded instances of dud shells coming from their own guns in reply. In January 1916 Percival lost his first subaltern to enemy shelling and the battalion suffered a dozen casualties from a gas attack, the last major event before 18th Division was transferred to XIII Corps, during which move Percival snatched a few days' home leave and then attended a month's course at the Army School at Flixcourt. It was the kind of deadlocked, slow-burning trench war which permitted such distractions. He did well on the course: 'a very good officer . . . keen and intelligent' wrote the course director, with the School Commandant adding, 'an excellent stamp of officer whom I have personally noticed'. General Maxse endorsed the 'excellent report'. The late starter in the Army was beginning to make his mark.[5]

By the time Percival returned from Flixcourt, the Bedfords had settled in at Corbie and taken their first tour in the trenches at Bray sur Somme amid rumours of plans for a major offensive. It was at Bray that 7th Bedfords first came to general attention with a most successful foray into the German trench system. The raid was planned with great care by Colonel Price and executed by a young second lieutenant, Harry Driver, and 30 men. It featured half an hour of hand-to-hand fighting and the use of 366 Mills bombs before the wounded Driver withdrew his party, leaving many Germans dead behind him. The raid had the unique distinction of a mention in Haig's despatch and a report in *The Times* and all the French newspapers. 'In publishing the name of the Regiment in the newspapers, which up to now has scarcely ever been done', wrote General Maxse, 'a great honour has been conferred on the battalion.'[6] The exploit earned Driver the DSO, his sergeant the DCM and a decoration or commendation for every man in his party. The service battalion of citizen soldiers had come of age and the men greatly enjoyed the limelight into which the exploit projected them as they began the meticulous planning and training for their part in the Somme offensive on which such great Allied hopes were pinned.

The battle of the Somme, the greatest trial and sacrifice of the entire war for the British Army, was also the first large-scale test of the offensive capabilities of the Kitchener Armies. It took place on a front of 18 miles astride the Somme river and lasted from the beginning of July 1916 until the third week in November. While only 19 British divisions were employed in the initial attack, by the time the opposing armies sank metaphorically to their knees and settled for a bloody draw, practically every division in the theatre had participated in one way or another. General Maxse prepared his division with his customary thoroughness. The Bedfords' officers had spent a full week in May taking parties of NCOs to see the trench system over which they were going to attack. The following month they spent 12 days at Picquigny training for the big attack by having, as Percival explained, 'an exact reproduction of the German trenches dug and practising an attack over it every day'. Given the tactics of the period, few battalions could have been better prepared.

By the evening of 30 June, the units of 54th Brigade were all crowded

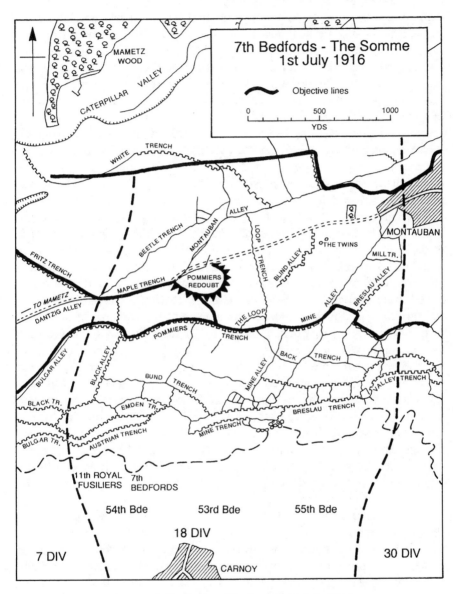

Map 1. 7th Bedfords – The Somme, 1 July 1916

together in the forward trenches with 11th Fusiliers and 7th Bedford designated as the attacking line and 6th Northants and 12th Middlesex in
support and reserve respectively. The artillery bombardment had been
constant, day and night, for five days. Casualties from German fire were
higher than usual because the lines were so jammed with men. Percival
and the other company commanders had drawn lots for their attacking
positions. B and C Companies were the assaulting companies with D
Company in support and Percival's A Company in reserve. The main
brigade objective was Pommiers Redoubt, a typical German strongpoint
set near the crest of a rise and featuring a circle of heavily wired trenches
mounted with machine guns and manned by two companies which shel-
tered in solid 50-foot dugouts in the centre, relatively immune to the fire
of the British guns, but supported by their own field pieces with which
they were in close contact.

The opening day of this long battle went remarkably well for the
Bedfords. The tactics laid down by Haig for overcoming the great strength
of the defence in trench warfare were as successful for them as anywhere
along the British line. If the British infantry was being reduced to a force
of 'barrage followers', as some critics have averred, then the Bedfords followed them particularly effectively. Colonel Price was determined to get
to Pommiers Redoubt as soon as possible so as to draw maximum benefit from the supporting guns. This was a wise tactic for five or six German
machine guns were active against the Bedfords' line from the very start of
their advance, 'which was rather disconcerting', wrote Percival, 'as we had
hoped they would all have been wiped out before that'. The Bedfords' sector was by no means the only part of the British line where this hope had
proved false. Although H Hour was set for 7.30am, Price had his assault
companies out of their trenches two minutes earlier so they could be well
through their own wire before the barrage lifted.[7] They managed this
very successfully and then doubled down the forward slope before the
enemy machine guns had a chance to switch their fire from the gaps in the
wire to the advancing bodies of men.

The companies re-formed at the bottom of the slope. From then on, as
they attempted to cross the German first and second line trenches, the
casualties began to mount. Between Austrian and Emden Trenches, B
and C Companies became practically leaderless, all their officers being
either killed or wounded. But so thorough had been the Bedfords' training that the NCOs knew exactly where their objectives lay and pressed on
doggedly with their tasks, cutting 'the wire as if there was nothing doing'
as the wounded Captain Bull later wrote of his company's nightmare half-
hour in front of Emden Trench. The support company also got through
the early advance at relatively little cost, but began to suffer heavily once
it crossed the second line of German trenches. It too was officerless before
it gained the last trench protecting the redoubt. But once there, it was able

to join the remnants of the attacking companies and rush forward in a confused but successful assault on the redoubt itself which fell to piece-meal attacks by elements of all three companies and the neighbouring Fusiliers. The battle was now little more than an hour old but so well had the attack gone that the advanced elements finally came under the fire of their own guns as they moved on to the final objective, Maple Trench, beyond the redoubt.

By the time Percival's reserve company went over the top at 7.40am (after many anxious, wakeful hours for the rum had been issued at 3am), the German defences were thoroughly roused and an inferno of artillery and machine-gun fire greeted the men as they got to the gaps in the wire through which 54 Brigade had advanced. Two of Percival's officers were out of action before their own fire trench had been crossed and half his company's casualties were sustained in getting through their own wire. They came under a fresh barrage once they had crossed Emden Trench and Percival had to call a halt in Bund Trench to reorganise his battered and thinning ranks before they moved forward again at 9.15am. Soon after, he received the order to make for the final brigade objective, since it was now clear that the redoubt had fallen. However, he had to take his men through a third barrage before they eventually reached the strongpoint where, as he wrote later in his company report, 'a state of great confusion reigned, men of four different battalions (Bedfords, Fusiliers, Essex and Berkshires), no officers and no NCOs'.[8] In fact Percival was one of only three Bedford officers who got through to the strongpoint unscathed.

As the Fusiliers were already pressing on to Beetle Trench, Percival sent three platoons forward under Second Lieutenant Colley, his remaining company officer, to help them, but with a strictly limited objective since the flanking brigade was still some way behind. He then set about con-solidating the position on the redoubt where, 'there must have been about 500 or 600 men and not a single officer besides myself!' He also ordered bombing parties to clear up Montauban Alley which was initially held by a strong party of Germans and needed a two-phase operation to clear. By 6.15pm it, too, was adequately defended and by 10pm Percival had men building defences on the newly gained objective. This was timely action, for at 10.30pm his covering troops reported Germans advancing over the ridge towards them. These were fired on and finally withdrew. Percival and his exhausted and much shrunken A Company were finally taken out of the line at 3.15am on 2 July.

A Company and its commander had been awake for much of the pre-vious 48 hours, active for about 22 of them, under fire for much of the time and taking casualties from the very start of the operation. They had withstood three artillery barrages as they advanced against a determined enemy. Percival's was one of three Military Crosses which the battalion won in the action. His citation recorded that 'during the advance he showed fine leadership and determination under heavy shell and machine gun fire. He worked unceasingly, with absolute disregard of danger, in completing every detail in the consolidation of the captured position.' It was an object lesson in what Maxse had been trying to achieve. He had written earlier of consolidation 'being left to too many individuals' and lacking system. 'We must put some fresh thought into the problem,' he had declared.[9] Percival was delighted with the way his citizen soldiers had come through the testing ordeal. 'Our Batt. was simply magnificent' he wrote, 'and the way the men went up the hill and took trench after trench was wonderful.'[10] The cost to the Bedfords had been great. They suffered 300 casualties including 81 killed. Percival lost two of his platoon commanders and nearly 70 of his men. The unit had more than earned the short rest which they enjoyed at Carnoy for the next few days.

They were soon in action again, if only in a supporting role, when 18th Division attacked and captured Trones Wood. While the Bedfords were holding the wood which the Northants and Middlesex had captured at great cost, Percival was hit in the back by a shell fragment as the Germans pounded the wood with artillery fire. It was only a flesh wound however and he stayed with the company to enjoy a small celebration on 26 July when General Maxse visited the battalion and 'spoke in very high terms of praise' of its action, mentioning in particular 'the splendid fighting spirit of the battalion in the Pommiers Redoubt operation'. By chance this was also the anniversary of the battalion's arrival in France the previous year and the surviving officers, now only 12 of the initial 31, marked it with a small celebration. 'A very good dinner and a festive evening', wrote Percival as he and the other 11 'originals' remembered their fallen colleagues and toasted their battalion's successes and their own good fortune in surviving. It had been an eventful second year in the Army and first at the front.

In mid-September 18th Division was preparing for its part in fifth Army's attack on Thiepval ridge and the Schwaben Redoubt. The Bedfords were to be the brigade reserve in 54 Brigade's task of capturing Thiepval village at the summit of the ridge. After some very heavy fighting the three leading battalions managed to secure much of the village but suffered heavy casualties and complete exhaustion in the process. Stubborn resistance in one corner of the village was holding up the advance of two whole brigades. General Maxse decided to use the uncommitted Bedfords to complete the clearance. The manner in which they ultimately managed this was a considerable testament to their courage and military skills, for the whole operation was laid on at short notice and without any artillery preparation. The culmination of the attack was the exploit of Second Lieutenant Tom Adlam, a pre-war schoolmaster and later founder member of the Army Educational Corps with only two months' experience in the trenches, who bombed his way through the right flank of the German defences with great dash and gallantry to earn the battalion's first Victoria Cross. But it was the skill with which the Bedfords hurriedly arranged their night relief and approach march in the dark for their dawn attack which made their success possible. Much of this was down to Percival.

The commander of A Company had been left in charge of the battalion while the colonel and adjutant went forward to be briefed at brigade headquarters on their unit's almost impromptu but critical task. Percival had the task of leading the battalion's night march to its start line for the attack. 'I consider that night march', Percival later tersely noted, 'was the most difficult thing I had to carry out owing to the lack of guides, impossibility of reconnoitring route beforehand, considerable shelling and uncertainty as to position of enemy'.[11] They finally arrived at this objective at 3.30am, having taken two and a quarter hours to cover one and a half miles. General Maxse was in no doubt as to the approach march's significance, describing it as 'the finest example of efficiency and battle discipline seen in the 18th Division during the course of the Somme and Ancre operations of the past five months'. This was praise indeed from a skilled commander who demanded high standards and was not generally lavish with his compliments. 'Only a well-trained and highly-spirited battalion such as the 7th Bedfordshire', the general's report continued, 'can accomplish such a feat and be ready for a day's fighting the same morning'.[12]

The clearing of Thiepval village was a remarkably successful minor operation of the utmost value, though it was an absurd parody of a village which the Bedfords beheld. 'Nothing but a mass of shell holes', wrote Percival, 'There was not one brick left on top of another.' After a day's delay the next attack, on the Schwaben Redoubt itself, went in with the Bedford's two relatively fresh companies, Wilfred Bull's B and Percival's A, leading the brigade operation. All began well enough, and the two companies went forward in perfect order covering the first 400 yards with few casualties; but then the difficulties began. German machine-gun fire began enfilading the attack's right flank just as the main enemy barrage came down on them. Percival had earlier written to his father after the first day's attack on the Somme, 'I came through the Great Battle all right . . . and was pretty lucky to do so'. It was just as the attack on the Schwaben Redoubt went forward that his luck finally ran out. Shrapnel from a shell-burst wounded him in four places: two pieces passed through his left arm, a third lodged in his back and a fourth penetrated his left side. Still able to walk, he made his way back to the advanced dressing station, had his wounds bandaged, went on to the headquarters and reported what he knew of the action and was finally evacuated through the medical clearing system now operating very smoothly due to its distressingly frequent use. The Bedfords finally consolidated their position on the objective after much bitter fighting, by which time the battalion was down to two officers, who by coincidence were brothers. It had been a tragically costly action. Four officers had been killed, five others besides Percival were wounded and 112 other ranks were also casualties. This was the last action of 7th Bedfords in the bloody Somme offensive.

Percival was away from the front for some time. His wound healed quickly enough but X-rays revealed a piece of shrapnel still lodged awkwardly in his hip which the doctors decided to leave in place. Two months' home sick leave restored him to reasonable health which his medical board confirmed, though Arthur was amused to note that the board president examined his X-ray upside down, declaring it very interesting! A major change to Percival's future was also confirmed during his recuperation in England. He had originally volunteered for the Army because of the national emergency and only for the duration of the war, like hundreds of thousands of others. However, a few days after the start of the Somme offensive, the brigade commander, Brigadier General Shoubridge, had visited A Company's trenches and offered to recommend Arthur for a permanent captaincy in the Regular Army if he wished to transfer. It was not a difficult decision; he enjoyed the excitement and challenge of Army life and his introduction, via the Inns of Court OTC and a Kitchener battalion, had been ideal for an older entrant. He was already impressing his senior commanders and had begun to realise that 'it would be rather hard to settle down to office work again' after all that he had experienced in the last two years, particularly since he could not see a great future for himself in the City. He accepted the brigadier's offer without too much heart-searching and on 13 October, while still a patient in No 1 War Hospital in Reading, he was gazetted as a captain in the Essex Regiment. The understanding was that he would serve out the war with the Bedfords and retain the temporary majority which he now had. The New Year found him on a ten-week course at the Senior Officers School in Aldershot. It was an interesting enough course, but the weather was foul and he was still not fully fit. No sooner had he returned home to prepare for his return to the front than he developed jaundice. In consequence he did not return to the Bedfords until mid-April 1917.

Soon after he was back in the line the battalion had its first reverse, and a serious one, as 54th Brigade played its part in the attack on the Hindenburg Line, to which defensive system the Germans had now retired. Though now a major, Percival was back in command of A Company. His old comrade Wilfred Bull, similarly recovered from his Somme wounds, was again in charge of B Company. Through a series of unfortunate mishaps and some poor staff work, the Bedfords' attack on the German trenches at Bullecourt was a failure. The dispirited troops were reduced to taking cover in shell scrapes and whatever other protection they could find from the merciless machine guns, a mere 400 yards in advance of their start point. The attack was one of the bloodiest reverses which they ever sustained: the Bedfords lost 14 officers and 242 other ranks. Two of the deaths Percival felt particularly keenly. 'Amongst the killed', he wrote, 'was my great friend Wilfred Bull, one of the best fellows who ever lived. He was a great loss to the Regiment and to me especially as I had been with him since the beginning of the war almost continuously.'[13] The two had indeed both stood in the queue to enlist at 10 Stone Buildings on the first day of the war and had had remarkably parallel fortunes ever since. There had been a great bond between the two company commanders: they had both given up positions in the City to enlist, were considerably older than the average volunteer officer and had followed very similar paths, even down to taking the Aldershot course together after their recovery from wounds. 'He was the most popular man in the Regiment', wrote Arthur disconsolately. The losses in this Bullecourt battle also included his own right-hand man, Company Sergeant Major Brands, 'a splendid fellow and a great loss', declared Percival, 'he was the best civilian soldier one could wish to have'. Death on the Western Front was always a lottery and when one's close comrades were struck down as they were in this terrible reverse, the odds against coming through it all alive seemed to be shortening dramatically. When the remaining officers of the original 7th Bedfords had their second anniversary dinner at Steenwoorde, only eight others of the original complement sat down with Percival, though his old CO, now Brigadier General Price, also managed to get over for the occasion.

Perhaps it was as well that a change of job soon afterwards helped to raise Percival's spirits, for the tactical circumstances certainly grew no better. He had a short spell as battalion second-in-command and then three weeks as acting battalion commander when a large draft of reinforcements arrived to replace the recent heavy casualties. Percival drew up a comprehensive programme of training and sports to get them ready for the front. Other costly actions lay ahead, for the battalion was also involved in the Third Battle of Ypres, Passchendaele, which, the Somme notwithstanding, was probably the most harrowing experience for the British Army of the entire war.

Conceived with the double objective of taking the pressure off the mutiny-ridden* French Army and of driving the Germans from their submarine bases at Ostend and Zeebrugge, the Passchendaele offensive involved a force of almost 12 divisions. The Bedfords were not committed until early August, by which time their strength and morale had much

---

* 'Mutiny' is perhaps too strong a word; it was really a military form of industrial action. Some units went on strike, refusing altogether to go back into the line; others worked to rule, content to stay in their trenches but refusing to go 'over the top'. The mutineers seldom harmed their officers, but their action gave a frightening fragility to the French line.

recovered, but they suffered another dreadful mauling. Their objective in Glencorse Wood was taken quite quickly; but holding onto the nasty, vulnerable salient in which they found themselves was tragically costly. The battalion won four Military Crosses in one day but its casualties were 284. The fighting spluttered and flamed for a further two and a half months on 18th Division's front before its weak, weary and dispirited battalions were finally pulled out of the line.

Percival had a spell as assistant to the brigade major during the battle, quickly discovering that the easy life that the 'gilded staff' were reputed to enjoy did not extend as far forward as brigade. He was kept very busy and the HQ dugout, far from being the well-appointed hideaway of subalterns' jokes was, he noted, 'one of the "dampest" spots I ever came across'. Returning to the Bedfords as second-in-command, he found morale further dented by the nightly bombing attacks which German aircraft had begun on the fragile hutted camps behind the line. The casualties were few but the moral effect was considerable; a case of 'bomb one, awaken a thousand' as Mao Tse-tung might have put it. Percival also noted that the latest gas attacks were causing concern. The Germans were apparently using 'a new form of gas shell which made the men very sick and caused blindness lasting for about a week. Having very little smell it was not always easy to detect and was frequently used in conjunction with HE.'[14] One such attack caused the Bedfords 85 casualties in just two days. It hit all the battalion's signallers, runners and medical staff at one go and caused Percival immense problems in dealing with casualties and keeping in touch with brigade.

It was a great relief when the 18th Division was pulled out of this fighting and took its battered battalions to the extreme left of the British line where they spent a miserable winter holding the part of the front at Houthulst Forest. 'Forest' had long ceased to be an appropriate description for what the divisional history described as 'a flat, low-lying 600 acres of broken stump and wreckage, a swamp with many a deep and treacherous hole to trap the unwary' with 'a smell of desolation and decay, of gas shelters, of dead men'.[15] The new location brought a new brigade commander and, for Percival, a spell as his brigade major. The new man was called Sadleir Jackson, a flamboyant, energetic character and a determined commander. He had previously achieved a degree of notoriety when commanding the Cavalry Signals for motoring around the battlefield rear areas in a blue Rolls Royce gathering up stragglers. He immediately set about trying to infuse a new spirit into his battalions and worked his staff hard in the process, not least his brigade major. 'During the three weeks I have been acting Brigade Major', was Percival's rueful note, 'I have had a pretty strenuous time, having on no single occasion been to bed before 1am.' But it was another valuable experience. The close working relationship which he developed with Sadleir Jackson bred a mutual confidence and trust which stood both in good stead in the emergencies which developed early the following year.

It was typical of the British soldier that he was able to find humour even in the atrocious living conditions which the Houthulst sector presented. Captain Vlasto, the Bedfords' medical officer, was based in a grubby little pill box which he described as 'Sky cottage with gas and water laid on' – the roof was open to the sky, it stood a foot deep in water and received a liberal allocation of gas shells from the Germans! Vlasto did well to see the humour in his situation for the poor man was very short-sighted and found the negotiation of the duckboarded walkways of this muddy waste-land a particular trial; but he was a courageous doctor who had won an MC for working unceasingly on the wounded in Glencorse Wood's forward positions during a gas attack. The 6,000-yard duckboard track which stretched from brigade headquarters to the forward trenches was a truly treacherous affair. Battalion reliefs took three hours to make the journey. Percival had a spell as acting commanding officer of the Bedfords during this period and wrote of one visit he made to the forward trenches: 'I made a fairly protracted tour of the front line posts. Before we had gone far I heard a splash and found my guide swimming in a shell hole.' The remarkable thing is that after their ordeal at Passchendaele the Bedfords bore these conditions with such stoicism.

THE TEST OF COMMAND

'No amount of labour – nothing short of a fairy wand – could have prepared all those defences in a few weeks.'

General Sir Hubert Gough

When Percival returned to France on 2 January 1918 after a few days' leave, it was finally to command the battalion with which he had served throughout the war. Still a substantive captain, he now became a temporary lieutenant colonel. The morale of the men he was returning to lead was holding up well; they had borne the miseries of the line in the Houthulst Forest sector and the dingy billets of the aptly named Dirty Bucket Camp with typical good-natured resignation. Spirits had been buoyed up a few days previously by an excellent Christmas dinner complete with turkeys despatched from Paris, hams, sweets and nuts sent from England and the issue of two pints of English beer per man. A draft of 75 reinforcements who had joined the battalion just before the festivities were greatly impressed at the spread laid before them. But the newcomers were mostly from Sussex: the towns and villages of Bedfordshire and Hertfordshire had few young men left to give.

The manpower situation on the Western Front as a whole was quite desperate. There was no way of making good the exceptionally heavy losses of Passchendaele. In order to continue the struggle, the expedient to which a straitened Army Council was now driven was the restructuring of Haig's armies, reducing the previously 'square', four-battalion brigades to ones of only three and breaking up some battalions to bring the remainder up to strength. The men of 8th Bedfords, the junior 'service' battalion of the regiment, were dismayed to learn that theirs was one of the units to be disbanded. Its casualty-wasted complement was sent as reinforcements to other Bedford battalions at the front. A company of seven officers and 174 men joined Percival's battalion. It was a far from ideal way of replacing his battlefield losses but the newcomers were at least joining county comrades and remaining with their own regiment. Their new commander found them 'a very good lot of officers and men'.

Manpower anxieties for the Allied High Command were much more worrying than even these dispiriting disbandments indicated. On the

Eastern Front Russian resistance had now collapsed entirely. Freed from these concerns, the German divisions from the east had been flooding into France and Flanders at the rate of one a week. Intelligence was mounting to the effect that the enemy was strenuously preparing a major offensive, and this at a time when the Allied armies had been further weakened by the need to provide reinforcements for the Italian Front. The Americans, it is true, were now in France in some strength but, as Percival well knew from his contact with them, they needed time to train. In any event, General Pershing would never allow his units to be absorbed piecemeal into the Anglo-French organisation. They were to fight as complete national formations. The French were already seriously weakened by losses and collapsed morale and were insisting that Haig should take over more of the line. The British commander reluctantly agreed. In consequence Gough's Fifth Army was switched to the British right flank, extending Haig's responsibility by some 28 miles of front. Percival's battalion now found itself in the Noyon region with only one further British division between its own 18th and the junction with the main French line. They arrived on 10 February, with the disconsolate company of 8th Bedfords joining them a couple of days later.

'It was very nice to get into clean country again after the mud and filth of Flanders', wrote Percival. The plains of Picardy which Fifth Army now occupied were not without their problems for defence; they had been systematically devastated by the Germans the previous year as they withdrew to the Hindenburg Line. 'All the villages here had been razed to the ground and all fruit trees cut down, bridges broken etc.', noted the Bedfords' commander, 'It was an awful scene of desolation in what must have once been one of the finest parts of France.' The battalion was soon involved in the Fifth Army's priority task of trying to fashion a coherent defensive system out of the ruined countryside, a task which its previous French defenders had by no means carried to completion. General Gough, seldom seen by the forward troops and surrounded by a staff bitterly disliked by the fighting officers, found it no easier. His new section of the line was thinly held (roughly two-thirds of the strength per mile of front that Third Army to his north enjoyed) and he lacked the manpower and transport to get adequate defence materials forward across the wasted countryside to form a continuous trench system. As a result the defence was based on a series of wired-in redoubts with incomplete trenches supplementing them, while his reserve divisions were held far from the front at the insistence of Haig's staff.

As the defensive preparations went desperately forward Percival's Bedfords grew more weary. The front was technically 'quiet' but the normal trench warfare irritations sapped their strength and when relieved in the line they generally found labouring duties rather than rest and retraining awaiting them. The increasingly frequent enemy air raids also

disturbed their nights. Just after the arrival of the contingent from 8th
Bedfords, a bombing raid scored a direct hit on one of their billets causing numerous casualties. Percival himself had a narrow escape when a wall
was blown down on him.

   The German offensive of March 1918 was one of the most widely pre-
dicted events of the war. The changed strategic circumstances made it a
German priority: they had a decisive numerical advantage which they
were anxious to exploit before the American forces could make their
presence felt. There were already four US divisions in France; their training was progressing and their numbers would soon justify their use.
Percival had an American officer with him under instruction when he
took over in the front line at the end of January. It was all very reminiscent of the Bedfords' first taste of the trenches. 'He was very inquisitive
to start with', Percival recalled later, 'and called everything an "outfit",
but very silent before he got to the front line (five miles!).'[1] The
Americans were numerous but they were still evidently very new.

   Meanwhile General Haig's intelligence department had been steadily
amassing evidence of the impending assault. Everyone knew it was coming. There had been 'a great scare on the evening of 28th [February] as
the Boche was expected to attack next morning but nothing came of it',
Percival noted, and by early March he was declaring that the attack 'now
seemed imminent although several officers in high places thought right up
until the last moment that he would not risk a big attack'. By the middle
of the month the staff were correctly forecasting not only the place but
also the actual time of the offensive, as Percival's diary recorded: 'On the
evening of 20th [March] we were carrying out a reconnaissance when we
were informed that a warning order had been given that the German
attack would take place the following morning.' He immediately returned
to camp where his unit was in brigade reserve north of Remigny, to find
everyone on the move as final preparations were made. He 'went to bed in
good time, everybody in a considerable state of excitement'.[2]

   In the light of this forewarning it may seem strange that the March
offensive achieved such surprise and engendered near panic in some of
the units and formations against which it was directed. The spectacular
initial German success was a result of the tactics Ludendorff employed
and the priceless good fortune he enjoyed with the weather. Warm showers had fallen over the front line the previous day, but the weather had
generally been good, ending a dry winter and beginning one of the finest
springs on record. The normally marshy Oise valley was now hard under
foot and the river easily crossed, while along its course and the Crozat
canal system which connected it with the River Somme, there lay a thick
blanket of white mist behind which the Germans were able to ready
their offensive. These ideal weather conditions were the accompaniment
to an artillery barrage which was as secret in its meticulous planning and

deployment by the Germans as it was devastating to the British divisions which suffered its effects. The German artillery specialist who devised it had discarded the laboured and extended preparatory barrage of the kind which had made the Somme and Passchendaele offensives so predictable and movement over the shell-torn ground so difficult. He opted for the tactical surprise of a short, intense and well-coordinated bombardment exploiting the use of gas as well as high explosive. His scheme worked remarkably well.

Percival awoke at 4.50am on 21 March to the clearest possible indication that the great attack was under way: 'There was a terrific roar of artillery – the biggest barrage we ever heard, but owing to the thick mist it was impossible to see much.' At 2.30pm that afternoon, with the brigade outpost line overwhelmed, Percival was ordered to put in a counter-attack and rode forward to a hilltop where he met Brigadier General Sadleir Jackson and from which they could see the Germans digging-in in the valley below them. The counter-attack went in successfully, but by 11pm the situation on General Gough's right flank was so desperate that he ordered a general withdrawal behind the Crozat Canal. Percival had great difficulty contacting all his subunits in the dark, but by 3am they had withdrawn the four miles behind the canal and were busy digging defences. He then gave the order for the bridges to his front to be blown. However at 5am the structures were still intact – the explosives were not strong enough (one account blames old French charges). Although it was now growing light a thick mist still shrouded the canal as Percival frantically tried to rectify the 'awful blunder' of the failed demolition, using all manner of devices from Stokes guns to hand-held picks to get the bridges down. They were all unsuccessful. As the mist began to thin the German units massed for their attempts to cross, bringing up trench mortars and machine guns in support. That afternoon the real fight for the crossings began and just before 5pm the Germans forced their way across the Montaigne Bridge on the Bedfords' left front and penetrated to within 22 yards of battalion headquarters where Percival and his adjutant Captain Browning set about burning the battalion maps and documents.

Sadleir Jackson ordered a joint Bedfords/Northants counter-attack which the Bedfords' Captain Browning led under intense artillery and machine-gun fire. After about three hours of heavy fighting the bridge was retaken, the canal line restored and a bridgehead established across it. Percival took some satisfaction from 'this very successful fight' after the botched demolitions; but the check to the German drive was localised and temporary. They were having the 'luck of the devil' with the weather, for the third day dawned again mistily. Percival soon discovered that the canal had been forced on both his flanks and that the Germans were already in the woods to his rear. He was again ordered to withdraw and managed to do so just as he saw the Germans 'coming through the woods in column of fours'.

This day and the next were among the worst of the war for the Bedfords' commander and his citizen soldiers. Reinforcements were moving forward and French units were being hurried north to help stem the German tide; but the advance now appeared to have gained an irresistible momentum created by the clever use of firepower, infiltration tactics and mustard gas, to which near panic in some Allied quarters served as an additional lubricant. The defending units, whose savagely reduced numbers were now nearing exhaustion, seemed never to have time to establish themselves anywhere before they were ordered to withdraw once more. The Bedfords were told to leave their new position when high ground to its left fell into German hands. Three hours later they received a fresh order to withdraw and re-form with the rest of the division around Caillouel to cover the withdrawal of the French and 1st Cavalry Division. There Percival and his exhausted troops spent the night of 23 March. They had suffered severely in their effort to hold the canal and in the subsequent withdrawal. Artillery, particularly gas shells, had thinned their ranks and the battalion had shrunk to six officers and 200 men.

The Caillouel position brought little respite: the French on the left were already falling back and during the following night the Bedfords were once again ordered back, this time to Crepigny. They reached the position at 10am only to find that the enemy were still two miles in rear of their left flank, so the withdrawal of the dog-weary troops continued. Their next position at Mont du Grandru proved equally untenable because of a 'blue on blue' incident, to use the modern phrase – they were being fired on by French artillery and machine guns in the belief that they were Germans. It was now noon and for safety Percival moved his unit to high ground a little further west. At 3pm new orders came through for a move to Varennes, south of the Oise, via the only river bridge which had been left intact. The exhausted Bedfords moved off in compliance, but had only gone a short way when a fresh message from Sadleir Jackson ordered Percival to turn about and, with 11th Royal Fusiliers, counter-attack the Germans in the town of Baboeuf about a mile away. It appeared that the enemy had pushed between a neighbouring brigade and the French to take the town and threaten several batteries of French 75's which had no infantry between themselves and the advancing Germans.

This was a moment of crisis for Percival. 'Order, counter-order, disorder' is a venerated military maxim. Repeated changes are demoralising enough for fresh troops but in the Bedfords' situation where, as their commanding officer noted, 'officers and men were alike dead tired after five days of incessant fighting', it was a doubly unwelcome countermand.

It had been a nightmarish withdrawal. When the men had marched they had been under fire, often having to withdraw by platoons as they struggled to break contact with the enemy; no sooner had they halted than they were digging in and rolling out wire under the hot spring sun, only to be pulled out of position again with the task half finished. It was a withdrawal, the 18th Division historian makes clear, 'compared with which the Mons retreat, with infinitely less shelling and machine-gun fire, was a skirmish'. Now, with the prospect of security behind the Oise denied them, they were being ordered forward again and into the attack though well below their proper strength and with their energy reserves almost exhausted.

Percival rallied his troops as best he could and they rose to the occasion magnificently. Sadleir Jackson had picked the psychological moment. The sudden change from morale-sapping withdrawal to counter-attack seemed to give the men fresh energy to which the excitement of an assault lent a new surge of adrenalin. The attack went in without artillery support and the Germans, bent on looting the Baboeuf wine cellars, were taken completely by surprise. Within half an hour the fight was over and ten machine guns and 270 Germans were captured. 'It really was one of the most extraordinary performances I ever saw and I hope will get the recognition it deserves', wrote a delighted Percival.[3] It certainly achieved its purpose, for contact with the French flanking unit was regained and the exposed batteries were able to pull out safely. The Baboeuf operation was one of the minor epics of the March retreat, the Bedfords' losses were light and their morale received a great fillip. This was one unit of Fifth Army which had clearly not lost its fighting spirit. Percival was awarded the Croix de Guerre for his unit's share of the action here in 'stopping dead', as the French citation put it, the German advance and covering the French gunners' withdrawal.

As night fell the remnants of the battered 18th Division resumed their withdrawal across the Oise. The Bedfords were the last to cross at 3am and directly afterwards the bridge was blown. 'Since then', Percival wrote home a few days later, 'we have had a rather more peaceful time.' They certainly needed it; every unit of the division was utterly played out. They had borne the brunt of an assault by almost three divisions of von Hutier's Army. The Bedfords had taken a hard knock: they had casualties of five officers and 160 men and many more were missing. The retreat was over on the Noyon sector of the front, but so dangerous did the overall situation remain that the Bedfords were several times called in at critical junctures to support the still crumbling defence further north around Amiens. After one desperate and ultimately forlorn attempt to stem the German advance, Sadleir Jackson wrote to Percival, 'I cannot express to you my admiration for the determination and gallantry shown by your battalion. The manner in which they held their ground is beyond praise and drew the whole of the enemy's strength.'[4] Maxse had been right about the potential of his service battalions.

By the end of April the main force of the German offensive in the Bedfords' sector was spent. The battalion took on successive drafts of reinforcements and Percival snatched a few days in England, less for the rest than to try and get Leslie Keep back to the battalion as his second-in-command. Keep was a brave and experienced officer, the surviving one of the two brothers who had distinguished themselves in the Thiepval action. He had later been evacuated wounded, but that had been over a year previously. Percival was now woefully short of experienced officers and needed a man of Keep's quality to help organise and lead the hundreds of 19-year-old conscripts who were being rushed out from England to replace the losses, not to mention the many young and untried subalterns who were arriving. A batch of 20, two-thirds of the unit officer strength, arrived on successive days at the end of April. His mission was successful and Keep soon rejoined the battalion, 'much to my satisfaction', wrote Percival, who got back to find the battalion already involved in another hard-fought action which climaxed in the struggle for Amiens.

This was the end of the great German spring offensive so far as Arthur Percival was concerned. It had caused his battalion countless casualties, given him much anxiety and little sleep; but the men had been first class. The battalion had never withdrawn unless ordered to and fought many fine little actions. He ended with a grudging admiration for what the enemy had achieved, as he confessed to his father, 'there is no denying that it was a wonderful piece of work on the part of the Boche and extraordinarily well organised; he also had all the luck with the weather . . .' Then, perhaps recalling his many forced withdrawals, he added, 'but at the same time he should not have been allowed to come through like he did'.[5]

In May 1918 Percival and his men learnt, 'much to our sorrow', that 7th Bedfords would shortly cease to exist. 'The 2nd regular battalion from 30th Division was coming to the 18th and would absorb us', wrote their commander resignedly. Another forced reorganisation, pressed upon the high command by the still horrendous attrition rates and the continuing manpower shortages, was about to take place. 2nd Bedfords had suffered badly in the Ypres Salient and were pitifully reduced in numbers. The remnants had been joined with those of 2nd Wiltshires to form a composite battalion. Now even that merger was overtaken and the depleted remainder was transferred to 18th Division to begin the work of absorbing the wartime battalion. Some saw it as the reverse process; the divisional historian wrote of the surviving officers and men coming 'one might say like a draft'. The question of who was to get command of the new unit proved, as Percival admitted, 'a delicate and difficult matter'. The brigade commander insisted, perhaps wisely in the light of the weakness of the senior unit and the stern fighting evidently still to come, on retaining Percival and his headquarters staff as the nucleus of the merged force. He had seen Percival's qualities at close hand in the thick of battle. It was testimony to the complete trust he reposed in the service battalion's commander that he should have preferred him to the 2nd battalion's regular CO who was a cap-badged Bedford and a substantive major. The latter 'behaved very well over the matter', Percival records, and went off to lead a training cadre for the Americans at Rogeant.

It was a time of mixed emotions for Arthur Percival. He was to have the honour of commanding a regular battalion (though at this stage in the war the distinction between 'regular' and 'service' was losing much of its meaning); but first he had the task of disbanding his old unit with which he had served throughout its 'short but glorious life'. Its two Victoria Crosses, numerous other gallantry awards and mentions both in official despatches and popular newspapers all testified to its fighting record. It was some consolation for Percival, as its commander, to be awarded the DSO for his part in its recent operations during which, as the citation recorded, he had handled his battalion cleverly and set a fine example during several critical periods.

Meanwhile the war had still to be won and a great deal of bloody fighting lay ahead, much of it very costly for 2nd Bedfords. At the end of June they took part in a single-division attack on German trenches opposite a feature called the Hairpin. Percival had kept two companies of his young and inexperienced force out of the line, training and rehearsing for this action. He prepared his men with a thoroughness reminiscent of his mentor General Maxse, 'every detail being gone through and rehearsed several times'. He incorporated several novel features in the attack which achieved complete success, taking the Germans wholly by surprise. But two days later the Bedfords were driven back by a strong German counter-attack delivered under an intense artillery barrage. The end result, Percival noted, was very disappointing given the care which had been invested in setting up the attack. Its outcome only went to prove what he 'had always thought to be the case – namely that local operations with limited objectives are not good propositions; the enemy can concentrate too many guns on a small area'.[6]

The Bedfords did not share in the victory of Amiens which Ludendorff declared to be 'the black day in the history of the German Army in the war', since they had beaten off a heavy German attack a couple of days previously. Instead they helped to get an American regiment to battle readiness, but by late August they were in action again, as part of a 54th Brigade attack just south of Albert. By mid-morning 2nd Bedfords had gained their objective and Percival, never far from the action, decided to go forward to C Company's position where the men were digging in on the newly won hill feature. At the start of the action Percival had been reconnoitring the position with one of his forward platoon commanders only to have the young man killed at his side by machine-gun fire. He now had to face the machine guns again and had a very nasty time getting up the hill to C Company for several were still firing and grazing the bank as he climbed it. He finally tumbled into the company dugout, breathless and perspiring from the hurried and dangerous climb. Hardly had he regained his wind when a message came in to say that the brigade commander, Sadleir Jackson, had been wounded and that Percival was to return and take command of the brigade. 'I was very sorry to receive the message,' he wrote later, 'sorry for two reasons, first that he had been wounded and second because I had no desire to leave that dugout for quite a long time.'[7]

Percival had earlier commanded the brigade when Sadleir Jackson was on leave, but this time a replacement brigadier general was in post within a few days and the Bedfords' commander was able to return to his battalion, but with what confidence in his successor we can only guess. 'The new brigadier', he observed dryly, 'was a most charming man, but did not know much about infantry work.' He was one of the numerous cavalry officers who were surplus to requirements in a war which had rapidly outdated their traditional role and competence. But Percival's belief in a successful outcome to the war at large was now increasing, for despite stubborn resistance from the Germans, it was clear that their losses in the Spring Offensive had been immense. They were at last reaching the end of their manpower resources at the very time when those of the Allies, thanks to the Americans, were growing greatly.

General Pershing's troops had had a great initial victory in reducing the weakly held Saint-Michel salient where they took 15,000 prisoners and 450 guns, but they still had much to learn and their later attacks on the main Hindenburg positions proved a different proposition. Percival was seeing a good deal of his transatlantic allies at this time and in an offensive being planned for them he provided a company for liaison duties with 27th US Division which was fighting as a formation for the first time. 2nd Bedfords were part of the force guarding the Americans' left flank and witnessed at close hand the horrendous baptism of fire which the division suffered.

The American staff work was poor, their communications were bad and their attack went in without a preliminary barrage against a still determined enemy. The division was savagely repulsed and Percival did not pull his punches in his judgement of them. Later in the day the beaten troops came dribbling back in twos and threes. '"Looking for their Lieutenant" was the invariable answer when you asked them where they were going', he noted, adding grimly, 'They were indeed learning real war by bitter experience as had been learnt by the Allies some years before.' Telling evidence of the deadly initiation which the Americans of 27th Division suffered is provided by the crumpled note, kept by Percival, which had been found pinned up in a deserted German machine-gun post. On it was scrawled: 'Many loves from the machine gun officer who has killed in the morning of 29.9.1918 50–60 Americans from hier[sic] himself. They were the greatest sheep I ever saw.' At the end of that day Percival was writing, '27th American division was a mere rabble'.[8]

It is clear that the famous 100 Days' Campaign which finally brought the Germans to conclude the Armistice was no easy triumphal march to victory; but now at last the Allies were advancing and with the gain of territory came prisoners. The 'exchange rate', the dehumanised jargon of relative casualty totals, was swinging rapidly in favour of the Allies. In the fighting at the end of September, 2nd Bedfords took 550 prisoners and 30 machine guns before being rested for what was to be their final bout of fighting of the war. Percival remained remarkably fit despite the trials of command, the long periods of action and his earlier wounds. After his battalion had won the brigade sports event he led its team to victory in the divisional cross-country race. The divisional history noted respectfully that 'the commanding officer was the first man home', but Percival's own comments made clear that this was because 'about ten men in front of me went the wrong way!' It was a welcome break, for the Bedfords were soon at the front again, joining in the general advance, but once more having to fight hard for their gains. In 18th Division's southward attack from Le Cateau, they mounted a successful night attack which netted 100 prisoners and 60 machine guns besides causing many German casualties. Even at this late stage the cost of victory was high, the Bedfords suffering 150 casualties themselves. This was no casual *promenade militaire*.

Nor was the last great action on the Western Front in which the Bedfords were once again engaged, the Battle of the Sambre. At 1.30am on 24 October, Percival received orders to have his battalion in position in front of the village of Bousies, about two miles distant, by 4am, ready to support an attack which the Northamptons were to lead. By quickly sending forward an officer to reconnoitre the village and putting in some rapid marching, Percival had his men in place a quarter of an hour before his deadline. So far so good. The unfamiliar enclosed country into which the advance had taken them, coupled with the pre-dawn blackness, caused the Northamptons to lose their barrage and falter. The men of the battalions following on, the Fusiliers and the Bedfords, were soon mixed up with those of the attacking unit. The enemy were still resisting stubbornly from the ridge near Bousies where they were bringing machine-gun fire down on the disordered forward troops and, more disconcertingly, taking the Bedfords in their flank. The brigade advance was grinding to a halt, putting the division's objective in jeopardy.

This was the situation when, as the regimental history records, the Bedfords' commanding officer came up and coolly sorted out the confused mass of men in the firing line, reorganising the battlefront, and formed a strong defensive flank on the right and then thinned out the forward line which by 9.15am was taking casualties from its own heavy artillery support.[9] Then a Bedfords officer who was commanding a Northamptons company led a small party with great courage and daring to deal with the machine-gun posts. He personally put four out of action from a total of six which his party cleared before the advance could be resumed. He won the Victoria Cross for his action. The fight continued throughout the day and into the night. Percival and his men were finally relieved at 2am after 24 hours of continuous action and taking 55 casualties. Later another daring little action took place at Preux au Bois where Percival and his men showed their growing versatility in mobile warfare and cooperation with tanks. At last, 2nd Bedfords were finally taken out of the line and moved back to Le Cateau for a much-needed rest. It was there that they finally heard the news of the Armistice. The juggernaut was finally sated; no further sacrifice would be demanded.

'Thus ended', wrote Percival, 'eight months of the most terrific fighting the world has ever seen. The situation more than once seemed desperate and now we had actually gained a military victory; it seemed almost unbelievable.' The campaign from the start of the German Spring Offensive onwards had been a most strenuous and almost continuous battle, with Percival's battalion in the thick of the action for much of the time. 'As an infantry officer it had, of course, been a very trying time,' he wrote, noting that the casualties suffered by his battalion in the final seven and a half months' fighting exceeded those suffered by 7th Bedfords in the preceding 32 months at the front. The campaign of 1918, with its return to a kind of mobile warfare, had been a particularly instructive period for him. It overturned all the predictabilities of trench warfare with its secure flanks and regular rest periods and exposed the psychological corrosion which repeated retreats can cause, the importance of initiative on the battlefield and the consequences of sheer exhaustion for fighting efficiency.

The Great War had been the most intense experience of Percival's life, and had produced a profound change in his personal circumstances and the direction his future would take. From the rather dull City backstreet where he had shared in the administration of a small office staff and played a minor role in Britain's trade in iron ore, he had moved to the command of an 800-strong battalion, and for a time the 3,000 men of a brigade. The nine-to-five working day and routine commuting existence were now a world away from the soldier's life of unlimited liability and the officer's of total responsibility. He had now led his men through the deadliest undertakings it was possible to imagine. His battalion had lost over 1,200 men who had either been killed in action or had died subsequently as a result of their wounds, among the highest totals in the division.

Thousands more had been wounded. The unit's ranks had been emptied and refilled time and time again. Fine soldiers and dear friends had fallen, like CSM Brands and Wilfred Bull; others like Lieutenant Whitburn at Albert had been shot down by his side. In common with every other infantry officer, Percival could count himself lucky to have survived. He had ridden his luck and done all he could to see that his battalion was as well placed as any in the division to cope with the rigours of the front and the lottery of action. He had kept his men fit and done his best to fill their leisure hours, working hard, for example, to get a cinema installed to lighten the off-duty hours at Dirty Bucket Camp. Over that project his luck had not held so well; the cinema hut had burnt down a few hours after completion. The lottery of war again.

Percival had been one of 106 eager young men who had enlisted in the Inns of Court OTC on the first day of the war. The fate of this group of aspirant officers starkly epitomizes one aspect of the national experience. Six of these volunteers had been discharged early in their training as unsuitable. Of the remaining hundred, 29 were now dead, killed in battle or dying later of their wounds, like Second Lieutenant Harry Creasy of the Devons, who had stood directly behind Percival in the queue to volunteer at Stone Buildings, but did not even live until the Somme. Of the 71 who survived the war (much shorter odds it might be noted than for those commissioned by other routes), 33 had been wounded, some twice over and one as many as three times. Percival was one of only three to achieve the rank of lieutenant colonel. Most of his intake had spent their war on the Western Front, but a few had tales to tell of campaigns in Salonika or Palestine, Italy or Egypt. Many had been decorated, but while Percival's DSO, MC, Croix de Guerre and three mentions in despatches were by no means singular in the Army at large, they were unmatched by his Inns of Court contemporaries.[10]

The war itself, better than any selection process, had shown how well suited he was to the military life. He had boundless energy and stamina, his leadership qualities and bravery were proven in combat and he had rapidly caught up with his longer serving contemporaries as far as knowledge of his chosen profession was concerned. Moreover, although the war had affected him deeply, it did not seem to have weighed him down as it had many others. 'I have had rather a dose of battle fighting and was glad of the rest', he had written at one point; but he came through the ordeal hale and balanced as ever. One contemporary, writing at the time of the final campaign of 1918 saw him as, 'a slim, soft-spoken young man, about twenty-four years of age [he was in fact 30] with a proven reputation for bravery and organisation powers.[11] His brigade commander, the ebullient, extrovert Sadleir Jackson, though of quite a different temperament to the undemonstrative Percival, had no doubt of his qualities as a fighting commander; few had been in a better position to evaluate them in the most testing of circumstances. Jackson's end-of-war confidential report on Percival summarised him as, 'An excellent and most efficient officer, beloved by his officers, NCOs and men . . . a very brave and gallant officer' whom he considered 'exceptionally gifted'.[12] A further acknowledgement of these qualities and his war performance came with the award of a brevet majority in the New Year Honours of 1919.

6

THE NORTH RUSSIAN
RELIEF FORCE

'Civilisation is being completely extinguished over gigantic areas, while Bolsheviks hop and caper like troops of ferocious baboons amid the ruins of cities and the corpses of their victims.'

Winston Churchill, November 1918

On 19 September 1918, when Percival's 2nd Bedfords were preparing for their part in the battle of Roussoy, in another sector of the Western Front, Brigadier General Edmund Ironside was being relieved of his command in France and told to report immediately to the War Office where details of a new assignment awaited him. He was a highly regarded officer, well placed for promotion to command of the next available division at the front. Now he suspected that a return to staff work awaited him; in his more melancholy moments he feared that the new post might be in the War Office itself. When he was finally interviewed by the Chief of the Imperial General Staff (CIGS), Sir Henry Wilson, his fears proved only partially ill-founded. He was to become Chief of Staff to the Commander-in-Chief of the Allied Forces in North Russia whose headquarters were in Archangel – a staff job indeed but a long way from Whitehall.[1] The reasons for the presence in North Russia of such a force, in which Arthur Percival would soon be serving, are not entirely edifying and require a little explanation.

Russia ceased to be an ally of Britain and France when, her armies defeated and her state in fragments, she concluded a separate peace with Germany at Brest Litovsk in March 1918. Long before this the two coastal towns of Archangel and Murmansk in the far north of European Russia had risen to prominence in the war as ports of entry for the vast quantities of munitions and supplies with which Britain had endeavoured to sustain her eastern ally in the common enterprise against Germany. Even when Russian resistance collapsed Allied interest in this northern front did not diminish. The port facilities at Murmansk, freakishly ice-free all year despite lying within the Arctic Circle, had been developed and a railway built southwards to connect it with the main Trans-Siberian Line.

Archangel too, though ice-bound for six months in every twelve, benefited from a railway connecting it with the main line and also lay on the banks of a major river, the Dvina, which was navigable in the summer for 400 miles from the sea. If both ports were used as a base for Allied forces, whether Russia was in the war or not, the German position in the east could still be threatened and her high command deterred from switching forces to France and Flanders. There were already considerable stocks of military stores at both ports where numbers of British nationals were residing. The difficulty was finding a pretext for intervention.

In wishing to protect the Murmansk railway and its stockpile of *matériel*, the Allies found common cause with the Murmansk Bolshevik authorities, for both feared the advance of German General Graf von der Goltz from Finland where he was rumoured to have a force of 15,000 at his disposal. With Finnish support, von der Goltz could perhaps topple the Murmansk Soviet and establish White Russian rule. He could also convert the important port into a German U-boat base, undermining the elaborate anti-submarine strategy which Britain had so painstakingly developed and on whose success the sustenance of her population depended. A telegram from Trotsky, the Communist Commissar for War, instructing the Murmansk Soviet to give the Allies 'all and any assistance', had been despatched on 2 March 1918. This provided the necessary pretext. The fact that the peace of Brest Litovsk was negotiated a few days later and that the telegram's message was later rescinded mattered little to the anxious Western Allies.

By May 1918 Royal Marines were in action alongside the Russians against the Finns on the Murmansk front. French and American contingents arrived. General F C Poole was appointed Commander-in-Chief Allied Forces North Russia. Soon a second force composed of Polish, French and British troops was sailing towards Archangel where they landed to the accompaniment of a naval bombardment of the Archangel defences. The previous day Allied diplomatic representatives had arrived in the town from Vologda further south, suspiciously soon after a *coup d'état* by former tsarist officers and the overthrow of the Bolsheviks. Clearly, Allied policy was developing. Aside from deterring any German moves, it now looked as though the Allies were intent on establishing a rallying point for all Russian anti-Bolshevik forces in the north, playing a full-blown part in the civil war. By the time Ironside arrived, General Poole had developed an ambitious plan for an attempt to link up this northern front with the anti-Bolshevik forces in Siberia. His idea was for an advance south as far as could be managed before the onset of winter, the establishment of defensive positions and then the resumption of the advance once the conditions were suitable. It was a plan to which the new Secretary of State for War, Winston Churchill, gave his enthusiastic backing.

Ironside was less than impressed with the motley assortment of military personnel assembled at King's Cross station to make the journey to Archangel with him. He was little more content when he arrived at the Russian port and was able to survey his command – for commander he rapidly became when Poole returned home. This front had been opened when the war with Germany was at a crisis point and few good soldiers could be spared for such a secondary theatre. Many of his men were low grade, reckoned to be unfit for service on an active front. It was, he confessed, 'a tiny army of not very first class troops sitting on the edge of Russia's vast territory, in which was being fought a bitter civil war'.[2]

On 11 November 1918 came the Armistice. This removed both the local anxiety concerning the German–Finnish threats to north Russia and the main strategic rationale for the presence of Allied troops on Russian soil. With the Armistice, almost to the day, came the north Russian winter. This shut down the Archangel front's river supply line to its forward posts, brought conditions of unparalleled cold and condemned the mediocre forces of Ironside's command to an isolated half-life with two murky hours of daylight in each 24 and the constant threat of Bolshevik guerrilla attack without any sign of relief and hope of return to their more temperate homelands.

Neither these local problems, nor the lack of a sustainable rationale for the force's continued presence, proved any brake on Churchill's enthusiasm for intervention or reduced in the least his optimism over a junction between Admiral Kolchak's White Russian forces in western Siberia and a British-led North Russian Army pushing down from the north. Churchill had neither liking nor respect for the Bolsheviks and held the enduring view that 'twenty or thirty thousand resolute, comprehending Europeans could, without serious difficulty or loss, have made their way very swiftly along any of the great railroads which converged on Moscow' and brought the Bolsheviks to heel.[3] The problem was finding sufficient men who met this exacting specification. Besides this, there was the not inconsiderable difficulty of the domestic opposition to this very questionable military commitment now that the war was at an end. The opposition came not only from the Labour Party, for whom the Bolsheviks represented the new dawn of their socialist aspirations, but also from a good deal of liberal opinion in Britain. Although the Army hierarchy remained generally enthusiastic, they were also becoming concerned at the resources involved in the venture and the countervailing demands for troops coming from both India and Ireland.

Ultimately, on 4 March 1919, the Cabinet decided that Britain should evacuate all her troops from North Russia by the end of the Russian summer. Bitterly disappointed, Churchill set about developing his proposals for covering the withdrawal; paradoxically, this involved a very substantial reinforcement of the troops already there. Churchill certainly had ulterior motives for making his proposal for reinforcements; but it was a wise decision nonetheless. The Director of Military Operations (DMO) was already concerned at 'the unreliable state of the troops composing the forces under the command of Generals Ironside and Maynard'. In his view they were, 'a heterogeneous assortment of all nationalities and . . . never of high quality. They are now tired, dispirited, homesick and inclined to be mutinous'.[4] It was a judgement from afar, but a sound one: the first mutiny occurred in the small Russian contingent within a month of Ironside's arrival; several more were to follow. A French unit from the railway front also mutinied, as briefly did a British regiment under the unusual leadership of two sergeants whose previous war service had been spent in England in the Royal Army Pay Corps. Churchill feared that the morale of the British contingent had become so fragile that it might break entirely before reinforcements could arrive. He therefore drafted a direct appeal to all the British soldiers of the force, interfering in the remit of a distant commander as he was wont to do. Ironside found the message an 'unfortunate telegram' which he declined to communicate in any form to his troops.

Despite these concerns about morale, Churchill still had more proactive tasks in mind for the reinforcements than merely organising a clean break and a safe withdrawal. He still dreamed of an active role for them in effecting a junction of the major anti-Bolshevik Russian forces. He discussed with the CIGS 'a good punch towards Viatka to join Kolchak before we pulled out'.[5] This was rather more than the Cabinet believed it had sanctioned. Notwithstanding the wavering of Churchill's ministerial colleagues, the continuing doubts of Lloyd George and, ultimately, bad news from Kolchak's Siberian front, it was a version of this plan with which Arthur Percival became involved. For the first time, but by no means the last, he was to be the instrument of the judgements and enthusiasms of his new political master, Winston Churchill.

Since the Armistice Percival had been learning a good deal about peacetime soldiering. During the war he had given virtually every waking moment to the well-being of his soldiers and the success of the battle operations of his battalion. Now, with the almost palpable sense of relief which spread throughout the Army, he was enjoying, if not the fruits of victory, at least some of the celebration and merrymaking which came with the end of this terrible war. There was a trip to the Rhine with Sadleir Jackson, a visit to inspect the fortresses of Liège and Namur and speculate on the manner of their fall, and a viewing of other celebrated parts of the scarred battlefield. There were partridge shoots, sports meetings, grand balls in the newly liberated cities and, of course, the novel experience of a Christmas spent with an Army based abroad but at peace. After the long and bloody ordeal the fervour of the celebrations may be imagined.

Percival was to savour at last the lavishness of the hospitality which a peacetime Sergeants' Mess can extend to its commanding officer. He was not the first or last to find it 'a very severe ordeal', for senior officers must try to retain some semblance of sobriety on these occasions.

Of more immediate concern, however, was the much less glamorous business of clearing up the battlefield after this 'war to end all wars'. The 2nd Bedfords stayed in the battle zone as a pioneer battalion, removing the detritus of the fighting and collecting the vast array of weapons which the great industries of Europe and America had concentrated in this relatively small area. Demobilisation began. In small parties men of the regiment went home again, to what kind of future they knew not. Steadily the strength of the battalion ebbed away. Percival did his best to give the returnees a good send-off, each man receiving a personal letter from his CO thanking him for his services and a stirring farewell from the corps of drums. The rest was up to the grateful government and nation. Percival's happy association with the Bedfords came to an end when the small regular nucleus of the regiment, commanded by the ever faithful Major Keep, went back to Bedford where a civic reception awaited.

Meanwhile at the War Office General Radcliffe was thinking about the relief force for Archangel. In the light of the morale problems of the existing troops he was determined that it should be a top quality contingent led by 'selected officers of the highest stamp'. Two brigades were ultimately decided upon, commanded by Brigadier Generals Grogan and Sadleir Jackson, both of whom met the DMO's criteria. Grogan was the holder of the Victoria Cross (whose ribbon his brigade major, the youngest man of that rank in the Army, also wore); Sadleir Jackson was a 'double DSO' and had been the dashing commander of 54 Brigade and Percival's chief. When invited by Sadleir Jackson to join his brigade of the relief force, Percival accepted with alacrity. Perhaps he, like others, was seduced by the Secretary of State's eloquent enthusiasm into believing that the expedition could well provide the opportunity for sightseeing in Petrograd and Moscow. Another volunteer from the Bedfords was Harry Driver who, like Percival, had gained his DSO and MC on the Western Front.

Grogan's brigade was composed of young regular soldiers, all volunteers, well trained and very fit; but none had seen service in the war. Sadleir Jackson's men were also very fit volunteers but were specially chosen for their combat experience. Some were drawn from the ranks of those still serving, but many were recently demobilised veterans who quickly volunteered once the call was made. They came, one of their officers noted, 'Dressed in civilian clothes, with medal ribbons on their waistcoats and red handkerchiefs round their necks. They have all seen previous service and look the most ideal material from which to form a battalion.'[6] As an *Evening News* reporter noted, it was 'the soldier without a medal ribbon who is conspicuous'. Many ex-officers also enlisted in the ranks: one was an ex-major with a DSO, another a wartime captain with an MC and the Mons Star, a third recently a pilot in the Royal Flying Corps. There were also many ex-subalterns among the rankers. The reasons were all too obvious. Employment was hard to find in depressed post-war Britain where there were soon to be two million men without work. Many of the volunteers had been having a difficult time as their appearance sadly testified: 'Worn clothes, jackets in which the pockets drooped pitiably, collars devoid of all ties, ties to which no collars give effect, baggy trousers, boots thin and cracked'.[7] But straitened circumstances were not the only spur; many missed the excitement of operations and the comradeship of the ranks. They had been unable to settle back into civilian life.

Percival journeyed down to Park Royal Camp in north-west London where Sadleir Jackson's brigade was beginning to assemble alongside Grogan's men in the sunshine and showers of April 1919, preparing for yet another campaign in the early months of peace. Sadleir Jackson's brigade had been embodied as 45th and 46th Royal Fusiliers and Percival found himself a major again in the 46th, whose men chafed impatiently at the delays in getting them equipped appropriately for their ill-defined and novel assignment. Frustrated at the hold-up, some failed to return from weekend leave. Ironside too was becoming concerned. The thaw in North Russia had already begun; by early May the port of Archangel would be open for reinforcements, but even earlier, as the river ice melted, the heavier Bolshevik batteries would be moving downstream to range against him. As yet no word had come of General Gaida's progress on Kolchak's northern wing, nor even that a spring offensive by him was being mounted at all. If there was the slightest chance of a junction with the Siberian Whites, Ironside could afford to make a bold thrust southwards; if not, a more prudential strategy would be needed. The latter circumstance would suggest a limited offensive simply to cover his own withdrawal and prepare the local White Russians to assume responsibility for their own defence. Above all he needed the reinforcements to relieve his dispirited conscripts.

Arthur Percival was second-in-command of the 46th, which had as its commanding officer Lieutenant Colonel Jenkins of the South African Infantry, an experienced soldier with whom he got on well. Percival was very busy sorting out the many requirements of the battalion for its unusual operation. There was fresh equipment to be acquired, a battalion band to be set up, canteen stores to be ordered and many additional problems to be resolved in this odd but high-quality unit, part regular, part civilian, all combat tested and bound for a war theatre of which they knew virtually nothing. In early May they moved to Sanding in Kent to pack their equipment, put in some more training and have the cholera and typhoid inoculations needed for their unusual destination. By the time General Rawlinson came down to inspect the brigade on 22 May, the transformation was complete; the shabby mufti of the veteran volunteers had been exchanged for the smart new uniforms of the Relief Force. The new formation sign of a bright white star against a black background looked a strange accompaniment for the medal ribbons of familiar campaigns, but it conveyed an appropriate message: a new test for the veterans. The North Russian Relief Force was ready to go.

Little more than a fortnight later Arthur Percival was gazing at quite a different landscape to that left behind at Tilbury docks where the battalion had embarked, after the mysterious reappearance of the absentees. 46th Royal Fusiliers were arriving at Archangel. Although it was after midnight as they approached the port which lay somewhat inland from the mouth of the River Dvina, it was nevertheless quite warm and light as midday. The green banks and newly leaved shrubs which fringed the great river gave little indication that this was the 'frozen north'. The journey aboard SS *Pretorian* had been uneventful. They had spent a night in harbour at Murmansk under the bow of HMS *Glory* and alongside two seaplane carriers and a hospital ship with a wireless balloon tethered nearby; all essential support for this isolated expeditionary force. The following morning the small convoy had left the warmth imparted by the Gulf Stream and headed for the cooler waters of the White Sea with its fast-melting ice floes. They had then moved into the Dvina estuary which had remained ice-bound long after the river was clear further inland, a phenomenon which had given Ironside's river flotilla a temporary 50-foot rise in river level to cope with, and the Bolshevik guns their short-lived advantage.

Now the estuary was navigable and the green and gold minarets, red roofs and white walls of Archangel cathedral came into Percival's view as the sun rose higher and picked out the individual small buildings of this largely wooden and rather depressing Russian city. He had heard that a boat was returning to England the following day and hastily scribbled a note home. They had been 'very comfortable on the boat and they have fed us well', he wrote, 'but we want some exercise badly. I have had to let my belt out a hole today'.[8] The convoy soon docked and Ironside viewed the arrival of this, the second brigade of his Relief Force, with growing confidence and satisfaction. 'As I watched them disembarking', he wrote, 'I felt they could walk through anything in North Russia.'[9]

The culture shock which followed their landing was, for Percival, as for the other Western Front veterans of the Relief Force, as much military as it was social, profound though this latter aspect was. Gone was the continuous fighting front from the Channel to the Swiss frontier, gone the elaborate logistical system of railways and motor transport and the heavy, land-based artillery barrages to support all advances. Gone also, alas, were reliable allies or even readily identifiable opponents. In their place there were immense distances, small forces of very assorted quality and a river lifeline. There were three main fronts to Ironside's command, all separated by scores of miles of trackless forest. The remotest was the river front, for which Percival's brigade was destined. It was over 300 miles from the Archangel base, with which its only secure communication was the Dvina. Vast tracts of forest separated the towns and villages in which a passive peasantry, caring little about the civil war, wished only to be left in peace to tend their crops and livestock in the short season of production afforded by the hostile climate. Artillery support, such as it was, came from the river-based monitors of the recently reinforced naval flotilla.

Sadleir Jackson's brigade made its way to the front by river barge drawn by a wood-burning paddle steamer. 46th Fusiliers in their entirety were crammed into a single huge barge which for five days and nights made its slow progress up the Dvina. The river was over a mile wide and occasional flights of duck, giving promise of sport to come Percival was not alone in thinking, provided the only variety in an otherwise uniform and featureless landscape which impressed only by its vastness. With his responsibility for unit canteen arrangements, Percival organised a lively barter trade with the local villagers at the nightly stops, exchanging the staple biscuit and beef ration for eggs and milk and buying butter and cream cheese. The brigade finally disembarked at Bereznik and Ossinova, the advanced bases at the junction of the Dvina and Vaga rivers, and camped with Grogan's brigade at Ossinova, hoping for some relief from the torment of the mosquitoes which had plagued their voyage up-river. Now at last Ironside was able to relieve his sorely taxed forces on the river front, the small Allied contingents which had borne the brunt of the attacks by the more numerous white-clad Bolshevik forces at temperatures of 20 degrees below freezing and with Russian troops of questionable loyalty as their only support. Some Russians could now be put in the front line itself with fresh British troops behind them preparing for an active campaign role.

A Russian battalion of the Slavo-British Legion passed through Percival's lines at Ossinova, moving on to take over a section of the front at Troitsa. This was Dyer's battalion, originally a disciplinary unit formed, in Ironside's words, 'of all the doubtful characters in the refugee population', many of whom 'were of the worst imaginable type, the very riff-raff of a revolution'.[10] The unit's CO, the Canadian Captain Dyer, had carefully sifted out the most undesirable elements and gradually transformed the remainder by training, reasonable treatment and a certain amount of propaganda, into a unit of the Slavo-British Legion with which Ironside hoped to augment the steadily developing White Russian forces. Ironside now intended to use Dyer's battalion in the coming offensive behind one of Sadleir Jackson's battalions. It moved to the forward village of Troitsa on 4 July. On the 7th it mutinied.

A small and determined group of Bolsheviks killed five of their British and four of their Russian officers, together with their orderlies. They imprisoned some of Sadleir Jackson's staff and were not subdued until fired on by artillery from a neighbouring village. Colonel Jenkins and two companies of 46th Fusiliers were rapidly transported to Troitsa aboard the GOC's river steamer to restore order. Percival was left in charge of the battalion, musing about the reliability of local allies and considering how he might dispose of the great cases of rubber thigh boots with which some thoughtful staff officer in the War Office had equipped the battalion, but which were useless in the dry summer and proving to be a great encumbrance.

The mutiny of Dyer's battalion had been Ironside's second piece of bad news. The first had been a telegram from the DMO bearing the information that Kolchak's situation in Siberia was serious, that General Gaida was being driven back and away from North Russia rather than towards it. The projected offensive for a junction with the Siberian forces was now out of the question. The river level had now fallen as dramatically as it had risen and there was no prospect of naval support much further upstream. In addition, some of Ironside's commanders were becoming restive, disgusted at having to put down mutinies. Sadleir Jackson was only with difficulty dissuaded from having nothing at all to do with the Russians and operating entirely on his own. At one point he was reported to have surrounded and forcibly disarmed 4th North Russian Rifles. This was actually a good move, one of the brigadier's officers thought, since they had been 'full of sedition for ages'.[11]

A further mutiny among the Russian forces at Onega on Ironside's right flank (to which Russians aboard the *Walton Belle*, a Margate paddle steamer now plying unfamiliar waters, made an incongruous contribution) persuaded him that the more limited offensive he was now planning, designed only to break the Bolshevik line and facilitate his Army's withdrawal from north Russia, should be brought forward to early August. The withdrawal itself would have to start at the end of the month. He left his forward commander Sadleir Jackson to plan the attack while he sorted out the fragile and querulous White Russian element in his command, about whose prowess Churchill was so misguidedly over-sanguine.

The plan which Sadleir Jackson drew up for the river offensive was characteristically bold and simple. About a quarter of his force would be used for frontal attacks on the enemy positions which extended for about three miles on each bank. The other three-quarters would attack from flank and rear after approach marches of as much as 12 miles through the unmapped forests. A short crash bombardment from the naval artillery would include smoke to cover the long approach marches and was to concentrate initially on the Bolsheviks' front line blockhouses. The front was divided into three sectors corresponding to the two river banks and the river itself. The sector commanders (the battalion COs and the naval commander) set up a separate planning headquarters while their seconds-in-command took over the training and administration of the forces.

No 3 Sector (46th Fusiliers) was the eastern arm of the offensive which was to attack along the right bank of the Dvina with three separate columns taking on the different fortified villages which the Bolos (in north Russia the Bolsheviks were universally if misleadingly known as 'Bolos', in preference to 'Bolshies', the term used by the War Office) held in some strength. The villages together formed a well-entrenched line along the river with positions heavily wired and based on strong log-built block-houses. The line extended into the forest itself for about two miles while the whole defence line was about ten miles deep, based, from front to rear, on the villages of Selmenga, Gorodok, Borok and the adjacent Ivanovskaya.

Major Percival was to command the most substantial force in the No 3 Sector attack, a mixed column of 46th Fusiliers and 1st/3rd North Russian Regiment. His objective was the village of Gorodok, the key to the Bolshevik defences. The other columns were to attack the front-line village of Selmenga and the more distant objective of Borok. At last Percival was able to get back to operational matters, putting aside the annoying corre-spondence with the fastidious paymaster at Archangel about minor details in his imprest account and the more diverting letters from Lady Macdonnel of Swinford whose Irish Women's Association had been pro-viding some of the more attractive canteen items for the battalion which had a strong Irish complement. Percival had dealt with these matters conscientiously enough, but they were a world away from the critical problem of getting his large mixed column right around the flank of the Bolo defences without detection.

There were two vital preliminaries to the offensive: sufficient pack ani-mals to support the forest approach march and the necessary intelligence to enable the column commanders to chart their way through the poorly mapped terrain. Eventually about 1,000 pack mules were requisitioned from the rear areas, their owners being paid, to their evident satisfaction, in flour, sugar and tea. For route guidance the existing forest charts were supplemented by information gained by reconnaissance parties which included local peasants impressed for the purpose. These operated with great skill, despite the contrary impression created by their brand-new and ill-fitting British uniforms. They needed and were given brave British patrol leaders; one, wearing the MC ribbon for his Great War service as an officer, later added the MM and DCM for his exploits as a patrol sergeant with 46th Fusiliers in the Gorodok column.

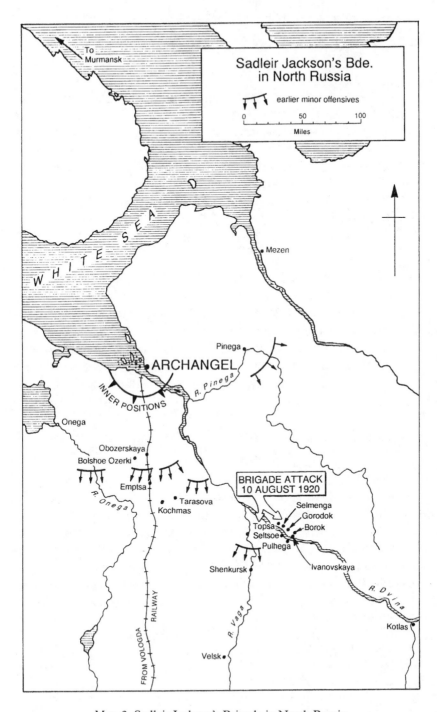

Map 2. Sadleir Jackson's Brigade in North Russia

Percival prepared a detailed appreciation for his column's operation, knowing how critical proper organisation and briefing would be for his mixed force. Eventually all was ready and the three columns formed up for the approach march which, for its first stage, they were to undertake together. As they did so the rain started. The attacks on the three villages were due to be put in simultaneously at noon on 10 August and the long outflanking march began at 9pm the evening before. The columns made slow progress on the little used narrow tracks and the pack animals had particular difficulties negotiating some of the marshy stretches which the downpour was turning into a morass. The crossing of the Selmenga river was hazardous and slow, the banks were steep and slippery and the depth at the crossing site increased alarmingly with the passage of hundreds of human and animal feet. The reluctant Russians were coaxed across with some difficulty. Only after four hours of dangerous vulnerability was the whole force across and the Selmenga column able to split off to prepare its attack on the nearest objective.

After an eight-hour march Percival's column reached his chosen assembly area. It was now 5am and the pack animals were at last unloaded and they and the men given a much-needed rest while Percival took the sub-unit commanders for a reconnaissance of their objective. This disclosed a ridge between the forest edge in which they were concealed and the village itself. The ridge was well protected with wire and defended by machine guns. A Bolo sentry could be seen pacing its perimeter about 300 yards from where Percival was watching. He decided that the ridge would be the first bound of the attack, after which his column would divide for attacks on different parts of the village. Artillery positions for the light guns were chosen and occupied. He ordered a five-minute bombardment of the ridge to cover the assault.

The artillery did its job well, one section of Stokes guns managing to get off 40 rounds in little over a minute as the infantry moved forward to the assault. The attack from this unexpected flank fulfilled its purpose, the column having little difficulty in overcoming the surprised defenders. 'With fire, dash and no hesitation', Percival recorded, both attacking groups moved on to their main village objectives. So quickly did they race across the 500 yards which separated ridge from village that the artillery support had to be stopped prematurely. Once again speed and unexpectedness carried the day. They had 'sprung a complete surprise on the Bolo in the village', noted the column commander, 'it was Sunday morning and he was just having his mid-day meal'.[12] Resistance stiffened as the attackers moved into the western end of the village and there was brisk hand-to-hand fighting before it was finally cleared at about 1pm. By this time about 300 prisoners had been taken. Later there was a hard fight to take a battery of 4.2-inch guns which the Bolsheviks had in action on the edge of the forest, firing on the British support flotilla. When the resistance was finally overcome the battery was found to be manned by German gunners.

Once the village had fallen, Percival set about organising his men in defensive positions to deal with the large numbers of enemy likely to withdraw from the Selmenga positions which his force had outflanked. These were expected to fight their way back in search of safety. At 3.45pm these desperate men emerged from the forest in extended order and attempted to fight their way through; but they immediately came under a heavy fire and retreated into the forest to try to work their way round the north side of the village. Once again they came under heavy fire, particularly from a well-placed outlying machine gun. Most then threw down their arms and surrendered. The remainder fled again into the woods and were rounded up later. By 10pm the fight was over on the Gorodok front; the Bolo had been routed.

The other right bank columns were similarly successful, though without the dramatic speed of the Gorodok force. The front-line Selmenga defence needed a sustained bombardment before it was finally subdued. However the attack did pin down the defenders for the vital hours while the Borok and Gorodok positions were being assailed. When its fleeing defenders finally reached Gorodok, Percival's defences were in place and awaiting them. The Borok position took longer to subdue: its defences were alert and the attackers met a heavy fire from the enemy entrenchments. They lost two officers in the early stages and had trouble with their artillery support. The position finally fell at about 3pm, but not before machine gun fire had claimed the life of Captain Harry Driver, Percival's old comrade from the Bedfords who had fought so valiantly on the Somme. On the other side of the river No 1 Sector's columns had a very shaky start, having a longer approach march and finding more alert defences. Two column commanders were killed and the Sector Commander and his staff were cut off by enemy movements and coordination became impossible. Despite these reverses, all the sector's objectives were finally taken. Once their resistance was broken the Bolsheviks appeared to lose all control. 'My men were digging Bolos out of all sorts of extraordinary places', one company commander wrote, 'such as up chimneys and underneath mattresses.'[13]

By nightfall the full extent of the Gorodok column's success, the most dramatic of the whole river offensive, was becoming clear. Percival had captured a regimental and two battalion commanders with about 750 of their men. Roughly 40 more had been killed. His men had taken nine artillery pieces, 16 machine guns, five trench mortars and 70,000 rounds of small arms ammunition, besides much equipment and secret documents. It was all testimony to the speed and surprise that the operation achieved which made an immense contribution to the success of the whole offensive. The Gorodok column took one-third of the prisoners, half of the guns and one-third of the small arms which the two battalions together had captured. Its casualties were 12, only seven per cent of those sustained by the two battalions.[14]

Sadleir Jackson had achieved a complete, if local, victory. The whole of the river front was 'enveloped and destroyed', Ironside declared. Six enemy battalions were crushed. The delighted Percival expressed it more colloquially in a letter to his father: 'We have scuppered practically the whole of the Bolshevik Army on this front,' he wrote.[15] In commenting on his columns' operations, Lieutenant Colonel Jenkins paid special tribute to the Gorodok force, 'splendidly led and organised by its commander'.[16] Later, at a ceremony at Lyavlya, further back down the river, Ironside presented Percival with a bar to his DSO for his leadership of the Gorodok operation. The citation noted the 'great gallantry and skill' with which he handled it and mentioned particularly his excellent leadership during the Selmenga counter-attack. As another of the 46th's officers recorded when he heard of the award, 'No one deserved it more.'[17]

The British North Russian Expeditionary Force was now able to withdraw from Murmansk and Archangel in relative safety, taking with it some 6,500 Russian refugees, people whose lives a future Bolshevik victory would put at risk. However, the speed with which the Bolshevik forces recovered from the Dvina reverse was ominous for the White Russian Army which remained under the ill-starred General Yevgenii Miller to continue the fight. Within a month fresh enemy troops from south Russia were launching bold but inexpert attacks along the river while the White Russians, true to form, were refusing to occupy their agreed positions. The difficulties which the British experienced in extricating their flotilla from the shallow Dvina made it abundantly clear that its support for a more ambitious advance would have been limited and unreliable. General Miller's Army did not have the stomach to resist for long. Lord Rawlinson, sent to Archangel to supervise the withdrawal, had quickly taken their measure. On the very day of Sadleir Jackson's offensive he had written prophetically of the Russians, 'Their troops won't fight alone and their officers are hopeless.'[18] It was no less than the truth. In early September, a 46th Fusilier officer recorded a confidence from a Russian colleague confirming that, 'the whole Russian Army here, (and there are thousands of them), are in such a bad state that as soon as the British are gone they will murder their officers and desert'.[19]

His Majesty King George later wrote to Lord Rawlinson congratulating him on the successful withdrawal. His message, compiled no doubt with the advice of Secretary of State Churchill, concluded with the words, 'It is especially gratifying to me to note that the withdrawal has been carried out in such a manner as to leave the loyal Russian forces in a favourable position for continuing an active and resolute defence.'[20] It was fond hope rather than sound judgement. On 27 September General

Ironside and his last troops left Archangel. Within three months General Miller's resistance had been totally extinguished and the port had fallen to the Bolsheviks. For Arthur Percival, however, it had been all in a day's work and another notch on the rifle butt of his military experience. As a fellow battalion officer put it, 'Certain things were asked of us, and those things we performed.'[21]

IRELAND:
THE INSURGENCY DEVELOPS

'Men who take up arms against the State must expect at any moment to be fired upon. Men who take up arms unlawfully cannot expect that the troops will wait until they are quite ready to begin the conflict.'

Winston Churchill, Secretary of State for War, 8 July 1920

It may seem strange, in the light of the terrible war which had so soon supervened in Europe, that Ireland rather than Germany should have been the focus of political attention in Britain during the torrid summer of 1914. It certainly appeared at the time that if the nation were to be involved in conflict at all, civil war in Ireland rather than international war in Europe was very much the more likely. If the pistol shot in Sarajevo soon sent its reverberations around the continent, it was some while before the Foreign Office brought its consequences to the forefront of the Cabinet's attention. The chronic Irish Problem which had bedevilled British politics for more than a century had once again entered a crisis phase, so acute on this occasion that it would not end until the problem had been entirely transformed, though hardly solved.

Despite the intensity of the fighting during the Great War, Ireland remained a source of grave anxiety and concern. In 1916, as preparations were quickening for the great offensive on the Somme, the Easter Rising in Dublin took place – a most unwelcome distraction for the military planners. In the event, the rebellion was put down in less than a week and drew no great public support. The Army garrison in Ireland rooted out 1,500 of the rebels and was reasonably satisfied with its performance. However the rising did prove a turning point: the execution of the ring-leaders shocked all Ireland, while political efforts to revise the Home Rule formulation kept the issue at centre stage. A rapid politicisation of Irish society took place; young men with no previous political consciousness became quickly aware of the republican cause. One such was Tom Barry, a young bombardier serving with the British Army in Mesopotamia, who was later to be a thorn in the side of the Essex Regiment based in West

Cork. He was to command the Irish Republican Army (IRA)'s West Cork Brigade 'flying column' and to have as principal adversary Major Arthur Percival, Intelligence Officer (IO) of 1st Battalion the Essex Regiment and the organiser of its anti-IRA operations.

Deeply involved in the European war, the Government attempted to administer Ireland on the basis of mild coercion – 'repression too weak to root out opposition, but provocative enough to nurture it'.[1] By the end of 1917 the faction of the Republican movement which believed in physical force rather than moral persuasion and political action, was gaining ascendancy. In April the following year, when the Ludendorff Offensive was in full swing, it received a decisive stimulus from the Government. The Western Front manpower situation was now so desperate that it was decided to extend conscription to Ireland. Reaction to the measure was immediate, wholesale and hostile. It united Republican opposition behind Sinn Fein and the Irish Volunteers. The Government finally acted decisively. Sinn Fein leaders were arrested and both it and the Irish Volunteers were declared dangerous associations. Viscount French was appointed Lord Lieutenant of Ireland. Talk of conscription and of Home Rule were dropped. The conscription decision and the violent reaction to it is said to have been 'the decisive moment at which Ireland seceded from the Union'.[2] However, an increasingly bitter campaign of nationalist guerrilla warfare and Government counter-insurgency was to hold sway for many months before that secession and the political compromise it involved were finally agreed to.

In January 1919 the Irish Volunteers were reconstituted as the IRA and the overall republican campaign matured, combining civil resistance and physical violence in an interlocking campaign against British rule. The campaign of violence had several phases. First came the efforts to capture arms, then their use for killing Royal Irish Constabulary (RIC) members and for attacks on smaller police posts, then raids and attacks on stronger police and Army installations and finally the establishment of 'flying columns' for larger anti-military operations. Control from Dublin was loose; the IRA secret publication *An t Oglach*, eventually a weekly publication, was the nearest thing that the IRA had to 'general orders'. It became a valuable coordinating blend of propaganda, intelligence and operational advice, comparable, in the view of one of Arthur Percival's Essex Regiment colleagues, to GHQ's 'Notes on Recent Fighting' issued in France during the Great War.[3] Behind the fighting men of the IRA stood the invaluable women's organisation *Cumann na m Ban*, composed of companies corresponding to the IRA's own and with the sole purpose of supporting the men of violence. It was all a far cry from the Bolos, mosquitoes and unreliable allies of the North Russian campaign.

1st Battalion the Essex Regiment, a much understrength unit of seven officers and 201 other ranks, disembarked in Ireland at the port of Kinsale in southern Cork on 31 August 1919. Arthur Percival was not among its complement; it would be another month before the battalions of the North Russian Relief Force even began their return journey from Archangel. Once home, he would enjoy the much-anticipated two months' leave which had been promised to all volunteers for the controversial Russian operation. Percival had now been in uniform for over five years, on active operations for much of the time, but had yet to serve with his regiment. He was to join 1st Essex in January 1920, by which time they were in the thick of operations against the IRA in West Cork which had become a particularly troubled area.

A campaign to boycott the RIC had been in progress for some time and attacks on them had started in July 1918. By the end of September West Cork had been declared a Special Military Area. The troop strength was increased and the local brigade commander was given powers to impose extensive restrictions. These measures quietened the situation temporarily but in 1919 attacks for arms and explosives began in earnest with the troops becoming more directly involved. In June 1919 at Kilbrittain a patrol of six soldiers and an RIC constable was disarmed and bound, the IRA escaping with their weapons. In November a haul of weapons was taken from a British motor torpedo boat in Bantry Bay when most of its crew was ashore. In Kilbrittain an RIC constable was shot dead in December, the same month in which Michael Collins' celebrated squad of terrorists made their dramatic assassination attempt on Lord French himself. The Army was now given extensive new powers of search and arrest and decided upon a policy of mass detention of all known IRA leaders. Percival joined his battalion at Kinsale as the plans for implementing this policy were being developed.

The enemy which now opposed 1st Essex was growing to formidable proportions. By the time of Percival's arrival, the Cork IRA was sufficiently strong to be divided into three brigades, with the West Cork Brigade operating in the 1st Essex area. It had seven battalions in all, based on the principal towns in the area and operating from Kinsale in the east to Castletown Bearhaven in the west, some 100 miles away. These 'battalions' were hardly the equivalent of the conventional British unit, but with their active supporters in the civil population they were a significant guerrilla force. The raids at Kilbrittain and Bantry had given them a nucleus of arms and they had managed to supplement these from a variety of sources for, incredible though it may seem, privately held weapons had yet to be confiscated by the authorities. Above all, they knew intimately the land over which they were fighting and their local intelligence was first class.

The main chronicler of the exploits of the IRA's No 3 West Cork Brigade is Tom Barry, according to whose account all the British troops who now began to hunt the IRA, 'had battle experience during the

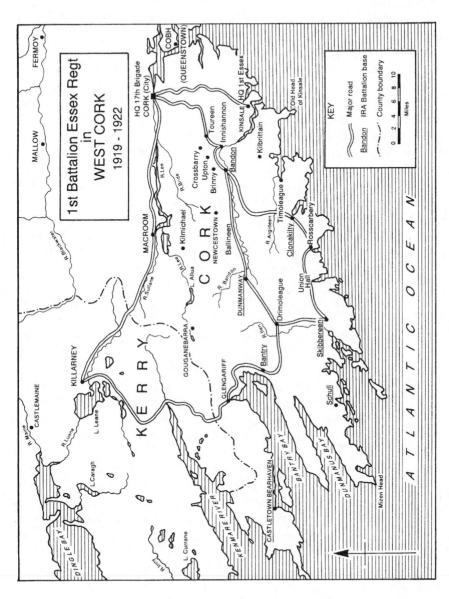

Map 3. 1st Battalion
the Essex Regiment
in West Cork

1914–18 war . . . were highly trained and well accustomed to fighting and to bloodshed' and had the 'finances of the world's largest empire behind them'.[4] So much for the perceptions of the IRA. It was hardly a description that Percival would have recognised when he joined the regiment. Ireland had been garrisoned throughout the war by Britain's reserve forces and only recently, with the great conflict at an end, were the depleted ranks of the regulars replacing them. Churchill's demobilisation policy of 'first in, first out' (replacing the disastrous expedient of releasing first the skilled men needed by industry who had invariably been the last to join up – a decision which had caused mutinies at the end of the war) meant that the regular units had lost their most experienced NCOs and men first. At the same time, they were endeavouring to absorb masses of new recruits, for by the summer of 1919 four out of every five men who had served during the late war had been discharged.

As for hunting the IRA, this was hardly the immediate concern of 1st Essex when they came ashore at Kinsale. They had first to absorb the personnel and equipment of their 3rd (Special Reserve) Battalion based at Castletown in the far west of the county, having already released their 483 wartime soldiers back to civilian life and, finally, begin the absorption of 300 new recruits, as well as the officers and NCOs returning from a variety of wartime appointments and foreign adventures – like Percival's in North Russia. The new recruits were young and inexperienced. 'Many of them were boys', the regimental history recorded, 'many of them, owing to insufficient education during the war, were ignorant and indisciplined to a degree.'[5] These were hardly the men to be thrown into the sophisticated soldiering required by counter-insurgency campaigning. This was the reality throughout Ireland, traditionally an area for military training and country sports, now the arena for an increasingly bitter anti-terrorist struggle.

Lieutenant Colonel Moffitt DSO, the commanding officer of 1st Essex, must have been mightily relieved at the arrival of Percival, an experienced, mature and battle-proven officer, whom he put in charge at the riverside market town of Bandon, for it was a particularly troublesome spot. He was extremely short of experienced officers, a number of whom had taken advantage of the gratuity scheme designed to reduce the Army's war-swollen officer establishment. As if that had not been enough disruption, he had only just got the men back to their scattered security posts after the false alarm of a move to the Plebiscite Area of East Prussia. One company had even got as far as Cologne before the move was cancelled. So much for Tom Barry's picture of the well-drilled military machine set against him.

As Percival looked about him and began to plan his anti-IRA operations he could well have been excused for being a little daunted at the prospect. Bandon, originally a Protestant stronghold and determinedly loyalist since the establishment of a settlement there in the time of Elizabeth I, was now much changed. Catholic and Republican influence had developed strongly and in recent times a local Catholic businessman had been the prime mover in the establishment of the Bandon Irish Volunteers. These had now grown into the strongest battalion in a particularly aggressive IRA brigade. Local society was deeply divided. The Essex detachment Percival commanded at Bandon was composed in the main of partially trained recruits. Even the few experienced NCOs and junior officers were quite unprepared for the irregular warfare they were to encounter. Massed assaults, trench fighting, tank and artillery support were all things of the past. In Ireland all was to depend upon fieldcraft, marksmanship, the seizing of opportunity targets and, above all, on local knowledge and sound intelligence. Great responsibility, patience and initiative would be required of junior NCOs who had seldom made much call on such qualities before. A particular concern for Percival as the local commander was that the challenges to discipline would be great in circumstances in which direct personal command would be difficult, for the operational unit would henceforth be the section or platoon rather than the company or battalion. It was all as different from Flanders and North Russia as it was possible to imagine.

Percival was now beginning an assignment which, aside from the Malayan campaign itself, was the most taxing and controversial of his entire career. If he had mixed feelings when taking over from Major Thompson the half of the latter's company which formed the Bandon garrison, he could have been little cheered by his first impression of the local RIC. They were not only total strangers to him, but also rather demoralised by their recent reverses. A priority task was to get to know these men for whose safety he was to be responsible and on whom he was, initially at least, critically dependent for local intelligence. In the latter regard he did not find them immediately cooperative. 'It took a lot of talking before you got very much out of them', he noted later. Besides, they did not always know a great deal, especially in a town like Bandon with a very active IRA presence. By the start of 1920 they were under regular attack and 'their morale, with very few exceptions gave way and they were of little assistance except to act as local guides'.[6] Hunting the IRA was to be largely down to Percival's own efforts.

By early February 1920, the local IRA brigade were strong enough to begin a more concerted offensive against the RIC. Simultaneous attacks were launched on the barracks at Allihies, Farnivane and Timoleague, all in the Essex area. The posts were resolutely defended and the attacks failed, as did one the following month at Durrus. After a lull in guerrilla activity the brigade switched to a policy of killing individual policemen. It was a decision which quickly angered and exasperated the military forces. In April a sergeant from the Dublin Metropolitan Police was shot dead by the Clonakilty battalion. The following day another group killed a sergeant and constable near Upton, taking their weapons and ammunition. Arms were again captured when three constables were killed and a fourth wounded near Timoleague. This was all on the Essex patch and not far from Percival's Bandon base. The troops seemed powerless to deal with an enemy whose intelligence was up-to-the-minute, whose methods were entirely ruthless and about whom it was difficult to obtain accurate and timely information.

There was one local IRA member about whom the authorities were apparently well informed. Tom Barry had by now been recruited as an under-cover member of the Bandon battalion, charged with acting as an intelligence officer in the town area; but in May he discovered that Major Percival already had him on his 'wanted' list, so he quickly left the town. Percival's own intelligence work was beginning to have an effect. In the light of Barry's military experience in the British Army and evident enthusiasm and determination, he was soon put in charge of brigade training.

It was one thing for Percival to resolve that his only option was to get out and hunt for information, but quite another to acquire it. Many townspeople were sullenly silent if not actively hostile, while the battalion's operational area was immense. The substantial ports of Queenstown and Kinsale absorbed the greater part of the battalion's manpower, but further west lay the open and wilder areas which the detachments of Bandon, Bantry and Clonakilty patrolled. The distances were considerable and the nature of the country greatly favoured the rebels: small fields surrounded by low stone walls provided excellent cover for guerrillas while restricting observation from the roads. These were in any case not difficult for the IRA to block. Further west still, mountain and bog predominated, with many areas quite inaccessible to the military wheeled vehicles. With these factors favouring the guerrilla, it is hardly surprising that Percival was to describe West Cork as 'probably one of the most disturbed areas in the whole of Ireland'. The task of pacifying the Essex's section of it was quite beyond the resources of a single battalion.

The manpower difficulties of both the Army and RIC prompted Churchill, still Secretary of State for War, to propose the enlistment of a special force of 8,000 ex-soldiers to reinforce the local constabulary. The idea of ex-soldiers from England becoming an organic supplement to the Irish police was a radical and questionable departure. The CIGS's view that the 'panic measure of raising 8,000 scallywags would, for some months anyhow, give us no military value but great anxieties', proved remarkably prescient.[7] These men became the infamous 'Black and Tans', exceeded in notoriety only by the similarly recruited Auxiliary Division RIC which was to follow. They were not drawn exclusively from 'a very dangerous type of unemployable' as some Irish accounts have implied, and the CIGS's own description might imply. Rather, they were a cross-section of the million or more veterans who could find no work at home on their return from the trenches. Similar men had performed nobly in North Russia, but Ireland was a different matter. These new recruits to the RIC had no experience of the civil restraints and individual responsibility of the police constable and little affinity with the Irish population with whom they had to work.

Percival's view was that they were 'generally a very fine lot of men', who 'would have done well in other conditions';[8] but the conditions of conventional warfare and military discipline were both absent from their hostile Irish environment. In the relaxed disciplinary regime of the RIC they were to take matters increasingly into their own hands when they saw their colleagues killed in cold blood. A contingent was soon stationed in Main Street Bandon, a few score yards from the barracks occupied by Percival's detachment.

Against this background the campaign continued: intimidation, arms thefts and killings of policemen on the one hand, patrols, house searches and the capture and internment of IRA members on the other. Both sides claimed a measure of success in the spring of 1920. Thirty IRA members were arrested in the Essex area, many as a result of Percival's raids and searches, and taken off to Belfast or Wormwood Scrubs. At the same time, IRA action forced the local RIC to abandon some of their smaller and isolated 'barracks', which were often little more than fortified houses. The West Cork IRA were also playing their part in the burning down of the 100 Inland Revenue offices which were put to the torch throughout Ireland. RIC morale was shaken and Army frustration increased when the Government, vacillating as ever, decided that the imprisoned IRA members should be released. Meanwhile the killings continued in the Essex Regiment's operational area. A constable was shot dead on 12 June, another was killed and a third wounded on the 22nd; a fourth was shot 'right under the noses of the British garrison at Bantry', Barry crowed,[9] and a fifth gunned down at Glengarry across the bay. On 27 June another was shot dead at Clonakilty. There were also attacks on RIC patrols and barracks at Skibbereen and Castletownbere. Maddening though this local action was for Percival's detachment, the most embarrassing coup had taken place on 26 June when the North Cork IRA Brigade had actually managed to capture the GOC and two staff officers of 16th Brigade, the Essex's superior formation, who were caught while out on a fishing trip. After this the troops at Fermoy ran amok in Cork city and Churchill himself had to warn that, 'officers and men who allow themselves to be deprived of their weapons or kidnapped . . . are liable to severe disciplinary action'.[10] An extensive drive failed to find Brigadier General Lucas and his fellow captives, though he managed to escape a month later.

Life was taken a little more seriously by the security forces at Bandon, where the potential of the opposition was becoming clear. A document captured by the local RIC at about this time showed that in early June the Bandon battalion IRA had amassed 29 rifles, 146 shotguns, 42 revolvers and a quantity of explosives,[11] though in the use of this latter commodity they were to demonstrate a particular incompetence. This was hardly to be compared with the hardware ranged against them, but the rebels' best weapons were their excellent intelligence and the quiescent or supportive population. They could strike where and when they wished and, in classic guerrilla fashion, avoid all action unless the circumstances favoured them. In plain clothes and to all intents peaceable, the IRA man could be asking the RIC constable the time of day at one moment and gunning him down the next. Their arms cache grew rapidly in early summer with two successful raids on the same coastguard station in the space of 11 days. This was at Howes Strand, ten miles south of Percival's base. The second raid was led by Charlie Hurley, the second-in-command of the Bandon battalion. The double blow netted the rebels 25 rifles and 20,000 rounds of ammunition.

The Essex troops were even more incensed by the murder in late July of a policeman in Bandon whose death had a direct impact on their anti-terrorist operations. RIC Sergeant Mulhern, the Crimes Special Sergeant at Bandon and a key collaborator with Percival in intelligence gathering, was gunned down on his way to church on the morning of Sunday 25 July. An armed guard of Black and Tans had escorted him to the church gates and he had just mounted the flight of steps to the churchyard when two gunmen struck. Hit by two bullets he staggered into the church porch where he died. The killers escaped unhindered. Members of the assembling congregation had no doubt witnessed the shooting and recognised the perpetrators, but they 'one and all refused to give evidence as to their identity', Percival noted grimly.[12] The circumstances of this murder, within the precincts of the church, accorded it a particular horror. A great outcry followed; there were denunciations of the outrage from the pulpit and the church had to be reconsecrated. The anger and frustration of the garrison may be imagined. It was feared that they might take immediate reprisals on the town as had happened after similar outrages at Fermoy and Thules, but they were held in check.[13] The IRA even underscored their triumph by firing an ineffectual volley of shots at the barracks the same night.

The following evening Percival, determined to suppress the local IRA activity and capture the ringleaders, ordered the searching of various IRA haunts in the locality and at about half-past midnight went himself to observe the activity at the house of the local IRA leader in Bandon. Despite the risks involved and hoping for an unobserved approach, he took with him only one member of the detachment, Corporal Maddox.

The two were just entering the garden of the house when a shot rang out and Maddox fell dead. He had been shot through the head by a slug-loaded shotgun. The house was obviously picketed, probably to protect an IRA meeting; but surprise was lost, no IRA were apprehended, and a valued NCO lay dead.[14]

Undaunted by this reverse but even more determined to capture the ringleaders, Percival switched to another known IRA haunt, Laragh, with a dawn raid the following day, without success. But when he raided the house once more in the evening after making searches at other IRA properties, the detachment arrived unseen and his persistence and surprise tactics at last paid off. He was met in the farmyard by two well-dressed gentlemen claiming to be on holiday from Dublin. While talking to Percival one of them was seen to be slipping papers from his pocket into the hedge behind – evidence which on examination made it clear that he was a local IRA leader. An arms dump was found hidden on the property and further incriminating documents within the house itself. The captives proved to be none other than the commander and quartermaster of the IRA West Cork Brigade, Tom Hales and Patrick Hart, the two men who, in Percival's view 'had doubtless organised the murder on the previous day'.[15] This capture was a signal triumph for his perseverance after the spate of dispiriting killings, a notable tit-for-tat for Brigadier General Lucas's capture and a great local coup. The capture, exulted the *Daily Mail*, 'has robbed Sinn Feiners of West Cork of two strong leaders and striking personalities'. Prior to this success not one noted Republican had been captured in West Cork since the start of the year. 'The arrest of these two firebrands will have an excellent effect', declared the GOC.[16] It is said that 'hale and harty' became something of a regimental catchphrase with the Essex.[17]

According to published Republican accounts, the two captives were beaten before and during their journey back to Bandon barracks and, once there, were beaten and tortured by the Essex detachment. These charges have been repeated in other accounts. The *Daily Mail* merely recorded that 'both men were injured while being taken'. If this was somewhat economical with the truth, it was typical of the press releases of the time, for an intense propaganda war accompanied the campaign which both sides, Government and rebel, were waging. It appears that Hart never recovered from his treatment (and principally perhaps from a blow to the head from a rifle butt said to have been inflicted during the lorry journey back to barracks) and died, in a mental hospital according to Barry, some years later.[18] Hales was sentenced to penal servitude and held in Pentonville until the truce was signed. He lived until 1946.

Given the prevailing circumstances there seems little reason to doubt that the two IRA leaders were beaten following their capture. 1st Essex were not the most complaisant of units from the IRA perspective and in view of the series of IRA killings in West Cork in June and July and the particular sequence of events in Bandon itself, from Sunday's horrific shooting to the capture of the two men on Tuesday evening, one can easily appreciate the upward ratcheting of anger, tension and frustration among the Bandon troops. The shooting of Corporal Maddox occurred, it must be remembered, when the IRA was still avoiding major contact with the Army. It was regarded as sufficiently radical a departure for it to be recorded in the list of outrages given in the GOC's post-insurgency report.[19] It is notable that the published Republican accounts do not connect the capture and treatment of Hales and Hart with the killings of Mulhern and Maddox, though they were consecutive events.

What then was Percival's role in the Hales and Hart affair? His determination and tactics were certainly directly responsible for their entrapment. Tom Hales' declared view was that Percival was the 'Chief Architect of the dastardly performance'.[20] In the sense that he was responsible for their capture, this is certainly true. As to any subsequent brutality, it is most unlikely that Percival was involved, even indirectly. Given the very clear General Staff HQ Ireland instructions on the treatment of prisoners during interrogation, mere expediency on the part of an experienced officer such as Percival, aside from his own strong principles, would have ruled it out. By this stage in the campaign Percival had handed over his local duties as OC Bandon detachment to a Major Neave. Colonel Moffitt had noted Percival's special aptitude for intelligence work and for planning field operations and had given him battalion-wide responsibilities for operations and intelligence.[21] One account records that the interrogation of the Bandon prisoners was in the hands of a Captain Kelly;[22] another that according to information sent to Michael Collins, IRA Director of Intelligence, the treatment of Hales and Hart was the action of Essex officers of Irish nationality, which Percival was not.[23]

Charge and counter-charge alleging excesses, brutality, illegality and ill-treatment flew regularly between the two sides in this increasingly vicious campaign, as they did between the new Irish Republican Government and the rump of the rejectionist IRA in the bitter civil war which followed it. Tom Hales' brother Sean, for example, was shot dead by the anti-treaty Republicans some time later and as a reprisal for his death four innocent anti-treaty men were immediately executed. The likeliest explanation of this particular Bandon episode probably comes from the confidential interview which the Unionist MP for Bromley, ex-officer Cuthbert James, had with the Commander-in-Chief Ireland, General Macready, in early December 1920. Macready was not noted for visiting his operational units, but the available records indicate that the three occasions when he did leave Dublin were all for visits to Cork where HQ 17 Brigade was based.[24] He would have been well briefed about 1st Essex. Macready confided that he 'knew all about' Percival and regarded him as 'an exceptional company commander'. However, 'the standard attained by his colleagues was – let us say– not high', James records Macready as confiding, 'If AP was present things worked smoothly, if not there was trouble'.[25] It seems that the Hales and Hart affair was one of the latter occasions.

That Percival was most energetic, determined, fearless and ruthless in his hunting of the IRA was beyond argument. He was, as Barry put it, 'tireless in his attempt to destroy the spirit of the people and the organisation of the IRA',[26] activities which were apparently not only to be deplored but, in Barry's view, were one and the same. In fact the Essex IO was careful to preserve the distinction between the two, arguing that, 'You must at all costs distinguish the sheep from the wolves. If you fail to do so you drive the whole population into the hands of the enemy.'[27]

Percival's reconnaissances, raids and searches for the IRA in his area continued unabated. He remained, in Barry's words, 'a leading instrument in the plan for our destruction'.[28] Kathleen Keyes McDonnell is bitter in her criticisms of Percival. Her home, Castlelack, was repeatedly subjected to raids and searches, often at night and sometimes when she, the children and their nurse were alone in the house. From this bald account of the circumstances one is tempted to sympathise with her position. However her husband was the father figure of the local IRA and, from his position as a prominent Bandon businessman, a key personality in sustaining its operations. In the opinion of one IRA member, 'he supplied all that was necessary for military activities'. He provided three cars for IRA use; the mill at Castlelack was a secret bomb-making factory; a principal ammunition dump was on its land and there were never fewer than 12 rifles hidden in the elevators and wooden shoots of the flour mill. The Bandon battalion often planned their operations at meetings at the McDonnell's. The lady of the house herself carried and hid messages for the IRA and had its members in hiding on the property.[29] It was inevitably a regular target for Percival's repeated searches and surveillance. It stretches credulity and compassion just a little to have Mrs McDonnell bemoaning the visitations and expecting gentlemanly civilities from Major Percival each time his party called. During one search Mrs McDonnell asked Percival to release the herdsman and his wife to attend to the cows. She recorded the subsequent exchange with Percival. '"The cows to hell!" he blurted out savagely; the words were out of his mouth before he could stop them. "You forget yourself!" I retorted, staring him out of countenance, but he could not rise to the occasion.'[30] Is one surprised?

After his narrow escape when Corporal Maddox was killed, Percival later had another one of which he remained entirely unaware. Because his activities were a constant source of danger to the IRA, Tom Barry resolved on a personal mission to shoot the Essex major. Barry learnt that on the three previous evenings at about 7.45pm Percival had left the Bandon barracks and walked 150 yards to have dinner at a house in the town. On the

fourth evening Barry and a comrade-in-arms waited in adjoining door-
ways, intending to shoot the major as he passed by. They waited until
8.20pm, but although several other Essex officers and soldiers were
sighted, Percival did not appear. Barry trudged disappointed out of
Bandon and back to his headquarters, only to learn that throughout his
dangerous vigil Percival had been out of Bandon, searching for the IRA
elsewhere.[31]

IRELAND:
THE MOBILE COLUMNS

'Don't blame these boys, don't blame their officers, but put the blame where it is due – put it upon the policy which has turned Ireland into a place where violence reigns supreme; where a man's house or his church are not secure from violence; where 50,000 growing lads are being demoralised and spoilt.'

Brigadier C B Thomson, *Military Adviser to the Labour*
Commission on Ireland

It was in the late summer of 1920 that the IRA headquarters in Dublin ordered the formation of full-time Active Service Units or 'flying columns' as they were more generally known. With increasing numbers of activists being convicted by court martial and the identities of others becoming known, many men had been forced to go 'on the run'. The logic was to form these into full-time guerrilla units – the flying columns. The North and West Cork flying columns, which became the most celebrated of the new formations, began assembling in mid-September. Most of the columns consisted of 20 or 30 men, but the IRA strength in West Cork was such that, with the training system which Barry devised, the flying column there reached a total of 110 men, 'twice as large as the next biggest in Ireland'.[1] Arthur Percival, now several months into his new appointment as battalion intelligence and operations officer, first became aware of the flying column operations in mid-October.[2] Their appearance signalled activities more dangerous than the arms raids, night attacks and isolated shootings on which the rebels had hitherto concentrated. They were now ready for active operations against the Army and the RIC with its detested supplements, the Black and Tans and the 1,000-strong Auxiliary Division, whose counter-terror activities made them particularly desired targets.

Aside from the difficulty of acquiring timely, accurate intelligence, the greatest impediment to Army anti-guerrilla operations was the road-bound transport system required to cover the vast tracts of territory for which the rural battalions were responsible. The fast Crossley lorries of the Essex could move rapidly over long distances, carry heavy equipment and reduce the fatigue of the troops. The downside was that their approach was all too predictable over the limited network of motorable roads and their noisy progress eliminated all surprise. They were notoriously prone to ambush. As one Essex officer noted, 'as the number of these vehicles increased, the success of the IRA increased proportionately'. *An t Oglach* drew the same conclusion, noting that 'the armouring and wirenetting of these vehicles has not increased their fighting value but diminished it'.[3] The uncomfortable fact was that the bursting of a grenade inside a lorry was lethal, the high armoured sides maximising the impact of the explosion on those confined within it.

Percival was caught in a lorry ambush in early October 1920 when the West Cork flying column attacked his two-vehicle force of 14 men, after dark at Newcestown Cross. The patrol had completed a search of the local public house, a suspected IRA haunt, and had just set off for a second objective, Castletown, where other searches were planned. The lorries had travelled no more than 400 yards when they came under fire. The vehicle lights were put out, they quickly halted and their occupants deployed under fire. Although Percival's men ultimately drove off the attackers it was not without considerable loss; an Essex lieutenant and an RAF flight lieutenant (the Bandon wireless officer) were both killed and three soldiers wounded. It was a considerable triumph for the IRA. Percival's men did well in difficult circumstances – the night was dark and half the patrol was composed of recruits. Percival himself received the Commander-in-Chief's commendation for 'his great personal bravery in carrying to safety the two wounded officers who were lying in an exposed position'.[4] Unfortunately his courage did not suffice to save their lives. The ambush had been set up by Sean Hales, OC Bandon battalion IRA, who had been at the public house at the start of the search but had managed to slip away unnoticed.

It was probably the Newcestown ambush which Secretary of State Churchill had in mind when he urged the Military Secretary to give standard campaign rewards for service in Ireland. 'Take the Essex Regiment, for instance', he wrote. 'They have had three officers killed and six men out of seven wounded in one small encounter. Why because they are shot down by Irish rebels and not by Mesopotamian rebels, should they be excluded from consideration?'[5] Perhaps a conflation of two separate incidents, but the argument was unassailable.

In November the West Cork flying column scored two further notable successes which both underscored the vulnerability of the lorry-borne operations. In the first a two-lorry convoy of Essex troops was attacked in broad daylight at Toureen on the Bandon to Cork road; an officer was killed and other men wounded. In the second it was the turn of the Auxiliaries to be ambushed on a deserted stretch of boggy land near Kilmichael. Two lorries were halted by an IRA ruse and a savage close-quarter fight followed. Three IRA men were killed, but the Auxiliaries paid with their entire force – 17 of their 18 men were killed and the eighteenth was severely wounded. This was probably the most devastating ambush of the entire conflict and a cause of particular satisfaction to the IRA. They had been eager to avenge the reprisal and counter-terror policy of the Auxiliaries who were based at nearby Macroom. This shocking ambush followed close upon Bloody Sunday, the day of multiple murders by the IRA in Dublin. It was inevitable that the military, held back hitherto by political wavering at Westminster, would now be given more extensive powers to deal with the rebellion. Martial law was declared in Kerry, Limerick, Tipperary and, of course, in Cork.

By this stage the Essex had been given some assistance in West Cork. The westernmost section of their area, Bantry and the countryside around it, was now held by 1st battalion The King's (Liverpool) Regiment, fresh from a pleasant posting in Jersey. The Queenstown area had been taken over by 2nd Cameron Highlanders. HQ 17th Brigade in Cork now had the operations of seven battalions or their equivalents to manage, a responsibility which devolved largely upon the brigade major, one Bernard Montgomery. Montgomery was the same age as Percival, like him still single and a similarly dedicated professional. Their careers were to have many interesting parallels and contrasts. Percival's operational area covered a total of 400 square miles. He had now seen enough of the IRA's *modus operandi* to be painfully aware of the difficulty of rooting them out, and of the limited value of military operations on their own. As he was later to explain with a realism borne of much hard experience, the rebel campaign in Ireland 'was not conducted by a few hired assassins as was so often supposed', but by 'a nationalist movement backed by a large proportion of the population'. He was also well aware from hard-won intelligence that 'the organisation of the Irish Republican Army was much more complete than was generally known'.[6] The military difficulties still centred on predictable movement, limited intelligence and the difficulty of identifying their suspects. The population was dominated 'by families of one surname, similar Christian names; even the same type of physiognomy and invariably the same West Cork brogue, pure gibberish in Sassenach ears'.[7] Recognising IRA members was one problem, finding them was another. The lorry-based sweeps were no answer, indeed they were actually 'playing the enemy's game pure and simple'.[8] The ease with which their progress could be abruptly halted by felled trees and the like was a critical weakness. Percival was involved in planning numerous such sweeps in the winter of 1920–21 and one in particular led to one of the biggest fights in the open to take place during the entire Irish war. This was the Crossbarry ambush of 19 March 1921. It exemplified all the shortcomings of the motorised strategy.

The ambush occurred during a major anti-terrorist sweep planned by Montgomery and involving about 120 men from two separate battalions as well as Auxiliaries from Macroom. The sweep was based on information passed to the brigade HQ by an informant, captured during an earlier ambush, to the effect that the IRA flying column was encamped in a group of farms based in the Ballymurphy townland. This hamlet was roughly equidistant from the two main British garrisons and their units quickly began an encircling movement. Barry was commanding the flying column and realising the difficulties that withdrawal would present, he decided to take on the troops, outnumbered though he was certain to be. The flying column had now grown to a strength of 104 men and included a medical officer and his assistant and also, somewhat bizarrely in a guerrilla campaign, a piper recruited to help the foot soldiers 'to fight even better still to the strains of their traditional war songs'.[9]

The ensuing action, a relatively minor one in terms of conventional warfare, was nevertheless a considerable tactical victory for the IRA. The manner in which Barry handled his force reflected great credit on his developing skills and the growing confidence of his men. The action also illustrated the difficulties for Percival and the other commanders in taking on a guerrilla force whose deployment and likely tactics were unknown and which, in the event, was to operate from cover on its chosen battlefield. The Army patrols, encumbered by their lorries, were committed to a slow and painstaking search of every farm building along their converging routes. At each turn in the road the concentrated firepower of the flying column might be encountered. Barry's scouts were able to inform him of the expected earlier arrival of some of the Bandon troops and the flying column commander resolved to ambush these first before redeploying to engage the remainder.

The lorries from Bandon, carrying only a small part of the Essex contingent, were successfully attacked; weapons were captured, including a brand-new Lewis gun, and many casualties were inflicted. The lorries were then burned. The noise of this action was heard by the other searching parties who quickly made for the scene, only to find a regrouped flying column awaiting them. Both Percival's men, and a separate force under Major Hallahan, were met by heavy fire and Barry was able to extricate his force before a cordon could be thrown around them. They then disappeared across country with remarkable speed. It was hardly a re-run of Stonewall Jackson in the Shenandoah Valley, but similar advantages of intelligence, time, distance and interior lines were exploited by the IRA commander. The flying column never stood and fought again throughout the campaign; but it had scored an important propaganda victory. It lost four men killed, including the West Cork Brigade commander in a preliminary skirmish, and others were captured or wounded but British casualties were considerably greater; 16 were killed or wounded according to the official figures, but the newspapers and the IRA claimed a higher number. The shortcomings in British tactics were now manifest and changes were on the way.

Percival had been well aware of these inadequacies for some time and had been doing his best to overcome them. 'To obtain surprise', he wrote, 'you must work well away from your transport, which on a still night can be heard miles off coming along the road.'[10] His surprise arrival at Laragh had borne fruit and IRA accounts spoke of him employing 'surprise tactics', or merely that 'Percival and a column appeared on the scene'. Now, at last, the general policy was changed and the Army introduced mobile foot columns and bicycle troops of their own. The columns were usually two or three platoons strong, manned by volunteers (there was no lack of these), lightly clad and equipped with rifles, bandoliers and haversacks. They moved noiselessly on rubber-soled boots and could cover 25 miles at a stretch supported by a transport system composed only of light carts. 'If our objective was a village', Percival noted, 'we would billet or bivouac 5 or 6 miles away, and then send off a bicycle patrol to make a sudden descent on the village at dusk.'[11] Travelling by night they were able to negate the customary advantage of the rebels' scouting organisation and avoid ambushes where the odds were stacked against them.

The weather of spring and summer 1921 also helped the new tactics. It was dry and sunny throughout, more than rivalling the glorious conditions that Percival remembered from the fateful summer of 1914. His mobile columns lived in the open from April until July 1921, a period when, remarkably, the south-west of Ireland had only two wet days. Percival enjoyed the outdoor exercise and the country air which the new tactics offered. The 'hide and seek' character of the operations also appealed to the young soldiers after the boredom and vulnerability of the lorry patrols and put fresh life and vigour into their work. Sweeps and 'round-ups' now lasted as long as three weeks and involved the coordinated activity of several columns. The additional martial law measures which were operating – more curfews, summary courts and the banning of cars and bicycles – were further pressures on the West Cork Brigade flying column. At one stage it was driven away from the principal towns of the county and forced to take refuge in the wild and roadless hills and bogs of the borderland with Kerry. The column was not brought to battle, but pushed to the limits of its endurance before the searching troops moved off and the rebels were able to slip back into familiar territory.

By this juncture, the casualties incurred in the limited conventional military actions were dwarfed by those of the many smaller assaults and isolated killings which were a daily occurrence. Burnings and lootings were routine activities in the reprisals campaign, with which the Black and Tans and the Auxiliaries were particularly associated. It was, moreover, a reprisals campaign which had Government sanction. The killing of IRA suspects without the formality of a trial was by no means unknown. On the IRA side the killings also continued; two unarmed Essex soldiers had been kidnapped and murdered in February, an outrage which General Macready denounced as a 'provocation such as would not be indulged in by the wildest savages of central Africa'.[12] The rebels were now burning the properties of loyalists in return for the torching of their own. Spies and informers were summarily executed; the West Cork brigade had shot 12 by the end of February 1921 and a further four would be dead by the time of the truce. Many others suspected of collaborating with the British were hounded out of the country. Bandon already bore the scars of the conflict; its hosiery works had gone up in flames the previous autumn and a large haberdashery, stationery and boot store was also burnt down. It had become a bitter and bloody war which deeply divided political opinion and drew much international condemnation. 'The whole country runs with blood', cried the *Irish Times*, 'Unless it is stopped and stopped soon every prospect of political settlement and material prosperity will perish and our children will inherit a wilderness.'[13]

In fact the war was approaching a state of asymmetrical deadlock and consequently inching towards a settlement. With a massive influx of additional forces the military campaign was moving steadily in favour of the British, but at the cost of the disappearance of all normalcy from civil life. The IRA was now hard-pressed, but the political struggle of Sinn Fein was within sight of achieving its major aim. Negotiation and compromise were in the air. The Cabinet met in Inverness Town Hall to deliberate on a settlement. General Macready arrived by destroyer to advise on the military situation. He took with him four regimental officers to give Lloyd George and Churchill a view of the insurgency from unit level. Major Percival of 1st Essex was one of those selected to speak.[14]

The West Cork Brigade remained deeply critical of the Essex Regiment in general and Major Percival in particular. The Essex men certainly seem to have been harsh and unruly opponents; but the IRA's anger was as much the result of Percival's unrelenting and legitimate determination to defeat one of the strongest IRA brigades in Ireland. The IRA knew that active intelligence officers were the most dangerous of the forces ranged against them and their HQ issued instructions to pinpoint the most 'aggressive' of these. Percival's name was high on the list. As a result of the effectiveness of his exploits, the Sinn Fein High Command offered a reward of £1,000 for his capture, dead or alive.[15] General Macready later noted that the rebels 'did all they could to scupper him'.[16] Michael Collins himself is said to have initiated an attempt to kill Percival when he went on leave in March 1921. An assassination squad was apparently set up for an attempt on 16 March, but had to disperse when police appeared on the scene.[17]

Commandant Barry remained Percival's fiercest critic. Barry was a brave, skilful and resolute Irish nationalist, but he was also a ruthless guerrilla fighter, unbending in his determination to succeed and harsh in his denunciation of those who stood in his way. Percival certainly did that and his reputation as 'the most ruthless of the English intelligence officers in the Brigade',[18] based probably on Barry's evaluation, is clearly not one which he would have wished to disown. It certainly seems the case that officers who were active in their district, as Percival was, attracted particular denunciation and vilification from their opponents. If an officer did little in the way of searching houses and so on and reported his district 'quiet', the IRA tended to leave him alone. Providing they were able to continue their policy of liquidating the police, negating the British machinery of government and substituting their own, they were naturally happy to let quiescent units remain in relative peace.

In his criticism of Percival (whom he seems to have regarded as commanding officer of 1st Essex and responsible for all its actions), Barry makes an illuminating comparison with Lieutenant Colonel Hudson, commanding officer of 1st King's who had taken over the Bantry area from the hard-pressed Essex in late July 1920. Hudson was 'a good type of British officer', Barry averred; his behaviour and that of 'his officers and men was exemplary in all circumstances'.[19] This judgement seemed rather to reflect the fact that Barry's activities were little troubled by Hudson. The flying column commander would have denied this, but nevertheless affirmed that 'We never had a vendetta with any of the King's Liverpools in any garrisons.' Hudson was an ardent angler, Barry recalled, 'and he had a permit from us to fish any river he wanted. His ghillie, of course, was an IRA man.'[20] Percival, too, was keen on country sports, but he was in Cork to catch the IRA.

Major Russell (later Lord Russell of Liverpool of war crimes trials fame) provides a fresh perspective on this evaluation. He was one of Hudson's company commanders and based at the workhouse in Bantry. He recalls arriving at the scene of the murder of four RIC constables, minutes after the shooting had taken place, to find a priest already on the spot administering the last rites to one of the dying men. Russell was furious with the priest whom he regarded, because of his miraculously speedy arrival on the scene, as complicit in the killings. He angrily berated the priest whom one of the King's men then booted down the steps. The following morning the local Sinn Fein leader (unusually a mason, as was Hudson) advised the King's commanding officer to get Russell out of the country because the IRA had sentenced him to death. Hudson immediately complied: Russell was on the next boat to Fishguard and did not return to Ireland until October 1921.[21] A remarkable capitulation to IRA threats, to which one could not have imagined Percival ever consenting. Little wonder Barry thought so highly of the regiment.

The King's also had a much less troublesome patch to control. Skibbereen in particular had only four IRA members in the whole town and three of these, it appears, had been arrested. If Barry is to be believed, the King's were not particularly active in defending it. He records that the IRA determined to shoot the place up to bring the supine population and still conformist local council into line. On 9 April 1921 a 12-strong IRA group advanced into the town to fire on the barracks, hoping to draw the security forces into a prepared ambush which they had set up on the out-skirts. For two hours the small IRA party held the town without response from the strong King's garrison. 'Everything was done to draw out the military', wrote Barry, 'but all failed.' The external sentries were merely withdrawn inside the building they were guarding. Although the ambush remained in place for a further four hours the garrison 'did not emerge from their barracks until the following day'.[22] Attacks in Bandon invari-ably drew a military response, providing an immovable impediment to the IRA designs.

In sitting in judgement on the Army's behaviour and complaining when traditional military standards were not observed, the IRA were perhaps forgetting that there was scant precedent for the kind of war in which they were engaged. It was fought between uniformed soldiers on the one hand and men in civilian clothes on the other. Even the Boers, with whose irregular warfare the Irish sometimes compared their own, wore slouch hats and bandoliers which instantly identified them as belligerents. The IRA however, except when operating openly in the flying columns, appeared as innocent civilians until they actually drew the gun. In these circumstances they always risked being fired on if their actions were suspected or misinterpreted, and the innocent could easily be confused with the guilty. It all made for a particularly unpleasant war.

Ironically, on the only occasion when Percival had the commander of the West Cork flying column at his mercy, he let him go. It was at the time of Barry's return from deliberations with the IRA high command in Dublin. His 'cover' of being a sick medical student had served him well throughout the trip. He had practically regained home territory and was about to turn his pony and trap into the drive of the local IRA headquar-ters when, according to his account, 40 steel-helmeted British soldiers rose from the ditches on both sides. 'My heart sank', Barry recorded, 'when I saw they were the dreaded Essex.' His cover story, supported by medical textbooks and study notes in his own hand, stood up well in his initial interrogation, but he was detained until the commander of the operation, Major Percival himself, should give a final decision.

The much-feared major did not arrive until two hours had passed, during which time Barry's fevered imagination led him to expect the worst. His recollections of the dramatic confrontation, recorded a quarter of a century later, are of a revolver-armed Percival dressed in the tunic and shorts of the Essex mobile column. 'The cruelty of his set face', recalled

Barry, 'was accentuated by the two buck-teeth which showed like small fangs at either side of his bitter mouth.' Anyone familiar with Percival's visage, somewhat marred by centrally protruding teeth giving him a somewhat rabbit-like appearance, will appreciate the extent of Barry's distorted recollections.

Percival listened carefully to his officers' account of their interrogation, examined Barry's belongings and then inspected the captive closely, staring into the young man's eyes 'as if he would read my mind', remembered Barry. He stepped forward, removed Barry's hat, took another long look at him, walked away a few paces, looked again at the prisoner and then spoke the only words he uttered in Barry's presence: 'Release him.'[23] As Percival was later to record, the identification of prisoners 'was one of the most difficult things in the whole campaign'; the key men were seldom known by sight and always gave false names. 'A number of them slipped through our hands after actually being captured.'[24]

The Sinn Fein Irish President, De Valera, had interviewed Barry during his Dublin visit and asked him how long the Cork flying columns could carry on the fight. Pugnacious optimism induced Barry to exaggerate and say five years providing the British were not reinforced. De Valera himself was clearly making a more realistic assessment. Michael Collins' oft-quoted remark, made admittedly after the Treaty had been signed, 'You had us dead beat. We could not have lasted another three weeks,' was no doubt a similarly purposeful exaggeration. Percival would have judged it nearer the truth. In his opinion the rapid movement and supply of the British mobile columns were having such a demoralising effect on the nerves of the IRA 'that in another few weeks the back of the rebellion would have been broken'.[25] The view of another Essex officer was that once the truce was signed, 'The few really wild men who remained at large were at their last gasp and frankly admitted the fact to our troops when they discovered that the latter had no further intention of hurting them.'[26] Richard Mulcahy, IRA Chief of Staff, fully recognised that the strictly military achievement of his force had been very limited and that 'the greatest success of which it had been capable was the taking of a moderate sized police barracks'.[27] What these military evaluations do not address is the extent to which the political situation had developed in Sinn Fein's favour during the fighting and because of it. Percival had merely played his loyal but dangerous part in the Army's holding of the ring until the politicians were ready to settle.

It had been a difficult campaign for Percival and the Essex: numerous scattered small detachments to supervise; raw junior officers, many without the benefit of Sandhurst training; inexperienced NCOs; fearful and indisciplined recruits; the boredom of guard duties to be countered; and time to be found for much-needed training. As Percival later noted, every man needed to be an expert skirmisher and sniper, but there were few opportunities to train for this role. Then there had been the difficult and delicate problem of discipline. As the GOC had himself privately admitted, troops without enough spirit to retaliate when their comrades were attacked were 'not worth a damn', yet harsh punishment might take the heart out of them.[28] One of Percival's solutions had been to focus their attention on hunting the terrorists, 'to try and make them interested in the proceedings, which we did by lectures and talks on local IRA celebrities etc.'[29]

Perhaps his most important contribution to the development of counter-insurgency warfare was the emphasis he placed on intelligence and an active policy at unit level towards its acquisition. He regarded the appointment of intelligence officer as critically important since 'the whole success of the conduct of operations in any given area really depends on him'. As his own activities made clear, he held firm views on how the IO should operate: 'Most important of all, an IO must move about the country and hunt for information. It will not come to him if he sits in his office all day.'[30]

Percival's views on tackling an insurgency such as had taken place in Ireland were later reproduced in two lectures which he delivered while at the Staff College. These formed a small but important step in the Army's development of practical measures for countering guerrilla warfare. From the perspective of the 1990s, with the experience of more than 25 years of a second IRA campaign and a monumental outpouring of theoretical and practical manuals on the subject, it is difficult to comprehend quite how undeveloped contemporary military thinking actually was on countering insurgency in that kind of environment. Percival's was an early and valuable contribution to a subject with which few within the Army, blessedly, had reason to be familiar.

However determined a hunter of the IRA he may have been, Arthur Percival was always at pains to distinguish between the rebels, who received no quarter from him, and the population at large. He deplored the way the Auxiliaries treated the whole population as hostile, writing, 'Personally, I was convinced that such an attitude was fundamentally wrong.' The views of Montgomery, the brigade major at Cork, were rather more primitive. 'I think I regarded all civilians as "shinners" [i.e. supporters of Sinn Fein]', he wrote, 'and I never had any dealings with any of them . . . My whole attention was given to defeating the rebels and it never bothered me a bit how many houses were burnt.'[31] His point seems to be that the British were not ruthless enough. One wonders in what terms Mrs McDonnell and Commandant Barry would have written about a Montgomery, rather than a Percival, as operations and intelligence officer in their local British battalion.

There can have been few regrets among the Essex soldiers when the campaign was finally at an end. It had been a world away from what the new recruits had expected or their NCOs had previously experienced. Percival recognised just how arduous the work had been for the troops, for there were few areas in which they could relax and 'walk out' in relative safety. Major Russell of the King's agreed, making the comparison with the Great War where, once out of the line, the men could relax in the rear areas in relative safety. 'In Ireland', he noted, perhaps a touch hypersensitively, 'there was nowhere that one could feel safe from the "enemy", who was here, there and everywhere'.[32]

In February 1922 Major Percival was present with 1st Essex on the railway station at Kinsale where the battalion was assembled for its journey north to Carrickfergus. Some of the battalion band, long since swept up into active service with the mobile columns, recalled with incredulity how on first arrival in Ireland they had fondly imagined they would be spending their time playing in the sunshine on the Kinsale front for the entertainment of the local citizenry. Now the weather was more in keeping with the bitter irregular warfare which lay behind them. 'Gales swept the platform with ever increasing violence, slanting rain beat pitilessly upon us all . . . blue lightning of dazzling brightness played intermittently across the sky, north and west; from the direction of Cork came mutterings of thunder.'[33] The war of bombings and assassinations, of burnings and reprisals was over. Percival had completed the only operational tour he was to serve with 1st Essex.

FROM STAFF COLLEGE
TO SINGAPORE

'It is the educated mind, contrary to the expectation of many, that adapts itself best to the strains of war.'

Field Marshal Lord Ironside

Carrickfergus, set in the heart of loyalist Ulster, was a total change from Bandon. The seaside town faced across the North Channel to the Mull of Galloway and mainland Britain, to which it looked for its political support and dominant culture. The stay here of 1st Essex, their regimental history records, was 'most beneficial and much enjoyed', blessedly free from that sense of being encompassed about by foes, from which they had never been entirely free in West Cork. In the pleasant tranquillity of the new battalion base, Arthur could look back on a job done to the best of his ability in an anti-terrorist campaign which no one had enjoyed. At least he had the satisfaction of knowing that his efforts had been recognised and appreciated. In addition to the Commander-in-Chief's commendation he had been awarded the OBE in the New Year Honours of 1921 for his gallantry in the operations against the rebels. Now at last came the opportunity to get on with some conventional military training. There was also the chance to relax a little and do some socialising. It was during his time at Carrickfergus that Arthur first met Elizabeth MacGregor Greer, 'Betty' to her intimates, the younger daughter of a family from Greenisland, a few miles along the coast road from the Essex base. Some years later Arthur and Betty were to marry.

The truce also gave Arthur the time to qualify for the Staff College. He achieved good scores in the military subjects of the examination but was rather let down by his performance in the subject 'Principles of Business Organisation and Administration', confirmation perhaps that his decision to leave the City had been wise! Although technically over-age, he was fortunate enough to gain a nomination for the staff course; but his selection to attend the 1923 course was an even more singular piece of good fortune. After neglect during the war years, the College had recently been refurbished and his joining coincided with the arrival of an invigorating and reformist commandant. The course of 1923 was quite unlike that attended a couple of years earlier by Bernard Montgomery before his tour in Cork. At that time the place was run-down and had few outstanding instructors. Apart from Gort and Dill, whom Montgomery pronounced 'a very fine character', he had found the rest of the course not to his liking and had departed 'profoundly disappointed'.[1]

Percival was 36 by the time his course at Camberley started. He succeeded in gaining a nomination, it was said, only because of the intervention of War Minister Churchill, to whose attention he had come as a result of his exploits in North Russia and most recently in Southern Ireland. At the Inverness Conference, Churchill, it appears, had been 'very impressed with Percival's grasp of a problem which had baffled so many'.[2] In any event, these were not times when regulations were too scrupulously observed; there had been no staff courses during the war years and there was a backlog of officers with considerable experience and distinguished combat service which, as with Percival, more than justified their attendance. A lingering minority of military backwoodsmen still regarded a move to the Staff College as a retrograde step since it involved 'turning one's back on the regiment'; but the reality, according to one of Arthur's fellow students, was that the college was 'the Mecca for all ambitious officers'. Arthur was certainly one of these and very keen to make up for the lost years spent in the humdrum routine of his London office. Although the letters psc (passed Staff College) which appeared after the names of all its graduates in Army records were not the *sine qua non* for high rank, significant advancement without them was not easy, particularly in peacetime.

By 1923 the material aspects of Staff College life had been improved immeasurably. Arthur was able to appreciate to the full the ambience of the place and the 620 acres of Surrey parkland and training area which it shared with the Sandhurst military academy close by. He now had a two-year stay at the professional base of the officer corps and the opportunity to flesh out his formidable fighting experience with some broader theoretical understanding, to absorb some of the cultural background of his chosen profession and to meet some other of its future leaders. The aims of the Staff College were as much social as educational and there was a great deal to be gained from getting to know a broader range of his most promising contemporaries.

Percival found the living conditions a delightful contrast to the muddy dugouts of the Somme, the tented camps and rough wooded huts along the Dvina river and the ugly, spartan barracks at Bandon. The manicured lawns and flower beds which fronted the college with its imposing italianate entrance hall bespoke a return at last to civilised standards and decent living. Since Arthur played most sports to a respectable standard he made good use of the excellent facilities which the college boasted. He soon had a regular place in the Staff College cricket eleven; indeed his first match score of 51 runs suggested he might become the mainstay of its batting, though this early promise was not entirely fulfilled. The college journal, *Owl Pie*, blamed the competing attraction of his other summer sport, tennis, but it is as likely to have been the needs of study. Dynamic new directing staff had taken the reins at the college and were radically transforming its curriculum.

General Ironside, the youngest major general in the British Army, was a great hulk of a man. Arthur remembered him well for his inspiring leadership in the uncertain conditions of North Russia. Ironside was destined to be the outstanding commandant of the inter-war years whose reforms were to have a lasting impact on the college's approach to the training and education of its charges. One of his first acts when he knew of his appointment as commandant was to request the services of Colonel J F C Fuller as his chief instructor. Fuller and Ironside had been at the college as students in 1914 and they shared the belief that the place should be turned into a true War College, adopting university methods of teaching and developing the syndicate system of instruction following the example of the university seminar.[3] This change was long overdue, for the students of recent courses were not bright-eyed inexperienced beginners but veteran campaigners who themselves had much to offer the courses if a participative regime was introduced. Almost all had been through the inferno of the Great War and 80 per cent of Percival's intake wore gallantry decorations; three of them bore the distinctive claret ribbon of the Victoria Cross. As it happened, Arthur Percival was among the most decorated of them all. For him, as for the others, Fuller's approach, as announced in his opening address, was just what was needed:

> As the director of your studies, the ideal I intend to aim at is that we should teach each other; first because we have a vast amount of war experience behind us, and secondly because . . . it is only through free criticism of each other's ideas that truth can be thrashed out.[4]

Fuller's contribution to Percival's military education stemmed from much more than this radical teaching philosophy. He also had the fruits of much original thinking to impart and had spent the previous autumn travelling around Europe with his wife, sketching out and writing up the series of 50 lectures on 'The Science of War' and 'The Analysis of War' which he intended personally to deliver to his students.[5] On his arrival at Camberley, Fuller summoned the chief clerk and ordered the burning of all existing schemes and documents, intending to replace them with his own. 'Boney' Fuller was a remarkable officer who had already made a considerable name for himself as a military reformer and original thinker about future war. He was a great apostle of the tank and proponent of armoured warfare. Small and balding with a messianic gleam in his eye and a ready, if often acid tongue, he came to the Staff College with an established reputation as a radical visionary and iconoclast. 'Our one and only military prophet', declared an *Army Quarterly* reviewer.

Other instructors working for Ironside in these vintage Staff College years included men of such mettle as the future Chief of the Imperial General Staff Field Marshal Lord Alanbrooke and a distinguished post-war Adjutant General, Sir Ronald Adam. It was a quality intake of students as well. In the senior division when Percival joined was the future Lieutenant General Sir Henry Pownall, whom he had known since their schooldays, while within his own junior division were the future Australian and Canadian generals, Horace Robertson and Harry Crerar, together with Loch, Macready, Firebrace Franklyn, Halsted, Stopford, Gambier-Parry and Smyth – all of whom served as generals during the Second World War. The methods and the men were such as could not but excite the interest, compel the attention and encourage the involvement of all serious and able officers.

Percival made his own distinctive contribution to the new college philosophy. His two lectures, 'Guerrilla Warfare – Ireland 1920–21' were born of hard experience and much reflection. They also benefited from an exchange of letters with Montgomery whom Percival consulted for a staff officer's perspective on the campaign. The lectures were a model of clarity, concision and sound judgement and no doubt as valuable a contribution to the developing body of operational doctrine on this most difficult form of warfare, about which no military manuals then existed, as they were to his fellow students' education. The influence of Fuller was also visible within them, for Percival was at pains to relate the counter-insurgency campaigning in Ireland to the principles of war which 'Boney' was currently endeavouring to define and develop. Percival's parting reference in his second lecture to Sir John Moore's time in Bandon over a century earlier was, no doubt, an astute diplomatic obeisance in the direction of the Chief Instructor who was then preparing his *Sir John Moore's System of Training* for publication. It is not clear whether Percival became as whole-hearted an advocate of armoured warfare as Fuller might have wished. His experience of tanks on the Western Front had been rather mixed. But this was to be of little consequence; when Percival received his next truly operational command, tanks would not feature in his order of battle.

The two years Percival spent at Camberley were not all lectures and sport. The students had all the latest weapons and equipment explained to them. They toured military establishments at home and abroad and carried out a combined operations exercise with the students from the RN and RAF staff colleges at Greenwich and Andover. In many ways the highlight of the course was the foreign tour which all students undertook.

Percival was teamed up with a Grenadier Guards officer for a tour of the countries of Eastern Europe and an evaluation of the defence forces of Poland, Czechoslovakia and Hungary on which a detailed report had then to be written. Defence issues in the Far East were also a topic for study. The Government had decided only the previous year to establish a naval base at Singapore. In consequence the question of the defence of Singapore was a topical subject for discussion. A fellow student recalled that while Japan was the designated enemy in one exercise considering the island's defence, the problem 'did not appear then as too much of a difficulty'. By the time the Japanese fleet and transports had got anywhere near the newly fortified base, the British Grand Fleet and many squadrons of aircraft were well on their way. The whole thing, he recalled 'would end in a bloody massacre – for the Japanese'.[6]

The Commandant and Chief Instructor were very impressed by the Essex Regiment's representative on the course. Among his other reforms, Ironside had instituted a system of earmarking for accelerated promotion the eight best officers from each intake. Percival was high on the list. Ironside considered him 'an officer of exceptional ability and intelligence', a natural leader whom he recommended for accelerated promotion.[7] Percival left Camberley with the satisfaction of having earned a first-class report, and as the member of a new regiment, for he had now taken up a vacancy for a permanent commission in the 22nd (Cheshire) Regiment with which he would be associated for the rest of his service. It was a fine regiment with, at that time, a very high-grade complement of junior officers. However it was a job 'on the staff' and the first genuinely foreign posting which was now planned for Percival.

It was to be almost 11 years from leaving the Staff College before Percival made his first visit to Malaya, ultimately the scene of the sternest examination of his military qualities. The intervening years were spent in tours with his new regiment, postings as student and instructor at staff colleges and tours on the staff itself, whence came his undeserved reputation as a 'staff wallah'. His first staff tour was spent in West Africa, on the headquarters staff of the Nigeria Regiment. After 11 years in uniform it was his first real experience of peacetime soldiering, his introduction to the long-established practice of raising troops locally to serve under British officers in defence of Britain's imperial interests, and his initial taste of tropical conditions.

Nigeria was Britain's largest African dependency, a vast territory encompassing great topographical and climatic as well as racial and religious diversity. It had proved more turbulent and difficult to pacify than most of the west African colonial territories and over 40 small expeditions, the lifeblood of regimental soldiering before the First World War, had been needed to bring it to order. As recently as 1921 punitive patrols had been required to deal with villagers who had warded off visits from the local tax inspectors with flights of poisoned arrows. However when Percival's tour began, British authority was well established throughout the region and peace was ensured with the aid of only five African battalions.

The military life at Kaduna was most enjoyable and Percival threw himself into all aspects of it with his customary energy. Recreational opportunities were excellent with plenty of guinea fowl to be shot and surprisingly good facilities in so remote a station for tennis, golf, racing, polo and cricket. However in a community of few more than one hundred expatriates the social life was stylised and restricted. Since their first meeting in 1922 Arthur and Betty Greer had conducted an extended and at times difficult courtship, separated as they soon were by the Irish Sea and subsequently by much of southern Europe and west Africa as well. Ultimately they decided to marry and the ceremony took place in 1927 during Arthur's home leave. The old parish church of Holy Trinity, West Brompton was the setting and Arthur's chum from his Essex days, Major Hassel, now of the South Staffords, stood as best man. The two officiating clergy were both Betty's uncles. The honeymoon was spent motoring in Devon, after which the new Mrs Percival was whisked away from the temperate civilities of the West Country to a clapboarded bungalow in Kaduna to begin her married life as an Army wife.

There were many worse places in which to have made such a start. The climate in Kaduna was more acceptable for Europeans than that in most other stations in Nigeria. The bungalow was large and modern by local standards. Airy and spacious, it was fronted by a long, wide verandah and surrounded by a substantial garden studded with local bushes and flowering species introduced by the Europeans, offering pleasant vistas and some privacy. It was a great contrast to Greenisland with all the amenities of Belfast close by. Kaduna's only contact with the outside world was the railway to Lagos many hundreds of miles to the south. Aside from that, two dirt roads took the traveller a mere 20 miles from the settlement to villages north and south before the tracks petered out. The furniture of the bungalow was good if somewhat basic, carpets and curtains having yet to penetrate to this colonial outpost, but the food was very acceptable. There was plenty of local fruit and vegetables, and ducks and other fowl were in good supply. For other delicacies the residents relied upon frozen supplies from Lagos or hampers ordered from Fortnum and Mason.

Social life centred on the club, an unpretentious tin-roofed building painted in regulation public service green. Community dances were held there to the accompaniment of gramophone records or, on the grander occasions, the West African Frontier Force band. Gardening was another local pastime. Each year the expatriate community (composed almost entirely of 'officials', military and civilian, there being few businessmen in the settlement) held a flower show which took place on the spacious

verandah of the Colonial Secretariat building. A cup was also presented
for the best-kept and most attractive garden compound. For years this cup
had been routinely won by the Chief Health Superintendent. The
Percivals' bungalow had a beautiful garden which Arthur enthusiastically
cultivated with the aid of his gardening boy so that, as a civilian official
recorded, 'his flowers and lawns were a sight for sore eyes'. He also had
the temerity, as a mere Army 'bird of passage', to enter his compound for
the 'best garden' cup which he surprised the old hands by winning. The
story goes that he was fined a fortnight later for having a dirty compound!
One can imagine the web of small-community expatriate intrigue and
the role perhaps of the Chief Health Superintendent within it, which produced this bizarre sequel![8] Despite this contretemps (or perhaps because
of it) Percival was very popular with the officials of the colonial service as
he was with his own officers. For them he had the additional appeal of
being a recent graduate of the Staff College and only too willing to help in
their preparation for its qualifying examination.

The Percivals' stay in Nigeria lasted four years, a year longer than normal. It was extended especially to enable Arthur to complete a project on
a revised defence system for Nigeria, a study which bristled with com-
plexities because of the great size and varied conditions of the country.
The plan he drafted was very well received by the Government's Overseas
Defence Committee, which recorded its appreciation of the 'able way this
scheme has been drawn up' and concluded that 'The Committee are of
the opinion that the work of this officer deserves special commendation.'
Percival was rewarded for his efforts with a brevet lieutenant colonelcy.
Betty and he returned to the UK at the start of 1929.

He had been a Cheshire now for four years and was at last to have an
opportunity to get to know the regiment he had joined. He was posted to
the 2nd Battalion which was stationed at Tidworth on Salisbury Plain.
This was the fourth battalion in which he had served and he was once
again a company commander, an appointment he had first held with 7th
Bedfords 14 years previously! Such was the stagnation in military affairs
during the inter-war years when funding was short and the baleful effects
of the 'Ten-Year Rule' included the blunting of most efforts at military
reform and found some able officers kicking their heels on half-pay.
Indeed, in the year before Arthur's return to England, Winston Churchill,
now an embattled Chancellor struggling with a worsening economic situation, proposed a 'revolving date' extension to the 'Ten-Year Rule' under
which the planning assumption for the Chiefs of Staff, that the nation was
to be free from war for another ten years, was effectively renewed each
morning. This made all prudent strategic planning quite impossible and
hardly encouraged an officer like Arthur who had made such a late change
of career and was anxious to make up for lost time.

His days with the 2nd Battalion were not many. Before the year was out he was selected to attend the 1930 course at the Royal Naval Staff College at Greenwich to which a few Army officers went each year. Staff training in the Navy was a recent introduction, forced on this, the most conservative of the Services, by inadequacies which the Great War had exposed. The one-year course which 20–30 middle rank naval officers attended had been hailed by Haldane as of 'far more value than a battle cruiser', but much die-hard naval opinion still resisted it for years to come. The Greenwich course was, on the one hand, an unwelcome distraction at a time when Percival was just getting to know the Cheshires, but on the other, it provided a useful extension to his military education, making him all the more employable in these days of slow and limited advancement. The RN directing staff found him an 'ideal attached officer' who brought a 'new and refreshing outlook to bear on naval problems'.[9] The experience certainly broadened his military understanding and fitted him well for his next move, which was the considerable distinction of appointment as an instructor at the Army Staff College. The commandant there was now Major General John Dill, one of the ablest soldiers of his generation and a future CIGS. Dill, it will be recalled, was one of the few instructors to have impressed Montgomery during his irritating and unhappy sojourn at Camberley after the war. Arthur developed a warm and enduring personal regard for Dill and a great admiration for him as a soldier. Dill was similarly impressed with Percival: 'the best officer I have met for a long time', he confided to the Director of Staff Duties. From this juncture onwards Dill's was the guiding hand in Percival's fortunes. But it should by now be very clear that whatever advancement Dill recommended merely echoed what all Percival's previous commanders had been urging. He knew that Arthur was due to command a battalion on his next move but considered that 'it would be really tragic if he did not get a nomination for the IDC' (Imperial Defence College) in due course.[10]

First, however, came Percival's battalion command, the most important and sought-after appointment for the keen infantry officer. Percival's time on Dill's staff at Camberley was reduced to one year so that he could take over command of 2nd Battalion of the Cheshires which, at the end of 1930, had exchanged Corunna Barracks Aldershot for the infinitely more congenial St George's Barracks in Malta. It was here that Percival joined them. The barracks stood on a rocky promontory alongside a pleasant little bay a few miles from the capital Valetta. The buildings had changed little since the battalion had last occupied them 80 years earlier, but this did nothing to dull the soldiers' enjoyment of their idyllic foreign tour. The status of the battalion in Malta was slightly anomalous. Since the 1st Battalion of the regiment was in India, the 2nd was regarded as the 'home service' battalion responsible for training and sending out drafts to India, although itself based half-way across the Mediterranean. It was far below its war establishment and remained at about 400 men all told, while the

1st Battalion which it supplied was several hundred stronger. The anomaly was that the Worcestershire Regiment's foreign service battalion was also in Malta but kept at full strength! This disparity made the Cheshires' success in local competitions all the more noteworthy.[11]

The arrival of a new commanding officer, particularly one not well known in the regiment, is an event attended with no little interest and often a certain amount of trepidation on the part of those who have to deal with him most directly. Would the new man be a fire-eater, forever shooting off orders in all directions, continually inventing new and not very important tasks to fill the soldiers' every waking moment and reducing life in the ranks to mild but extended misery? Or would he be like not a few commanding officers in the stagnant inter-war years, only too content to leave the running of the unit to the warrant officers and NCOs while he and the other officers engaged in an unending series of gentlemanly pursuits? The main lineaments of Percival's military character and leadership style were now well established and his running of the battalion epitomised neither of these extremes. Perhaps the most outstanding feature of his approach to command was the personal example he set and his sheer professionalism. His commitment to the battalion was total and he worked unceasingly for its effectiveness and the welfare of his men. This was all the more noticeable at a time when national economic difficulties were serious, the administrative system was cumbrous and not every officer, by no means every commanding officer, believed it necessary to lead an arduous life. Percival imposed upon himself a stern personal discipline, working a full day and seldom missing a platoon or company sporting event. Although he was now in his mid-forties, the weekly battalion cross-country race often saw him in the lead. He ran the battalion on an assured but light rein and seemed to take it for granted that all his officers would, without question, emulate his own very high standards of soldiering and not need any forceful direction from him. The men at first found him rather quiet and a mite austere; but after a short acquaintance his friendliness and concern became clear, as did his stubborn determination to get things done. He seemed to know everyone's name, and nothing that happened escaped his attention. Whatever went on, whatever problem needed solving, 'Percy' would know.[12]

He was supported by an unusually able RSM, Mr Sharpley, who had been the youngest RSM in the Army when first promoted to the rank in 1921. He remained RSM until 1938 and put a remarkable personal stamp on the regiment. With his depth of regimental knowledge he was the ideal executive for the new CO with whom he shared, strangely for a RSM, the personal characteristics of reserve, an undemonstrative manner and superb, unhurried efficiency.

Percival's low-key personal style emphasising leadership by example rather than by *diktat*, produced a happy and efficient unit. Any backsliders who thought that his lightness of touch betrayed weakness were soon to appreciate the firmness beneath. But it was his personal involvement in every activity of unit life and the freedom he gave his junior officers to learn their jobs which contributed most to the development of the battalion – something of a vintage one. Percival's period of command in Malta provided the early exemplar for at least one future general, Sir Charles Harington, two major generals, Tom Brodie and John Cubbon, as well as a future brigadier. As might be expected of a unit led by so keen a supporter and participant as Percival, his battalion excelled in sport. 'So far as games are concerned', wrote Malta's Governor General in his farewell message at the end of the battalion's tour, 'I doubt if any battalion which has been in Malta could show a better or more varied record than that held by your battalion.'[13] In general he concluded that Percival had 'improved his battalion out of all recognition'.[14]

There could hardly have been a greater contrast in leadership styles than those shown by Arthur Percival and Bernard Montgomery, who was commanding his regiment, the Royal Warwicks, across the Mediterranean at Alexandria at much the same time. In the Royal Warwicks visiting senior officers found 'officers and men in a state of barely concealed hostility to their commanding officer'. Similarly dedicated but distinctly more austere, Montgomery was exhibiting the opposite leadership style to Percival: leaning on his officers and men so heavily that the unit was on the point of exploding. Only the intervention of superior officers of unusual insight, indulgence and understanding enabled Montgomery to survive.[15] By contrast, Percival's emphases were on the encouragement of his officers and personal example rather than autocratic fiat. 'To my mind', he declared in a leadership lecture to his officers, 'there is nothing more degrading than to see an officer standing by and allowing his non-commissioned officers to carry on for him.' His lecture concluded with a characteristic admonition to his subalterns 'to display a greater determination to be helpful', adding that he and they, 'were all part of the same concern and our job is, each in our different spheres, to make the wheels go round'.[16] These were sentiments which, a few years later, would have benefited from public display in the meeting chamber of the Far East War Council in Singapore.

Percival was indeed nominated for the IDC course as Dill had recommended and in order to get back to England for the start of the 1935 course, he and Betty left Malta immediately after Christmas 1934 to a great send-off from the regiment which itself returned to the UK the following week. The IDC course was intended for selected senior officers of all three Services and for specially chosen civil servants. It was aimed particularly at fostering mutual understanding of the roles and perspectives of the fighting Services and civil governments in emergency situations. It was another valuable training experience, as courses which mix together people from a variety of professional backgrounds generally are, but it scarcely prepared Percival for the type of civil-military problems which he was soon to meet.

Towards the end of the course he heard from the Military Secretary's department that he had been selected as General Staff Officer 1st Grade, Malaya Command, effectively the Chief of Staff to the commanding general there, General Dobbie. Although the post involved promotion to full colonel, the prospect did not at first appeal to him; six of the last ten years he had spent on foreign service and virtually all his time in England had been at staff colleges of one sort or another. It was the prospect of being abroad again and once more on the staff that he found unattractive. He particularly wanted to serve again with troops, and in England. The discussion with the posting authorities soon made it clear that the proposed position was a new and important one for which he had been specially selected. His lengthy overseas service had been taken into account before the decision to appoint him. Arthur correctly saw the hand of General Dill, now Director of Military Operations, behind his selection. Dill might not have taken Percival's argument for serving with troops as keenly as Percy did himself. Dill was in a key senior position at the centre of military affairs, but he had not commanded even one battalion, let alone Percival's three! In a decision which effectively sealed his fate, Percival accepted the position but asked for a return to the UK after two years in Singapore rather than the customary three.[17] With matters thus arranged the prospect of a tour in the Far East began to appear rather more appealing.

FIRST ROUND IN MALAYA

'The Naval Base gives a sense of security – it is a visible, concrete symbol of our power and, let us hope, a deterrent to war.'

British expatriate, the Singapore Club, 1936

The question of revised arrangements for the safeguarding of British interests in the Far East had come to the fore at the conclusion of the First World War when Russian and German threats to the region declined and Japan gradually emerged as the local power competing with the British and American position there. The second major factor was that the United States was now a naval power of the first rank. This changed strategic situation was signalled by the abrogation of the Anglo-Japanese Alliance under American pressure in 1922 and by British acquiescence in the same year to US equality in capital ships which was agreed at the Washington Conference. Even before the alliance was at an end Admiral Jellicoe had recommended the construction of a naval base at Singapore as a counterweight to Japanese influence, since Britain had no dockyard east of Malta capable of handling capital ships. The Imperial Defence Conference which assembled in London in 1922 confirmed Jellicoe's recommendation (having rejected the possible alternative locations of Sydney, Hong Kong and Trincomalee) and decided that the base should be constructed in the north of Singapore island on the Johore Strait. The fact that the base was being built seemed to guarantee that a fleet would be available to occupy it when the need arose. All that remained to be determined, it appeared, was how the base itself was to be defended.

These radical changes in Britain's international security situation were much discussed in military circles. In consequence, the problem of the defence of Malaya and Singapore was not entirely a closed book to Arthur Percival as he prepared to take up his new appointment at the conclusion of the IDC course. Now that the question of the length of his tour had been resolved he went off to Malaya 'full of enthusiasm for the new job'. He had been promoted to full Colonel, he knew that the Singapore appointment was an important new one and that a key element in his responsibilities would be the development of defence plans for Malaya Command which he had first studied as a student at Camberley and examined afresh on the course which he had just completed. The defence of the naval base was clearly a complex problem. Indeed, from the time of the 1922 Imperial Conference argument had raged about the most appropriate defence arrangements for it. Then there was the even greater conundrum of how they might be funded.

The protracted inter-Service arguments over the most effective defence system to be provided totally overshadowed the more fundamental question of whether the creation of a naval base at Singapore was a satisfactory single mechanism for protecting British interests in the East. Many of these interests lay in Malaya, Britain's richest colony, which produced half of the world's tin and one third of its rubber – both vital strategic commodities. The assumption from the start had been that any threat to the base would come from the sea. It was too readily assumed that the Malayan jungle would prove an impenetrable barrier to any hostile southward advance by land. This was observably not the case. West coast Malaya was flat, largely jungle-free and well served by road and rail. As early as 1922, Army Staff College students in both England and India, few with the benefit of any local knowledge of Malaya, had suggested a Japanese offensive down the Malayan peninsula in their appreciations of hypothetical war scenarios. One such student, the future General Lord Ismay, was to become Senior Staff Officer to Churchill and a member of the Chiefs of Staff Committee, when war finally came.[1] In 1925 the GOC Malaya, General Sir Theodore Fraser, was taking much the same view. His opinion was that all of Malaya, and Lower Thailand as well, would need to be defended if Singapore was to be safe. For some reason these views never penetrated to the senior defence planners of the early 1920s.

The Royal Navy would have much preferred a permanent Far Eastern Fleet as well as the base to maintain it, but the lack of money, the Ten-Year Rule philosophy and the restrictions imposed by the Washington Naval Treaty ruled out that possibility. The Army and Navy Chiefs of Staff would have settled for the siting of fixed, heavy 15-inch guns, supported by medium and close-defence artillery as adequate seaward protection for the base. However, the newly independent Royal Air Force was flexing its young muscles and the Chief of Air Staff Sir Hugh Trenchard was arguing as much for his Service's permanent status and the acceptance of proper roles for air power when he claimed that the best defence against an enemy assault from the sea would be that provided by RAF torpedo bombers. These, supported by fighters and reconnaissance aircraft, would be more effective, cheaper and more mobile than fixed guns. The aircraft could also be based elsewhere until required. It was a seductive argument for a penurious Treasury but, as the other Chiefs of Staff argued, the aircraft might not be available at the critical moment; only if based in the region permanently would they serve to deter. This was true enough, but it was an argument which applied with equal force to the Fleet itself, on whose availability for eastern waters the whole security edifice was founded. It might be added that Trenchard was being unjustifiably optimistic about the future capabilities of RAF aircraft against moving ships: at no stage in the Second World War did they manage to sink a single undamaged capital ship with free-falling bombs.[2] On such uncertain foundations were Britain's plans for the defence of its interests in the Far East slowly taking shape.

If the Chiefs of Staff could not agree on the Singapore Defence arrangements, successive Governments were to add to the ambiguity of Britain's commitment. The project for the base itself was cancelled by the short-lived Labour government in 1924 and renewed only half-heartedly by the Conservatives in 1926 after Churchill, now struggling to balance the books as Chancellor of the Exchequer, had queried the pace at which the Navy's project was developing and demanded reductions in defence expenditure generally. The arch-interventionist of 1920, at whose insistence much blood and treasure had been poured into a variety of anti-Bolshevik schemes, was now acting with all the cheese-paring parsimony of a monastic chapter. He argued that there was no urgency about developing the Singapore base and no need to station a fleet in the Far East. The result of the Government's financial strictures and the Services' failure to agree was the inevitable half-measure compromise. Three 15-inch guns were agreed but a decision on the optimum gun/plane mix for the remainder of the defences was shelved. Trenchard got agreement to the Air Reinforcement Route (the chain of airfields which terminated at Calcutta) being extended to Singapore, and to the development of the torpedo bomber.

In the years which followed, the rift between the Services was not closed. A new Chief of Air Staff, Sir John Salmond, argued, with some justice, that improved aircraft performance and weapon techniques added further strength to the air defence argument. His fellow Chiefs still opted for fixed guns as the main deterrent to naval attack and the Government tended to agree. Meanwhile, the embryo of a Far East Air Force was established in Singapore and a programme of airfield construction slowly pushed forward as the naval base itself was developed. No priority was given to this work, however, since Chamberlain, the Chancellor in Baldwin's National Government, who was to begin the rearmament programme, argued that the country could not provide for hostilities against both Germany and Japan, and since Japan would not attack unless Britain was embroiled in Europe, a deterrent against Germany would be a deterrent against Japan. With this persuasive logic from the future Prime Minister as the context for their efforts, the difficulties facing the Service authorities in the Far East may be imagined.

The defining moment in the troubled history of the Singapore Naval

Base and the entire defence philosophy, however flawed, which it represented, came on 21 June 1935. This was the day when the First Lord of the Admiralty announced to Parliament the conclusion of the Anglo-German Naval Agreement. This permitted Germany to build a navy one-third the size of Britain's. This was a ratio much more favourable to Britain than she had enjoyed at the time of the Great War; but then the Japanese Navy had been in firm alliance with Britain's, now it was a real and growing threat. The freedom as to categories of warship which the agreement allowed made it virtually certain that once Germany's programme was completed, the British Fleet would, in Churchill's words at the time, 'be largely anchored in the North Sea'. It mattered little that Germany might have pursued the same naval programme without Britain's assent; the point is that from mid-1935 onwards it became increasingly unlikely that the Royal Navy would be able to send to Singapore a fleet capable of deterring Japanese attack. As Churchill clearly realised, 'the whole position in the Far East has been very gravely altered'.[3] The Japanese were themselves denouncing and ignoring all naval limitation agreements, making the size of any deterrent British naval force in the east all the more critical. The uncomfortable but inevitable conclusion is that from the summer of 1935 onwards Britain's entire Far Eastern defence arrangements were resting on as uncertain a footing as that provided by the mangrove swamps which fringed the north-west coast of Singapore. 'What a windfall this has been to Japan!', Churchill declared. It seems to have been some years before the significance of the agreement dawned upon the Admiralty, but Churchill's subsequent actions may be judged from what he understood of its implications at the time, while a vociferous back-bencher opposing any abdication of Britain's imperial power and berating the Government for the nation's unpreparedness which, as an earlier Chancellor, he had played such an important part in continuing.

Little of this would have been any more evident to Arthur Percival than it apparently was to the Navy. The favourable capital ship ratio with Germany was apparently the important thing. Neither he nor the Naval Staff could have known that when war finally came, the French Navy would cease to be an asset, Italy would be in the lists against us and Germany would control most of the Atlantic coast of Europe. The prospect of a tour in the Far East was an exciting one and Singapore was an excellent family station. 'Family' the Percivals had now become, for Betty had had a daughter, Dorinda Margery, while Arthur was attending the Greenwich course and a son, James, would be born during their time in the Far East. There could scarcely have been a better posting in which to have a young family. Domestic help was readily available and very cheap. Betty had two Chinese *amahs* to help with the family and they were able to afford other house staff as well as a gardener. The Percivals took over a spacious white-washed house in as airy a district of suburban Singapore as that tropical island affords. Facilities were excellent for shopping in the local cold storage establishment and the famous Robinson's department store, while clothes for every occasion could be run up by local seamstresses very cheaply and in a matter of days. The local clubs provided excellent facilities for sport, social events and for eating out. The climate, at first enervating for those accustomed to the bracing air of Britain, was something to which one grew accustomed; children in particular adapted quite quickly. In short, life was most enjoyable, at least for the representatives of the imperial power, in this, the richest of Britain's colonial possessions at the hub of a developing and prosperous commercial and industrial region.

The Malayan defence scene, however, was a rather different matter, even in the context of the flawed conception which lay at its heart. After the many early delays, by 1936 the facilities of the Naval Base itself were developing well, and the RAF had established major airfields on Singapore island and set up its headquarters at Seletar. On the Army's side, the fixed defences of heavy, medium and close-defence guns were also nearing completion. But Percival was soon aware of some disquieting features. Before he left for Singapore he had been given a briefing note prepared by an officer recently returned from a tour spent developing the artillery defences of the island.[4] The note concentrated on the close protection of the base and confirmed that the seaward defences were approaching adequacy, but it also touched upon several issues which were to run like leitmotifs throughout the pre-war Singapore drama. The RAF were unwilling to cooperate over air defence, the note recorded, while the older and more influential civilians on the island 'bitterly resented the influx of the three Services' and opposed the defence priorities being urged upon them. The note also mentioned that Johore was vulnerable and, employing a metaphor that was later to acquire considerable notoriety, 'the defence of the back door needs addressing'. There was much here for Percival to think about.

Arthur's boss, the GOC Malaya Major General Dobbie, was also a new arrival. He was a man of strong principles, firm religious faith and imbued with a proselytising zeal. Percival found him 'a delightful man to work for'. The GOC gave his GSO1 a free hand and found Percival 'extremely hard working' and, despite the difficulties and frustrations which the appointment soon brought, 'quite imperturbable'. He was soon deeply involved in all aspects of defence planning. His efforts were given additional urgency by the growing evidence of Japanese hostility and the scale and technical sophistication of her military activities. The passage of time appeared to have done nothing to soften the Japanese resentment at the ending of Britain's alliance with her, while her war with China and the growing scale of her commercial and industrial operations in the region were a major cause of friction. Authoritarian extremism was also casting a long shadow over her domestic politics. But it was her military capabilities which gave Percival most concern. In her war with China she was using, he noted, 'equipment which was far in advance of anything we had at the time' and was showing considerable sophistication in landing operations. The Japanese had developed special landing craft and were using them in large numbers; they had built landing ships to carry them and had adapted tanks for use in their combined operations. They were building a fleet of fast 18-knot merchant ships for which a military purpose seemed as likely as a commercial one. These worrying advances were mirrored by similar developments in their other Services.[5] Each improvement in offensive capability, Percival believed, meant that the defence of the Naval Base would have to be pushed out further from the territory of the base itself.

He had little difficulty in convincing his GOC of the significance of these developments, but the colonial government and the civilian community were a different matter. Although Percival had been told before leaving England that one of his principal tasks was the improvement of civil-military relations, it was no easy matter. Many of the senior colonial officials had missed the Great War entirely and discounted any threats to local security. They saw no need for any military preparations beyond those which the Naval Base itself represented. The Governor, Shenton Thomas, although married to a lieutenant colonel's daughter, was hardly an enthusiastic supporter of the military arguments. Prior to his appointment in Malaya he had spent all his colonial service in Africa, where the last war had touched him only at its most gentlemanly extreme – in the civilised sideshow of a campaign which was waged from Kenya against General von Lettow-Vorbeck's force in Tanganyika. The nearest he had come to military service had been as an auxiliary policeman doing the occasional night guard duty.[6] As for the civil community generally, Singapore had seen peace for over a hundred years and their view was that nothing should interfere with its commercial activities. It appeared to Percival that the colonial government, instead of adjudicating between the competing priorities of defence and commerce, saw its role exclusively as that of protecting the latter against the former. 'I have regretfully come to the conclusion', he wrote to his GOC, 'that the Local Authorities have no intention of cooperating with us', adding that, 'I feel sure that the views I have expressed are held by the whole of our staff and also by the staff of the other Services.' It was plainly a problem that Dobbie had been grappling with for some time, for he scrawled across his GSO1's memorandum, 'The points raised are, like the poor, always with us.'[7] Percival recommended that the issue should be referred back to the War Office to be taken up with the Colonial Office at departmental level. He was right; the colony was working to a policy of commercial priority which only fresh Government instructions to Thomas were likely to change. However, he also proposed local initiatives, regular meetings of the local Defence Committee (there had been a lengthy hiatus since its last deliberations) and agreement on a common defence objective, to help matters along. It accorded with his general philosophy of 'trying to be helpful'.

The main difficulty from the Army viewpoint was that the garrison was pitifully small. There were only two British battalions on the island itself in addition to the artillery and engineer units, while Malaya was defended by a single Indian battalion. Aside from this regular unit, the peninsula had only the Malay Regiment which was just forming and the local volunteer forces, the Federated Malay States Volunteer Force (FMSVF) and the Straits Settlements Volunteer Force (SSVF). Both were very much under strength, under trained and seriously under financed. The peninsular dimension of the defence problem was giving Percival increasing concern. The territory was, after all, virtually the size of England without its West Country extremity and had hundreds of miles of vulnerable coastline. Since the defence would have to rely largely on the efforts of the volunteers, the inadequate funding of these forces was a serious concern. They were paid for locally by the colonial government and the funding was fixed for a number of years ahead, a ridiculous restriction in the context of the growing threat. Yet there was opposition to increasing the funding. The local civilians paid no income tax and feared that with increased defence expenditure they would have to.[8] 'If the attempt to work the present system is continued', Percival advised Dobbie, 'the result will be a lack of security for some time to come.' Again his recommended solution was the referral of the problem to the Government in London so that the Colonial Office could instruct the Governor appropriately. Only Whitehall could make the appropriate assessment of priorities based on the arguments which GOC Malaya supplied. He recommended that 'the problem should be tackled on the highest plane'.[9]

The internal security of Malaya Command was another matter to which Percival and General Dobbie were giving a deal of thought. The commercial prosperity of Malaya and Singapore meant that both were awash with immigrants, many of whom were on period contracts and had no citizenship rights. Their fundamental loyalties were to their countries of origin rather than to the colonial regime. There was already some disaffection and unrest among some sections of them. Of much greater concern was the large number of Japanese engaged in commercial and industrial activity throughout the territory. Their numbers had grown despite worsening Anglo-Japanese relations. Dobbie was already aware of the existence of an espionage network among them and had, as one of his first acts as GOC, persuaded the War Office to appoint an Army officer as Defence Security Officer (DSO). The man appointed, Colonel Hayley

Bell, was a great benefit to the counter-intelligence effort. Percival was under no illusions about the internal threat which the Japanese represented. 'The Japanese are members of a disciplined nation', he warned in a memorandum on the island's defences, 'and are, practically one and all, prepared to do desperate things for their Fatherland'. He regarded them as 'a real danger to the security of the fortress'.[10] The same year as Percival had arrived in Singapore, Major Arisue from the Japanese embassy in London (later to be head of Japanese Army intelligence) returned to Tokyo and advised the immediate stepping-up of intelligence-gathering activities in Malaya.[11]

Unfortunately for the counter-intelligence effort, the newly appointed DSO in Singapore received less than whole-hearted cooperation from his opposite number in the Civil Police, the head of the Japanese section of the Special Branch, a Major Morgan. Morgan was an odd man, sickly, secretive and paranoid, who steadfastly refused to share his intelligence with the Services, despite its direct relevance to many of their operations. In Percival's view Morgan had 'an eccentric mentality, ill-balanced judgement, muddled thought, lack of general common knowledge and uncalled for reticence . . .', and was 'not fitted for the appointment he holds'.[12] The trouble was that he had a long contract and, in the civilian regime then operating, it would have been particularly difficult to get rid of him. Percival advocated instead the building up of the DSO's organisation and developing maximum cooperation among all the intelligence-gathering organisations. He urged strong measures to achieve this, writing, 'I do not believe that this organisation will have any chance of success unless a strong lead is given right from the top.' He suggested that the Governor, as Chairman of Defence Committee Malaya, should order its implementation and that individuals should be sacked if they did not cooperate.[13] Despite Morgan's intransigence and unsuitability he remained in post. Hayley Bell, however, was less fortunate. During his two and a half years in Malaya he uncovered an extensive Japanese network and made an accurate forecast of Japanese actions. Indeed so disturbing and unpalatable was the information he provided that Shenton Thomas later arranged for his removal and the dismantling of the organisation he had developed.[14] Percival later recalled, 'I have a vivid recollection of Dobbie saying to me one day shortly before I left Singapore in 1937: "That man [Sir Shenton Thomas] will break my heart."'[15]

During his all-too-short 20-month tour Percival travelled extensively in Malaya, getting to know the geography, visiting units and examining the possibility of an attack on Singapore from the north. On one such trip north he gave the closing address to a course for one of the volunteer units. His speech emphasised their role in the defence of Malaya and warned of the danger of the Japanese trying to 'burgle Malaya by the back door'. The phrase found its way back to Britain and into a national newspaper. It was by no means a baseless fear. Up to this time the general view was not only that Malaya was 'impenetrable jungle' but also that a landing by an enemy on the east coast of Malaya during the north-east monsoon was impossible. Dobbie had determined to put this assumption to the test and during the monsoon season of 1936–37 he and Percival set up exercises to do this. They proved to Dobbie's satisfaction not only that landings were possible during the monsoon, but that they were actually more likely then since the weather conditions would prevent defensive air reconnaissance.

By the middle of 1937 Percival's ideas on the defence of Singapore had hardened to the point where he was virtually discounting an attack from the island's seaward flank and seriously considering the possibility of Malaya's defences being neutralised by an enemy acquiring forward air bases in Siam. 'The use of Siamese territory by an aggressor', he believed, 'is a contingency which demands our careful study. The occupation of Southern Siam would enable him to cut off the bulk of our food supplies from that country and would also place him within air striking distance of Malaya.' He said that more infantry units were needed and emphasised that they should be sent to Malaya 'before, not after, the crisis develops'.[16]

This new strategic possibility was one to which the RAF was, quite independently, developing its own response. Up to this time the airfields of Malaya had been built, for sound commercial reasons, on the western side of Malaya's mountain spine, where the main industrial and trading activities were located. On this flank, too, the RAF had built its own airfields at Alor Star and Port Swettenham as part of the Air Reinforcement Route from Calcutta. But air reconnaissance and possibly defensive action were now clearly required in the north-east, out across the Gulf of Siam. Given existing aircraft capabilities this was impossible from the airfields in the west. The AOC Far East therefore recommended, and the Air Ministry approved, the building of east coast airfields sited to give maximum range, close to the coast itself. No consideration was given to how the GOC, with his small garrison, was to defend them, nor was his advice taken as to their siting, which proved to be tragically vulnerable. This was a factor which Percival 'never ceased stressing' at the time. He argued the case with the local RAF commanders, Tedder and Peck (and Slessor from the UK) but, as he later confessed, 'I am afraid we did not get much change out of them.'[17] Percival's view was that the main eastern airfield should have been at Kuala Lipis, with only refuelling strips further to the north-east. The proposed sitings only made sense if the RAF was to be sufficiently strong to be able to deliver 'such a shattering blow' to any invasion flotilla that it could only put weak forces ashore. It never was and it never did. In Percival's view, this was a serious failure 'to face realities'.[18]

In retrospect we can see that the strategic situation in which Malaya and Singapore were now placed was becoming alarming. The Naval Base had been developed at huge cost to accommodate a main fleet; but a fleet could not be based there in peace and was unlikely to be available to utilise it in war. Yet the defence of this base was still the priority of the other two Services. A seaward attack on the base, against which much defensive effort had been expended, was now the less likely contingency. It was clear that Malaya was vulnerable to attack from the north; but there were very few troops in Malaya and the RAF, the other Service with a commitment to defend the base, was siting its new airfields without any consideration of the Army's ability to defend them. The civil authorities for their part were proving very hostile to the intrusion of defence considerations into the local scene at all. Dobbie confessed that he 'never approached the civil administration without meeting complete indifference or active opposition'.[19]

It was now November 1937 and Percival's tour was coming to an end. He asked his GOC if he could draw together all his work on the defence arrangements for the Command by writing an appreciation and plan of attack on Singapore from the Japanese point of view. Dobbie readily agreed and the plan was drawn up. It proved remarkably prescient. The document discounted the possibility of the British Fleet being able to reach Singapore in 70 days (the current planning figure), it warned of the probability, in the event of a Japanese attempt on Singapore, of preliminary operations to seize the airfields of South Thailand and Kelantan state. The defence of northern Malaya was therefore of prime importance. Percival wrote also of the threat from 'the enemy within our gates' – the Japanese intelligence activities within Malaya. The paper stressed the need for more infantry and for air forces strong enough to prevent the Japanese landing ships closing with the coast. It emphasised the requirement for more naval craft, destroyers and the like, and argued for the building up of the volunteer forces and of larger food stocks, against the possibility of supplies from Thailand being interrupted. The completed appreciation had Dobbie's full approval and on his instructions Percival took it back with him to England when the family sailed for home aboard H T *Dilwara* in mid-December 1937. He dutifully handed a copy to the relevant department in the War Office.[20]

Back in Singapore, General Dobbie sent a copy of Percival's appreciation to his opposite number in the Navy, Commodore Clarke, at the Naval Office on Collyer Quay. The Commodore's opening response was complimentary. 'Thank you for letting me see Percival's swansong', he wrote, 'it is a masterly document and I would like to send a copy to the C-in-C.' However, the comments which followed highlighted much that was wrong with defence perceptions in pre-war Singapore. Clarke believed that Percival had overestimated Japanese capabilities and 'brushed aside too lightly' the naval side of the business. 'I rather feel', he added, 'that the civilian members of the Defence Committee may regard the whole as too pessimistic, and take the line that we are scaremongers.'[21] It is not clear what the RAF Commander thought of the appreciation or indeed whether he received a copy. But then the RAF had their own plans for defending Singapore.

FRANTIC INTERLUDE

'I am looking to you to keep the Japanese quiet in the Pacific, using Singapore in any way convenient.'

Churchill's first message as Prime Minister to
President Roosevelt, 15 May 1940

Arthur Percival returned to England by no means content with the defence arrangements in Malaya, but at least secure in the knowledge that he had done all he could, at his level, to develop them. General Dobbie had been more than satisfied with his efforts, writing of his GSO1 that his work had been 'of the highest order' and that 'the improvement in the defence organisation here and in the training of the garrison is largely a result of his efforts'.[1] Percival was returning with promotion to brigadier promised, and an appointment in command of a regular brigade. He had been recommended for such a promotion since his days in Malta. However, on the voyage home from Singapore he received a wireless message asking if he would be willing to take up the post of Brigadier General Staff (BGS) Home Command in Aldershot. This was another staff job rather than the expected command post, but in every other respect it was one of the best opportunities in the Army for an officer of his rank. More than that, it would involve working again for General Dill, who was now the GOC-in-C Home Command. Percival accepted with alacrity and the family moved to a pleasant house off the Farnborough Road in Aldershot.

Dill's Home Command was at the centre of the Army's efforts at arming and training itself for war after the years of neglect. The basic rearmament decisions had been taken as long ago as 1935, but so pernicious and long-lasting had been the effects of the extension of the Ten-Year Rule that the enervated defence industries were in no position to meet the Army's requirements even when the Treasury finally made the money available. Besides, the Army enjoyed neither the traditional esteem in which the Royal Navy was held, nor the sparkling cachet of the junior arm, the Royal Air Force, of whose developing technology so much was expected. These were the days when strategic bombing theories reigned supreme, when the general belief was that the threat of massive retaliatory bombing was the only defence for the nation against a hostile air force. For this reason the RAF budget, which in 1935 had been less than half the Army's, had easily overtaken it by 1939, when it became larger than the Navy's as well. Even within the War Office, the preparation for a major continental commitment of the kind which it was eventually to undertake received no priority. In December 1937, when Percival had been packing his bags for home, the Minister for the Co-ordination of Defence had declared the provision of anti-aircraft defences at home to be the Army's first priority and 'cooperation in defence of the territories of any allies Britain might have in war', the last.

But all was not gloom. A new and reformist Secretary of State for War, Hore-Belisha, was now in post and there was every sign that he would be an effective new broom. He purged the Army Council of some of its less cooperative members, replacing the CIGS General Deverall with General Gort who skipped the rank of lieutenant general and several senior officers, including Percival's new chief Dill whom Hore-Belisha also interviewed for the position, to reach the Army's senior post. Hore-Belisha also began to tackle the conditions of service and living standards for soldiers and the officers' career structure. One could not but admire the zeal with which he rapidly turned to preparing the small, badly organised and ill-equipped Army for war on the continent of Europe which, in his view, the Government's appeasement of Hitler did not make any less likely. The Munich Agreement convinced him that Britain would indeed be sending an expeditionary force to France. The Government finally accepted this continental commitment in February 1939 and frantic efforts were begun to train and equip the first four regular and Territorial divisions and to recruit the many more which were now authorised. Much of the work associated with this fell on the shoulders of Dill and his staff at Aldershot, with Percival in the key position for orchestrating the manifold activities in which the staff were involved.

General Dill had always worked himself too hard, indeed he was to work himself to death in the strain of the early war years. At Aldershot he was mightily relieved to have Percival to coordinate his staff's operations. Dill was an outstandingly able soldier and an experienced higher commander, but he lacked the robust constitution of his BGS, who also had the invaluable background for this hectic period of expansion and training, including his time in the hurriedly raised Kitchener's Army and his wide experience of commanding men in action at battalion level which Dill, surprisingly for one who had risen to the pinnacle of his profession, had not. Percival's energy and stamina were immense, and his commander found him, as all his predecessors had done, 'a most loyal and disinterested worker' who was quite indefatigable in getting things done. These differences aside, perhaps Dill saw something of himself in 'Percy'. Both men had a selfless loyalty to the Army, coupled in each of them with a natural reserve and absence of flamboyance which some mistook for a lack of decisiveness and leadership. This was a dangerous and superficial mis-judgement in both cases. However, while Dill always looked the part of the assured and experienced commander, the same could not be said of Percival. His raw-boned and rather angular frame was not constructed for best display in uniform, while he lacked the strong jaw-line which made such commanders as Wavell and Slim appear the epitome of will and determination. Dill had always been aware that his subordinate was less than prepossessing when first encountered and some years back had noted, 'He has not altogether an impressive presence and one may there-fore fail on first meeting him to appreciate his sterling worth.'[2] This had not prevented Dill, whilst he was commandant at the Staff College, from reaching the judgement that Percival was the best officer of his rank whom he knew. There is no evidence that his opinion had changed in any way over the intervening years. During the time they served together at Aldershot this high regard blossomed into a warm friendship.

The main task at Aldershot was training: formation training of the kind which had been neglected while the Government had refused to countenance a continental entanglement, and training with the new weapons that were at last coming through from the factories. It was a daunting task, for at the very time that the regular units were being pre-pared for war, they were being stripped of many of their most experienced men to provide basic cadres for the 26 new territorial divisions into which recruits were now flooding. General Lloyd, one of Dill's divisional com-manders, tackled Percival about the difficulties being created and Percy duly informed his chief, giving as an example the situation in 1st Cheshires, his own regiment, which had been so milked of its experienced NCOs that it now had only five trained corporals instead of its war estab-lishment of 36. It was a problem which only time would solve and there was not to be a lot of that precious commodity left.

General Dill was much admired and respected professionally. Many had been surprised when he had not become CIGS as part of Hore-Belisha's initial stable-clearing. But not many of Dill's juniors could claim to know him well in personal terms. Percival was one of the small number who could. In the intervals of their more immediate concern of getting the field force ready for war, the two often discussed the Singapore situation. Dill asked Percival if he thought the island was impregnable. Percival confessed that, 'far from being impregnable it would be in imminent dan-ger if war broke out in the Far East unless there was an early realization in high places of the complete change in the problem of its defence which was then taking place'. He added that the system then relied on, of holding overseas garrisons with skeleton forces, relying on the arrival of the British Fleet to make them secure, was out of date and needed revision. Dill, it seems, agreed and never had any doubts about Singapore's importance.[3] Percival also found time to give his views on the security of the Far East to wider audiences. At the end of 1938 he lectured to the Camberley Staff College on the defence of Malaya Command, as part of the students' Far Eastern Study. He repeated then what he had emphasised the previous March in a lecture at the Aldershot Study Period, about the importance of Siam to Singapore's security and the likely enemy objectives in northern Malaya and southern Siam in the event of an attack. He spoke in similar terms to other officers' courses during his time in Home Command. The message of the island's vulnerability to an attack from the north, and the consequent need to defend all of Malaya, was being emphasised by at least one senior officer, and if it only reached a restricted military audience, it was not an insignificant one.[4]

When Britain finally declared war on Germany, India and the colonies were automatically involved, while the governments of Australia and New Zealand loyally followed Britain's lead without the formality of a parliamentary vote. The BEF duly went off to France. It had been understood for some time that Dill would command any BEF that was formed, but once again Gort was preferred. By this juncture the War Minister and his CIGS were hardly on speaking terms. Hore-Belisha was perhaps relieved to be able to ship his Chief off to France; but his choice of Ironside as Gort's successor as CIGS was as poor a judgement as that of Gort had been. Dill took command of the 1st Corps in a BEF which embarked for the continent initially only four divisions strong. Percival continued as Dill's BGS.

The 'miracle' of the campaign which followed is customarily regarded as being the evacuation of the trapped divisions from Dunkirk; but that was the second miracle, the first being that the BEF which went to France did not contain a single horse. The French and German Armies still depended to an enormous extent on horsed transport and horsed cavalry. But the BEF was far from being either fully mechanised, properly equipped or adequately trained. It was 'woefully deficient in what really mattered in modern war – aircraft and armoured fighting vehicles', wrote Percival. What is more, the force had only managed to be 'motorised' by large-scale requisitioning from civilian firms whose broken-down vans and lorries were soon littering the countryside of France. But at least the BEF had the period of the 'phoney war' to complete their defences and improve their training. It was hardly an easy task with all efforts frustrated at first by torrential rains and then, as winter advanced, by abominably cold weather with severe frosts. Thus the construction of fieldworks proceeded slowly, and often in positions where, as things turned out, the BEF was not destined to fight. Perhaps the most successful aspect of this preparatory period was the 'blooding' of successive batches of BEF units in the lines of the Maginot system, much as, Percival remembered, the Kitchener units had been in the trench lines of France and Flanders. Here at least they grew accustomed to enemy shell-fire without the cost of many casualties.

Before the German blitzkrieg struck, Percival had been recalled to England. In February 1940 he was promoted to major general and given command of 43rd (Wessex) Division which was then training in Wiltshire. The division was to have an eventful war in north-west Europe, but Percival did not remain long enough to lead it at the front. Dill had hoped that Percy would be selected for a different post when his promotion was announced. He had recommended him to be Major General, General Staff of 3rd Army, but during Dill's absence in France the selection board had put someone else in the position.[5] It is interesting to speculate how Percival's fortunes might have prospered if he had been selected for the 3rd Army post. In fact his next move was not to a fighting formation at all but to Whitehall. Dill had been recalled from the Front, initially as Vice-CIGS, but little more than a month later he was given the Army's senior post, that of CIGS. He hardly had time to begin sorting out the 'complete chaos' he inherited in the War Office after Gort's tenure when he found himself serving a new Prime Minister and Minister of Defence, Winston Churchill. At the end of April 1940 he summoned Percival from Salisbury Plain to rejoin his team at the War Office as one of three Assistant Chiefs of the Imperial General Staff (ACIGS) and with responsibility for coordinating the Intelligence and Operations Directorates.

This was Percival's one and only experience in the War Office and though his was the key ACIGS post of the three, he did not particularly enjoy it. Of course it was stimulating to be at the very centre of the nation's affairs at this time of supreme danger and he attended many top-level meetings, even meetings of the Cabinet itself. He was able to bring some reassurance to Sir Anthony Eden, who felt very keenly the loss of the garrison at Calais, with the confirmation that it had not been a worthless sacrifice. 'Here is the justification for your decision', confided Percival, handing the Secretary of State a copy of an intercepted German message which had ordered the transfer of a panzer division which had been threatening Gort's vital communications, for a renewed attempt on Calais. This, the signal declared, had to be reduced at all costs.[6] The delay which the defence of Calais imposed was one of the several factors which saved the BEF.

Percival was also involved in an attempt to persuade the vinegary and anti-British US Ambassador Joseph Kennedy to have more faith in the nation's cause against Germany. Percival called to his office the young GSO1 from Gort's headquarters, Gerald Templer, who had been sent back from France in advance of the main evacuation as one of the *bouches inutiles*. Since his return Templer had been hanging about the War Office hoping for a useful job and railing against all that had gone wrong in France to any senior officer with the patience to listen. Percival arranged to put Templer's caustic tongue to good use by getting him to speak to Ambassador Kennedy in a similar vein, in an interview that had been specially organised. Templer delivered a half-hour tirade to the ambassador with his customary passion and directness. When he finally ran out of steam Kennedy gave his considered judgement: 'Young man, England will be invaded in a few weeks' time and your country will have its neck rung by Hitler like a chicken.' Quivering with fury, Templer told Kennedy exactly what he thought of him and marched out.[7] The gambit had not worked.

Despite the interest of such episodes, Percival did not relish his position of Assistant CIGS. However necessary the post had been during the crisis in France, he felt it was becoming an unnecessary link between the Directors of Operations and Intelligence on the one hand, and the CIGS or his deputy on the other. Besides, life behind a desk while the war was going on did not suit him. He asked for a move to a field formation and was appointed to command 44th (Home Counties) Division which had recently been evacuated from Dunkirk. The next nine months he spent reorganising his division which had lost all its baggage and heavy equipment in the evacuation, and in developing the coast defences, ready for the invasion which Ambassador Kennedy was certain would soon be launched. His responsibility was first of all the east coast defences in Yorkshire with his divisional headquarters near Doncaster. In fact the staff at Doncaster did not see a great deal of him as he 'spent many weeks touring the divisional anti-invasion defences tirelessly day after day'.[8] In September he organised a major divisional anti-invasion exercise which General Sir Alan Brooke, C-in-C Home Forces, flew up to observe. The division later moved to the Kent and Sussex coast where many of the soldiers came from and where Percival had the responsibility of 62 miles of front – a long stretch for a single division, even though he was given an extra brigade. Once again his time in the post was short, for towards the end of March 1941 he received a telegram summoning him to the War Office the next morning and advising him, rather ominously, to get his tropical kit together. When he got to Whitehall he received the news that he was being promoted temporary lieutenant general and appointed GOC Malaya. He had to be ready to leave by flying boat in three days' time.

Percival was delighted at the promotion (for he was still a relatively junior major general) and particularly pleased at the prospect of an independent command. But command in Malaya! It was true that of all the officers of his rank he knew more about the situation there than any. He was after all the author of the most perceptive paper on where the major threat to the territory lay and what needed to be done about it. On the one hand, there was the chance that the European war might rage on and his future command remain inactive; but the reverse possibility was just as likely. Britain's fortunes were at their lowest ebb; there would be few resources to spare for the distant Malaya Command if the Japanese did attack. It could be, he noted in the understated language of the time, 'a pretty sticky business'. And if there was a better example of Clausewitz's 'frictional forces' in war against which the commander continually had to struggle, than the apathy and obstruction Percival had met from the colonial bureaucracy during his first tour in the command, he would like to have known about it. There was much about the new job to give one pause. At least the CIGS understood what was required. Percival had every faith in Dill's judgement and was confident that his old chief would do his best for him.

In fact, much had changed in the Singapore defence scene since Percival's last tour in Malaya Command. General Dobbie had long since moved on, but not before he had followed up the appreciation on which Percival had worked, with a fresh one in July 1938, warning that a landing in Johore followed by an attack on Singapore from the north was now the greatest threat. A quite inadequate sum of £60,000 was allocated for the construction of Johore defences, but it was given no priority by Dobbie's successor, Major General Lionel Bond. However the fact that the money was allocated at all, and that the Indian battalion based at Taiping and due for relief by the newly raised Malay Regiment battalion, was allowed to remain in Malaya, made it very clear that the War Office authorities at last recognised that the Naval Base was vulnerable to attack from the north.

The coming of war with Germany and the fall of the Low Countries and France, for all that they heightened the risks and dangers to the security of Malaya and Singapore by increasing the vulnerability of Indo-China to Japanese influence, failed totally to produce the unity of purpose and cooperation among those locally concerned with their defence. The old Defence Committee which the GOC had controlled during Percival's first tour had now been put under the chairmanship of the Governor as titular Commander-in-Chief. General Dobbie had offered no objection to the reorganisation. In theory it provided improved machinery for the coordination of the local defence, but it took little account of the personalities involved, the conflicting priorities they attempted to apply and the meagre resources which the London authorities were prepared to allocate them. Before long an irreconcilable disagreement had developed between General Bond and the new Air Officer Commanding Far East, Air Vice Marshal Babington. Babington continued to press the view that until the Fleet was available, the defence of Malaya was a matter for the RAF. The main task of the Army should be the defence of the airfields which had now been constructed in the north and north-east of the peninsula. Bond steadfastly refused to comply, arguing that with his weak forces he should concentrate on the defence of the Johore area. The meddlesome civilian Secretary of the Defence Committee, a Mr Vlieland, supported the RAF line and persuaded the Governor to agree.

The situation, then, was one in which Babington was insisting on a role for the RAF which, with only 88 obsolete aircraft available in the whole of Malaya, it was quite unable to fulfil. Bond, on the other hand, was restricting the Army's responsibility to a task more suited to its very modest capabilities but which made less and less strategic sense as each day passed. Vlieland, charged with coordinating the civilian defence effort, was doing little in that direction but interfering notably in the Services' affairs and keeping the Governor in general support of the RAF position. To complete the picture of strategic unreality, there was the position of the keystone of the security edifice, the Naval Base itself. This had been finally opened with some ceremony by Sir Shenton Thomas on 15 February (a fateful date) 1938 before a large gathering of civil and military dignitaries from Britain and the Empire. However the doubts about the Fleet ever being available to occupy it, which Churchill had expressed as long ago as 1935, had been more than confirmed by events since. Substantial naval losses and fresh challenges at sea in the early months of the European war were to confirm the hollowness of the 'main Fleet to Singapore' deterrent. Yet the key calculation on which the planners in Singapore were basing their defence arrangements continued to be 'the period before relief' by the Fleet.

So obvious and so worrying was the lack of defence preparation by the civil authorities in Singapore, and so deep and public the disagreement and personal animosity between the Army and RAF commanders, that successive local naval commanders (Commanders-in-Chief China Station whose headquarters were moved from Hong Kong to Singapore) reported the critical situation back to London. They advised that the two men be replaced. They were finally, but the Government's first reaction, in October 1940, was to appoint Air Chief Marshal Sir Robert Brooke Popham as Commander-in-Chief Far East.

By this stage the competing Army and RAF Commanders in Singapore had put their separate cases to their chiefs in London and the Governor had sent his, backing the RAF line, to the Colonial Office. General Bond's memorandum, based on a theoretical 'period before relief' by the Fleet which was now extended to 180 days and a Japanese threat which had advanced as close as Hainan Island, recognised at last that all of Malaya would need to be defended. For this he would need a minimum of three divisions, two tank battalions, two machine-gun battalions and a pool of 20 per cent reinforcements. If an invasion of southern Siam were contemplated to forestall a Japanese landing there, he would need at least two further divisions. The Overseas Defence Committee met to consider the Governor's and General Bond's messages on 16 May 1940. Two days earlier the Dutch Army had surrendered; two days later the German blitzkrieg would break through to the English Channel. It was the blackest hour of the entire war for Britain and plainly not a juncture at which the Chiefs were likely to be able to spare forces for Malaya. They advised the conscription of local manpower resources and said that they were reviewing the situation in the Far East as a matter of urgency. Meanwhile the Governor, Sir Shenton Thomas, departed for his home leave, to be spent in a charming country house in Littlebourne near Canterbury, leaving his Colonial Secretary as Acting Governor to take charge of civil defence preparations and attempt to reconcile the opposing views of the land and air commanders. Thomas did not return for eight months, during which time Malaya's situation turned from grave to critical.

At the end of June 1940 the Chiefs of Staff produced their promised appreciation for the Far Eastern strategy in the light of the changed situation in Europe and the strengthening position of Japan in Indo-China. They recommended the withdrawal of the strategically useless British garrisons in China, declared Hong Kong not to be a vital interest and recorded their opposition to its reinforcement. With Italy now in the lists and posing a substantial Mediterranean threat and Germany as dangerous as ever, there was no question of an adequate Fleet being sent to Singapore. The Chiefs of Staff were at last signing the death certificate of Britain's Far Eastern strategy. It had been a sickly infant when the naval base decision was first adopted in 1922, terminally stricken since 1935; now it was declared stone-cold dead. Furthermore, in the changed circumstances, the Chiefs accepted that the whole of the Malayan peninsula would have to be defended. Without a fleet, this would be largely a task for air power. Given the other regional commitments, a total of 336 first-line aircraft (against the 88 obsolete ones in theatre) would be needed. They recommended the despatch of the first of these without delay. Once this total was achieved (and it seems to have been more a statement of the total possible than the number necessary) the Chiefs calculated that Malaya could be defended by six brigades of ground troops. Until such a time, they accepted General Bond's figure of the equivalent of three divisions plus attached troops as the necessary reinforcement. These were important decisions and the first of a series of benchmarks against which the ultimate failure in Malaya needs to be judged. Since Percival had been serving in the War Office when this appreciation was being prepared, he would have drawn some small comfort, when he learnt of his appointment the following March, from the realistic attitude that the Chiefs were now taking. Had he been privy to Churchill's thinking on the issue he would have been considerably more disturbed.

With the management of the war his prime responsibility, Churchill's unrivalled knowledge and experience made his position virtually unassailable. He had fought as an officer in two wars, been First Lord of the Admiralty in two wars and run both the War Office and Air Ministry in times of crisis and of peace. He had substantial experience both as war correspondent and military historian. He was consequently able to direct the war with an imperious assurance. Few had the experience, authority or support to gainsay him. As the Prime Minister himself admitted, 'All I wanted was compliance with my wishes after reasonable discussion'.[9] The task of tempering his strategic enthusiasms and dissuading him from his wilder schemes was a daunting one for the Chiefs of Staff and particularly for the CIGS. The RAF probably had least trouble with him, since he supported their dominant policy of strategic bombing, while the Admiralty was virtually an operational headquarters and able to retain more independence. It was the Army, with no set plans and an ignominious defeat in France behind it, on which the Prime Minister and Minister of Defence leant hardest, and CIGS Dill who took the pressure most of all. His keenest disagreements with Churchill were about strategic priorities and these came into sharpest focus in their contrasting attitudes to the defence of Malaya and Singapore.

Four days before the Chiefs of Staff announced their reinforcement proposals, Churchill was writing to the Prime Ministers of Australia and New Zealand assuring them that the reinforced Eastern Mediterranean Fleet, 'could of course at any time be sent through the Canal into the Indian Ocean, or to relieve Singapore. We do not want to do this, even if Japan declares war, until it is found to be vital to your safety.'[10] In October, long after the War Cabinet had approved the Chiefs' recommendations, Churchill was writing to General Ismay, his watchdog on the Chiefs of Staff Committee, in a slightly different tone, 'The prime defence of Singapore is the Fleet. . . . The defence of Singapore must therefore be based upon a strong local garrison and the general potentialities of sea-power. The idea of trying to defend the Malay peninsula . . . cannot be entertained.'[11] The Prime Minister and the Chiefs of Staff seemed to be singing from different hymn sheets.

Once their appreciation was produced, the Chiefs of Staff at once set about getting together such reinforcements for Singapore as they could amass. The two battalions withdrawn from China were sent to Singapore, and much larger reinforcements from India, the products of the first phase of its remarkable wartime expansion programme, began to arrive. 12th Indian Infantry Brigade was already in Malaya, and the Indian authorities now agreed to send 11th Indian Division (two brigades only and no artillery) to join it. This meant that the infantry of a full Indian Division was in Malaya by the end of November 1940, but it had done very little training and was quite unprepared for close-country, tropical warfare conditions. These reinforcements scarcely approached the totals of land forces the Chiefs believed necessary, even if the air force strength had reached the requisite levels, which at the time it fell lamentably short of doing.

The local commanders had already produced their tactical appreciation, indicating that much more was needed than what London was proposing if Malaya was adequately to be defended. They accepted that the air arm was the main weapon of defence for Malaya, in the temporary absence of the Fleet, but argued that 566 first-line aircraft (200 more than the Chiefs proposed) would be required to assure this defence. Even then, they believed, the Army strength could not afford to be reduced below 23 battalions (five more than the Chiefs believed necessary). They also pressed for three flotillas of motor torpedo boats (MTBs) to prevent Japanese moves along the coast of Malaya. At the end of October, Admiral Layton, C-in-C China Station, chaired a conference of local commanders which also included representatives from India, Australia, New Zealand and Burma. This conducted a regional strategic review based on the Chiefs of Staff's appreciation and the response of the local commanders. It endorsed the local commanders' views of the force levels necessary, but in view of the gross disparity between these figures and what they actually had on the ground, it recommended further cooperation with India, Australia, New Zealand and Burma in an attempt to put matters to rights.

The ultimate result was the commitment of a brigade group from Australia (later to be expanded to 8th Australian Division) and a further division from India, 9th Indian Division. Steps were also now in hand to send from the UK the specialist additions which would turn the Indian divisions into more balanced fighting forces. However, it was in the air that the defending forces remained lamentably weak, and it was the Air Arm which was still designated as providing the main defence of Malaya. The local commanders had asked for twice as many bombers and fighters as the Chiefs had suggested, and for 44 Army cooperation aircraft as well. In January the request was turned down, the reply from London noting that the Chiefs' original figure of 336 'should give a fair degree of security' and that the provision of aircraft specifically for Army cooperation was thought to be uneconomic. However, they hoped to be able to provide five fighter squadrons by the end of 1941, by which time they planned that the overall total of 336 first-line aircraft would be achieved. They also agreed the higher total of infantry battalions which the local commanders had called for.[12]

Whatever the Chiefs were trying to do for this distant theatre, the attitude of the Prime Minister to its reinforcement and defence remained unchanged. 'I do not remember to have given my approval to these very large diversions of force', he wrote to the Chiefs when he had read their reinforcement plans.[13] His dispute with Dill on strategic priorities came to a head with Churchill's directive of 28 April 1941. Churchill had been stung into writing this by the chance discovery of what he believed was 'defeatism' among his senior military advisers. Produced without the advice of the Chiefs, the directive emphasised the primacy of the Middle

East in overseas defence commitments, and at the same time made crystal clear Churchill's views on the Japanese threat to Malaya. 'Japan is unlikely to enter the war unless the Germans make a successful invasion of Great Britain', was the Prime Minister's opening postulate. He concluded with the observation that, 'it may be taken as almost certain that the entry of Japan into the war would be followed by the immediate entry of the United States on our side', adding that any change in the conditions he was laying down would be notified to the Chiefs of Staff 'in good time'. Dill's response was that if Churchill's assumptions proved false, there would be no 'good time' in which to recover; it took three months to get reinforcements to Singapore. Moreover, since the rest of Churchill's directive was already committing such reinforcements elsewhere, there were unlikely to be any available. But there was no convincing the Prime Minister.[14]

Churchill never wavered from this basic political position about the Japanese threat and supported it with views on the defence of Singapore which were equally adamantine and notably at variance with those of the Chiefs of Staff. Singapore was a protected 'fortress' whose general defence remained the responsibility of the Fleet; no substantial UK-based air or land reinforcements were to be provided for its defence, the Middle East being the higher priority theatre. Behind these determinations lay the hope (and there were few grounds for it ever hardening into an expectation) that the USA would, in the end, pull Britain's Far Eastern chestnuts out of the fire. However hard Dill worked to alter the Prime Minister's views he was unable to shift him. Unsurprisingly, when General Brooke later took over from Dill as CIGS and discussed the Japanese menace with him, Dill had to confess 'frankly that he had done practically nothing to meet this threat'.[15] Percival's confidence in the support which Dill would give him was well-founded, but it reckoned without the unyielding opposition of the Prime Minister. The result was Dill's replacement rather than any change in Churchill's priorities.

GOC MALAYA COMMAND

'God knows where we should be without him, but God knows where we shall go with him.'

General Sir Alan Brooke on Churchill, 4 December 1941

When war had first been declared in September 1939, Betty Percival had realised only too clearly that she would soon be parted from her husband as he went off to France with the BEF. She no doubt had a clear idea of the danger and the hardship which might be his lot in war. Perhaps she also had a presentiment that years of separation could lie ahead for them and even the sickening fear that he might not return at all from the battlefront. Ten days after the expiry of Chamberlain's ultimatum, she had sat down in their Aldershot home and written a simple testament to her husband as their parting loomed.

> My darling Arthur,
> I am writing this as I could not have said it with a dry face. Thank you darling for your love, our lovely children and the happy years we have had together. Partings are always sad but we have nothing to look back upon but happiness and good comradeship.
> I commit you to God's care sure that he will do what is best for you. I pray for your safe return but should it be otherwise I shall try to carry on faithfully till we meet again.
> The children shall be cared for as you would wish and you need not worry about anything.
> All my love darling now and forever.
> Ever yr faithful wife
> Betty M Percival.[1]

In the event, Arthur was soon called back from France, but Betty's words must have been a considerable comfort to him as he set off for his more distant destination of Singapore the following year. Perhaps similar letters were being written in Japan, as they might have been written for almost a decade, since the Imperial Armies first moved against the Chinese. But in Japan there were also more unusual, and to western eyes, quite incomprehensible ceremonies as the menfolk went off to war. Some families arranged the full formalities of a funeral for their departing sons so that they would be prepared to die for the Emperor without concern for their relatives' feelings. There were wives who killed their children and then committed suicide themselves, lest their existence might be a hindrance to their husbands in risking death in the Imperial cause. Such a show of selfless devotion to the Japanese national purpose was a foretaste of the culture shock, martial and social, that awaited General Percival's army.

When Percival was selected as the next GOC Malaya and promoted to acting lieutenant general he occupied the 28th position in the seniority list of major generals printed in the spring 1941 edition of *The Army List*. He had plainly been chosen over the heads of many more senior officers, though the list over-dramatises the jump he had taken; some names on it were of specialists ineligible for a command appointment, others were of those on the verge of retirement, still more were holding posts from which they could not be spared. It was, nevertheless, a considerable promotion and one for which General Dill had specifically selected him. Dill had every faith in Percival's qualities, in his knowledge of Malaya Command and in the direction of his strategic thinking in regard to its defence. If anyone was likely to pour oil on the troubled waters of the Far East High Command and get people working together, it was Percy.

Churchill would also have sanctioned the nomination, as he did all matters of consequence in the conduct of the war (and many of very little). He remarked pointedly to his Secretary of State for Air in relation to another move, a couple of months after Percival's selection, 'As Minister of Defence I am bound to take a direct part in all high appointments in the Fighting Services. No important appointment has been made during my tenure without my being consulted.' Besides, he knew Percival well; his signature was on the certificates of the four mentions in despatches which Percival had gained, he knew about Percival's exploits in Russia and especially in Ireland and had interviewed him with Lloyd George at the Inverness Cabinet which prepared the truce negotiations with the Irish. He would have been content to note that Dill's selection for Malaya Command was a man of high personal courage, a quality which Churchill always admired. *The Army List* of spring 1941 also featured an interesting sidelight on the painfully slow adjustment which the country and its Prime Minister were making to the threat in the Far East: the Japanese Emperor Hirohito still featured on its pages as an honorary field marshal. It was not until the first 1942 edition (correct as at 25th December 1941, the day Hong Kong fell) that his name was unceremoniously expunged.

Despite the urgency of Percival's original summons to the War Office and the haste of his preparations to be on his way, it was five weeks before he finally flew off for Malaya, an interval which gave him the opportunity for lengthy briefings in London and for a lunch with Dill. At the time, the

CIGS was in the midst of his bitterest struggles with Churchill over strategic priorities, though how much of this he was able to pass on to his old BGS from their 1st Corps days is not clear. A much sadder event in Arthur's final weeks at home was the death of his mother in early April. Old Mrs Percival, then 84, had borne the bombing in Hertfordshire with great resolution, but the impending departure of her younger son for a distant land had been an additional anxiety which perhaps hastened her death. Alfred Percival was now left alone, but by this time Betty and the children had moved back to the county and were close at hand.

The flight to Singapore took a fortnight with refuelling stops at Gibraltar, Malta, Alexandria, Basra, Karachi and Rangoon, where Percival transferred to a RAF plane from Singapore for the final stage to Alor Star and on to Singapore itself. The long initial delay and the lengthy flight are both reminders of the rudimentary state of air travel at the time and the general perception at home of Malaya as a very remote theatre. It would not be easy to reinforce it quickly, as Dill and his DMO had stressed to the Prime Minister. However the journey did give Percival the opportunity to renew his acquaintance with General Dobbie, now Governor of a beleaguered Malta, and Air Marshal Tedder in Alexandria whom he also knew from their earlier Malaya days; and the chance for a discussion with Major General Macleod in Burma who was even worse placed for balanced forces than Percival was to be in his new command.

The C-in-C Far East, Air Chief Marshal Sir Robert Brooke Popham, was considerably relieved when his new GOC finally arrived. News of General Bond's impending replacement had leaked out early to that unfortunate officer and Brooke Popham was keen to have his successor in post at the earliest moment. Not all the messages about the delays to Percival's flight had got through to his headquarters and he had been sending signals around the world trying to discover what had become of his new Army Commander. He was very glad of this reinforcement 'from the seat of the anti-invasion preparations' in the UK, as he put it, for a similar threat was now developing to Malaya as well as to Hong Kong and possibly even Burma, which were also part of the C-in-C's extensive command. It was true that he had no responsibility for the Navy (which had a separate C-in-C China Station, Admiral Layton) and only 'higher direction and control' of the other two Services, but it was an immense command nonetheless, for which a parsimonious Whitehall had authorised him a staff of only seven. Brooke Popham was 62, rather old for such a demanding post. He had been retired from the RAF since 1937, which meant that he was also rather out of date professionally. But his experience as a colonial governor in Kenya gave him the ideal perspective from which to view the state of civil-military relations in Malaya which, even in the second year of Britain's war, were depressingly reminiscent of those of Percival's earlier tour.

'The main thing that stands out about Singapore', wrote Brooke Popham, 'is the lack of touch and indeed the latent hostility between the Central Government, the Services and the Civilian Community'. He found that the government officials were 'closing their eyes to defence realities and war possibilities', but nevertheless claimed that he 'got along well' with the Governor, Sir Shenton Thomas. One significant achievement already lay to the C-in-C's credit: he had managed to force the resignation of the civilian Defence Secretary, Mr Vlieland, about whom he had been briefed before he had left London. 'I have seldom met anyone who is, with two or three exceptions, so universally distrusted', he wrote, averring that Vlieland had established 'procrastination as a fine art'.[2] It was perhaps symptomatic of the Governor's judgement and sense of priorities that he had appointed Vlieland in the first place and plainly trusted him, although the War Committee for which Vlieland was responsible managed without an agenda, issued no minutes and had proved an obstacle rather than an aid to improved defence arrangements. Neither Vlieland nor anyone else had bothered to produce the Defence Plan for the C-in-C's information when he first arrived. Unfortunately Brooke Popham seemed to have an ill-founded optimism on several key defence issues, like the defensibility of Hong Kong, the capabilities of the Far East Air Force and the general inferiority of the Japanese armed forces, about whom he asserted to Sir Arthur Street at the Air Ministry, 'I do feel that as regards landings from the sea they have never been up against any opposition and as regards air bombing they have never been up against fighters.'[3] Percival would have been a good deal more cautious about Japanese combined operations, but nevertheless found his new Chief very accessible, declaring that his 'personal relations with him throughout were of the happiest'.[4]

The second major figure on the Singapore scene with whom Percival had to deal was, of course, the Governor himself, whom he knew quite well from his first tour in Malaya and slightly from even earlier days in Nigeria. Shenton Thomas had always been, in Colonial Office jargon, a 'Secretariat man' and had never served as a District Officer, the key training post in which officials 'roughed it', gaining up-country experience. He seems to have been initially opposed to any defence build-up in Malaya,[5] was ill-disposed to the upsetting of his bureaucratic routine which war preparations required and ill-prepared for the hard decisions which war itself brought. His seven years in Singapore had been preceded by 24 in Africa and even before this earlier period was completed he seems to have grown weary of colonial government and been ready for a quieter life. 'I wish to goodness I could give up all this and retire', he had written longingly to his wife during his time in Nyasaland.[6] It would have been wiser if he had been replaced when the European war had first broken out, but the Colonial Secretary had asked him to stay on and see it out in Singapore. He and Lady Thomas entertained the incoming senior military people with an unforced affability, but Shenton Thomas was not the man for the tempest which broke on all their heads. He and his officials seemed wedded to the pace and routine of peace. Even Percival, who seldom offered public criticism of his superiors, was forced to admit, in his characteristically understated way, that Thomas's seven years in Singapore were 'a long time in that trying climate'.

There were also significant potential difficulties with Percival's direct subordinates, the most important of whom was Lieutenant General Sir Lewis Heath. Heath had been appointed by HQ India to command III Indian Corps, into which 9th and 11th Indian Divisions had now been formed. In terms of command experience he was a good choice for this post, just as Percival, selected in London, was for the overall Army Command; but they would scarcely have been put together in their respective positions if a single decision-maker had made the selections. Percival and Heath were as different as chalk from cheese and had risen to stardom at opposite poles of the military firmament. Heath was two years older than Percival and senior to him until the latter's appointment as GOC (though he appeared on the Indian rather than the British Army List). It did not make matters easier for the GOC that Heath had arrived in Malaya before him, already with a knighthood and the considerable cachet of having conducted the first British offensive of the war. He had taken 5th Indian Division to victory against the Italians at Keren in the Eritrean campaign. Most of Heath's service life had been spent with Indian troops, he had virtually no staff experience and had even declined a place at the Indian Staff College in favour of a command appointment.[7] The contrast with his new GOC, graduate of three staff colleges, could hardly have been greater. Heath was the Indian frontier soldier *par excellence*; Percival was a 'westerner' who knew nothing of the Indian Army and was not very impressed with its ill-trained recruits who formed the bulk of his new command. To complete the picture of their differences, Percival had been a bachelor until he was 40 and had now left his wife and young family on the other side of the world in England. Heath was very recently remarried to a New Zealand nurse many years his junior whom he had 'smuggled into Malaya', as he put it, as his fiancée. By the time operations began she was expecting a child and was consequently allowed to stay. It was, in all conscience, hardly a satisfactory basis on which to face the traumas of a campaign, or a good example to his juniors. Percival and Heath were both men of considerable courage and military experience, but their appointment to serve together in the circumstances of 1941 was singularly ill-advised. All seemed well in the relations of GOC and Corps Commander until the Japanese struck. They rapidly deteriorated thereafter.

Another direct 'subordinate', if that is the appropriate term for someone to whom subordination did not come easily, was the hot-tempered and prickly commander of the 8th Australian Division (at this stage only one brigade strong but soon accorded the status of Australian Imperial Force at its commander's urging), Major General Gordon Bennett. Like many of his officers and the majority of his division, Bennett was not a professional soldier. He had gained a commission in the militia as a young man and gone off to the First World War as a major in the Australian Imperial Force. His undoubted bravery and leadership had seen him rise rapidly to the command of a brigade by 1916 which he held until the end of the war, except for two short periods when he had command of 1st Australian Division. The end of the war had seen him return to civilian life, but he retained his militia interests and with his considerable military reputation had become in 1930, at the age of 43, the youngest major general in the Australian service. That rank he had now held for 11 years. He was a controversial figure, ambitious, opinionated, outspoken ('rasping, bitter, sarcastic' was how *The Times* correspondent described him) and an accomplished self-publicist. He had failed to gain command of any of the first divisions, 6th, 7th and 9th, which were formed and despatched to the Middle East. In the opinion of the Chief of the Australian General Staff, Bennett had 'certain qualities and certain disqualities' for an active command. Only when an unfortunate air crash robbed Australia of three government ministers and the CGS at one blow did this controversial figure get the command he sought.

Gordon Bennett was not an easy subordinate for Percival who had no instructions defining his authority over the Australians. While the GOC did all he could to reduce the differences between the various elements in his command, for example in relation to rations and recreational travel, Bennett insisted on retaining the special conditions which his men enjoyed, having them always serve under Australian officers and refusing even to have their off-duty behaviour regulated by the British military police. His many statements to the Press, often given in praise of the qualities of his force, inevitably reflected on the remainder. Bennett agreed to take orders from Percival without hesitation and to cooperate with British units, but his insistence on the separateness of the Australians, his abrasive personality and his lack of recent military experience led to many difficulties. When the Australian CGS, General Sturdee, visited Malaya in the autumn of 1941, he seems to have appreciated the problems which Bennett was causing for Percival and suggested to his own authorities that Bennett, who was 'very senior', might be sent to command Australian Home Forces and be replaced by an 'energetic junior commander' who would fit in better with Malaya Command's requirements.[8] Unfortunately the change did not take place. Relations between Percival and Bennett were never easy throughout the campaign, nor were they always harmonious between Bennett and his own subordinates. This did not bode well for effective action under the strain of combat. The Press loved Bennett;

his readily proffered and outspoken pronouncements were always news-worthy and he 'talked a good war', comparing favourably in the eyes of the newsmen with the more reserved Percival and Heath.

The third commander who worked directly to Percival was Major General Keith Simmons, in charge of the fixed defences of Singapore. Here at least was an uncomplicated relationship. Simmons had been com-manding in Shanghai and had moved to Singapore when the China garrison was withdrawn. Percival found him tactful, courteous and able, all important qualities for a commander whose men were in regular con-tact with the civilian population and himself with the colonial authorities of Singapore. Among the latter, despite the growing Japanese threat, there was still an attitude of 'business as usual'; commercial activities took pri-ority, in accordance with London's wishes although, as Brooke Popham kept repeating, 'I realise the importance of rubber and tin but there won't be much of either if we don't hold Malaya.'[9] Percival had made a similar point in a personal letter to Dill in October, when he had written, 'life is still so comparatively easy here it is difficult to get them to understand what war really means'. In the same letter he had repeated his need for tanks, adding, 'It's safe to assume that if our friends [the Japanese] decided to come this way they would bring some with them.'[10] Nevertheless, the C-in-C continued to make the most optimistic public pronouncements. He was particularly impressed by the Australians and quoted one commanding officer whom he had met up-country as saying to him, 'Don't you think they are worthy of some better enemy than the Japanese?'. Meanwhile the Singapore social round continued. Megan Spooner, wife of Rear Admiral Spooner who was Layton's deputy for Malaya, arrived in the city with her husband in late August 1941 and kept an intimate diary of her impressions. It recorded an unending round of social events and supper parties with scarcely a mention of the possibility of war until the moment of the Japanese attack. She found Percival, 'a nice shy man who blossoms slowly in conversation'.[11]

'With the arrival of Lieutenant General Percival', recorded the official historian General Kirby, 'a new spirit entered every sphere of activity, including training.'[12] For a start the old Army/RAF antagonisms were put aside. Brooke Popham had done his best to set the tone with a tri-Service and civilian exercise the previous December. However the AOC had not participated but left for Malaya on tour. The exercise was a valuable start but it had merely emphasised 'to the highest degree the lack of under-standing between the Army and the RAF'.[13] Air Vice Marshal Pulford, Babington's successor as AOC, had arrived shortly before Percival. From the time the new GOC joined him in Singapore there was the most com-plete cooperation between the two. Since they were both unaccompanied by their families, Pulford shared Flagstaff House with Percival and they began the creation of a joint operational headquarters at Sime Road alongside the Royal Singapore Golf Club. The two thought alike 'on most matters military and non-military', noted Percival and quickly developed a close comradeship. This was a sea change from the situation only weeks earlier when the animosity between khaki and light blue had been so great and the personal dislike of their chiefs so pronounced and public that hostesses took care to see that they were not invited to the same parties. It had been made very clear to Percival, both at the War Office and by the C-in-C himself, that air power was to have the key role in the defence of Malaya and he was doing his damnedest to follow that policy. Immediate action was taken 'to put the matter of defence works and schemes at aerodromes in place throughout the country'. The trouble was that the Japanese clock was already ticking and this vital work had been neglected by the earlier commanders. In consequence, as one of Percival's staff was later grimly to recall, the works 'were not completed, nor were denial and demolition schemes, before the outbreak of hostilities'.[14]

'Aerodromes sprang up in Malaya like mushrooms', wrote the same officer in evident bafflement. His exasperation was understandable; but it was the policy of the Chiefs of Staff that two-thirds of the air strength of Malaya should be able to concentrate in the north or south of the country at any one time. Since the Chiefs had planned that their recommended first-line strength of 336 aircraft would be in theatre by the end of the year, airfields to accommodate them had to be provided. In fact the first squadrons of fighters had already arrived. 'It must be a great comfort to you to have some effective SS fighters which the Japanese would simply loathe to meet', Ismay had enthused to Brooke Popham.[15] The reality was that the US Brewster Buffaloes of which the new squadrons were composed had already been rejected as first-line fighters for use in Europe.[16] Percival was certainly a little puzzled at his colleague being supplied with fighters 'of a type which I had not heard of as being in action elsewhere'. However, he was much more disturbed by the total absence from the armoury of the RAF in Malaya of heavy bombers, dive-bombers, transport and Army-cooperation aircraft. But at least there was now full consultation with the Army before the location of any new RAF airstrip was decided upon. The unenviable task fell to Percival of deciding how best to protect those (and there were many of them) sited with no thought at all to the problem of their defence.

This was but one aspect of the strategic conundrum which confronted the new GOC. The threat from the Japanese was clearly approaching from the direction which he had first envisaged in his 1937 appreciation; but in practically every respect in which it was possible to envision it, the threat was now much more menacing. When Percival arrived in Malaya, the Japanese were already in occupation of northern Indo-China where the Vichy French authorities were in no position to resist further Japanese demands. Tokyo had also concluded a neutrality pact with Soviet Russia the previous month, securing their northern front in Manchuria should they wish to concentrate on a further drive to the south. From Indo-China an attack could be mounted on Malaya without the warning signal of an expeditionary force setting sail from the Japanese home islands. It all made the defence of the naval base infinitely more problematical, particularly since the Fleet could not now be expected to arrive for the relief of a besieged garrison for as long as six months. How much of any invading force could Percival expect the Far East Air Force to deal with if a Japanese attack were launched? Despite having the main responsibil-ity for the defence of Malaya, it still seemed to be remarkably weak. What were the most likely areas for a seaborne assault? What proportion of his force could Percival afford to allocate to airfield defence and how much to the vulnerable coastline and to Singapore itself? How best could he defend the land frontier with Thailand which meandered irregularly across the peninsula? Had he forces enough for an advance into Thailand to forestall the Japanese at Singora and Patani if they tried to capture the airfields at these coastal towns before invading Malaya? Brooke Popham had already proposed an outline plan for such a pre-emptive move. Finally, what support could he expect from the civil authorities in preparing Malaya for war?

When Percival arrived, he found Lewis Heath's III Indian Corps in operational control of northern Malaya with 9th Indian Division around Alor Star on the plains of Kedah in the west and 11th Indian Division on the east coast, split between Kota Bharu near the Thai border and Kuantan, a coastal town roughly 150 miles further south. Each division had only two brigades and lacked heavy weapon support. Their disposi-tions covered likely Japanese thrusts towards the northern and eastern groups of airfields. Heath had his headquarters in Kuala Lumpur. The AIF of Gordon Bennett, only one brigade initially, was in the Malacca/Negri Sembilan area. It formed the Command reserve, ready to move to any threatened area. There were also three unbrigaded battalions in the north of Malaya and some Indian state battalions of dubious qual-ity disposed for airfield defence. Finally there were the forces of Keith Simmons comprising the artillery and fortress troops of Singapore itself and the three brigades of field troops defending the beaches of Singapore and east Johore. On paper it seemed a substantial force, yet it contained only six regular British battalions and only one brigade which had been in Malaya for any length of time and was trained and reasonably prepared to fight there.

There was an immense amount to be done; yet the main instrument through which the GOC could achieve things – his Command Headquarters – was pitifully small for the task. It was, in effect, an Army as well as a Command HQ, responsible for a multinational force and preparing to defend a territory embracing the 12 different political units which Malaya Command embraced. Yet it boasted only a handful of staff officers more than General Dobbie had been given to run the defences of tiny, if beleaguered, Malta which was also thousands of miles nearer home. What was worse, its recent enlargement had been achieved through local promotions and additions since the War Office had refused to post in qualified and war-experienced staff from elsewhere. Since the rates of pay and tax situation of officers on the British, Indian and Australian establishments were all different, Percival had little flexibility in getting the right men into key appointments. When one officer returned in September 1941 to the HQ in which he had served a year earlier, it was to find it considerably expanded, but largely because, 'most of the original staff had gone up a rank or two'. The lack of enough staff of the right quality and experience was not the least of the problems with which Percival had to cope. Pulford was as badly placed, Percival noted, with 'only one officer on his staff who had been trained at the RAF Staff College'.

A second basic difficulty was the stranglehold which the Treasury maintained, via the War Office, on every aspect of expenditure in Malaya Command. There had been little relaxation in this detailed control from the centre, even in this, the second year of the war and despite the mounting crisis in the Far East. The policy, which bore equally hard upon the RAF, had two clear and disastrous consequences for Percival's preparations for war. It deprived him of the opportunity to use a civilian labour force to build fixed defences in the vulnerable areas of his defences; and it prevented him from purchasing locally the earth-moving and pumping equipment he desperately needed. The Treasury sanctioned a ridiculous 45 cents a day for the hire of local labourers when the Labour Controller in Malaya advised that $1.10 plus rations was the going rate. There was already labour trouble in Malaya over rates of pay. An alternative scheme which Percival put to London, to hire labour more cheaply from Hong Kong, also fell foul of Treasury parsimony, while the request to buy urgently needed equipment was refused on the grounds that it could be supplied from the UK. It never arrived. The delay in the processing of requests before they were finally refused was a further complication. As many suspected, though no one of course knew, preparations for war in Malaya were a race against time. The bureaucratic processes of the Treasury and War Office were forcing Percival to run that race under the severest of handicaps.

Soon after his arrival General Percival was asked to review the Army strength he required for Malaya's defence. He completed this review after visiting all the main defence locations, studying the problems on the ground and agreeing or amending the local dispositions and defence plans. He also tasked a joint staff study group with examining the strategic defence problem for him. One particular question he put to them was for an estimate of the damage which 'the Air Force *at its existing strength* [author's italics] might be expected to inflict on a hostile sea-borne expedition before it reached the shores of Malaya'.[17] The figure he was given (provided by the C-in-C's principal RAF staff officer, Group Captain Darvall) was 40 per cent of the attacking force.[18] Taking this vital statistic into account, Percival framed his response to the Chiefs of Staff. He requested what he regarded as 'the absolute minimum in view of the greatly increased threat to Malaya which was then developing'.[19] He asked for a complete division as a reserve for III Corps (a prudent request in view of the plan for the Corps' pre-emptive move into south Thailand should a Japanese attack be clearly on the way), an extra brigade for 9th Division, to bring it to full divisional strength, two regular battalions for Penang and a brigade group instead of a single battalion for Borneo. He also repeated the request, which had first been made as long ago as 1937, for tanks. He wanted two tank regiments. These, and two heavy anti-aircraft regiments to defend the airfields of Malaya, completed his requirements. It was a modest and realistic shopping list. Percival knew the national predicament and was far from demanding the levels of over-insurance insisted upon in other theatres. In terms of infantry troops on whom the fighting in the close country of Malaya would largely depend, he was asking for a total of 48 battalions. The request had the full backing of Brooke Popham and was telegraphed to London in early August.

The completion of his review and the arrival of some anticipated rein-forcements gave Percival the opportunity to make some improvements to his dispositions. The despatch of the second Australian brigade enabled him to give Bennett the operational responsibility for which he had long been chafing. The AIF became responsible for the defence of Johore and Malacca. 12 Brigade took its place as the Command Reserve. Percival also strengthened the Kelantan defences by the addition of two battalions and he took two anti-aircraft batteries from the Singapore defences and allocated them to General Heath, for no air defences had been provided for the all-important but very vulnerable airfields in Malaya and on Penang. He also took control himself of the anti-aircraft defences of Singapore so that they could be coordinated with the fighter defence now that Pulford had an experienced specialist officer in charge of this. Thus a coordinated gun/plane air defence of Singapore was at last achieved. Given the priority role of the air arm in the defence of Malaya, there was little more Percival could achieve by reorganisation until his request for reinforcements was met.

From the very start of his time in command Percival gave a high prior-ity to training. The circumstances made it vitally necessary but at the same time exceptionally difficult to organise. Aside from 12 Brigade and the fortress garrison of Singapore, virtually all the other units of the command were new to the theatre and only partially trained as soldiers, let alone

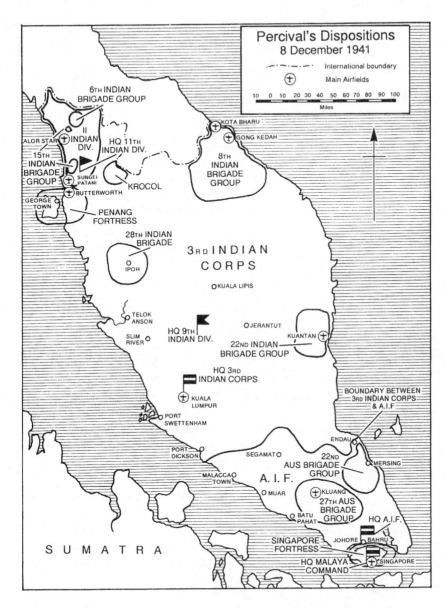

Map 4. Percival's Dispositions, 8 December 1941

trained for close-country combat in a tropical climate. The dispersion of units to guard the vulnerable airfields and coasts of Malaya meant that formation training was virtually impossible; while the need to build defences drastically reduced the time that could be devoted to developing weapons skills and unit tactical training. Under previous regimes, training had had a low priority and had lacked realism. When 2nd Argylls had arrived from India and made known their intention to get on with some jungle training, one of their officers recalled, 'we received very little encouragement from Malaya Command and they assured us that if we were not drowned in the seasonal rains we would be decimated by malaria'.[20] In General Bond's era there had been a lack of direction in training and, aside from 12 Brigade's efforts, not a great deal of it went on. With Percival's arrival the headquarters quickly adopted a more positive attitude and 'a series of sound and valuable directives on training were issued'.[21] There had been none at all until the previous December. The new GOC wisely concentrated on individual and sub-unit training which could, to some extent at least, be carried out concurrently with the construction of defences. He stipulated that wherever possible the training should take place in 'bush country'. His plan was that in the period from December to February the following year, with most of the defence works complete and unit tactics practised, they would move on to formation exercises based on a scenario of repelling a Japanese attack launched from southern Thailand. Of course, in Malaya there were none of the well-provisioned training centres and schools through which all formations and reinforcements in the Middle East passed before they were allowed anywhere near an enemy.

While these preparations were under way, news began to come in of Operation Barbarossa. Hitler had launched three massive Army groups supported by the forces of his satellites against the Soviet Union. Over 2,500 tanks rolled forward on a front which stretched from the Baltic to the Black Sea. The scale of this gigantic undertaking, presaged for some weeks by the 'Ultra' decrypts passed daily to Churchill, and coming on top of the RAF's victory in the Battle of Britain the previous autumn, made it abundantly clear not only that Britain was safe from the threat of invasion until the titanic struggle in the east had been concluded, but also that the much-feared possibility of a German pincer movement in the Middle East was now remote. This was Churchill's opportunity to reorder his priorities and sanction at last the action for which his CIGS had long been arguing: the despatch to the Far East of the troops, tanks and aircraft of which the commanders there stood in such need. If this was Percival's hope it was a fond one.

Churchill now became as fervent a supporter of the Soviet Union's struggle for existence as he had been an ardent advocate of strangling the state at birth 22 years earlier. On the day the news of Barbarossa broke,

Churchill broadcast to the nation and promised that 'Any man or state who fights against Nazidom will have our aid.' Almost immediately tanks and planes began to flow to British ports, destined for Archangel and Murmansk to succour the Soviets, just as in 1919 Percival had sailed north to assist Ironside in squashing them. The first convoy moved out on 21 August, the old aircraft carrier *Argus* carrying 48 Hurricanes with more stacked in crates aboard the accompanying merchantmen. Tanks followed; 280 in the October quota and 446 by the end of the year. Just under 500 fighter aircraft were supplied in October alone, 676 in all by the year's end.[22] Two hundred aircraft and 250 tanks were promised each month until June 1942. It was ironic that Russia already had 39 armoured divisions against the Germans' 36, and in the T-34, which first appeared at the front in July, the best tank in the world.

It was not as though Churchill was acting with the full support of his military commanders. In October, when General Sir Alan Brooke was still C-in-C Home Forces, he warned the Prime Minister 'of being very short of tanks if we went on sending them to Russia as proposed'.[23] Even the faithful Ismay had to admit that 'it was equipment that we most grievously needed for ourselves – tanks, aircraft, anti-tank guns, anti-aircraft guns. We were giving away our life's blood.'[24] As for CIGS Dill, aside from any strategic considerations, he was temperamentally opposed to support for the Russians. He regarded the Communists 'as so foul that he hated the idea of any close association with them'. He and his DMO did try to reduce the supplies to Russia, but with Churchill so determined and Eden and Beaverbrook (who controlled the Prime Minister in such matters)[25] in strong support there was little chance of Dill prevailing. This meant, Ismay noted, 'that we would be unable to do very much to strengthen our position in the Far East'. The possibility of reinforcements for Percival was made even less likely by the Prime Minister's determination to quicken the pace of operations in the Middle East with an invasion of Sicily to which his military advisers were strongly opposed.

Percival was confident that his old boss Dill would do all that was humanly possible to send him the necessary reinforcements, but although the Chiefs of Staff agreed with his estimate of the forces needed to defend Malaya, they declared, understandably in view of the Prime Minister's obduracy, that they would be unable to send them in the foreseeable future. But the Chiefs' message embodying this unwelcome news included a most misleading rider: the need to augment the Army garrison would gradually diminish as British naval and air strength there increased! How could they possibly increase with so much being convoyed so expensively to the Soviet Union, with forces being garnered in the Middle East for Auchinleck's offensive and with Churchill violently opposed to sending men and equipment to lie idle in Malaya? If anything was designed to inspire a misleading confidence in the plans for the defence of Malaya, and confirm the Army's subordinate role in them, it was this message from London.[26]

In fact the only significant reinforcement to be sent to Singapore from the UK before the Japanese attacked was not military at all but a Cabinet Minister, Duff Cooper, the Chancellor of the Duchy of Lancaster, despatched to the Far East by the War Cabinet to investigate how Britain's civil activities throughout the region might best be coordinated for the needs of war. Was this a sign of the growing importance being attached to the defence of the region? Hardly. Although Duff Cooper had run both the Admiralty and the War Office in the 1930s and had the unique distinction of having resigned over Munich, he was now a politician in decline, after an unfortunate stint as Minister of Information. Furthermore he was a politician better known for his 'blazing indiscretions' as Chamberlain had described them, than for his diplomatic skills and the latter were at a premium in the atmosphere of intrigue and back-biting that still characterised the higher echelons of the colonial administration of Malaya. He also took with him his famous actress wife, Lady Diana Cooper, inevitably turning what might have been a relatively brief working visit into a more extended social sojourn. 'It will create the worst impression among the poor soldiers and sailors who cannot have their wives', commented one of the officials involved.[27] The reception of the Coopers, as described by Lady Diana, is eloquent of the pace and style of civil affairs in the premier British colony three months before the Japanese attacked. 'Commander-in-Chief Brooke Popham on the jetty and the whole set up entirely to my liking – liveries of ostentatious gold and white and scarlet on Malay and Indian servants, A.D.C.s, movie-men, gaping coolies . . . God's acres being mown by the fingers and thumbs of natives advancing on all fours in a serried row and plucking the growing grass-blades.'[28] No matter that Percival still lacked a civil labour force to dig his defence works. Duff Cooper had a personal staff of six, one fewer than Brooke Popham was initially permitted for the running of his entire Command.

Little more than a fortnight into his review, Duff Cooper convened a high-level conference in Singapore attended by the Governor, the Commanders-in-Chief, the Ambassadors to China and Thailand and the Australian envoy to the British War Cabinet. Percival and Pulford were not invited. The conference concluded by doubting that Japan could be contemplating war in the south for some months, largely because she had mobilised her forces on the Manchurian front and was therefore thought to be preparing to attack Russia, but also because it seemed unlikely that Japan would attempt a landing on the east coast of Malaya during the impending north-east monsoon! This was a truly astonishing conclusion, which Percival and his chief General Dobbie had shown to be false in 1937. Nothing was less likely to wring the necessary land and air reinforcements

from the determined grip of a reluctant Prime Minister than this optimistic conclusion. Duff Cooper's ignorance was understandable; Brooke
Popham's acquiescence was inexplicable.

It did seem however, as the weeks of training and preparation went by,
that Churchill might at last be recognising the key role that land forces
were to play in the defence of Malaya. On 5 November he wired Brooke
Popham, 'It has been decided, in view of developments in the Far East,
that the duties of C-in-C Far East, should be entrusted to an Army Officer
with up-to-date experience.'[29] The possible implication was not lost on
Brooke Popham. In a reply to the Chief of the Air Staff he asked the question, 'Am I right in assuming that the policy of relying mainly on air
power for the defence of this area has changed. This makes a difference to
the alignment of certain projects.'[30] It certainly did. If true, it meant that
Percival had disposed a whole division for the defence of the east coast airfields to no particular purpose. It meant that MATADOR (the pre-emptive
move of his force into Thailand) was a much chancier affair. The matter
was not resolved, for Brooke Popham was not immediately replaced owing
to a dispute among the Chiefs over the powers of his successor. He
remained in charge for the critical weeks of November and December
knowing that his assignment was almost at an end; hardly a situation
likely to sharpen the mind.

On 2 December Percival, just returned from a visit to the meagre forces
in Sarawak, joined Air Vice Marshal Pulford in the garden of Admiral
Layton's residence to watch the arrival of the nearest thing to a Fleet that
ever occupied the Naval Base at Singapore. The Brooke Pophams, the
Duff Coopers, the Shenton Thomases were all there as the two great
British ships, the battleship *Prince of Wales* and the battle cruiser *Repulse*,
steamed up the eastern channel of the straits to anchor at the Naval Base,
after an intentionally public progress around the island. The arrival of
Force Z, as Admiral Phillips' squadron was called, did have an effect on
the Japanese, but hardly the one intended. It induced Admiral Yamamoto
to strengthen the force that was to strike Malaya. He immediately
despatched to Saigon from Formosa 27 of his most advanced torpedo
bombers.

Percival knew all the new naval commanders well. Admiral Sir Tom
Phillips had been at the Admiralty during his own time at the War Office,
while the captains of both ships, John Leach and Bill Tennant, he remembered from his days at the Greenwich Staff College. However, he also
recalled from his Greenwich studies the importance that the Navy placed
on having a balanced fleet for operations. This latest reinforcement was
hardly that. There were no submarines, no heavy cruisers, just a couple of
destroyers and above all, no aircraft carriers, without which, he had been
told, 'a battle fleet loses most of its value in modern war'. The Admiralty
would have preferred to send a much larger force of older battleships, but

against this reinforcement the Prime Minister had also set his face, believing in the greater deterrent effect of the *Prince of Wales*. 'Today a little fleet arrived to help', was how Diana Cooper innocently put it; it was, she judged, 'a lovely sight but on the petty side'.[31] The following morning Admiral Phillips decided to send *Repulse* to Australia, to have the *Prince of Wales*'s boilers cleaned out and himself to make a courtesy call on the American commander, Admiral Hart, in Manila. Thus was the naval deterrent, inadequate even when concentrated, so quickly dispersed.

13

THE JAPANESE INVADE

'Personally I should be most doubtful if the Japs ever tried to make an attack on Malaya, and I am sure they will get it in the neck if they do.'

General Wavell C-in-C India to Air Chief Marshal Brooke
Popham C-in-C Far East 13 November 1941

Since the Chiefs of Staff had declared Army Cooperation aircraft to be unnecessary for Malaya, General Percival made his way about his extensive command by whatever alternative means were available, often by train or civil aircraft, later frequently by the single-engined Moths of the Malayan Air Force Volunteers, once they had been mobilised. 30 November 1941 had found him boarding a destroyer at Kuching for the return journey to Singapore from Sarawak (like the more distant Christmas Island, Sarawak was part of his extensive command). The destroyer's captain had received urgent instructions to return to Singapore with all possible speed. They made the journey back in 24 hours. Percival now heard the news which dramatically overturned the fairly general belief that the Japanese would not attack in the near future: the US–Japan negotiations in Washington were on the point of breakdown and a southward drive by Japan might occur at any time. The opportunity for formation training for Percival's troops was rapidly disappearing; the chance of strengthening the northern defences significantly with equipment from the UK was fading from the scene; the possibility of timely reinforcement seemed equally remote. It looked as though they might have to fight with what they had. Just the sort of 'pretty sticky business' he had been hoping to avoid. He arranged for the whole of Malaya Command to be put on the second degree of readiness and for the Volunteer Forces to be mobilised. He asked the RAF to intensify their reconnaissance over the South China Sea. It was the following day that he watched the arrival of the *Prince of Wales* and *Repulse*. The pace of events was quickening.

The plan for the pre-emptive advance into Thailand had long been absorbing Percival's thoughts. Of course the idea was not a new one; in many ways it was merely an extension of the assumptions which had informed his appreciation of 1937. Later General Bond and then Air Chief Marshal Brooke Popham had suggested to the Chiefs of Staff that British forces should cross the Thai border to seize Singora and Patani as soon as it was clear that the Japanese intended to attack, for these places would be their natural first objectives. Brooke Popham took the idea up with considerable enthusiasm and a somewhat inappropriate concern with its detail.[1] The potential benefits of the operation were obvious to Percival. It would give him the opportunity to deny the Japanese the use of the airfields at the two coastal towns and a good anchorage at Singora, and prevent them from controlling the communications which led directly south to Malaya's west coast arterial road and rail system. Besides, conditions for defence were difficult further south at the frontier itself. Most appealing of all was the possibility of destroying any attacking force at its most vulnerable, as it emerged from its landing craft, already seriously weakened by the attacks of the RAF.

The success of the operation depended critically on getting to the beaches in sufficient time and strength to deny them to the enemy. Therein lay the difficulty, for III Corps still lacked the reserve division which Percival, and Bond before him, had requested for just such circumstances. Moreover, any advance into Thailand, however limited, would itself be an act of war, not to be undertaken lightly. Nevertheless the best chance of safeguarding Singapore from the Japanese would be to defeat them on these northern beaches. The Chiefs of Staff were doubtful about the feasibility of the scheme and Churchill did not like it. Authority for MATADOR, as the projected operation was called, would have to come from London, with the inevitable delay which that would impose. Consequently, while Brooke Popham and Percival continued planning for a possible advance, they also planned a defensive position within Malaya itself at which to hold up a Japanese offensive. The need to protect the airfield at Alor Star determined the choice of Jitra, where road and rail routes south converged and river lines gave some modest additional protection. It was far from ideal and as Percival admitted 'nobody ever really liked it', but given the constraints all the alternatives were worse.

If war came, the circumstances of the moment would determine whether 11th Indian Division would advance with all speed to implement MATADOR, or else occupy the defensive position at Jitra. It had to prepare for both roles, though in truth it had sufficient troops for neither. Percival was not happy with the options but did not have the luxury of other choices, since the initiative, especially in regard to timing, would lie with the Japanese. Much would depend on what the main arm of strategic defence, the RAF, could achieve by reconnaissance and pre-emptive action and, now that the small nucleus of an Eastern Fleet had arrived, what help Admiral Phillips might give. It was, after all, the security of the naval base around which all the defence planning revolved.

General Heath had reservations about the practicability of MATADOR from the very start, though the divisional commander concerned, General Murray Lyon, was keen to undertake it. After much discussion the plan was modified: the main advance, Operation MATADOR, would be to Singora alone; a separate subsidiary thrust along the Kroh/Patani road was planned, but only as far as a position called 'The Ledge', 30-odd miles inside Thailand. This was the best defensive position available between the frontier and the coast at Patani. Because of 11th Division's critical and difficult role, Percival's staff saw to it that it was the best armed and equipped division in Malaya.[2] The news on 1 December when Percival got back to Singapore seemed to suggest that it might soon be in action.

After extended negotiations with London about the operation, on 2 December Brooke Popham asked for authority to launch MATADOR on his own initiative and received a surprisingly rapid reply. Churchill had now gained an assurance of US armed support in certain contingencies, one of which was the launching of an operation such as MATADOR to forestall a Japanese landing. 'Accordingly you should launch MATADOR', the Chiefs of Staff told their C-in-Cs in Singapore by signal on 5 December, 'without reference home in either of the following contingencies . . . (a) you have good information that a Japanese expedition is advancing with the apparent intention of landing on the Kra Isthmus. (b) the Japanese violate any other part of Thailand.' The signal was brief and to the point. It gave Brooke Popham the freedom that he needed, though with the naval C-in-C also an addressee, it seemed to suggest an equal share for Admiral Phillips in the decision-making. 'They've now made you responsible for declaring war', Brooke Popham's Chief of Staff noted. The weighty implications of the C-in-C's delegated responsibility were beginning to sink in.

So far as Percival was concerned the signal made MATADOR at last a practicable proposition. On Saturday 6 December he took the early civil flight to Kuala Lumpur to discuss the new situation with Heath. At about 3pm the two were at the HQ of the newly-mobilised FMSVF when a phone message came in for General Percival informing him of air reconnaissance reports received in Singapore a little earlier in the day to the effect that two Japanese convoys (merchantmen accompanied by warships) had been sighted 80 miles south of Cape Cambodia, heading westwards. This surely was the invasion force! He told Heath to bring his Corps to the first degree of readiness and, believing that MATADOR might soon be ordered, had him put 11th Division at short notice to move. He also arranged with the railway authorities for the trains required for the advance to be held at the agreed entraining point. Little more than an hour later Percival was on the afternoon flight back to Singapore, musing perhaps at how soon after being granted the discretion to launch MATA-DOR, Brooke Popham was having to exercise it. He felt sure that when he reached the Combined Operational Headquarters at Sime Road he would find that the C-in-C had already set MATADOR in motion, for the timings were critical and speed was of the essence.

However, Brooke Popham had not given the order. Having consulted Admiral Layton and the Chief of Staff of the absent Admiral Phillips, he had concluded that the convoys were making for the shelter of Kao Rong Bay whence their destination could be Bangkok or any of the eastern Kra Isthmus ports. Since a move to Kao Rong Bay would take the convoys further away from Singora than they had been when first sighted, he had felt he could defer a decision on MATADOR until he had more positive information. Brooke Popham ordered further air reconnaissance; but no other sightings were made on 6 December. By 7pm the long wooden hut at Sime Road which housed the Combined Operations Room was fully manned and ready for action. Percival conferred with the C-in-C and the Governor and then waited; 200 miles to the north, in Kuala Lumpur, Heath waited; 250 miles further north still the brigades of 11th Division waited, their transport ready, their requisitioned trains allocated and the defence stores loaded. It was raining.

Throughout the next day, Sunday 7th, Percival waited anxiously for news of positive sightings of the elusive convoys, but none came. Then, in the evening, the crucial reports finally came in: one Hudson reconnaissance aircraft had been fired on by a Japanese cruiser and, despite the bad weather, a second had seen Japanese warships 70 miles off Singora, steaming south. Percival's view was that the evening's sightings were sufficiently definitive to meet the Chiefs of Staff's conditions for launching MATADOR (indeed he had held that view of the sightings made almost 30 hours earlier). The decision was no longer political but strategical; and in his opinion it had now become too late to launch MATADOR. The result of an advance now could only be a messy encounter battle with a Japanese force already securely ashore. Percival met the C-in-C in conference at Sime Road and confirmed to him that he 'considered Operation MATADOR in the existing circumstances to be unsound'.[3] He conferred by telephone with Heath and then travelled with Brooke Popham to the Naval Base where the C-in-C and Admiral Phillips had their headquarters. Brooke Popham was still undecided. III Corps was informed that the GOC hoped to have a MATADOR decision for them by 11pm. At 11.15pm the GOC rang through; after discussion with Admiral Phillips, just returned from his trip to Manila, the C-in-C was still undecided: the message for III Corps was that MATADOR was not to be operated that night but that they should be ready to put it into effect the following morning if so ordered.[4] It seems that after this first conference at the Naval Base Percival returned to his own base. Within little more than an hour of the GOC's message Japanese troops had landed at Kota Bharu. Percival was awakened to receive this news and immediately reported the landing to the C-in-C and the Governor. By 4.30am the Singapore airfields and the city centre itself were under air attack. Still Brooke Popham did not release the land forces from the MATADOR commitment. As it happened, a Japanese attack on Malaya itself was the one circumstance for the launching of MATADOR which the Chiefs of Staff's signal had not covered. In the morning Percival's staff, eager for a decision, telephoned Brooke Popham's, but the C-in-C was still waiting for the results of the morning's air reconnaissance over Singora and Patani. 'Do not act' was the message that was passed down at 8.20am.

It was now too late for MATADOR. Percival spoke to III Corps at 9.30am, told them of the reports indicating that the Japanese were already at Singora and Patani and authorised Heath to operate the prearranged harassing and demolition activities and to 'watch northern frontier'.[5] This was the clearest message that MATADOR was not to take place. The cancellation decision by Far East Command appears to have been passed to Percival's headquarters shortly before 10am. By this time the GOC had gone off to report the outbreak of hostilities and the emergency measures taken to the Straits Settlements Legislative Council which met that morning. While he was away Brooke Popham's message came in, formally releasing 11th Division from MATADOR and authorising Percival to send forces to occupy the Ledge position. Percival's despatch records these orders as being passed on to Heath 'at about 1100hrs'. Percival's telephone call to Heath also suggested sending a mobile covering force across the border to delay the Japanese advance, giving the division more time to prepare its position at Jitra.

The decline in the personal relations of Percival and Heath dates from this disastrous delay in the release of 11th Division from the MATADOR commitment. In the bitter post-mortems on the military tragedy which ensued, it was to become, however unjustly, a focus for Heath's recriminations. 'I find it impossible to excuse General Percival for permitting Air Chief Marshal Sir Robert Brooke Popham not to arrive at a decision on 7th December when everything pointed to the certainty of Japan initiating the war in Malaya', he wrote years later.[6] The delay on the morning of the 8th, especially when Percival's BGS, Brigadier Torrance, apparently fobbed Heath off at one point on the grounds that Percival was at a Legislative Council meeting, merely increased Heath's bile; 'Ye Gods', he wrote, recalling the moment, apparently forgetting the GOC's 9.30am message, which made the situation pretty clear. In fact, for some reason which has never been made fully clear, the vital message 'MATADOR off, man Jitra' was not received by 11th Division until 1.30pm on 8 December, despite Percival's telephone call to Heath over two hours earlier.

Brooke Popham's delay in acting on Percival's advice had given the Japanese who landed at Singora and Patani a start of ten hours. For this the blame must lie with the C-in-C. Others, besides Heath, have blamed Percival for not insisting on the cancellation on the evening of 7 December; but his advice was clear enough and he had the privacy of the car journey with Brooke Popham from Sime Road to the Naval Base to reiterate his views. In the end it was Brooke Popham's decision. MATADOR was his responsibility and he seems to have been consumed by the fear that the Japanese convoys might have been making merely a demonstration to induce him to invade Thailand first, giving Japan the pretext it wanted and bringing the Thais in on its side. To keep such a large invasion force 'cruising around', as General Brooke put it, for so long for such a negligible purpose made little strategic sense. Yet he seems to have been unable to bring himself to cancel the operation by which he had set such store. There was not merely delay; there seems also to have been muddle. As late as 10.40am on 8 December Percival's headquarters was still being warned by Brooke Popham's that 'We may still have to do MATADOR'.[7] But Brooke Popham was not the sole decision-maker: the responsibility was shared with Phillips. This must have made it even more difficult for Percival's advice to have carried the day.

There is a further factor in Brooke Popham's indecision which may be of considerable importance. Before the Pacific War began British intelligence was already reading the Japanese diplomatic and naval codes. Decrypts were available to the Prime Minister and no doubt relevant ones to Brooke Popham, perhaps even to Percival. The possibility certainly exists that the C-in-C, if no other local commander, already had precise details of the Japanese convoys and their targets at the time of the first sightings. But since the intelligence sources themselves were so secret and sensitive, it seems that no action could be taken on the reports without their corroboration from orthodox channels.[8] This was the working rule which applied in other theatres to such highly classified information whose sources could never be compromised. If this factor did nothing else, it would have presented an additional agonising dimension to an already difficult decision for a tired and overburdened Brooke Popham. The factors he was wrestling with had already been coloured by an impassioned plea on 7 December from the Ambassador to Thailand for the British not to be the first to invade. If Percival had any hint of the existence of this factor behind his chief's reluctance to release Heath's Corps from MATADOR, it might have given him pause in pressing for its release. It is a tantalising speculation. Both sets of *Despatches* skate over this episode.

Heath himself would have been ignorant of much of this.[9] He remained in Kuala Lumpur, far from Singapore and even further from the military action, leaving Murray Lyon to control both the eleventh-hour preparations at Jitra and the operation of 'Krohcol', the separate force which was to advance to the Ledge position. Despite the lengthy delay, under which Heath evidently chafed, and the fact that III Corps should have been at the first degree of readiness since the afternoon of 6 December, even by the 8th not all of his men were at their start line. Krohcol had not been concentrated on the frontier, ready for its vital move forward, when the order finally came. The column commander, Lieutenant Colonel Moorehead, had neither the second battalion due from Penang[10] nor the full complement of Volunteer gunners who were supposed to support him. In blaming his GOC for the delay, Heath had perhaps also forgotten that until the disasters of the first four days of the campaign turned everything haywire, the land forces were very much the junior partners in the defence enterprise. Following Brooke Popham's and Phillips' joint decision on the evening of the 7th not to launch MATADOR, the two commanders went on to consider how the Navy and the Air Force might respond to the Kota Bharu landings, which Percival had reported to them in the early hours, and to the other reported sightings. This second deliberation was followed by the belated and fatal commitment of *Prince of Wales* and *Repulse* to a dash north to deal with the Japanese transports. Their deterrent purpose had failed and they were now committed to action.

When the Japanese invasion was launched General Percival was deficient by 17 battalions of the total which the Chiefs of Staff had declared was a 'reasonable figure for land forces required in the present circumstances'. He was also without four anti-aircraft regiments, two tank regiments and many anti-tank guns. His Army still contained only six regular British battalions. Of the ten brigades in his force only two could be regarded as anything like trained for the kind of warfare that was about to engulf them. Air Marshal Pulford, on whom he was relying to blunt the edge of the Japanese attack, was even worse placed. He had 158 operational aircraft rather than the 336 which the Chiefs of Staff had suggested would give 'a fair degree of security', but which the Singapore air staff reckoned gave them only half the bombers and fighters they really needed. Pulford's bid had been for 566 front-line aircraft. Of his operational machines, 60 were the Brewster Buffalo fighters whose arrival had given such confidence to an island which had never seen fighters before. But they were to be piloted in the main by Australian and New Zealand aircrews who were straight out of flying schools. Many had never even seen a monoplane fighter before, let alone one with the formidable climb rate and speed of the Japanese Zeros they were soon to confront.[11]

Lieutenant General Tomoyuki Yamashita, Percival's opponent in Malaya, was similarly from a non-military background. His father was a doctor, as was his brother, and both his sisters had married into the medical profession. But there the similarity ended; Yamashita senior, unlike Alfred Percival, guided his younger son into the military profession from the very start. Tomoyuki did well at the Military Academy, later passed out of the Staff College near the top of the list and showed such promise that he rose from captain to lieutenant colonel in three years. The two commanders were also physically very different; Yamashita was as squat and well-fleshed as Percival was tall and raw-boned. He was unusually well travelled for a Japanese officer, having held attaché posts in Switzerland, Germany and Austria. If Percival was the unswervingly loyal subordinate of both military and political masters, Yamashita, by contrast, had long been deeply involved in Japanese military politics. By 1926 he was a major general and a leading member of the 'Imperial Way' military faction which carried out the bloody but unsuccessful *coup* of 1936. The taint of implication in the *coup* drew the enmity of the opposing 'Control' faction to which Premier Tojo belonged. Yamashita had succeeded Tojo as Inspector-General Army Aviation, a particularly important post in view of his later employment, but once Tojo became Premier, Yamashita was shunted back to Europe for a tour of Germany and Italy. After that he was moved to take command of the relatively unimportant Kwantung Defence Army in Manchuria.

It was not until the eleventh hour, November 1941, that Yamashita gained command of 25th Army, charged with the invasion of Malaya and the capture of Singapore. Fortunately, intensive planning and training for the offensive had been taking place for some months, guided by the Commander Southern Army, Count Terauchi, and masterminded by 25th Army's chief operational planner, Colonel Masanobu Tsuji, both members of the opposing 'Control' military clique. So Yamashita, too, did not enjoy the smoothest of relations with superiors and subordinates. However in 5th and 18th Divisions he had fully trained and battle-hardened troops well prepared for their Malayan assignment. His third division, the Imperial Guards, was accustomed only to ceremonial duties and untested by combat. Yamashita did not like the ways of the Guards and distrusted their commander Lieutenant General Nishimura, but both served him well, by and large. His fourth division, 56th, he never needed.

Brooke Popham had been correct in surmising that the convoys might have been intending to head north when his planes first sighted them. But they were heading not for the shelter of Kao Rong Bay but merely for a prearranged assembly area where the six separate elements of the invasion force could be coordinated for their separate tasks, and timings could be synchronised so that no forewarning could be passed to the defenders of Pearl Harbor who were to be subjected to the vital surprise attack. It was the success of this central element of the Japanese plan which so confounded Churchill in his hope that the Americans might save Singapore for him. Three Japanese invasion forces were headed for Singora, Patani and Kota Bharu, objectives which Percival had pinpointed in his 1937 plan, and three for minor ports further north, sealing off Malaya from the hinterland of south-east Asia and capturing Victoria Point airfield, an important link in the air reinforcement route to Malaya. The spearhead of the invasion was General Matsui's 5th Division, experienced in landing operations, which was to strike at Singora and Patani. A detachment of General Mutaguchi's 18th Division, Takumi Force, was to land at Kota Bharu and the third division of Yamashita's force, the Imperial Guards, was to make its way south overland once Bangkok had been occupied. In reserve (though never used) was 56th Division. The key task of securing the Victoria Point airfield and occupying southern Siam went to Uno Force, a regiment of 55th Division, loaned to Yamashita for the operation. Yamashita had the support of over 230 light and medium tanks with more on call. He also commanded the 3rd Air Division which contained more bombers than Pulford had aircraft altogether. Over one-third of the Japanese fighter aircraft were of the latest Zero type. In addition, 180 aircraft of the 22nd Air Flotilla were also supporting the invasion. This was a formidable total of 534 modern machines against Pulford's 158, many obsolete or second-rate. The initial Japanese objective was not the destruction of the opposing land forces, but the neutralisation of Pulford's planes and the capture of airfields, first those at Singora, Patani and Kota Bharu, then the others at Kelantan and Kedah. Air power was to be the key to the campaign.

Some critics, notably Major General Kirby who carries the authority of having written the earlier Official History volume on Malaya, have criticised Percival's defensive dispositions on the grounds that by August 1941 it was clear that the weakness of the RAF made it highly improbable that it would be able to carry out its defensive task.[12] That being the case, it is argued, Percival was unwise to commit virtually half his infantry force to the defence of the northern airfields. He should instead have concentrated his battalions in depth at defended localities on the western arterial route to Singapore, which was certain to be the Japanese line of advance. These positions, and the key maritime base of Penang, should have been strongly held and supported by mobile infantry counter-attack forces. The northern airfields, only lightly defended, would have had demolitions prepared ready to crater the runways once the RAF no longer required them. It is a seductive, if narrowly military argument, but it is heavy with hindsight.

There was no reason to believe, in August, that the Japanese would attack in December, and every cause for hoping that by the time they did invade, the RAF strength would have been built up. This could have happened quite speedily via the air reinforcement route. The argument also ignores the assurance Percival had been given of what the RAF might achieve with its *existing* strength. Britain was used to winning the air battle with inferior resources in other theatres and Brooke Popham's correspondence with the Air Ministry indicated no dissatisfaction with the quality of his fighter defence. He certainly seems to have believed that the Buffaloes were superior to the Japanese fighters and well suited to Malaya.[13] There was thus every reason for Percival to be required to protect the northern airfields at which two-thirds of Pulford's aircraft might need to concentrate. After the bitter inter-Service struggles of the 1920s and 1930s, Pulford and he had achieved a remarkably close cooperation and much was expected of the support of each for the other. In any event it would have been politically unacceptable to have left the northern states of Perlis, Kelantan and Kedah virtually defenceless. Shenton Thomas would never have accepted it from Percival, any more than he had from General Bond. As it was, when the troops in Perlis withdrew to occupy the main Jitra position, the Sultan of Perlis protested that the British were abandoning him in violation of their treaty of protection.[14] It was no less than the truth. Finally, Percival was drawn ineluctably to a northern defence by Brooke Popham's enthusiastic commitment to MATADOR. The surprise for the GOC was that his chief never ordered it.

As soon as it was clear that the Japanese offensive against Malaya had begun the two force commanders took some concerted action. Pulford ordered a dawn reconnaissance of Singora and sent his bomber squadrons from Alor Star, Sungei Patani and Kuantan to attack the Kota Bharu invasion force, while Percival moved one battalion of his Army reserve north to Kuala Krai in support of the defenders of Kota Bharu. In the disastrous opening engagements of the Malayan campaign, the one which began least badly for Percival and Pulford was the defence of Kota Bharu. The Hudson bombers from the base nearby began their sorties at 2am and by 5am they had flown 17. One Japanese transport was totally crippled by the bombing, two others were damaged and numerous landing barges were sunk. A subsequent torpedo attack by the ancient Vildebeestes caused little material damage but contributed to the turmoil in the Japanese landing operation. Brigadier Key, defending the beaches with a pitifully weak force, did not manage to prevent the Japanese from getting ashore, nor to drive them back into the sea once they had done so; but there was fierce fighting for the beaches and a hard-fought counter-attack in the driving rain by Key's Frontier Force battalions in the afternoon. This failed to close the gap which the Japanese had created and when news came in that Pulford had ordered the evacuation of his bombers from Kota Bharu airfield, Key got Heath's permission to withdraw from the beaches and from protecting the now useless airfield and took up a new line defending Kota Bharu town. Though badly disorganised and with many casualties, his force was more or less in place by dawn the following day. The Japanese were securely ashore but at a cost as great as any they were to bear for a single day's fighting in the entire Malayan campaign. Successive attacks by Pulford's squadron at Kota Bharu had caused havoc among the Japanese transports. This foothold on Malayan soil, the first land battle of the Pacific War, cost Takumi Force almost 500 casualties,[15] the loss of one merchant ship and damage to many other vessels. The loss inflicted by one modern and one obsolete squadron of Pulford's force, manned by acclimatised and trained crews, based close to their targets, makes it very clear what might have been achieved if the RAF commander had received the 566 planes he had asked for, or even the 336 which London thought sufficient.

Elsewhere in the air the story was much worse. The Kota Bharu landing force operated without cover from Yamashita's aircraft for the simple reason that his priority was to gain the air mastery he needed for subsequent operations. During the morning of 8 December 150 aircraft of 7th Air Brigade, two-thirds of them long-range fighters and all flying initially from southern Indo-China, made heavy attacks on the seven major airfields in north Malaya, often catching Allied aircraft returning from their own sorties or refuelling in preparation for further ones. The irony was that on the Allied side the bulk of the offensive sorties which were flown against Kota Bharu from the more distant airfields arrived there too late to do any damage, when the Japanese transports and their protection force had already moved off after their battering. One squadron which flew on to Patani to raid the landings there was specifically briefed not to overfly Thailand since that country was not involved. This squadron was caught on the ground just after returning from its unsuccessful mission and was rapidly reduced to two serviceable aircraft. Brooke Popham's reluctance to 'declare war' was costing the defenders dear.[16]

While the Allied squadrons were concentrating on Khota Bharu, the main body of the Japanese 5th Division and 25th Army Headquarters came ashore at Singora and Patani virtually unmolested – a staff officer's sprained ankle was said to be its most serious casualty.[17] Further north, Uno Force landed on the Kra Isthmus without serious Thai opposition and was soon able to take the vital reinforcing airfield at Victoria Point. When the Allied aircraft returned from their sorties they often found their own airfields under attack. The Japanese used light bombs to cause maximum damage to planes and personnel, but leaving runways intact. Pulford had started the day with 110 operational aircraft in northern Malaya; he ended it with 50, 40 having been destroyed and 20 seriously damaged.[18] The Japanese had won their fight for air superiority in a single day. Pulford was forced to order his remaining aircraft to fly to safer airfields in the south. But it was infinitely worse than that; the one opportunity he had had of doing serious damage to the invasion force had been lost when the squadrons had concentrated on Kota Bharu instead of Singora and Patani. By the time the error was realised, it was too late and the squadrons were too weak and disorganised to launch a fresh offensive. 'The Air Force promised us that they could dispose of 40 per cent of any ships coming this way', was Heath's bitter comment when addressing his troops imprisoned in Changi.[19]

There was little more land action on this first day of the Malayan campaign. The demoralised brigades of 11th Division occupied the Jitra position and started to develop its defences, and one battalion was sent forward as Percival had ordered, to delay the Japanese advance. It moved some ten miles into Siam and then halted to await developments. An armoured train also moved north, attempted to destroy a major bridge in the main line and then withdrew, destroying further bridges as it retired. Krohcol, or at least the single battalion which Heath had ready, similarly advanced into Thailand at about 3pm; but it was immediately fired on by Siamese frontier guards and had gained only three miles by nightfall, when it decided to halt 'owing to darkness and heavy rain'.[20] It was not an encouraging start.

The next day brought no good news to brighten the gloom of the first contacts with the Japanese. Since the RAF had no further use for the Kelantan airfields and the population had already evacuated Kota Bharu town, Brigadier Key got permission to disengage from the Japanese who were already pressing his forward units near the town, and prepared to move back to Machang. His divisional commander and General Heath thought that a more decisive break would be better and proposed to move Key's brigade back as far as Kuala Lipis. This was a withdrawal of over 100 miles for a brigade that was much battered but by no means defeated and which Percival had already arranged to reinforce. He refused to sanction the move. It was only the second day of the campaign and here was his Corps Commander proposing to surrender 100 miles of territory to the Japanese. How could the Naval Base be protected if the enemy was allowed to advance at this rate? Here was a second major disagreement with Heath, and battle barely joined. Percival offered to go up to Kuala Lumpur to discuss the issue, but Heath insisted on going himself to Singapore.[21]

By the time of the withdrawal of Key's brigade from Kota Bharu town, Admiral Phillips and his squadron were at sea. He had made a brave but foolhardy decision to take his ships up towards the Gulf of Siam to attack the Japanese transports. By this time it was abundantly clear that the main landings at Singora, Patani and Kota Bharu had already taken place, that fighter cover would not be available to him off Singora, that the RAF was unlikely to be able to operate from any of the northern airfields and that the Japanese had large bomber forces in southern Indo-China. Yet Phillips was determined to make a positive if belated naval contribution to the fight to defend Singapore. The result is well known. The Japanese sighted the unprotected force and began their bombing attack on it at 11.18am on 10 December. Two hours later the *Prince of Wales* and *Repulse*

Officers of 'A' Company 7th Bedfords with their frail-looking 'dug-out' commander. Second Lieutenant Arthur Percival standing, second left.

Above Wavell's pre-war visit: with Percival and Commanding Officer
2nd Gordon Highlanders. *Imperial War Museum.*

Below Air Chief Marshal Sir Robert Brooke Popham and
the Rt. Hon. Duff Cooper. *Imperial War Museum.*

Air Vice-Marshal Pulford welcoming Dutch reinforcements.
Imperial War Museum.

Lieutenant General Sir Henry Pownall.
Imperial War Museum.

'British Commander Percival'. Drawn in Changi Jail.
'He seemed extremely tired; his eyes looked dazed
and the muscles of his face twitched repeatedly.'
Miyamoto Saburo.

A gaunt Percival on release from captivity, with GOC British Troops China, Major General Hayes.

A FEPOW partnership: Percival with Brigadier Jackie Smyth VC.

Percival as Colonel 22nd (Cheshire) Regiment, 1950.

lay at the bottom of the shallow sea off Kuantan. Down with them went Admiral Phillips, Captain Leach and over 800 of their men. Residual Japanese naval chivalry permitted over 2,000 sailors to be rescued. Many of them went on to give valiant service as temporary soldiers; not exactly the reinforcements for which the GOC had been hoping.

14

JITRA AND AFTER

*'Speaking to an English engineer officer taken prisoner, I asked,
"How long did you think this fortified position would hold out?"
He replied, "Held by the full strength of the 11th Division I
believed it would hold out for three months at the least."'*

Masanobo Tsuji, Singapore: The Japanese Version

The Japanese did not attack Percival's main Jitra position until about midnight on 11/12 December. However there had already been enough calamities on this Kedah front for the defences on the Jitra line, on which so many hopes were pinned, to be less than the rock-steady rampart the GOC required. It was a worryingly extended position, stretching for 13½ miles from the hills on the right to the sea on the left. The right-hand sector of the position, which included the two main roads and was the likeliest to be first threatened, was held by 15 Brigade with two battalions forward. The frontage on the left was twice as extensive but much of it was marshy. It was held by 6 Brigade whose situation had already been seriously compromised. During its withdrawal from Perlis a bridge had been prematurely blown behind it and the brigade had had to abandon most of its carriers, mountain guns, transport and precious anti-tank guns, on the wrong side of the stream. Hardly a good start for the brigade which had then to get back to Jitra, erect barbed wire on the marshy ground, lay fresh telephone cables and make ready for a defensive battle. Not the rapid advance into Thailand they had been expecting.

On the main road axis down to Jitra one would normally have found the divisional reconnaissance regiment operating, passing back information about the size and composition of the advancing Japanese forces. But the 'mechanised' 3rd Indian Cavalry, which was all the divisional commander, General Murray Lyon, had for this purpose, was without either horses, which it had already given up, or armoured cars, which it had yet to receive and which its partially trained recruits would, in any event, have been unable to drive. Murray Lyon sensibly left this unfortunate and useless covering force out of his battle line. Instead, on the main road running up towards Patani, he had strengthened his one-battalion covering force with a second in an effort to impose further delay while the Jitra defences

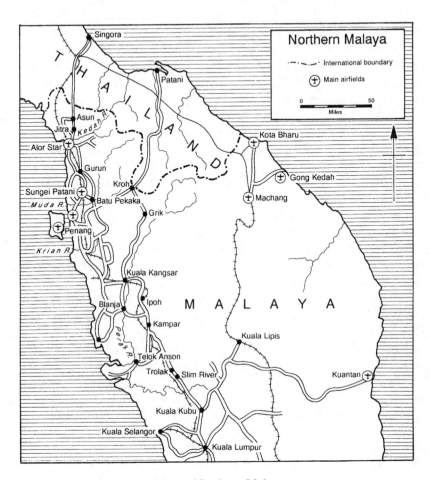

Map 5. Northern Malaya

were strengthened. At the very moment when the order for the withdrawal of the most advanced of the two battalions to a position behind the
second was changed to an order for a further delaying action in an intermediate position, the Japanese struck. A force of medium tanks followed
by light tanks and lorried infantry tore down the main road, filleting the
poor Punjabi battalion and later smashing the Gurkhas who were holding
the bridge behind them. Courageous action knocked out some of the
tanks, but the two battalions were soon finished as a fighting force. What
was more, Brigadier Garrett, the 15 Brigade commander, was wounded
and missing for a time so that his section of the Jitra defences had now to
be commanded by Brigadier Carpendale of the reserve 28 Brigade whose
own formation had now been allocated to the Jitra position, though it was
the only Corps reserve which General Heath had. Carpendale was understandably unfamiliar with the terrain in which his new units were
disposed. The final misfortune for 11th Indian Division was the capture
by the Japanese during the first engagement along the road down from
Singora, of a marked British map which showed in detail Murray Lyon's
defensive dispositions.[1] Heath was later to write of the Japanese commander's 'almost uncanny sense of directing his attacks against the most
profitable targets' at Jitra.

To these important but local misfortunes for General Murray Lyon
had been added the worrying knowledge that the Japanese had beaten
Krohcol in the race to the Ledge position. Krohcol had at last been
strengthened by its second Punjab battalion, but the first had already
been halted by the Japanese whose tanks had made a surprise appearance
on this front as well. After two days of hard fighting against the Japanese
and one of skirmishing with the Thais, Krohcol had suffered over 200
casualties. Its commander was finally given permission to withdraw to
Kroh, where his resistance had to be a determined one: if the Japanese
were not stopped there they could get south of the main position at Jitra
and the whole front would be compromised. News of the shock sinking of
the *Prince of Wales* and *Repulse* had also spread to the Jitra front. 'There
was no denying that its moral effect was great', wrote Percival, 'as few
people, even in the Services, knew that the fleet had put to sea.' To this
dismaying realisation was added the mounting evidence of the superiority of the Japanese air arm. The opposing bombers had not yet turned
their attention to the ground forces defending Malaya, but it was clear
that they were winning the air battle. The Allied squadrons had already
vacated the airfields which the unsatisfactory position at Jitra had been
occupied to defend. Even as they pumped out their waterlogged defences,
the weary and dispirited defenders could see the pall of smoke from the
blazing stocks of fuel at Alor Star. Brigadier Carpendale telephoned his
divisional commander: 'The RAF have hopped it. They seemed to be in
a great hurry. What's happened? You might have let me know.' The fact

was that the RAF had not notified 11th Division of their intention to evacuate.

When the Japanese tanks were finally checked on the main road in front of Jitra their infantry began to probe the line just east of the main road, where they found gaps between the defended localities and promptly launched a reckless attack in this area with all their available troops. They were driven back, but attacked again and this time held their gains. Brigadier Carpendale was passed a series of reports that the Japanese were attempting to turn his right flank and so he borrowed reinforcements from his neighbouring brigade which he moved into what he believed was the threatened area. An attempt to counter-attack the Japanese the following morning went badly wrong with two Indian battalions mistaking each other for Japanese and then missing the artillery support programme when their error had been sorted out. There were serious casualties. When Murray Lyon took stock of the night's events he was in an unenviable position. All his reserves (and they were the Corps reserve as well) had been committed either to the delaying action, the defensive line, or else to these failed counter-attacks. He had no fresh troops left with which to influence the battle, empty airfields to his rear and a force whose morale was already badly shaken. Krohcol had also withdrawn before a superior tank-armed force. Conscious that his division was the only force available for the defence of northern Malaya and that the main Japanese invasion force could be expected to move on Jitra before too long, he decided to withdraw to a good defensive position south of the Kedah river at Gurun where defence would be easier. He telephoned Heath for authority but the corps commander had already set off for Singapore to discuss the east coast strategy with the GOC, and his train was late. His message was therefore relayed directly to General Percival.

Percival's reaction was that such an early and long withdrawal from a main defensive position, which he had never contemplated in any of the pre-war planning, was unacceptable. To pull back all of 30 miles at this stage, before the Japanese main force had been engaged, would have had a devastating effect on the morale of the whole Command, not to mention the civilian population. Some of the intermediate positions would offer better anti-tank obstacles than Gurun. The War Council which met shortly after Murray Lyon's brief message came in, endorsed Percival's view of the likely effect on morale. The GOC told Murray Lyon that the battle had to be fought out in the Jitra position.

Murray Lyon and his staff seemed relieved that they now had a decisive order to stay and fight; only Carpendale seemed unhappy, and his subsequent indecision betrayed his anxiety. He first planned a counter-attack and then changed his mind in favour of a limited tactical withdrawal which caused considerable confusion. Much of this got back to Murray Lyon in the form of incorrect reports indicating that the situation was infinitely worse than it really was, though Japanese pressure was continuing with fire support from the road-based tanks and later from deployed artillery. Once again the situation of Krohcol played on his mind; a report came in that the one battalion that had got anywhere near the Ledge position was now back at Kroh, reduced to half its original strength. The worry of being outflanked rose again, for Kroh was over 50 miles to his south-east. Once more he asked for permission to withdraw and his message was again relayed to Singapore where Heath and Percival were still conferring. This time they let him go, confirming that his task was to fight for the security of North Kedah and suggesting that he should dispose his force in depth on the axis of the north/south roads and based on good tank obstacles. At 9pm Murray Lyon issued his orders for the withdrawal from Jitra.

In this anti-climactic manner, without a major action or his troops being driven from their lines by the Japanese main force, Percival lost what was perhaps the crucial land battle of the Malayan campaign. The three brigades of 11th Indian Division had been defeated by what was little more than an impetuous probing attack by the Japanese advance guard, Saeki Detachment, about two battalions strong, supported by ten tanks and some guns and at the cost to the Japanese of 110 casualties.[2] Some of Murray Lyon's units had suffered heavily, especially the battalions of the delaying force, but it was demoralisation and fear which had done most damage; the much-despised Japanese had tanks (which most of the poor Indians had never seen before), a formidable air force and their infantry seemed to be everywhere. Infiltration and 'jitter' tactics had worked well. The withdrawal from Jitra proved, as the battle itself had been, an almost unmitigated disaster. The confusion of the rapid night pull-out added immeasurably to the scale and significance of the reverse. This withdrawal, Percival noted, 'was too fast and too complicated for disorganised and exhausted troops'. Orders went astray, many of the troops scattered into the rubber plantations seeking safety from the tanks, others headed for the coast. The division, once it was again concentrated, was hardly fit for operations, but had perforce to be kept in the front line for a further four weeks. Percival had to give Heath his sole Army reserve, 12 Indian Infantry Brigade, to stiffen his corps' evaporating determination. He had nothing left with which to influence the north Malayan campaign. The first, decisive moral victory had gone to the Japanese.

The huge stock of booty discarded at Jitra testified to the haste and disorganisation of the withdrawal and the completeness of the Japanese victory. The Japanese captured 50 field guns, 50 heavy and light machine guns and 210 trucks and armoured cars, together with, according to the bombastic Colonel Tsuji, enough 'provisions and ammunition for a division for three months'.[3] One of Percival's senior staff candidly admitted that 'the losses in arms and equipment were almost fantastic'.[4] What they called 'the Churchill supplies' became a not insignificant factor in the Japanese logistics. The statistic most eloquent of the problem now facing Percival was that of the 3,000 Indian troops whom the Japanese claimed had surrendered to them after scattering into the jungle in despair. It may have been an exaggeration, but from Jitra onwards the concern for the morale and steadiness of his troops, particularly his Indian troops, and for the morale of the native population of Malaya, was an ever present concern for the GOC. The Japanese had created an organisation headed by Major Fujiwara designed specifically to spread disaffection among the Indian communities of South-east Asia. It found fertile ground in Malaya where the Indian Independence League (IIL) was already at work among the estate workers and had begun to extend its efforts at disaffection to the Indian Army units even before the campaign opened. Leaflets bearing the powerful Japanese propaganda message were already fluttering down to Malaya's Asians, in and out of uniform: 'Malays and ali Asiatics take up the torch of liberty against the white devil and drive him out of your country with a flaming sword.'[5] It was a siren call for the many half-trained sepoys who had now seen the myth of Britain's invincibility rudely shattered. From the ranks of the disaffected Indian soldiers whom they captured, the Japanese were to create the Indian National Army, under the leadership of one of the early captives, Captain Mohan Singh.

Within the space of four days, each of the British Services had suffered a disastrous reverse and, perhaps the crowning insult for the 'white devils' themselves, in the opening hours of the campaign the Japanese had managed to bomb not only the Singapore airfields but also Raffles Square and Robinson's, respectively the meeting place and premier British department store in Singapore, potent symbols of Britain's imperial supe-riority. In evaluating the Army's failure at Jitra it is all too easy to blame the commanders: Carpendale who too readily took counsel of his fears; Murray Lyon who, in the opinion of one of Percival's operations staff, had been 'obsessed with this [MATADOR] plan to the detriment of the frontier defences';[6] Heath, who went off to Singapore and left his divisional commander handling the three-brigade defence at Jitra and the separate Krohcol operation 50 miles away despite Murray Lyon's protestations that it was too much; Percival himself who would not countenance the first withdrawal request with the result that a daylight retirement was replaced by a disastrous one at night. Was he too demanding in expecting three brigades in a defensive position to hold off two battalions of Japanese for longer than 15 hours? Should he not have trusted the judgement of the general on the spot? Could he be held responsible for the disorganisation and disarray of the withdrawal?

The true, if undramatic, explanation for the disaster of Jitra was that the troops did not have the training, the weapons or the time to put up a respectable defence, nor was it a good position at which to try to mount one. All were factors of which Percival was well aware, but they were all beyond his control. Most of his men had never seen a tank until those of Colonel Saeki were bearing down upon them. How did all this square with the C-in-C's Special Order of the Day, long prepared in all the vernacular languages and issued the moment that the Japanese attacked? It was designed particularly 'to make an effective appeal to the Indian troops' and had attempted to encourage the men by explaining that Japan was drained by 'her wanton onslaught on China', whereas Malaya's 'defences are strong and our weapons efficient'.[7] This was not how the Indian troops viewed things at Jitra. Their platoon commanders could do little to stiffen their resolve: many were recently commissioned, quite raw and had yet to learn their soldiers' language. The battle would not have been fought at Jitra at all but for the need to protect the airfields around Alor Star. Without the need to defend those in the east at Kota Bharu, both divisions could have been kept together for a concentrated defence.

That his own arm, the RAF, should so rapidly have lost the battle for air superiority in northern Malaya was a great disappointment for Pulford. What made things worse for his fellow commander Percival, whose Army units had, perforce, to remain and fight, was the manner in which the RAF ground staff scurried back to safety. Kota Bharu airfield was hastily vacated in the false belief that it was under ground attack. The runway was left uncratered and stocks of bombs and petrol untouched as the staff made off to the railhead, leaving Brigadier Key's men to witness 'the disorder and near panic' of the evacuation and cope with the mutiny of some troops of the airfield defence battalion, 1st Hyderabads, and the murder of their commanding officer. Similar, if less dramatic, scenes were enacted at the other northern airfields with stores, bombs, fuel and runways generally being left intact. The worst case of all was Kuantan, a key airfield since once Japanese fighters were based there they would have Singapore and the islands beyond within easy range. Kuantan aerodrome, way behind the front line, was abandoned in panic after an attack on it by nine Japanese aircraft, while the opposing ground troops were still three weeks away, and before a single casualty had been caused. This was the only station where the unseemly stampede of the ground staff seems to have afflicted some of the aircrew as well in their precipitate flight south. So serious and widespread were these evacuations that Pulford set up an official court of enquiry. This appeared to draw a discreet veil over the entire episode, concluding, according to its president, that 'the evidence revealed no instance where disciplinary action was called for'.[8] However Brooke Popham was so angered and ashamed by the events that on Christmas Eve he took the unprecedented (and scarcely seasonal) step of personally handing to Pulford two copies of a confidential letter to be issued to all RAF units. This spoke of 'instances where the aerodromes appear to have been abandoned in a state approaching panic' and where a 'general state of chaos has been evident'. It went on to make the emphatic point that, 'In the majority of cases the bombing of aerodromes has been of a far smaller scale than that suffered calmly by women and children in London . . . and aerodromes have usually been vacated whilst still well out of range of enemy land forces.'[9] It all came particularly hard for Pulford who was not a well man and desperately overworked. Despite the great courage of most of his squadrons, he was poorly served by some of his men in his efforts to shoulder the task of the main defence of Malaya which the Chiefs of Staff had so unfairly laid upon him.

This depressing episode had important consequences for Percival. It meant that the Japanese squadrons were quickly able to establish themselves in the northern airfields, complete their mastery of the air, and then turn their attention to the support of the ground forces. This in turn was to speed the contagion of demoralisation and panic which had been witnessed at the airfields. Could Indians remain steady if Europeans had already fled? 'How is this possible? They are all sahibs', one Indian driver queried incredulously when told of the flight from Kuantan.[10] If the morale of his troops was an increasing concern for Percival, it was much more of a worry for Heath who knew the Indian soldiers better. 'The trust of the Indian in his leaders is sensitive and basically is dependent upon the belief in British supremacy', he was later to write.[11] How could that trust be retained when that supremacy was being so successfully challenged? Heath soon came to believe that too much was being asked of his men.

The strategy for the defence of Malaya had now been turned on its head. According to the Chiefs of Staff, the plan had been that during the period before relief by the Fleet, 'reliance for the defence of the Far East was to be placed upon air power'. But that power was now well on the way to being destroyed. As for relief by the Fleet, the protection of whose base facilities at Singapore provided the entire rationale for the presence of the other two Services, Churchill sent the new battleship the *Prince of Wales* as 'the best possible deterrent' to Japanese aggression. But the deterrent had not worked and the great ship now lay on the sea-bed with its sister ship *Repulse*. A few destroyers remained, but despite valiant efforts they were unable to prevent Japan's free use of the seas to the east of Malaya. Some were themselves sunk, others were withdrawn to the relative safety of Ceylon. Yamashita was able to move forces by sea where and when he chose. There was little to prevent him attempting, if he so wished, an improvised landing directly on Singapore itself; but in the event he chose to stick to the original plan. Nevertheless, the possibilities of further landings on the east coast of Singapore were a constant concern for the embattled GOC.

Percival's army, whose subordinate role the Chiefs of Staff had emphasised as recently as mid-September when they declared that, 'as naval and air strength increase so would the need for land forces diminish and that material increases in both were likely to occur before his requirements could be met',[12] was all that now stood between Yamashita and his Singapore objective. It had already suffered a signal defeat whose character was to set the parameters for virtually every other battle of the campaign: weary and demoralised troops, no tanks to support them, too few anti-tank weapons and the ever-present fear of infiltration and of flanks being turned. As a result of the sensational reverses, the British Press was now beginning to take an interest in this remote theatre and the man on whose shoulders the entire burden of Malaya's defence had so unexpectedly come to rest. The GOC Malaya 'is a tall, very thin and bony officer who walks with tremendous strides – and can go on doing it indefatigably in any climate', the *Daily Mail* informed its readers, adding that 'in appearance he is more like a lean scholar than the traditional soldier'.[13] It left the impression that Percival did not look like a resolute commander. Certainly he was not at his best in tropical uniform, with baggy shorts of indeterminate length famously emphasising his long and bony legs. Like many tall, slim men Percival had developed over the years a slight stoop about the shoulders which reinforced the *Mail*'s 'lean scholar' impression.

If there was no Fleet to make use of the vaunted Naval Base, what on earth were the troops fighting for? There was no easy rallying cry for Percival to employ. Indeed his own Special Order of the Day issued on the eve of the Jitra battle had been a good deal less sanguine and complacent than Brooke Popham's, speaking rather of the possibility of the struggle being 'long and grim' and of the need for the Army to prove 'worthy of the great trust' which had been placed in it. Percival now had the task of keeping the Japanese as far north in Malaya as possible for as long as possible, so that the port of Singapore could be kept open for the desperately needed reinforcements. Singapore was a major city, already swelling with refugees from the north. The rapid move of air and land reinforcements to the island represented the only hope he had of denying the Naval Base to the enemy. The situation was already exceptionally grave, for all that the campaign was only four days old. The full weight of Yamashita's forces had yet to be felt. The troops had yet to come under the lash of the Japanese air arm.

There was a further disadvantage with which Percival had to contend. This was the use the Japanese were making of their excellent intelligence system. Long before the war, during his first tour in Malaya, Percival had inveighed against the threat from the enemy 'within the gates'. But throughout the period before the Japanese struck, her agents in Malaya had unfettered opportunity to gather information about the topography and military dispositions in the country and to set up fifth column cells. Their varied business interests in the tin, rubber and fishing industries and their positions as village barbers and photographers, provided ideal activities for acquiring the information they needed. Action against them was prevented by the pre-war Foreign Office policy of permitting nothing to be done which might cause offence to the Japanese. When the Argylls had been busy building defences on the east coast at Kota Tingii, their work had been watched by local Japanese who, according to Captain Rose, 'would follow behind us taking all the measurements and carefully writing them down in their notebooks'.[14] General Heath explained that Jitra was not fully wired as it would give too much away to locally-living Japanese.[15]

The civil authorities were very prompt in rounding up all Japanese nationals once war began; but by then it was too late, the information was in their hands and 25th Army had already been designed to meet the particular needs of the country and the campaign, strong in bridging and railway engineers, ready for the countless demolitions they knew they would meet. Evidence of a fifth column at work was clear from the start of the war, when the residence of the C-in-C was found to have been ringed with marker fires lit before the opening air raid on Singapore.[16] Then there was the notorious Captain Heenan, a British officer spying for the Japanese. Heenan was serving as an air intelligence liaison officer for Murray Lyon's headquarters. It was no doubt partly a result of Heenan's treachery that the Japanese air force was so spectacularly successful in its early operations.[17] Suspicion also attached to some Malay officers in the Johore Military Force and a radio transmitter was known to be operating clandestinely in the Johore area where Japanese influence had long been strong. A bizarre metaphor of the extent of Japanese influence came from Lady Diana Cooper: 'The Sultan of Johore gave me a mynah bird, a loquacious talker, but only in Japanese'.[18]

When Churchill first heard the news of the Japanese attacks, he derived from it a certain grim satisfaction. Final victory was at last assured by the involvement of the United States but, as Brooke appreciated, 'the manner in which it had been brought about had greatly increased the chances of immediate and perhaps irretrievable disaster. Churchill's vision was on the horizon rather than on the shambles at his feet.'[19] The moment the first defeats had been suffered, Brooke Popham signalled the Chiefs of Staff urgently for large air reinforcements, including long-range bombers. One of the early responses he received from an uncomprehending Whitehall was the priceless advice, 'All war experience shows the uselessness and wastefulness of attempting to gain air superiority by bombing aerodromes at long range'.[20] This was precisely what the Japanese had just tried with exemplary results! An urgent request followed from Admiral Layton for all the naval forces that could be spared from other theatres. Percival's own demand came after his land forces had suffered their early disasters. He asked for the despatch of a brigade group from India as soon as possible, together with 6,000 reinforcements for the battalions of 11th Division.

The Chiefs of Staff's response to the grave situation in the Far East was to transfer Burma from Brooke Popham's operational control to that of Wavell in India and to give Wavell the next available major troop rein-forcements, 17th Indian and 18th British Division, both originally destined for the Middle East, against an expected Japanese thrust into Burma. Aside from the promise of some artillery units, Percival was to get nothing.

The Chiefs seemed to imagine that the GOC's weak force would man-age to hold the Japanese despite air superiority and command of the sea having already been lost. He was to get no tanks, although Brooke noted that the Defence Committee had met to discuss sending them: 'Many were going to Russia and Churchill would not stop sending them nor divert any to Singapore.'[21] Substantial air reinforcements were agreed: within a few days an encouraging total of 58 bombers and 51 fighters had been promised to Malaya. But few were likely to arrive quickly. The fall of the Victoria Point airfield to the Japanese on 15 December closed down the air reinforcement route. The longer range bombers would have to fly in via Sumatra, while the fighters would have to come all the way by sea. The fighters in question were crated Hurricanes, already at sea *en route* to Russia via the Cape before their diversion to Malaya. So much for the RAF's belief that the inherent mobility of air power would permit the rapid reinforcement of any threatened locality. After the disasters of the first days of the land campaign the Chiefs of Staff quickly changed their minds about Army reinforcements. By the middle of December, Percival learnt that they had decided that two brigades of 17th Indian Division would now go to Malaya, as would the 18th Division. 17th Division was in training in India, 18th was part way through a long voyage to the Middle East via the Americas. The Australians also agreed to provide a machine-gun battalion and some reinforcements. The trouble was that none of these forces could get to Malaya until well into January at the ear-liest. Had not Dill warned Churchill that to await the arrival of the crisis in the Far East before sending reinforcements from a pool held elsewhere, was to court disaster?

The outbreak of war had changed the higher direction of Britain's affairs in the region. Churchill appointed Duff Cooper as Resident Cabinet Minister for Far Eastern Affairs in Singapore; much the sort of post Duff had himself recommended in his report to the Cabinet at the end of October, about which Churchill had done nothing.[22] In any event it would have been too late; it was now certainly beyond the point at which the Resident Minister could do anything to help Hong Kong or Singapore. Duff Cooper quickly set up the War Council in Singapore and assumed its chairmanship; but he did not have the temperament or indeed the time to weld together the disparate elements in the manage-ment of Malaya's defence affairs, with which he rapidly became almost exclusively concerned. He was very critical of most of those around him and his manner tended to encourage them to stand on their dignity rather than to cooperate. His appointment did little to make Percival's task any easier. Indeed the fact that the War Council meetings were held daily meant that Percival frequently had to miss them; the fact that they met as early as 9am meant that when he was able to attend them, it was generally before he could be properly briefed by his staff or have discussions with his service colleagues. This did not make for the rapid despatch of business. Duff Cooper was unable to provide for Percival the only service that would have helped: getting reinforcements to him more quickly.

15

TERRITORY VERSUS TIME

'The deeper the chronicler shall delve into the history of the Malayan Campaign the heavier he shall find the weight of responsibility on those at home for its disastrous outcome.'

Compton Mackenzie, Eastern Epic

By midday on 14 December the units of 11th Division, or what was left of them, had reached their positions at Gurun. The hope which Percival must then have entertained, that the troops would get some rest after their withdrawal, was dashed by two great disappointments, shortly followed by a third. The first was that the Gurun defences, which Heath had ordered Murray Lyon to have prepared at the same time as he was to occupy the Jitra line, were by no means ready: the labour battalion which the Kedah authorities had undertaken to provide had not turned up. The dog-tired troops had to start the digging themselves. The second was the dismaying speed with which the Japanese were able to switch their air force to the support of their ground troops. The third disappointment was the similar promptness with which the attackers were able to follow up the withdrawing units of Murray Lyon's division after the Jitra débâcle. By 15 December the Japanese were already upon them, first with an aerial bombing of the crossroads in advance of the main position and then, as at Jitra, by driving in darkness straight down the road, with tanks supporting the lorried infantry. It mattered little that Gurun was by nature one of the strongest defensive positions in Malaya with the massive Kedah Peak rising sheer on the left of the narrow road and rail corridor and with rubber plantations flanking it on the right. There was no natural tank obstacle at Gurun and there had been no time to construct one. The Japanese drove straight through a battalion and then a brigade headquarters, killing most of the staff at both and scattering the units concerned. They were not checked until they had penetrated two miles down the road and met the men of the reserve brigade. Surveying the plight of his exhausted and battle-shocked troops in the early hours of 15 December, Murray Lyon ordered an immediate withdrawal. By the following day the division had at last got itself behind the substantial tank obstacle provided by the Muda river. Was this finally the respite the troops so desperately needed? Alas not.

In attempting to account for the loss of Malaya which followed so rapidly from the landings in Thailand and at Kota Bharu, it is all too easy to ascribe the disaster to the air and sea ascendancy which the Japanese quickly established, and to the fact that they were soon able to deploy tanks in support of their major thrusts. All this was true, but would not have sufficed without the superb quality of their infantry fighting soldiers. Battle-hardened in the main, brave to the point of foolhardiness, they formed an excellent fighting machine. Against the polyglot assortment of half-trained national contingents ranged against them, they brought a racial and national homogeneity and a unity of purpose to their fighting despite the political manoeuvring of their senior commanders. Elated by their early successes they fought with verve, tenacity and improvisation and a disregard for the laws of war which struck fear into their unprepared opponents. They pressed the locals into service for labouring duties without a second thought, disguised themselves often as civilian Malays or Chinese and travelled by road where they could and by track and river where they could not. They used lorried infantry to good effect, commandeered bicycles from the villages they passed through, but also marched well in formed units when they needed to. Percival recalled one Japanese prisoner (there were not many) explaining that his unit had marched 26 miles from its landing place at Kota Bharu and then gone straight into action. Their infiltration tactics were particularly effective, especially at night, when a single intrepid fighter who had penetrated a defensive position could produce fear, rumour and panic reactions out of all proportion to the threat he posed.

Murray Lyon and Heath did not regard the Muda river position as anything more than a very temporary solution to their difficulties. Murray Lyon had already argued for a substantial withdrawal much further south to a point where the whole Corps could be concentrated. General Heath tended to agree with him and on returning from a visit (surprisingly his first) to Murray Lyon on the afternoon of 14 December he rang Percival to argue the case for a withdrawal behind the Perak river. This was about 100 miles to the south. Percival would not hear of it and ordered Heath to cover Penang and not to withdraw south from the Muda position without his authority. This was how things stood when Murray Lyon's force finally got behind the Muda river barrier.

Percival's refusal to agree with Heath's urgings was not born of an obstinate refusal to face the tactical facts and thereby risk the destruction of the division, but of the need to respect an overriding strategic imperative. It had been crystal clear to the GOC ever since he had produced his August review of the forces he needed, that Britain's hold on Malaya and Singapore depended critically upon the arrival of reinforcements, particularly fighter and bomber aircraft, but troops as well. The sea routes to the island had to be kept free of the predatory Japanese air force so that the convoys bringing them could get in unmolested. That meant keeping the Japanese as far north as possible for as long as possible, so as to deny them the use of the airfields in central Malaya. It was the traditional military problem of territory versus time, posed to Percival in the starkest terms. The safe arrival of reinforcements was the overriding concern; but there were also great quantities of military and air force stores at various centres in north Malaya which would take some time to backload if the troops were finally to pull back. Large stocks of tin and rubber, both important war commodities, had also to be got away. Indeed, it was the existence of these strategic resources which had made the argument for the defence of all Malaya rather than Singapore alone so inherently sensible from the outset. The blunt military fact was that the Japanese would not be stopped, or even slowed, unless they were given battle again at some point and forced to take casualties. To achieve all these purposes Heath's divisions had to make a stand – not a fight to the finish, but at least a substantial delaying action in north Malaya. Percival was only too aware that Heath's Corps was the only force he had to delay the enemy in the north, but expected a rather better showing from it than had been given so far.

Withdrawal, however, was the military operation with which Percival was to be most immediately concerned, despite the great reluctance with which he was considering it. He had already reviewed his east coast, Kelantan, strategy and, at Heath's urging, sanctioned the withdrawal of 8th Indian Brigade, since it now seemed certain that the main enemy effort was in the west. The brigade's move could have been a hazardous operation, for it had no road behind it, only the single line railway which meandered precariously through the wild country of central Malaya before it met road communications once more at Kuala Lipis, 100 miles to the south. In fact the withdrawal was successfully undertaken; stores and most vehicles were backloaded and the troops, all but the rearguard, travelled back by train after which all the major bridges were successfully destroyed. The Kelantan campaign was over. Another pull-out it may have been, but one whose orderly yet secret execution gave some pride and satisfaction to the GOC. The Japanese never did repair the east coast permanent way, but later used its rails and fittings for the Burma–Siam Railway.[1]

For all that the Muda river line represented a substantial tank obstacle, it did not provide the safe lodgement around which Heath could base the operations of his Corps in the west for very long. The basic tactical problem was that the Japanese were making two thrusts down the west side from north Malaya, and as Heath attempted to halt them, a failure with one blocking force threatened to expose the flank or the communications of the other. It was the inevitable consequence of having to defend too much with too little. The withdrawal of 11th Division as far back as the Muda was already giving him concern that the flank of 12th Brigade which was blocking the Japanese Patani/Kroh thrust might soon be threatened. It was now clear that this thrust was not being pushed directly west along the main road to the coast, but instead was heading south-west along an unmetalled track, the Grik road, which Heath and his staff had not considered viable for lorried troops. This advance, if successful, would get the Japanese to the west coast arterial communications much further south at Kuala Kangsar. This was well to the rear of the main body of 11th Division.

There was now another decision which Percival never imagined having to take this early in the campaign: what to do about Penang. This beautiful and prosperous island, part of the Straits Settlements colonial administration rather than one of the protected states, had a tiny garrison. Like Singapore it was officially a 'fortress', and had been so designated in 1936, but in common with Singapore it had few fortress characteristics. The anti-aircraft defences approved in 1936 had never been provided, nor had the two regular battalions which Percival had asked for as the nucleus of the garrison defence. The island had only a single volunteer battalion, two batteries of guns guarding the approaches to the anchorage, a company of 5/14th Punjab and a few engineers. A force of 70–80 Japanese bombers had struck the capital Georgetown on 10 December and a smaller force repeated the bombing the following day in the worst sustained terror attack of the Malayan campaign. Many people were caught in the streets by the attacks which set half the town aflame; the casualties ran into thousands. Much of the town's population took to the hills for safety, taking most of the municipal work force with them, leaving the public services in disarray and the small garrison and civil defence volunteers, who stood firm, hopelessly overburdened. The decision was taken locally to evacuate the Service families and to arrange to evacuate all civilian European women and children. Percival then put to the War Council in Singapore the case for evacuating the military garrison from the island. Such troops as he had there were desperately needed on the mainland and the fighter defence at nearby Butterworth had lasted only a day. Admiral Layton confirmed that he had no further use for the island's anchorage. The ferries to the mainland were already being operated by survivors from the *Prince of Wales* and *Repulse*, the civilian crews having fled. The War Council accepted the military necessity of Percival's case and decided that the garrison might be withdrawn as the military situation on the mainland demanded, accepting the effect on morale that this was bound to have.

Percival sent the orders to Heath by telegraph, leaving the timing of the evacuation to his discretion and telling him to get away such military stores as he could, but to destroy everything else of military value. The local commander had little time to put the denial scheme into effect and was given no priority for destruction by his corps commander. The fixed defences and stocks of petrol and oil were largely destroyed, but two serious omissions were the boats lying at the anchorage and the Penang radio station. Both were used to good effect by the Japanese. The two dozen self-propelled craft left undamaged were a valuable addition to the landing craft which the Japanese brought laboriously across Malaya to the west coast from Singora. The day after their occupation of the island the Japanese had the radio station on the air. The broadcasts in English would usually begin, 'Hello, Singapore, this is Penang calling; how do you like our bombings?' They included special talks for Indian troops, which fortunately few were able to listen to; there were already enough pressures on the loyalty of Percival's Indian soldiers.[2] The evacuation of Penang became a major local scandal because of the decision to bring out the Europeans but leave the Asians to their fate. However, the military could do little else, as the improvised ferry service was quite inadequate and a wholesale evacuation was not a realistic option: the mainland was, in truth, no safer. But that was not how the locals saw it. Shenton Thomas was indignant at the way the Asians had been abandoned and a major row developed in the War Council.[3] The realities of the war had yet to get through to the Governor; but he was soon to appreciate their force. Later, when the crowds of civilian Asian refugees were ordered south from the fighting in Perak by the military, they found a telegram from the Governor awaiting them at Kuala Lumpur station saying that no more people could come to crowded Singapore.[4] It was all a consequence of having to fight a major campaign, not in an empty desert or a foreign land, but in a prosperous British dependency which was largely unprepared for war and totally surprised by defeat. Few battlefield scenarios could be worse for a GOC.

The disagreement between Percival and Heath persisted. With his concern for the preservation of his Corps, Heath maintained his argument for a withdrawal to what he considered to be a defensible line. He urged the surrender of northern and central Malaya and the concentration of the forces on a shorter front somewhere along the boundary of northern Johore. Percival knew that with the defence line as far south as that, both the expected convoys and the Naval Base itself would be vulnerable to constant Japanese attack. There was no alternative to his present strategy. On 18 December Duff Cooper held a conference in Singapore which was attended by the Commonwealth and Dutch military representatives. This gathering endorsed Percival's strategy of holding the Japanese as far north as possible. It also reported the situation as being very grave and emphasised the need for reinforcements. That the conference should have asked the Chiefs of Staff for a complete division, a brigade group, reinforcements for both 9th and 11th Divisions, five anti-aircraft regiments, an anti-tank regiment and 50 light tanks, as well as substantial air reinforcements of four modern fighter and four bomber squadrons, gave a clear indication of just how grave they regarded it.[5]

Percival had already taken other hard decisions in support of his general strategic aim. Once Pulford's remaining squadrons had reorganised after the first Japanese air attacks, their operational priority became the support of the Army in the north-west. The aircraft were outnumbered and outclassed and despite the heroism of their crews, little was achieved and more planes and their crews were lost. With reinforcements the key to the recovery of the Allied position in the air and on land, Percival grimly agreed with Pulford over the husbanding of his remaining fighter squadrons for convoy protection work and for the defence of Singapore itself, and for priority in the use of civil labour to go to the construction of alternative airstrips from which the fighters could operate. Support for Heath would henceforth be restricted to reconnaissance missions alone. This decision required great moral courage, for Percival realised how badly mauled Heath's troops had been and how bitter their commander was becoming. The sacrifice was made bearable by the knowledge that reinforcements really were on the way. At Percival's urgent request the Chiefs of Staff had agreed that 53 Brigade of 18th British Division, aboard the fast American transport *Mount Vernon*, should be detached from the main divisional convoy, at this time on its way around the Cape *en route* to the Middle East, refuel at Mombasa and then head straight for Singapore with the convoy bringing the Hurricanes. This would get it to the GOC two weeks earlier. He was also promised a second brigade from 17th Indian Division, 44 Brigade, since it was now clear that the Japanese intended to concentrate on Malaya before turning their attention to Burma, about which Wavell was rightly concerned. The knowledge that the fighters were on their way was particularly cheering. 'I was prepared to make almost any sacrifice to get these fighters in safely and to get them into the air', Percival was later to write.[6]

There were soon to be even more reinforcements on their way to Pulford. At last realising the gravity of the Far Eastern emergency, Churchill asked Auchinleck to part with four of his Hurricane squadrons which the aircraft carrier *Indomitable* (the much-missed absentee from Admiral Phillips' original squadron) was ordered to pick up from Port Sudan and later fly off to Java or Sumatra and thence to Singapore. Auchinleck also promised 50 light tanks and made ready a full armoured brigade equipped with light cruiser tanks. Much more was promised and got ready, particularly as Australia began to feel her own direct vulnerability and pressed for the withdrawal of her substantial forces in the Middle East. It was surprising how so much that had been declared quite impossible to supply only weeks before, suddenly became available to the beleaguered garrison of Malaya. Churchill and the War Cabinet now quietly assented to the strategic priorities for which Dill had unavailingly argued during the summer. On 1 January the Chiefs of Staff cabled the commanders concerned telling them that 'the security of Singapore and the sea communications in the Indian Ocean were second only to the security of the United Kingdom and the sea communications thereto'.[7]

The change of heart in London was now complete; all that remained to be determined was whether the reinforcements produced by it would be sufficient and arrive in time to save Percival and his Army.

On the day of Duff Cooper's conference Percival went up to Ipoh to review the situation with Heath. The pressure seemed to have eased temporarily both on the Krian river front where 11th Division now was, and the routes to the west coast from the Patani road. However, he confirmed his earlier instruction giving Heath the authority to withdraw behind the Perak River when necessary and instructed him to prepare defensive positions in depth between Ipoh and Tanjong Malim on the main route south. He still insisted on keeping General Barstow's 9th Division in eastern Malaya. He was determined to deny the Kuantan airfield to the enemy for as long as possible. Heath was keen to concentrate his Corps as quickly as he could. Some critics have since supported his view, arguing as Kirby has done, that 'the complete demolition of Kuantan airfield and its installations' would have sufficed,[8] and permitted the concentration of all Heath's forces against the thrust in the west. But, as the experience with the northern airfields had already shown, and Air Vice Marshal Maltby's *Despatch* was later to make clear, the 'demolition of aerodrome surfaces had little more than nuisance value' since stocks of road metal had already been gathered at each one ready for repairs and these could not be removed or destroyed.[9] The Japanese did not hesitate to impress the locals for rapid repair work. Airfields had to be denied, not disabled.

After their Ipoh discussions, Heath and Percival went off to reconnoitre the Perak River, fast flowing and one of the largest in Malaya. They then went north to Kuala Kangsar on which units were now falling back after the fighting up-country. From there they returned to Heath's headquarters based in a special train at Ipoh and talked and planned far into the night. By the time Percival left for the south the following morning they had discussed and agreed a range of issues, mostly concerned with the reorganisation of the battered 11th Division. The weary remnants of 6 and 15 Brigades were to be taken out of the line and reorganised as 6/15 Brigade. Their component battalions were similarly merged, the Leicesters and East Surreys, for example, becoming 'the British Battalion'. It was a sad necessity, but had worked well enough on the Western Front in the last show, Percival recalled. Three new brigade commanders were appointed to take over from those who had become casualties. Percival also decided that the time had come to replace the divisional commander, Murray Lyon, 'a brave and tireless leader', as he called him, but one who had limited experience of bush warfare. He chose for the post Brigadier Paris whose 12 Brigade was the best trained and most experienced in Malayan conditions. Stewart of the Argylls moved up to take charge of 12 Brigade. To give some rest to the troops whilst continuing the defence, the two commanders agreed to a plan for a defence in depth by brigade groups once the Perak river had been crossed. Heath travelled down with Percival for part of the GOC's return journey and they made a provisional selection of some defensive positions, concentrating on the use of tank obstacles and finding positions which gave cover from Japanese bombers, to which the troops were now very vulnerable.

On the way back to Singapore Percival met Barstow and confirmed the instructions for his 9th Division to continue covering Kuantan airfield and protecting 11th Division's communications from a possible attack from the east coast. Before leaving Heath he also discussed with him the plans for a special west coast raiding party which, with the assistance of a light flotilla based on Port Swettenham, was to attack the ever-lengthening Japanese communications. Percival had arranged with Bennett for 50 Australian volunteers, joined by a couple of platoons of Royal Marines, survivors from the east coast sinkings, to form the basis of this force. It was stimulating actually to have an offensive operation to organise, but the raiders only managed one successful strike against Japanese transport west of the Perak river. Nothing more was possible because of the enemy's domination of the air over northern Malaya. They bombed and sank the raiding flotilla's base ship as well as five fast motor boats which had been obtained from the Americans specifically for this kind of operation. The Japanese then had unrestricted use of the coastal waters for their own operations with no chance of reply by Percival.

Meanwhile, changes in the higher direction of the war in the Far East were complicating life for Percival; each fresh incumbent had to be met, briefed and taught the uncomfortable lesson that their Japanese adversaries were far from being the Asian incompetents of popular belief and that Malaya was very different from the Western Desert. Duff Cooper had visited the Combined Operations Room at Sime Road on 9 December, 'together with panama hat, Brigade of Guards tie and Personal Assistant', as one of the GOC's staff put it, for a tour and briefing. Towards the end of the month Lieutenant General Sir Henry Pownall finally arrived, after many delays, to take over from Brooke Popham. He reached Singapore on Christmas Eve and took over as C-in-C on 27 December, by which time his command was already collapsing. Hong Kong had fallen to the Japanese two days earlier. He made a visit to the front in northern Malaya before he took over, quickly registering how deceptively the distances were viewed in London on the War Office's small-scale maps and how militarily immature were the troops and junior commanders. He found Heath much aged since he had last seen him years earlier in India, and 'not "full of fire"', but knowing 'what needed to be done to pull the troops around'.[10] However, apart from discussing the situation with his predecessor, whom he found 'pretty tired', and with Percival, Duff Cooper and Shenton Thomas, he had little chance to do more than confirm the correctness of Percival's strategy before he was himself superseded by General Sir Archibald Wavell who was given the task of setting up the mould-breaking ABDACOM – the American, British, Dutch and Australian Command – thus becoming the first Allied Supreme Commander of the war.

On the day of Pownall's arrival, 11th Division was beginning its withdrawal across the Perak River. Murray Lyon's increasing concern over the threat to his communications posed by the Japanese thrust along the Grik road had forced the decision on him. Behind the troops the permanent road and rail bridges at Kuala Kangsar and the pontoon bridge carrying the road at Blanja were all successfully blown. Heath was planning the defence in depth by brigade groups which Percival and he had discussed earlier. He was hoping to mount the first main defence at Kampar, after which the brigade there would withdraw behind the second at Tanjong Malim, some 60 miles further south. There were also intermediate positions at Tapah, Bidor and Slim River. The terrain was starting to funnel the Japanese advance along a single north–south axis; there were no further lateral communications in their hands from the east coast which they could exploit. The difficulty for Heath and Percival was that since the Japanese air force had put paid to the possibility of amphibious operations against their communications, the enemy were now free to consider seaward strikes of their own. Their air arm, meanwhile, was able to give full support to their land forces.

On 27 December General Paris decided to bring his most advanced brigades back to the Kampar position. 12 Brigade had already suffered severe casualties resisting the advance of a regiment of the Imperial Guards Division, and Paris could not risk its security any further. After what was unfortunately becoming the customary confusion over bridge demolitions, by the morning of 30 December the entire division was south of the Kampar River in a position which Percival considered 'probably the strongest occupied in Malaya'. It was the first prepared position that the division had taken up since Jitra and the four-day battle which took place there illustrated what could be achieved by steady troops in good defensive positions with effective artillery support.

On 30 December Percival decided to go north again and see the situation for himself. The time was fast approaching when important decisions would have to be taken about the withdrawal of 9th Division from the Kuantan front, since the sole road linking it with the west coast front at Kuala Kubu was now getting uncomfortably close behind 11th Division's battle line. The timing of any further withdrawal would be critical. Percival went up by road and spent the night with Heath at Kuala Lumpur. The following morning they motored on to Paris's headquarters at Tapah, passing on the way a large civil labour force gathered from the nearby estates which was preparing a defensive position north of Tanjong Malim. Further north, beyond the Slim River, they met Stewart, the 12 Brigade commander, who was reconnoitring a position for his brigade. Defensive possibilities there were good, for the road and railway lay close together and were hemmed in on each side by a dense jungle belt. Outflanking moves would be difficult and tanks would, as usual, be restricted largely to the road itself. On the other hand, there was no natural tank obstacle and much would depend on such artificial ones as could be provided for the anti-tank defence. Up at Tapah they met Paris who was confident that he would be able to hold the Japanese in the 70-mile stretch north of the vital Kuala Kubu junction until 14 January, thus coordinating with Percival's plan for the conclusion of the defensive action on the east coast at Kuantan. The timing of the action on both flanks had as its ultimate objective the security of the convoys due in Singapore during the first two weeks of January. After an overnight stop at Fraser's Hill the two generals motored on to Raub, where General Barstow had his 9th Division headquarters. Percival confirmed to Barstow that he needed to hold the Kuantan airfield until 10 January: the latest date by which he could still be sure of getting his force away to the west coast, yet still offer maximum safety to the precious convoys. Then it was back to Kuala Lumpur for the night before the GOC made his return journey to Singapore, making detours *en route* to check on the situation at Port Swettenham and Port Dickson on the west coast itself. He got back to Flagstaff House shortly before midnight after a busy trip and a long and exhausting final day, 250 miles on the road as well as numerous conferences with local commanders.

Before Percival had even crossed the Causeway to Singapore the situation in the north was already unravelling. Although on New Year's Day the Kampar position was still intact, numerous heavy attacks having been successfully repulsed, its integrity was already being compromised by what was happening on the coast. Japanese activity there had been reported earlier and by 2 January General Paris felt his position was so threatened that he was forced to give up the Kampar position and move back to the Slim River. That day the Japanese troops were ashore at Telok Anson, 20 miles to the rear of Kampar, having travelled south down the Perak River and then joining up with others landed from the sea. The same day they attempted to land at Kuala Selangor, but were repulsed. However, some other Japanese troops had already reached the port by pressing along the coast road. This coastal threat was developing some 50 miles behind Percival's front line! Such was the advantage which command of the air and sea conferred. Paris was thus forced to send the already weary 6/15 Brigade (very much the heroes of Kampar) to deal with the Kuala Selangor incursion and begin a hastier occupation of the intermediate Slim River position than he had planned. 12 Brigade Group occupied the forward sector at Trolak, with 28 Brigade behind it in the Slim River village area. Paris's troops reached the Slim River position on 3 January.

Two days later, Percival called an important conference at Segamat to consider the next stage in the fighting withdrawal which was to take his forces into a narrower, more populous part of Malaya, less divided by the mountain spine and with much better communications. At Segamat were Heath, Bennett and Brigadier Duncan, commanding the newly arrived 45th Indian Brigade, together with principal staff officers from the three headquarters. The three commanders agreed that the new conditions would favour the Japanese use of armour and their now customary outflanking tactics. An amphibious hook onto the key communications centre of Tampin, from which the roads radiated in all directions like the spokes of a wheel, was also a possibility. Percival now took the uncomfortable decision that they should not fight for the states of Selangor, Negri Sembilan and Malacca, but withdraw right back to Johore state when the need arose, making their defence along the line Muar–Segamat–Mersing. It was a radical retrenchment, but Heath needed little persuading; nor did Bennett, whose main concern was now to get into the action, for which he had already suggested that he should be allowed to take charge of operations in Johore, or at least that his fresh troops should replace those of the weary 3rd Corps. Percival rejected this proposal on the sensible grounds of the administrative problems involved in switching formations, the weakening of the east coast defences that it would cause and because Heath's Corps would by then be concentrated and have at least one fresh brigade, 45th, which he planned to move forward as soon as possible. He no doubt realised as well that the Australian was doing his best to see, as the junction of the various forces approached, that his division did not have to serve under III Corps. The GOC's decision was to make Heath responsible for the western sector and Bennett the eastern. However, he was determined that the airfields at Kuala Lumpur and Port Swettenham were to be denied to the Japanese until 14 January, after which Heath might implement the plan they had just discussed. It was at this point that the Japanese gathered themselves to inflict on III Corps what was probably the decisive defeat of the campaign.

Yamashita's forces had followed up the withdrawing units of 11th Division with their customary speed and had begun probing attacks on the Trolak sector of the Slim River position on 5 January. These were repulsed without too much difficulty. Then, during the afternoon of the 6th, the Japanese force commander, Colonel Ando, was persuaded to allow the tanks to lead a night attack. This was against his better judgement since they were restricted to a single road through the narrow defile which was bound to be protected by wire and obstacles.[11] In fact the tank attack succeeded beyond all expectations. The engineers managed to clear the obstacles by moonlight and the tanks quickly broke through the forward battalion which Stewart had already decided to withdraw at first light once he knew armour was massing to the north. The battalion in the main Trolak position shared a similar fate, though it stopped some tanks with mines and anti-tank fire. By first light the tank force, followed by lorried infantry, had broken through the road block hastily erected by the third battalion of the brigade, the Argylls. Here the tanks paused for a few minutes, as they had while the earlier obstacles were negotiated and alternative ways forward discovered, and then ploughed forward again, across a bridge where the demolition had failed, out into the open country beyond the obstacle zone. Stewart's reserve battalion was caught moving up the road and scattered. Both Trolak and Kampong Slim itself were now in Japanese hands and the Gurkha battalions of the rear brigade proved little hindrance to the reckless career of the tanks. They brushed past the first battalion and then took the second from the rear as they were marching non-tactically eastwards along the road to their allotted positions, believing they were well away from the nearest Japanese. They, too, were overrun and scattered. Before 9am the Slim River bridge itself had fallen to the Japanese tanks, which were finally brought to a halt at 9.30am, two miles beyond the bridge, by the guns of a field regiment firing at a range of less than 100 yards.

The achievement of the impromptu Japanese mini-blitzkrieg was remarkable: the tanks had covered 19 miles through 11th Division's lines, 'heedless of danger and of their isolation', the divisional history noted ruefully. 12 Brigade and much of 28 brigade had ceased to exist as fighting formations; anti-tank guns and parked artillery had been shot up; much of the division's transport and many of its guns were now trapped behind Japanese lines. Several thousand of Paris's men became prisoners. About 1,000 stragglers are said to have been collected by members of the INA and IIL for recruitment to their organisation. Percival's plans for an orderly and measured withdrawal to north Johore were in ruins. What had gone wrong?

The natural tendency is to focus on the errors made by the local commanders: Paris, who gave his forward brigade commander only a fraction of the anti-tank mines and guns he had available; Stewart, who gave none to his forward battalion although the unit was covering the obstacles with which the sappers had blocked the road. He also had one battalion and two batteries of guns out of his battle line, resting the one and believing the other was unsuitable for use in the local conditions. These were serious failings, but they were not fundamental. The true battle winners were the Japanese command of the air and the sea. The latter priceless advantages had enabled them to turn the strong Kampar position and hustle 11th Division into a hasty defence of Slim River, from which position General Paris was forced to remove his third brigade in response to the next amphibious threat to its rear. Once at the Slim position the troops had no rest: they worked on the defences by night to escape the air attacks which disturbed what little rest they got by day. The bombing destroyed the communications between the brigades and back to General Paris, who lacked both information and control when the tanks began their charge. And of course they had no tanks themselves.

16

FAREWELL TO MALAYA

'All were weary. Many had been fighting, and withdrawing to fight again, in an exhausting climate and cruel country for seven weeks on end and in the face of a powerful enemy equipped with every advantage. The most remarkable thing perhaps is that so many of them were still full of fight after such an ordeal.'

Percival, The War in Malaya

General Wavell's Catalina made a perfect landing in Singapore Harbour at first light on 7 January, just as Major Shimada's tanks were ploughing through the unfortunate 12 Indian Brigade. There on the quay to greet the new Supreme Commander was General Pownall, his own brief reign as Commander-in-Chief at an end. Later that day Percival was to meet his new chief, the third he had had in a little over a fortnight. These rapid changes seemed an odd way to manage a war; their 'general effect was far from healthy', was Percival's typically restrained comment. Wavell was, however, the most experienced senior commander Britain had; tough as teak, he was determined to create some order out of the chaos into which the Japanese offensive had thrown the widely spread territories of his new command. The trouble was, as his biographer readily acknowledges, he had 'only a superficial, limited and long-distance knowledge of the country in which the campaign was being fought, of the enemy, and of his own troops and their commanders.'[1] The same had been true of Pownall, though at least Percival and he had known each other well since their school days. Wavell also apparently harboured a 'complete contempt for the Japanese as soldiers – an attitude of mind which he retained right up to the fall of Rangoon'.[2] As a result of this misappreciation he had already made one unfortunate contribution to Percival's problems and was about to make a second. The first had been to raise no objection to the despatch as reinforcement to Singapore of the 45 and 44 Brigades of 17th Division; his own Director of Military Training had declared it unfit for operations against anything but a second-class enemy, and it had been preparing at the time for service in Iraq, for which purpose it had been the first Indian division to be issued with heavy battledress. Available at Secunderabad was 19th Indian Division, whose

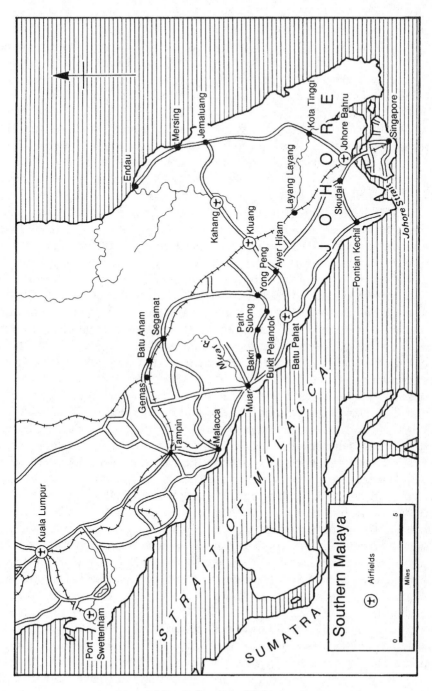

Map 6. Southern Malaya

48 Brigade (all Gurkha regiments), would have been a much more sensible reinforcement for Malaya.[3]

Wavell spent the 7th in discussions with Duff Cooper, who was being recalled by Churchill after less than a month as Resident Minister, with Pownall and with Percival himself, about whom Pownall reported Wavell as being, after the briefest acquaintance, 'not at all happy'.[4] One is reminded of Dill's cautionary remark on Percival's 1932 confidential report about misleading first impressions. Wavell decided, in view of the disturbing reports coming in from the north, to go up and have a look for himself. He decided, unwisely, to fly. This deprived him of the 'feel' of trying to exercise command over such vast distances, besides absorbing almost the entire fighter resources of Pulford's meagre and hard-pressed air force.[5] He arrived at Kuala Lumpur at dawn the following morning and after a bad breakfast with a disconsolate Heath, the Corps Commander took him forward to 11th Division where he met Paris and then the desperately tired Brigadiers Stewart and Selby, the battle-shocked commanders of 12 and 28 Brigades, who had struggled down the railway line from Kampong Slim with the remnants of their units, past Japanese-held positions. Wavell listened attentively to what the exhausted Stewart had to say and afterwards remarked to Heath, 'Well, I have never listened to a more garbled account of an operation.'[6] He also met the commander of 9th Division and the third of Paris's brigade commanders. He concluded that III Corps was no longer fit for active operations and should be withdrawn to Johore as soon as possible. He told Heath as much in the verbal instructions he gave him, and then flew back to Singapore. He had already had a discussion with Bennett and had been impressed with his fighting spirit and aggressive ideas. That night, he wired the Chiefs of Staff to the effect that after seeing Percival and Bennett the following morning he would send a 'plan to meet what has become a somewhat critical situation in Malaya'. In fact he had already formulated his plan without seeing them. Percival was summoned to Wavell's temporary headquarters, kept waiting in an ante-room for a considerable time and then, without further discussion, handed a plan which Wavell had written out in full and which he instructed him to put into operation forthwith.[7] It was a cavalier way to treat a subordinate commander, as well as offending the principle of not interfering with the tactical plans devised by the man on the spot, particularly on the basis of such a short and superficial visit.

Wavell's plan for a clean break and a withdrawal to the Muar–Segamat–Mersing line in Johore was much the same as Percival's, though it was now obviously a matter of greater urgency. The difference was that he was proposing to give Bennett the front-line command that the Australian general had long been seeking and which Percival, knowing much more about the man and his relations with his commanders, had rejected four days previously. The action did nothing for Percival's authority and not a little to exacerbate his subsequent difficulties. Wavell's redeployment plan involved a layered command, with Bennett taking charge of the front-line forces in the west and Heath withdrawing his Corps behind them to refit. The Australian was to command his own 27 Brigade which would move to the west, 9th Indian Division withdrawn from the east coast and the newly arrived 45 Brigade under Brigadier Duncan. This combination was to be designated Westforce. Heath's III Corps would refit behind it in south Johore and would also take command of 22nd Australian Brigade on the east coast. Percival later loyally wrote that he did not see 'how any better plan could have been evolved in the circumstances', and quickly acted to put it into operation. However the plan did split the Australian division, something which he had been trying to avoid; it did not dispose the formations in depth and permit them to withdraw on their own communications and it gave Bennett a very extensive front – from Muar to Segamat – to control. Bennett had no experience of Indian units or of dealing with the Japanese. Close control was not one of his strengths: even Duff Cooper had been 'surprised that his nearest troops were distant eighty miles from his headquarters'. But Wavell believed that the Australian had 'studied [the] theatre and trained his division in appropriate tactics' and would be able to delay the enemy until reserves could be collected and a counter-stroke delivered in about the middle of February.[8] He also foresaw the Navy preventing landings on the Johore coast and the RAF attacking the enemy's shipping, road columns and northern airfields. Having apparently restored the situation by this burst of positive thinking, Wavell flew off with Pownall and his staff to set up his headquarters in Java. At Batavia airport he found a long line of admirals and generals awaiting him. He was to have eight of them in his short-lived headquarters. Perhaps they could tell him what resources his new command would have; his own Chiefs of Staff had been unable to.

The GOC was not sure that the Supreme Commander understood just how dominant the Japanese position was, or how demoralised the Indian soldiers were becoming. After his next conference with his commanders he sent a personal message to Wavell making the point very clearly: 'Am NOT repeat NOT happy about the state of morale of some Indian units. Believe Garwalis and Dogras will continue to fight but some others doubtful. On 10 January two coys 2/9th Jats surrendered without fighting.' This was a serious business: both Indian divisions seemed affected. Percival put the blame on their extreme fatigue, 'enemy propaganda working on fertile ground' and, of course, the complete Japanese domination of the air.[9] The worrying thing was that there was little he could do to alleviate the situation; only fresh troops and some respite from the air attacks would do that. At Heath's suggestion he agreed to promote Brigadier Key, an Indian Army officer, in place of General Paris (who was not) to command of 11th Indian Division. Perhaps Billy Key could do something to turn the Indians around.

Events at the front were by no means Percival's only concern, though they inevitably predominated. Civil government considerations were constantly occupying his attention and that of his staff. There were continual difficulties in getting the full cooperation of the authorities in Singapore, though the provincial officials were generally quick to adjust to the realities of war which seemed to percolate through to Shenton Thomas and his staff only slowly. It was not until 15 January that the Governor finally awoke to the need for urgent action and issued his famous edict, 'The day of minute papers is gone. There must be no more passing of files between departments. . . . The essential thing is speed of action. Nothing matters which is not directly concerned with defence . . .'[10] Percival had found the colonial officials particularly proprietorial and Thomas too readily influenced by them. Duff Cooper was critical of virtually every aspect of the civil administration in Singapore and of the military commanders for that matter. Reading the gracefully written character assassination of all and sundry in his confidential letter to Churchill,[11] one suspects that Duff Cooper was endeavouring to ensure that if Singapore were to fall, he was not going to carry the blame for it. His criticism of Shenton Thomas, however, that he was 'the mouthpiece of the last person he speaks to', was one with which Percival would certainly have agreed. So used had he become to the Governor changing his mind over something that he had previously agreed with Percival (particularly after being advised by Colonial Secretary Jones) that the GOC always took a stenographer to record the decisions at meetings with him 'and would not leave the building until he had the Governor's signature to them'.[12] Of Brooke Popham, Duff Cooper wrote that he 'sometimes seems on the verge of a nervous collapse'; he considered Pulford a very likeable man but, 'worried to death and rightly determined to preserve his small resources as long as possible'. Of the GOC he wrote that he was 'a nice, good man who began life as a schoolmaster [sic]. I am sometimes tempted to wish he had remained one. He is a good soldier too – calm, clear-headed, even clever. But he is not a leader, he cannot take a larger view.' All this criticism caused Churchill to wonder why none of it had appeared in the Minister's earlier report. The verdict of one of the most perceptive and balanced historians of these events is that 'Duff Cooper made little impact, and that little was not all gain.'[13] The Governor's views of Duff Cooper were decidedly uncomplimentary: 'A rotten judge of men, arrogant, obstinate, vain; how he could have crept into Office is beyond me'.[14]

Percival saw both men in the War Council meetings to which he went for sanction of the major civil-military decisions that came his way. He had urged on it the evacuation of all Europeans from Penang because of their great value to the war effort, but a major row had ensued between

Governor and Resident Minister, with Duff Cooper backing the military line. The basic problem was that there had been no pre-war policy on the evacuation of refugees and making one up as the campaign progressed was bound to create difficulties and injustices. Civil defence now loomed large as the bombing increased and the battle lines drew closer to Singapore. The existing organisation headed by Jones had left much undone and the military found him bureaucratic and obstructive. Duff Cooper's solution was to appoint Percival's enthusiastic and voluble Chief Engineer, Brigadier Simson, as Director General of Civil Defence with full plenary powers. Percival did not like either proposal. He could not afford to lose Simson's services at this stage in the campaign. Furthermore he would much rather have seen the existing civil defence machinery properly utilised, 'strengthening it as necessary with men of character and proven ability', rather than an attempt to create a wholly new one at the eleventh hour. He had no great love for Jones and was not averse to his replacement; but he had always belonged to the 'cooperative' rather than the 'destructive' school of management. In the end he reluctantly agreed to Simson taking the job, but kept him as titular Chief Engineer, partly to protect Simson's financial position, but with his deputy doing most of the strictly Army work. Simson tackled the task with his customary energy, but like most things in this sorry tale, it was too late to do very much, particularly as the Governor fought hard to restrict the Director General's independence and to restrict his authority to the island itself. The change merely added to Percival's particular burdens.

Duff Cooper called for a further change with which Percival did not agree: he pressed for the introduction of martial law. Percival knew all about the circumstances in which martial law is appropriate from his tour in southern Ireland; but law and order had not broken down in Malaya and the military were not engaged in restoring normal conditions. There was plenty of apathy among the Asians and a *sauve qui peut* attitude had long since developed among many, but there was no internal disorder and the troops were quite busy enough attempting to hold back the invader. However, martial law was eventually declared in Singapore only and Keith Simmons, the Singapore commander, became its administrator. Heath and Bennett were given the powers to introduce martial law in their respective areas of Malaya, but never found it necessary.

Another problem for the GOC which the peculiarities of the Malayan theatre produced was the implementation of an unrestricted scorched-earth policy, for which he received instructions via Duff Cooper in mid-December. Churchill and the Chiefs of Staff probably had in mind the scorched-earth policy applied in Russia by both sides; but ordering its implementation in Malaya and Singapore bespoke a lack of understanding of the local situation. There was the world of difference between scorched-earth as ordered by the world's two most powerful dictators in their struggle and what was practical politics for a benevolent colonial power in Malaya and Singapore. Early in 1941 a 'denial' scheme had been prepared, directed principally at the destruction or removal of every-thing that might facilitate the movement of the invading forces; but this plan had not envisaged 'scorched-earth'. Percival understood the military arguments for such a policy, but neither accepted them all, nor was entirely convinced of their practicability. Road and rail bridges, stocks of rubber and tin, machinery in European-owned firms were one thing, but food, water and power supplies for hospitals for an Asiatic people whom Britain was bound by treaty to protect, were quite another. At a time when he was doing everything possible to sustain the morale of his battered for-mations, the noise and smoke of explosions to their rear were likely only to lower it further and convince them that the line they were holding was to be given up in any event. As for the locals, there was no better market-ing ploy for the Japanese 'Asia for the Asiatics' slogan than the destruction by the British of their means of employment and sustenance. Eventually Whitehall agreed to a more sensible and moderate policy.

It was no doubt Percival's objections to what Duff Cooper was trying to get agreed which led him to comment on Percival's failure to 'take a large view'. As it was, the 'denial' policy sucked in engineer and other military resources, for the civil authorities and business heads were in no position to implement it alone. Now that the withdrawal to Johore was to be so hurried, there was little that could be done about the vast quantities of stores and *matériel* in the Kuala Lumpur area. In anticipation of finally having to give up central Malaya, Percival had ordered the backloading of military stores when Heath had begun the withdrawal behind the Perak River, but the rapidity of the collapse at Slim River meant that there was much that could not be got away. The early evacuation of Kuala Lumpur resulted in great congestion on the single-track railway, which was now manned by volunteers and sailors as well as the remaining FMS Railway staff. The tragic result was that 13 trainloads of military stores fell into Japanese hands. These included a consignment of maps of south Johore and Singapore where the next stage of the campaign was to be fought.

The withdrawal from the Slim River position to north Johore was the most dramatic demonstration of the reversal of the Army's fortunes that could be imagined. Its effect on British prestige in the eyes of the local population was immense; it was no less serious for the morale of the troops. Two of Malaya's most prosperous states, Selangor and Negri Sembilan, the ancient Straits Settlement of Malacca and the federal cap-ital Kuala Lumpur, were all being handed over without a fight. With them went the airfields at Kuala Lumpur and Kuantan, from which Japanese fighters would be able to range freely over Singapore and the seas around it. Behind the withdrawing troops lay a desolated Malaya: bridges blown, airfield installations wrecked, plantations deserted and everywhere monster fires as rubber factories, mine installations, petrol and rubber stocks were 'denied' to the enemy. The wealth of Malaya was being bled away, its local population left to their own devices and the tender mercies of the Japanese who were 'liberating' them.

But at least the convoys were getting in. The first, carrying 45th Brigade from India, had docked safely on 3 January. Three days later a second had brought the brigade's transport and stores. Then on the 13th had come the vital convoy, bearing 53 Brigade and the Hurricanes. Their protection had required a great effort by Pulford, involving wide reconnaissance sweeps into the South China Sea, close anti-submarine patrols from the Banka Straits onwards and a fighter escort for the final approach to Singapore. Two Catalinas, six Hudsons, four Glenn Martins and every available fighter were required for the escorting of each convoy, with every other plane kept at instant readiness. It was not surprising that nothing was left to support Percival's Army. But the sacrifice seemed to be worthwhile. Security was good and the convoys carrying 45th Brigade and its equipment got through without Japanese interference. The indispensable convoy on the 13th, carrying the British brigade, three artillery regiments and the precious Hurricanes, was protected by even stronger air defences and, fortuitously, by bad weather as well. These kept at bay the 81 bombers and 20 Zeros which the Japanese had waiting to attack.[15] They did get through to Singapore town but with gallant interception by 20 British fighters the raid was largely ineffective. Maltby, Pulford's deputy and successor, later wrote, 'It is difficult here adequately to convey the sense of tension which prevailed as these convoys approached Singapore, and the sense of exultation at their safe arrival . . . many confidently expected that the Hurricanes would sweep the Japanese from the skies'.[16] Percival was equally optimistic, 'We had seen what they could do in the Western theatre', he wrote, 'and we saw visions of them clearing the navy 'O's out of the air in a very short time'. Unsurprisingly, the ships discharged as speedily as possible and got away unscathed. For Percival the reinforcement of British troops was particularly welcome, especially coming from 18th Division. The predecessor to this 53 Brigade had fought alongside his own on the Somme. What would their successor be like after being at sea since October? At least the idea of fighting for the British Empire would have a meaning for them which was quite lost on the Indians. Two fresh brigades and 51 Hurricanes might not turn the tables, but they were a damned good start.

Percival wasted no time in putting Wavell's orders into operation. The morning after he received them he confirmed that Bennett was to command Westforce which would defend the area from Muar on the coast road to Batu Anam and Segamat on the trunk road. Bennett would initially have his own 27th Brigade Group and the new 45 Brigade for the defence, with 9th Indian Division coming under his command as soon as it got across to Johore. III Corps would withdraw through Westforce and become responsible for south Johore, besides taking over command of the remaining Australian brigade, 22nd, at Endau on the east coast. The following day Percival motored up to Segamat to discuss the details of the handover, the allocation of supporting arms and to arrange the transfer to the battle front of two battalions from the Singapore garrison. He then made a quick reconnaissance of the locations to be occupied, including a position forward of Gemas where Bennett was planning an ambush. Percival thought that the spot chosen by Bennett was too far in advance of the main stand, but Bennett was adamant and it was his operation after all.[17] Percival had long been advocating aggressive ambush tactics,[18] and here the terrain was ideal and at last there were troops fresh enough to take it on. He stayed the night at Segamat, where Heath and Bennett were occupying adjoining houses; Lady Heath, now pregnant, had moved down to Singapore some days earlier. The following day Percival visited the troops in the forward areas. Then it was back to Singapore where the argument over the powers of the Director General of Civil Defence and the need for a Military Governor was still rumbling, though Duff Cooper was about to leave for the UK.

On 13 January Percival was at Singapore airfield to meet Wavell on his second visit. He quickly briefed the Supreme Commander and lent him his ADC, Ian Stonor, as a guide for his trip to the front. This time Wavell travelled by car and got a more realistic impression of the command problems over the great distances involved and of the state of the campaign. Wavell's party travelled up to Segamat in two brand-new Ford staff cars with a pair of motor cyclist escorts. They were hardly into south Johore when one motor cyclist had an accident and the other's machine broke down. The second car took the casualties back to Singapore and Wavell went on unescorted, protected only by Stonor's revolver. He had an hour's discussion with Bennett and an exhausted Heath, whose troops had taken further casualties as they withdrew. He also noted with concern that the Japanese were following up much more quickly than he had anticipated. He returned to Singapore down a trunk road choked with military vehicles and evacuee traffic. It had been a long day. This time Wavell's signal to the Chiefs of Staff was more realistic: 'Battle for Singapore will be close-run thing', he wrote.[19]

The ambush west of Gemas was a great success. Over 700 Japanese cyclist troops were in the ambush area when the bridge was blown behind them. Hundreds were killed. The success could have been even more complete, but the telephone line which snaked back a full three miles to the main Australian position was seen and cut by the Japanese so that the planned artillery programme against the lorries and tanks piling up beyond the blown bridge did not take place, nor did the Australian battalion headquarters know what was going on. The Japanese engineers had the bridge repaired in six hours and the following day they were attacking the main position with tanks, but were repulsed with considerable losses. It was the first notable Allied victory and led General Bennett to declare that his troops were confident that they would not only stop the Japanese but put them on the defensive. Alas, it was not to be.

Unknown to Percival the Japanese had now concentrated two divisions on the western route to the south. The coastal sector around Muar, which Bennett seems to have regarded as a subordinate concern, was now coming under pressure. Here the fresh but raw 45 Brigade was defending a 20-mile stretch of the Muar river and the coast on their left flank. This brigade, and its sister formation 44 Brigade which was to follow it to Malaya, were candidly not fit for operations against the Japanese. Both had been formed in July 1941 with battalions composed of one-third regulars, plus reservists and recruits. Over the next few months each battalion had been 'milked' of 250 men for the next Army expansion, receiving in December 250 recruits in their place. They had fewer than three regular officers per battalion.[20] Soon after, 45 Brigade left for Singapore and within three days of their arrival the men were moved up to the front. One of their commanding officers, admitting that he 'knew nothing whatever about this jungle warfare business' allowed a more experienced officer from a British battalion to make his dispositions for him.[21] This was the force that Gordon Bennett imagined was sufficiently skilful to conduct a fluid defence and arrange ambushes on the north bank of the Muar with the bridgeless river behind it. It was now under attack by the Japanese Imperial Guards Division. The town of Muar had been bombed daily from 11 January and on the 15th the Japanese overran the north bank defenders of the river line, then crossed to the south on captured boats, cut the Muar/Bakri road and took Muar town after some resistance, particularly from the Australian supporting battery. The defending unit, a Rajputana battalion, was no longer a fighting force: it had lost its commander, second-in-command and all its company commanders. A second battalion was cut off upstream and the reserve battalion could not break through the block which the Japanese had put across the road. The coastal defence line had been breached in two days. Bennett did not seem overly concerned by this reverse and sent the reserve battalion of his forward brigade from Gemas to restore the situation. He expected it back in a few days.

Percival found the news rather more disquieting, for he heard in addition that Japanese forces had been reported landing near Batu Pahat. This was the next major river line, over 20 miles south of Muar and more than twice that distance to the rear of the forward Australian troops. Must there be another demoralising withdrawal after the excellent fight-back the Australians had started? He hoped not, and motored up to north Johore on 17 January to confer with Bennett. He was concerned at the way heavy pressure was coming on both Bennett's widely separated fronts, and at the Australian's ability to control them with his small divisional staff. He decided to give III Corps responsibility for protecting Westforce's communications, including the threat at Batu Pahat, and ordered up the newly arrived 53 Brigade to deal with it. It was to be another formation thrown into an action for which it was ill-prepared. Percival's hope had been to train and acclimatise its men in Singapore before they saw any action. The following day he went forward to see Bennett again and decided on the next moves. He ordered an Australian battalion across from the east coast to strengthen the counter-attack force gathering at Bakri, south of Muar, replacing it with one from 53 Brigade. He could not risk weakening the east coast defences any further, as patrols had already reported Japanese moving down from north of Endau. Then there was the pressure on the trunk road itself which the Australian ambush had only temporarily halted. At least they had had some help from the RAF, freed temporarily from its convoy protection duties, which had bombed and strafed the Japanese columns now piling up between Gemas and Tampin. Percival's fateful decision to rely on these moves to hold the Japanese effectively sealed the fate of the reinforced but badly battered 45 Brigade. It was not until 18 January that he learned from his intelligence services that these green and already demoralised battalions had the full weight of the Imperial Guards Division ranged against them. By this time the enemy had got a block across the road to the east of Bakri, cutting off 45 brigade's line of retreat.

These were days of the most desperate anxiety and strain for Percival. Wavell's peremptory instructions had forced him into the role of operational Army Commander as well as GOC Malaya; the 'layered command' plan was complicating defence in depth. But the root cause of his predicament was the speed and resourcefulness of the Japanese advance. With their command of the air and the sea any position he occupied could be turned and his raw Indians were quite unfitted for any kind of mobile response. They knew nothing of the awful responsibilities of defending the outposts of empire which Percival had been left to cope with; their still-embryonic loyalties stretched no further than the regiment. With so few officers who could speak their language and engage their spirit, there was little loyalty to rely on. There would be the smell of mutiny among some of the Indians before the Johore campaign was through.[22] The GOC was working an 18-hour day throughout this period. He was rising at 6am, receiving the latest reports from the front, briefing his deputy for the War Council meeting, and then motoring the 80 miles to the front to confer with his commanders – the tired and increasingly resigned Heath, the unpredictable and edgy Bennett with his 'private line' back to Canberra and irritating habit of publicly blaming the earlier disasters on the lack of positive leadership among his fellow commanders. It was all rather alien to Percival's philosophy of positive cooperation. But Generals Barstow and Key were towers of strength. Then, with the gaps in the Johore defence somehow plugged, it would be back to Singapore for an evening conference with senior staff and perhaps government authorities before he drafted the daily report to the Supreme Commander. There were also responses to Wavell's queries to be drafted. Churchill was now bombarding the Supreme Commander with questions about the defence of Singapore itself, an objective with which the GOC had not originally been concerned. Then it was back to Flagstaff House for a very late meal served by his loyal and imperturbable Chinese staff, a momentary thought of Betty and the children in the no-less beleaguered England, and finally sleep at last, when the next day had already begun. No commander would have chosen to operate like this; few others ever needed to.

With the Muar flank turned, withdrawal was again inevitable. Percival issued the necessary orders to Gordon Bennett to get his 27 Brigade back down the trunk road to Kluang and took immediate steps to stop the Japanese incursions on the coast preventing him from doing so. Bennett himself was powerless to help the coastal forces, so Percival reverted temporarily to the vertical division of command that had been his original intention. III Corps was made responsible for the coastal sector, with Bennett commanding the force disposed on the central trunk road. However, the coastal situation had deteriorated dramatically, the Japanese 4th Guards Regiment (equivalent to a British brigade) had now got itself firmly in position astride 45 Brigade's escape route to the south and its efforts to break through the succession of road blocks were causing heavy casualties, more delay and enabling the Japanese tanks to close up on the brigade's rearguard. 53 Brigade was having no success in its attempts to break through to the beleaguered force from the south. One effort to do so was heavily bombed and strafed just as the troops were gathering on their start line. The commander of 45th Brigade, Duncan, was killed and the Australian battalion commander, Anderson, took over. He soon realised that his only course was to take the remnants of the brigade across country to safety. They received an air drop of food and medical supplies, destroyed their transport and heavy weapons, left their wounded to the care of the Japanese and struggled across country to the Allied lines. Nine hundred got back of the original 4,500. All 45 Brigade's battalion commanders had been killed. The brigade disappeared from Percival's order of battle. The Muar battle, in Percival's words, 'one of the most sanguinary of the Malayan campaign', had been an epic struggle. The brigade had held up the advance of the Imperial Guards for nearly a week, without tanks and with nothing to protect it from air attack. Its resistance had probably saved the central front.

Percival was already doing the tactical equivalent of trying to breathe in and breathe out at the same time: devising plans and issuing orders for the occupation of the next defence line which was to be held at all costs, while at the same time sending out secret instructions for the withdrawal to Singapore island if the line did not hold, and arrangements for its defence. Wavell had signalled him on the need for this on 19 January, generously offering to visit again if Percival thought that would help. Percival replied that he would be glad to see the Chief again and Wavell flew over from Java the following morning. He arrived at Flagstaff House just as the day's first bombing raid was starting. Three heavy raids struck the island that day during the discussions he had with Percival and his commanders over the continued defence of Johore and plans for carrying on the struggle on Singapore. The visit ended with Percival drafting his orders for a possible withdrawal to the island. These included the cautionary note: 'This instruction is for your personal information. It will not be reproduced and will be shown only to such senior officers and column commanders as you may think necessary. The intention is to fight and hold the enemy in Johore.' Percival signed the order. Wavell took a copy, put it in his briefcase and set off back to Java.

The Army now took up positions for holding the last defensible line on the Malayan peninsula. This followed the course of the lateral road running from Batu Pahat on the west coast, via Ayer Hitam, Kluang and Jemaluang, to Mersing on the east coast. It was a front of some 90 miles, which Percival's orders were to hold for as long as he could. There were still airfields at Batu Pahat, Kluang and Kahang and a string of observer posts to be denied to the enemy for as long as possible. Further reinforcements were due any day – a machine-gun battalion and 3,500 reinforcements from Australia and 44th Indian Brigade from Bombay. Then a few days later would come the main body of 18th British Division. Holding the line in Johore was an important part of the convoy defence plan. As from 24 January, Percival put Heath's III Corps in overall command of the three sectors, Eastforce, Westforce and 11th Indian Division on the west coast itself.

The withdrawal to Singapore island was beginning to seem inevitable, largely because the revival in the fortunes of the air force, on which all hopes were set, was not taking place. There had been momentary gleams of optimism, first with the action Pulford managed to arrange in support of the Australians at Gemas and against the Japanese landings at Muar, and particularly when the Hurricanes first took to the air. Within four days of the arrival of the convoy bearing the crated planes, 21 had been assembled and on 20 January, the day of Wavell's visit, they were in action for the first time with encouraging results. Twenty-seven Japanese bombers were caught unescorted on one of the bombing raids over Singapore. The Hurricanes shot down eight without loss; but their opponents did not make the same mistake again. Every subsequent bombing raid had its full escort of Zero fighters, against which the limitations of the Hurricanes were dismayingly apparent. Not in any event the most modern models and not modified for operation in the tropics, they were slower than the Zeros below 20,000 feet, less manoeuvrable at all heights and invariably seriously outnumbered. The day after their initial success five Hurricanes were shot down without loss to the Japanese. Thereafter the attrition continued; by the end of the week one-third had been destroyed. Maltby commented bitterly, 'the false hopes which had been placed in them reacted keenly when they were not realised'.[23] More Hurricanes were to take part in the fight, flown off the *Indomitable*; but only 15 of the promised 52 Hudson bombers and seven of the 18 Blenheims ever arrived.[24] It was all a grave disappointment to the defenders, particularly to Percival who had made such sacrifices to give the RAF Reinforcement Plan the chance to work.

It was Percival's view that the crisis of the campaign had now arrived. Within a few days his final major reinforcement, the bulk of 18th British Division, would be nearing Singapore. Holding the line until it had safely disembarked was the main aim; keeping it out of action until it was fully acclimatised and had done at least a little training would be the ideal. Somehow the Japanese bombers had to be kept away from the sea lanes until the convoy was in. He signalled Wavell: 'Hope you will press for continuous attacks by Fortress bombers on the Kuala Lumpur and Kuantan aerodromes. I feel that if we can drive back his fighters we can then deal with his bombers.'[25] More than anything else, it was the enemy's domination of the air that was breaking the spirit of his troops. If one experienced British major could write of the effects of being dive-bombed, 'I frankly admit that this experience shook my nerve and I was in very poor order for two or three hours afterwards,'[26] what must it have been like for the raw Indian teenage reinforcements? Percival hoped they would hold for long enough. By 24 January the brigade commander in Batu Pahat was asking for permission to withdraw: a Japanese force was threatening his position from the inland road and attempting to get around to the coast road to the south as well. He was told to hold on until the GOC could be briefed that afternoon; Percival had reserved any further withdrawal decision to himself. The following day there were road blocks already in position on the brigade's withdrawal route. When Percival heard of the strength of these and that Westforce had already repulsed heavy attacks on the trunk road and railway front, he agreed with a heavy heart to General Key's repeated request to withdraw and ordered Westforce to pull back ten miles to conform. Heath was told to ensure that Eastforce drew back as well. The last line of air stations would now fall to the Japanese. A withdrawal to the island itself was the only recourse remaining.

On the east coast the campaign ended without the disasters that had occurred elsewhere; but with the clearest illustration of why Percival had been for so long concerned about its vulnerability to seaborne assault. The Mersing beaches had been regarded as a likely Japanese landing option since long before the war and quite strong coast defences had been developed along them. The Japanese knew all about these and chose to make their landing further north at Endau on the extremity of the road that led directly down to Johore Bahru and their Singapore objective. The Japanese assault convoy was spotted at sea and on 26 January Pulford's remaining air resources were gathered to attack it. The ancient Vickers Vildebeeste bombers, little faster than a modern motor car, lumbered valiantly to the attack. Both Japanese transports were hit but the landing was not prevented and 11 Vildebeeste were lost as well as three of the accompanying fighters. 'Our Air Striking Force in Malaya, even such as it was, had now vanished', wrote Percival. The following evening the two ancient destroyers, *Vampire* and *Thanet*, sailed up from Singapore to attack the transports, but were met by a superior Japanese force and *Thanet* was sunk. That was the end of the naval striking force, such as it was, as well. Lightening this depressing episode was the action which followed it against the landing force which had pressed on southwards from Endau and was now beyond Mersing. 2/18 Battalion of 22nd Australian Brigade, with artillery support, put in such a successful ambush of elements of a Japanese infantry regiment that it was forced to withdraw. 22 Brigade then continued its own withdrawal in accordance with Percival's plan.

The Batu Pahat force withdrew at much the same time but was unable to break through the blocks established by the Japanese. Percival had delayed authorising the pull-out just too long. General Key hastily organised a force from 53 Brigade to attempt to break through to them from the south. This was ambushed, badly mauled and dissolved in some confusion. Conscious that his force was cut off and without relief, the Batu Pahat force commander did what was becoming a despairing routine against these Japanese tactics – he destroyed his guns and transport and ordered his units to make their way south as best they could across country. One exhausted column of 1,200 men, guided by local police, got through to Allied lines two days later. The remainder, blocked by a river they could not ford, were trapped in the two-mile coastal strip until Percival got to hear of their plight and arranged their evacuation by sea on four successive nights. Batu Pahat had been the base of the coastal flotilla and this successful evacuation of 2,700 men to Singapore was the only service that the residual British sea power in Malaya was able to perform for the hard-pressed Army; but it saved it from another major disaster. However, even as the naval rescue was being hurriedly put together, disaster was overtaking Westforce.

Throughout this traumatic period Percival had been keeping Wavell in touch with the deepening crisis. On 26 January he had written, 'Consider general situation becoming grave . . . may be driven back into the Island within a week.' The following day, as the Japanese trapped a second brigade and the air force sustained further losses over the east coast land-ings, he wrote, 'Very critical situation has developed . . . We are going to be a bit thin on the Island unless we can get all remaining troops back.' Wavell now gave him the discretion to withdraw to Singapore if he con-sidered it advisable. Early the following morning Percival met Heath and Bennett at III Corps headquarters. It was no longer a question of whether, but when, the move onto the island would occur. Both he and his Corps Commander considered 11th Division would be unable to hold the enemy on the west coast any longer and that to attempt a further defence in south Johore would hazard the whole force. They were right; Yamashita had high hopes of cutting off III Corps by a rapid west coast advance down to Skudai in the division's rear.[27] Although the Japanese commander did not manage this, the plans for an accelerated withdrawal on the night of 30–31 January were almost put at hazard by the situation of Westforce on the central front.

27th Australian Brigade, with 2nd Gordons under command, was fighting a number of local engagements as it withdrew along the trunk road. On the railway front it was a different story; not for nothing is withdrawal described as the most difficult operation of war. 8 and 22 Brigades of 9th Indian Division were withdrawing down the railway corridor, in conformity with the Australians a few miles away, when a series of errors, impossible to excuse in an experienced if very battle-weary commander,[28] allowed a gap to develop between the forward brigade, 22nd, and 8th which was supporting it. A flank move through estate roads enabled the Japanese to penetrate the gap. When General Barstow, the divisional commander, discovered the mistake he went forward to find the forward brigade, but was ambushed and killed. This was a grievous loss to Percival and the Army; Barstow was a very able commander and, moreover, one of the few who seemed to get on well with Bennett. After one effort to break through the Japanese block, 22 Brigade took to the jungle west of the railway in a desperate effort to rejoin the rest of the withdrawing division. Several days and nights of struggle through difficult country encumbered by their wounded ended when the brigade commander and the remnant of his brigade still under command, surrendered to the Japanese. It was a tragic affair. Some of the troops had fought well right to the end; some were in no fit state to fight and had refused to go on; some had gone over to the enemy in a formed body.[29] Self-preservation seemed the only concern of the rest of the withdrawing force which continued its move south despite the plight of 22 Brigade. Percival delayed the final withdrawal and sent out air and ground reconnaissance to try to locate the brigade, but without success. Some parties did struggle through to the coast near Johore Bahru and were later rescued by small boats.

The withdrawal to Singapore island was remarkably successful. The convergence of the road and rail routes on Johore Bahru and the narrow 1,100-yard Causeway linking it with Singapore made this an obvious choke-point and target for the Japanese bombers. Despite a brilliant moon on the night of the main crossing there was little interference from the air and the Japanese ground forces did not follow up closely after the failure of their repeated attacks along the trunk road 30-odd miles north of Johore. Maximum air defence was arranged around the Causeway and the traffic control arrangements worked smoothly. By 7am on 31 January the outer bridgehead composed of the Australians from Mersing were making their way across to Singapore, played over by the two remaining Argylls pipers. The Gordons followed them and then the Argylls themselves, whose shrunken battalion of 250 men formed the inner bridgehead. After they were safely across, the Causeway was blown. Percival's plans to protect the Naval Base had failed; all that now separated it from the Japanese was the mile-wide eastern channel of the Johore Strait.

THE FANTASY FORTRESS

'Of all the failings in Malaya certainly the most outstanding in the eyes both of the troops who fought there and the world at large, was the failure of Singapore as a fortress. The explanation is that Singapore was not a fortress, though this was a thing which few were allowed to know, or if they knew, to admit: for this would have been imperial heresy.'

Lieutenant Colonel FRN Cobley, GSO1 Malaya Command,
Changi Jail, 1942

In 1959 General Lord Ismay was drafting his memoirs of the momentous years when he had been Churchill's wartime chief of staff and a member, with Generals Hollis and Jacob, of the triumvirate which the Prime Minister dubbed 'My Secret Circle'. Ismay sent his draft to Jacob for comment. In one particular chapter he had written: 'I had always envisaged that Singapore was a self-contained fortress.' About this Jacob had recorded the comment, 'Had you really? I never had. After all the naval base was actually between the island and the mainland. The COS had always said that Singapore was untenable if the mainland was lost.'[1] There, in a nutshell, was the enormity of the task with which Percival was now faced. He was to defend the island which the Chiefs of Staff regarded as indefensible. General Kennedy, the Director of Military Operations, confirms what the military advice provided to Churchill had been. 'Our view, however,' his memoirs recorded, 'was that the "last ditch" would have to be on the mainland in Johore, and not on Singapore Island. The island had never been considered defensible from close attack.'[2] Needless to say, Ismay later removed the erroneous assumption from his draft. But the change in strategy was more fundamental than even these views indicated. These military judgements were essentially about the defensibility of the Naval Base on Singapore, not the whole of the island. As another of Percival's staff officers later put it: 'It does not seem to be realised generally that the object of the military forces in MALAYA was "in cooperation with the Navy and Air Force to defend the Naval Base at SINGAPORE" and not the island of SINGAPORE itself.'[3]

However, for Percival all this was now in the past, as was the possibility of a complete strategic withdrawal to a base elsewhere once Malaya was lost. It had been the view in the War Office, 'that the forces at Singapore, or as many of them as could be extricated, would be better employed in holding the islands to the southward'.[4] This mattered not. Churchill had decided, for political reasons rather than military, that the island was to be defended. Australian anxieties had to be addressed. Prime Minister Curtin had got wind of the Whitehall discussions of a possible abandonment of Singapore and transfer of reinforcements to Burma. This would be an 'inexcusable betrayal', Curtin cabled to Churchill. Besides, with the Americans resisting stoutly in the Philippines, the British could not be seen to be withdrawing. Churchill, 'stuck to his view that Singapore Island should be held to the last man; and Wavell acquiesced'.[5]

Completing Percival's discomfiture was the common belief that Singapore was indeed a 'fortress'. Like Penang, it had been given that designation merely on account of having a protected harbour; but it never had been, nor ever could be, a fortress in the conventional sense. The channel which separated it from Malaya was so narrow that the Naval Base and the whole island could be dominated by artillery based in Johore and indeed aircraft located much further north. This was why he had advocated the defence of the northern 'back door' as long ago as 1937; a strategic principle which the Chiefs of Staff had long since accepted. The concept of 'fortress Singapore' was as flawed as that of a 'chocolate teapot'. Yet the Prime Minister, expert on fortress warfare that he was (and admired biographer of his ancestor Marlborough who never 'besieged a fortress that he did not take'), and surrounded by military staff who were only too aware of the situation, seemed to believe that Singapore was prepared for all-round fortress defence. 'The possibility of Singapore having no landward defences no more entered my mind than that of a battleship being launched without a bottom',[6] was his response to the news from Wavell that there were only embryonic defences on the north coast. Wavell explained that, 'Until quite recently all plans based on . . . holding land attack in Johore or further north'. It scarcely seems credible that Dill (whose removal from office had much to do with his disagreements with Churchill over Malaya's defence and who understood the local situation perfectly), Kennedy, Jacob, or even new-man-in-post CIGS Brooke, should not, at some stage, have disabused the Prime Minister of the fortress illusion which he had expressed with great clarity in his minute to General Ismay as long ago as 10 September 1940.[7]

Whatever those in charge of Britain's strategic planning knew or did not know, for the man in the street (and this term included the troops in Malaya), Singapore was a 'fortress'. British pre-war propaganda had been directed to convincing the Japanese of the impregnability of her position in the area and 'fortress Singapore' was part of that campaign. 'Fortress' was the military label for the island, used commonly by Whitehall and the local leaders alike. The nation and the Press believed it; perhaps Churchill too had come to believe his own government's propaganda.

The island which Percival was now charged with defending is much the same size and shape as the Isle of Wight. It is separated from Malaya by a shallow, mile-wide channel and in 1941 its northern coast was fringed with mangrove swamps which created problems for the construction of defences and impeded the fire of those holding them. The island's aerodromes, water supply and most of its vital military installations were in the north or centre, within artillery range of the mainland. At the apex of its diamond shape lay the 1,100-yard Causeway which carried the road, railway and water pipeline from Johore; to the south lay the port and city with a peacetime population of about half a million, but now swollen with refugees to twice that number. In the south also were the major gun emplacements and defences designed to protect the Naval Base from a seaborne assault. The guns did indeed point out to sea, though many had all-round traverse and could fire northwards; but their flat trajectory and provisioning almost exclusively with armour piercing ammunition made them less than ideal for engaging inland targets. Why indeed did they need to? Once an enemy was in possession of Johore, the Naval Base was not only untenable, but useless. It was for this reason that Percival had not considered developing any north shore defences before the war, or in the early days of the campaign when there was still a serious prospect of holding the Japanese in the north and the withdrawal for an island siege had not been determined.

Percival's distaste for fixed defences went rather further than those with which the Prime Minister's imagination had castellated the island's northern shores. His Chief Engineer, Brigadier Ivan Simson, has since blamed his GOC for the consequences of not agreeing to construct defences in north Johore and elsewhere in Malaya.[8] This apparent failing has become part of the folklore of the campaign. During his short period of pre-war command, Percival had given a whole morning to a consideration of Simson's proposals for fixed defences. He had also agreed unhesitatingly to Simson's recommendations for the condensing into a single pamphlet and immediate issue by the Chief Engineer himself to all formations, of a series of War Office instructions on defence methods against tanks; he even went 'thoroughly into the letter and pamphlet' himself. The instructions had apparently lain unnoticed in Malaya Command until Simson unearthed them. But on the fixed defences which Simson was proposing he was much less keen, as indeed was his Commander-in-Chief. Brooke Popham had declared: 'Not having more defences on West side of Malaya and North side of island was a problem of morale and man-hours. I was always on my guard against the fortress complex.'[9] On 26 December Simson had called on Percival at 11.30pm, just as the GOC was about to retire for the night, to pass on a request

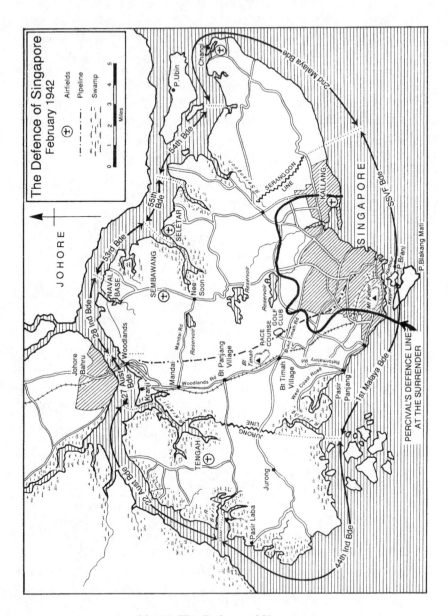

Map 7. The Defence of Singapore

from General Heath for the construction of 'successive lines of defence by the time he had retreated by stages to the Johore area',[10] and also to argue his own case for the construction of fixed defences on the northern coast of Singapore. According to Simson, whose account of this meeting is the only one we have, the discussion lasted two and a half hours, during all of which time Percival apparently advanced only one reason for rejecting the requests: 'Defences are bad for morale – for both troops and civilians.'[11] This sentence became a mantra for Percival's critics; yet consider the circumstances. At the time of this late-night meeting, 11th Division had only just crossed the Perak River; it had yet to mount a defence of the immensely strong position at Kampar; reinforcements for the theatre were expected soon. What message would have been passed to troops and civilians alike if the Army engineers had at that moment been concentrated to build fixed defences 200 miles to the south in north Johore? Percival could hardly have told Simson that he was already disturbed by Heath's wish for a clean break and long withdrawal from the north. Besides, there were the many demolition and denial tasks to which the sappers were already fully committed, as Simson recognised.

As to the proposal for defences on Singapore island, Percival had the same reluctance on grounds of morale. It would be a further 12 days before the Slim River disaster shattered his plans, and with fresh troops little more than a week away, a decision for large-scale overt preparations for a siege of Singapore itself seemed ill-advised, though he was aware of the need to think ahead. Some days earlier Percival had instructed Keith Simmons to 'arrange for reconnaissance of the north shore of Singapore Island to select positions for the defence of possible landing places.'[12] As late as mid-January, when Wavell was giving Percival instructions for the withdrawal to the island, the morale factor was clearly in the Supreme Commander's mind as well. 'Your preparations must of course be kept *entirely secret*', he wrote. 'Under cover of selecting positions for garrison of island to prevent infiltration of small parties you can . . . undertake some preparation such as obstacles or clearances, but make it clear to everyone that battle is to be fought out in Johore without thought of retreat.'[13] By then Percival had already given orders for the preparation of the northern defences 'to be undertaken at once as an urgent measure'.

Thereafter the progress in the development of the defences was limited by the very morale factor about which Percival was so concerned: it was difficult to get a labour force of frightened locals together, and harder still to keep them at their work under the bombing and shelling. Megan Spooner recorded that mere gunnery practice caused the Tamils who were camouflaging her roof to disappear, never to return.[14] That was before the withdrawal to the island, by which time the Japanese bombing had greatly increased in intensity, with two or three raids by formations of 27 to 54 bombers becoming a daily occurrence. In these circumstances practically all the native labour disappeared. Percival also gave priority to the repair of the Singapore airstrips over his defence works until the position of the defending squadrons became so desperate that they were withdrawn to Java. By this stage the original Hurricanes had been supplemented by a further 48, of the latest type, flown off the *Indomitable*. These did splendid work but were fatally outnumbered (at this time the Japanese were maintaining in Malaya a force of 250 bombers and 150 fighters) and their airstrips were precariously placed because of the increased bombing and shelling. At Percival's urgent request one Hurricane squadron was left on the island after Wavell had ordered the departure of the rest, as much for morale reasons as anything else. All the airfields on the island, except the civil one at Kallang in the south, were subject to observed artillery fire from Johore.

   In preparing for the final, forlorn phase of the campaign, for which Percival correctly reckoned he would have about a week's grace before the Japanese attacked, he had two important issues to address. Where would the Japanese mount their assault and how best could he defend against it? So great was their superiority in the air and at sea and so considerable the moral ascendancy they had established that Percival considered no part of the island's coastline safe. The Official History, following the account in Wavell's despatch, records that at their meeting on 20 January Wavell had advised Percival that he thought the Japanese would attack the north-west of the island and suggested that he should dispose his freshest troops, 18th Division, there to meet them. Kirby records that Percival believed the attack would come in the north-east and so disposed 18th Division there.[15] Percival's own accounts contradict this and confirm that, 'As regards the attack from the mainland, everything pointed to this developing from the west', though he did consider the possibility of a subordinate attack developing down the Johore river to the Changi area.[16] After the war, Percival wrote to Kirby and admitted that the statement that 'he expected the Japanese attack to be made in the north west was incorrect and based on hindsight.'[17] It would not have been surprising if his memory had failed him after the years of incarceration, but the issue is not nearly as clear-cut as this 'Wavell was right, Percival was wrong' interpretation would suggest.

   Both General Keith Simmons, to whom Percival had given the task of recommending the detailed dispositions for the defence, and the experienced Brigadier Paris whom he had appointed to help him, believed the attack would come on the north-west of the island.[18] Percival was consequently very concerned about this possibility and also about the threat of a larger sea-borne hook from the Straits of Malacca, as well as a thrust in the north-east. Nor were Wavell's recommendations quite as prescriptive as his *Despatch* suggests. His confirmatory note to Percival after the visit merely says, 'My idea of the best layout of the defences would be for the Australian Division and the 18th Division each to take one of the eastern or western sectors'.[19] Percival promulgated his plans for the defence of the island on 23 January when his old First World War Division, the 18th, was still on the high seas and a week away from a safe disembarkation. All he knew for certain was that it had been at sea for many weeks, was only partially trained (and that for the Middle East), and would have little time to get acclimatised. Might he not have considered this too risky a resource to put in the area of likeliest assault, preferring the Australians who were fully trained, battle-tested and available?

There is the strongest evidence that on 29 January, the day when the main body of 18th Division began its disembarkation at the bomb-pocked and debris-strewn dockside, Percival believed the attack would come in the north-west, the Australians' sector. That day he chaired a conference attended by Admiral Layton, Heath and all the divisional commanders. He spoke with a large map at his side. One of his staff officers, Lieutenant Colonel Ashworth, recalled the occasion: 'I well remember his short appreciation of the probable Japanese plan of attack. The GOC did in fact point to a place on the map and turning to the Comd AIF he said, "I think this is the most probable place for the enemy attack" . . . Actually when the attack did come the enemy had selected the exact place pointed out by the GOC.'[20]

The following day Wavell arrived on another visit, accompanied by Air Marshal Pierce, his new Air Chief, fresh from the resource-swollen Bomber Command and rather shaken at the paucity of his air resources in ABDACOM. There was no one at Kallang airport to meet them, Wavell's biographer records, perhaps implying a disorganised headquarters at Malaya Command. The fault rather lay with Wavell's Dutch pilot who, on this occasion as on his chief's final visit, misjudged the timing of the journey and arrived in daylight, against all advice, as there were too many Japanese aircraft about.[21] There was a brief tri-Service conference with the shipless Admiral Spooner, the almost planeless Air Marshal Pulford[22] and the exhausted Percival, still making the daily journey up to Johore to command the battle and returning to Singapore each evening to do his work as GOC. The situation was explained to Wavell. The plans were outlined: the last of the troops in Malaya would withdraw that night to their assigned positions on the island. Wavell accepted Percival's dispositions. He then went up to Johore to see Heath, whom he found 'taut and grey with fatigue', and Gordon Bennett who was 'edgy and abrupt'. He returned again to Percival's headquarters, later saw Shenton Thomas at Government House who had at last agreed to the imposition of martial law in Singapore, and then returned to Java. He had seen nothing to alter his view, expressed privately to Churchill ten days earlier, that he doubted the island could be held for long once Johore was lost, nor anything to gainsay the clear evidence of the Japanese' overwhelming superiority which they were using with great skill and boldness.

Once the Army had withdrawn to the island, Percival took operational command of the garrison and became the martial law administrator. Morale was now a critical problem. The clear evidence of the withdrawal of the Air Force and the evacuation of the Naval Base were already denting the resolve of the tired troops. Moreover, to quote an Australian view, 'It did not take long for the average officer or man to discover that the Fortress was in no fit state to resist a determined attack from an enemy possessing the ground and air resources and the fighting calibre of the Japanese.'[23] They probably did not have the detachment to appreciate, as did the Australian representative on the War Council, Mr Bowden, that 'with the naval base and all natural resources in Malaya gone', Singapore had, 'nothing more than sentimental value'. That was plainly true. Percival had sat silent in the War Council meeting when Mr Bowden made these remarks. But fighting on was still imperative. Percival's stand was occupying the full attention of three Japanese divisions (he thought even more) and a large air force. He was buying time for Churchill and the longer he could hold out, the better for the Allied cause.

Once again, he had no great rallying cry to which his motley forces could eagerly respond, but he wished to scotch all rumours of a withdrawal and his press release reflected this determination:

> The battle of Malaya has come to an end and the battle of Singapore has started. For nearly two months our troops have fought an enemy on the mainland who has had the advantage of great air superiority and considerable freedom of movement by sea.
>
> Our task has been to impose losses on the enemy and to gain time to enable the forces of the Allies to be concentrated for this struggle in the Far East. Today we stand beleaguered in our Island fortress. Our task is to hold this fortress until help can come – as assuredly it will come. This we are determined to do. . . .[24]

The GOC also held a press conference to squash the rumours and generate confidence in a determined defence. It was not a success. The departure of the RAF squadrons, anti-aircraft regiments and unwanted support troops took some explaining, as did the difficulties with civil labour which was evaporating from docks, airfields and the native-crewed ships in the harbour. The venue for the press conference was a long, dark room and the overburdened staff had plainly been taken by surprise at the numbers attending. Chairs had to be brought in hurriedly from elsewhere; but many of the Press people still had to stand. Percival was never at his best on large, public occasions and now, wearied by a month of constant crisis, he could do little to lift the mood of depression and foreboding which gripped his audience when he called for whole-hearted cooperation between military and civilian in the defence of Singapore. As

The Times correspondent Ian Morrison wryly noted, 'One of the minor lessons of the war in Malaya is the folly of public pronouncements unless the speaker really has something to say'.

The scorched-earth policy was making things even worse; it seemed the most blatant public indication that the Army was giving up. Percival did his best to postpone the most visible of the wrecking activities until the last possible moment. The War Office had asked for his personal assurance that if the worst came to the worst, nothing of military value would be left intact for the enemy on Singapore island. He could give no such guarantee: coast guns, for example, could not be destroyed until the last minute, nor could the 11,800 mustard gas shells which had to be kep for possible reprisal use; installations near hospitals could not be blown up. 'The fact is', he wrote, 'you cannot fight and destroy simultaneously with 100 per cent efficiency in both.' A detailed scorched-earth policy was nevertheless worked out and instructions issued, but it was all very time-consuming and took soldiers away from defence work. There were similar problems on the civil side, where Simson was arranging for the destruction of industrial installations, not without opposition from their owners.

Some of the help of which Percival's press release had spoken was now on the island. Between 24 and 29 January three convoys had docked, the first carrying the Australian 2/4th Machine Gun (MG) Battalion and 3,500 reinforcements for Bennett's Division, the second bringing 44th Indian Infantry Brigade and the third, as we have noted, bringing the bulk of 18th British Division and also a pathetic last-minute attempt at an armoured reinforcement – 18 light tanks collected from various training establishments in India. Some went straight into workshops and never took to the road. However, the troops constituted a significant reinforcement – if only in quantitative terms, for they were almost all inappropriately and inadequately trained. Many of them had already suffered something of an ordeal by sea. The 2/4 MG Battalion had embarked at Darwin, had then journeyed clockwise, away from their destination, trans-shipping at Port Moresby, taking on the raw reinforcements at Sydney and later standing infuriatingly at anchor off their home port of Fremantle, with no shore leave allowed, after virtually circumnavigating their continent. The indiscipline which resulted in this trained unit boded ill for their behaviour, and that of the raw recruits travelling with them, when they finally came under Japanese fire. Then came 18th Division, with Percival's fondly remembered 54th brigade, together with the 55th, after their astonishing 20,000-mile voyage which had begun the previous October. Finally, on 5 February, came the last convoy of Indian reinforcements, weapons and support units for the 18th Division. Despite the efforts at secrecy and security, Japanese dive bombers attacked the convoy and managed to sink its slowest ship, *Empress of Asia*. It was a sad end to a successful convoy programme for which Percival had risked so much. The ship's human cargo was rescued, but the weapons and equipment went down with her.

These were particularly unwelcome losses for the GOC, coming on top of those suffered by III Indian Corps during the long withdrawal down Malaya which Lieutenant Colonel Ashmore described as 'absolutely staggering'. His notes recorded that the Corps had lost 30,000 rifles, 1,500 light machine guns, 70 per cent of the units' scale of anti-tank rifles and 1,000 15-cwt trucks, with the result that 'the small and quite inadequate reserves were wholly depleted in the first ten days of the campaign'.[25] The sinking of the *Empress of Asia* meant that Percival could not arm all the men in the expanded force of Chinese irregulars (Dalforce) with which he was hoping to augment his defence, and had to rely on other units of 18th Division for the re-equipping of 53 Brigade.

In the week that Percival guessed he would have before the Japanese were ready to attack, there were a multitude of things to do. He had first to set about the reorganisation and re-equipment of his Army, part battered, weary and demoralised, part raw and untested. He appointed some new commanders at brigade and unit level, broke up 9th Division and used its remaining brigade to bring 11th Division up to strength. The loss of 22 Brigade also compelled him to put 18th Division, which he had hoped to keep as his Command Reserve, into III Corps. He was left with only the weak two-battalion 12 Brigade as his Command Reserve, with 6/15 Brigade as the III Corps reserve. The Australian brigades, three of whose six battalions were still virtually intact, were brought up to strength with the new recruits and reinforced by the companies of the MG battalion. He also ordered back to the fighting units all junior staff officers who could be spared and ensured that the support units were in a position to defend themselves. The garrison totalled between 90,000 and 100,000 men, but combat troops formed a much lower total, and trained and reliable ones a lower figure still. In simple numerical terms it was a substantial force, but the numbers concealed the gravest weaknesses.

Percival divided the island for defence purposes into three areas. Northern Area, covering all the north-east coast from east of the severed Causeway down to Changi, was held by Heath's III Corps. Western Area included the Causeway itself and all of the west coast and was the responsibility of Bennett's 8th Australian Division, strengthened by the newly arrived 44th Indian Infantry Brigade. Southern Area covered virtually all the south coast of the island and was held by Keith Simmons' fortress troops, the two Malaya brigades and the Volunteer Forces. Thus the north-east coast was now the more heavily defended with four brigades along the coast, against the three in the north-west; but it was a strange mix – two brigades had seen heavy fighting and two were straight off the boat. Of Bennett's three brigades, two had fought successful actions on the mainland; but each of these had one battalion which had absorbed large numbers of the rawest reinforcements and all battalions had taken some of these recruits, from which an extra platoon had been formed in each company. Such men had no place at the front; some had reputedly never handled a rifle. Bennett's third brigade, the Indians, were new and green. As a reserve he had only two battalions, one raw and one of scratch support troops. These dispositions, and that of the artillery supporting them reflected Percival's growing belief that the Japanese assault would come on his north-eastern flank.

In considering the second of his defence problems, how to deal with the Japanese assault when it came, Percival had an option fraught with difficulties. He could either hold the coastline in strength and attempt to repel the enemy before they had a chance to get ashore, or else hold back a large part of his force as a mobile reserve to drive back the Japanese once their main assault area had been determined. He could not do the first adequately since he had too few troops for all 70-odd miles of coastline, much of which, especially in the north-west, was too swampy and broken by rivers and creeks to be held at the waterline. On the other hand, the second alternative was hardly viable, since the close nature of the country favoured the enemy and the positions lacked depth because many of the vital military dumps and depots, and indeed the water reservoirs, lay in the centre of the island. Besides, to allow the Japanese to get a foothold in the fortress would have a demoralising effect on troops and citizens alike. He settled for a modified version of the first alternative with the troops occupying previously reconnoitred defended localities along the coast and with local mobile reserves ready for counter-attack. He intended to create fresh reserves once the direction of the main Japanese attack was certain. In trying to defend everywhere, he was not strong enough anywhere; but being faced by an enemy who had total command of air and sea and defending what the Chiefs of Staff recognised was indefensible, it was clear that any plan could be readily countered by his opponent.

The development of the Japanese strategy for the capture of Singapore clearly exemplified this advantage. In the first plan which Yamashita's staff devised in mid-January, they envisaged a simultaneous three-division assault along a broad front from east of the Naval Base, right across the Johore Strait to the west of the island. Subsequently intelligence reports of the strength of Percival's defences in the Northern Area and a more realistic appraisal of their own strength caused the Japanese to revert to the pre-war plan for a main two-divisional assault in the north-west, with diversionary moves in the north-east by Nishimura's Imperial Guards Division. They were fully aware of the weakness of the field defences in their chosen sector and reckoned on their artillery barrage crushing these easily, forcing Percival to make his last stand on the Jurong Line.[26] To keep his opponent guessing, Yamashita had cleared the population from

a ten-mile strip along the Johore Strait and had ordered 5th and 18th
Divisions to assemble well back from the coast.

The Jurong Line was one of two 'switch lines' which were of particular
importance for the defence. It consisted of a narrow neck of land between
the headwaters of the Kranji and Jurong rivers which ran respectively
north and south from their inland source, almost severing the western
quarter of the island from the rest. Percival had recognised the importance
of this position before the campaign started and it had been cleared of
cover, though defence arrangements along it were now the responsibility
of the Area Commander, General Bennett. However, the Australian
'would give no consideration whatsoever to the preparation of the
Kranji–Jurong Line, nor its incorporation in any plan', his Chief of Staff,
Colonel Thyer recorded. Thyer thought the line so important that he
authorised a reconnaissance and defence plan of the area himself, without
the knowledge of his commander. When Bennett heard of this he flared
up, declaring 'it was a defensive line, and went into a tantrum about the
withdrawal complex'.[27] The construction of defence works along the
Jurong Line was the responsibility of a Chinese contractor but there were
problems in feeding his workers who also disappeared as soon as Japanese
aircraft were sighted.[28] As usual, Bennett had his headquarters well
behind the front, in the corner of his Area furthest from the troops: a mile
further east and it would have been outside his area altogether. Maxwell's
27 Brigade headquarters was close to his divisional commander's and
well behind his troops. Taylor's 22 Brigade headquarters and that of
Ballantine, commanding the 44 Indian Brigade, on the Australians' left
flank, were both well sited.

The Japanese artillery barrage which began on 5 February seemed to
confirm Percival's fears of an attack in the north-east, since it was directed
against the 18th Division area. The Japanese even managed to shell
Government House that day, at a range of 24,000 yards while Percival was
visiting 44 Brigade with Bennett, stressing to the Australian the importance of counter-attack if the enemy got ashore. From his vantage point in
the west he had the mortification of seeing the *Empress of Asia* sinking in
flames, the last vessel of the final convoy. That evening he visited the survivors at the docks. The following morning his fears seemed to be
confirmed by a reconnaissance report of a Japanese invasion convoy
anchored off the Anambas islands north-east of Singapore. Wavell's headquarters confirmed that they believed its destination was elsewhere; but
they had been wrong before.[29] On 7 February the artillery increased its
fire on 18th Division and extended its range to the outer suburbs of the
city. In the early hours of 8 February, Percival signalled Wavell, 'Present
indications show main enemy strength north of Pulau Ubin.' This was an
island off the north-east coast which the Japanese had occupied during the
night.

Percival had ordered Heath and Bennett to send night patrols across into Johore to discover what they could about Japanese locations and strengths. He had great difficulty in getting Bennett to comply; indeed one of Percival's staff noted that 'there were no records of such patrols having operated' on the Australian front.[30] This was not quite true; 27 Brigade sent none over, but at the eleventh hour 22 Brigade did. Two patrols returned in the early hours of 8 February with the news that large enemy concentrations had gathered in the rubber plantations opposite the western shores of the island, though no landing craft were seen. By this stage Percival's intelligence staff were concluding from various indications that the main attack might well be in the north-west. This vital confirmatory information was with HQ 22 Brigade at dawn on the 8th, but Bennett knew nothing of it when Percival visited him at about midday and the information was not passed to Percival's staff until about 3.45 that afternoon.[31] It was then too late for any significant counter-action: the main Japanese artillery bombardment, supported by aerial bombing, had already begun on the Australian front. At 10.45pm that night Percival's staff received a report from Bennett's headquarters to the effect that the artillery fire was continuing but reports from the brigades indicated, 'Everyone vigilant and quite happy. The heavy fire was . . . doing no harm to speak of.' Twenty-six minutes later the next report came in: the Japanese had landed and 22 Brigade's 'forward positions pushed out.'[32] This rearward movement was perhaps aided by a brigade instruction, quite contrary to Percival's orders to Bennett, that if strongly attacked, the forward posts should fall back on the company and then the battalion headquarters positions. Soon it was clear that the Japanese were ashore along the entire frontage of 22 Brigade. The first of the 21 battalions of the Japanese 5th and 18th Divisions were struggling forward towards their first objective, Tengah airfield. The Australians inflicted considerable losses on the first waves of the assault, but they were swamped by its scale and intensity. The Japanese lodgement on Singapore was rapidly secured.

A GRIEVOUS AND
SHAMEFUL BLOW

'There must at this stage be no thought of saving the troops or sparing the population. The battle must be fought to the bitter end at all costs. The 18th Division has a chance to make its name in history. Commanders and senior officers should die with their troops. The honour of the British Empire and of the British Army is at stake.'

Prime Minister to General Wavell, 10 February 1942

It was midnight before Taylor had a clear picture of the critical situation on his brigade's front and made an urgent call to Bennett for reinforcements. In the course of the night Bennett sent him his two available reserve battalions. When Percival got the news of the Japanese landing, he asked for the remaining Hurricane squadron to be ready at first light and, after confirming in the morning that the Northern Area was quiet, he allocated 12 Brigade, his Command Reserve, to Bennett and ordered it to the Jurong Line. The final heroic action of the Hurricanes illustrates the intensity of the aerial onslaught that the troops were now suffering. The first sortie of eight fighters engaged 84 Japanese planes and later sorties faced similar odds. They had successes but the task was hopeless. Maltby, Pulford's deputy, visited the squadron, reduced to six serviceable fighters, that evening and ordered their evacuation to Sumatra at first light. During the campaign the RAF had lost virtually its entire original air strength; the cost in fighters was 122 Buffaloes and 45 Hurricanes.[1] What had been intended as the main defence of Singapore had disappeared.

In the afternoon, Percival went forward to confer with Bennett and confirmed that the other Australian brigade, 27th, was to remain defending the Kranji/Causeway area while the rest of Bennett's reinforced command, 12th Indian, 22nd Australian and 44th Indian brigades, would hold the Jurong switch line. He also allocated 6/15 Brigade, withdrawn from III Corps, to Bennett and brought it forward to the Racecourse area. Since the Jurong Line was 4,000 yards in length rather than the 40,000 yards of coastline originally defended by the Western Area troops, and now had four brigades allocated to it, there was some hope of the front being stabilised, at least temporarily. Percival also ordered the destruction of the oil storage tanks near the Causeway and the final demolitions in the Naval Base which Admiral Spooner had left to the Army. This done, he returned to his headquarters and worked out a plan for a shorter perimeter defence in case the Japanese broke through the switch line and got across the Bukit Timah road. This perimeter would cover the airport at Kallang, the MacRitchie and Pierce water reservoirs and the important military depots near Bukit Timah. Behind it would lie the city. The plan was issued as a 'secret and personal' instruction, Percival explained, 'so that responsible senior officers might know my intentions in case the situation developed too rapidly for further orders to be issued'. However, when General Bennett received the instruction he immediately issued the gist of it as an operation order to his brigadiers. This was an inexplicable action by a commander who customarily railed against anything which might cause his subordinates to 'look over their shoulders'. It had disastrous consequences.

It was not long before the other Australian brigade, Maxwell's 27th, exacerbated the problems in Bennett's Western Area. Brigadier Maxwell was already concerned about his left flank being uncovered, and when the Imperial Guards Division launched their assault on his sector on the evening of the 9th he allowed his battalions to pull back, despite the heavy casualties that the Japanese assault force had taken from the defenders' fire and the burning oil of the demolitions. With his headquarters six miles behind his battalion positions on an island only ten miles deep, Maxwell was out of touch with the real situation and his unauthorised withdrawal endangered both the flank of the Jurong Line along which the rest of the reinforced division was now disposed, as well as that of the Indian brigade to the east of the Causeway. At this point Brigadier Taylor received Bennett's operation instruction for the occupation of the inner perimeter and pulled the remains of 22 Brigade back from its sector of the switch line. The two Indian brigades to his south took similar action when they received their copies of Bennett's instruction; both had suffered some bombing but neither had been attacked. The Causeway area and almost five miles of the road south had been given up. Tengah airfield and the Jurong Line had been surrendered. The Japanese now held a substantial section of the island and were close to the important depots. The battle for Singapore was effectively lost, as it inevitably would be, but a good deal earlier than Percival had hoped.

Wavell's arrival in Singapore on 10 February, for his final visit, caused some surprise, as Percival had signalled him advising that the flight was unsafe. Again the Dutch pilot arrived in daylight. Wavell wisely flew by Catalina, as Kallang airport was now 'deserted, its hangars gutted, the landing strips pitted by bomb craters'. During the journey to Percival's headquarters it became clear to the Supreme Commander that the GOC was struggling with rather more than simply tactical errors on the part of the Australians. 'We had already passed groups of Australian troops streaming towards the harbour, shouting that the fighting was over and that they were clearing out', recalled one of Wavell's staff.[2] Discipline and morale were cracking; troops were deserting. Wavell found Percival 'composed, very tired, and presenting a controlled stoicism in the face of the harsh realities of his situation'. The pair then set out on a series of visits, starting with Bennett whom Percival was to visit twice again that day. Bennett had now established a new headquarters south-east of Bukit Timah village, a fact which the Japanese seemed already to have discovered for the house was heavily bombed while the generals conferred. All three unceremoniously went to ground under tables, Bennett later rather condescendingly recording that 'throughout this blitz both Wavell and Percival exhibited exemplary coolness'. It was clear that Bennett knew little about the dispositions of Taylor's units and was in ignorance of Maxwell's withdrawal; as one of the Australian battalion commanders later confided, 'Bennett did not go forward during the campaign.'[3] Perhaps Wavell now realised that he had been as wrong about Bennett as about the Japanese.

The two commanders discovered the gaping hole in the Causeway sector of the front when they reached Heath's headquarters. Percival decided to put Maxwell's brigade under command of 11th Indian Division, through which its communications now ran, once he had seen Bennett again. He also sent Maxwell a personal order to move forward again to control Mandai village and the vital crossroads on the trunk road leading south. Realising how threatened the Bukit Timah area was becoming, he also ordered Heath to withdraw three battalions from 18th Division (they became 'Tomforce') to strengthen Bennett's position. The two were back at the Australian headquarters by 2.30pm where they received the definitive news of the loss of the Jurong Line. Wavell emphasised the importance of re-establishing it, and on getting back to his headquarters Percival prepared orders for a three-stage offensive by Bennett to take it back. Further disturbing news came in to the effect that 44th Indian Brigade had broken from its position at the southern end of the Jurong Line and was streaming back through the garrison defences. He made yet another visit to Western Area headquarters and then to the West Coast road, to find the Indians being led back to their positions by their officers. The poor men had been bombed and shelled into a panic which had also affected 6/15 Brigade to their north. 44 Brigade had been reliant on the Australian headquarters for their supplies, but had received nothing since the Japanese attack had begun and had 'depended solely on their own skills in scrounging'.[4] Admiral Spooner complained privately to one of Wavell's accompanying staff that Percival was delaying the authority for him to destroy large stocks of naval oil on the grounds that it would discourage the troops. Given the eggshell fragility of morale among the defenders, one could understand Percival's point. Parts of the island were already like Dante's *Inferno*: 'the troops looked more like miners emerging from a shift in the pits than fighting soldiers', Percival remarked of one group; it was 'another example of the difficulties of combining scorched-earth and battle fighting'. Whilst Wavell was visiting Keith Simmons a call had come in from a naval duty officer saying that a party of Australians was making off in a commandeered motor launch. The officer was 'asking for permission to shoot them up'. It was not granted.[5] With such scenes fresh in his mind Wavell rejoined Percival at Flagstaff House.

Percival showed Wavell the counter-attack order he had given Bennett. A short while later the Supreme Commander received a telegram from the Prime Minister which he read without comment and then passed to the GOC. 'The drafting of this telegram was not an easy one', the CIGS, Brooke, later confessed. The message noted that Percival had over 100,000 troops on the island and vastly outnumbered the Japanese who had crossed to Singapore. It contrasted the Singapore situation with the heroic struggle being waged by the Russians against the German invader and by the Americans at Luzon. Churchill demanded a defence in which there must 'be no thought of saving the troops or sparing the population' and in which 'Commanders and senior officers should die with their troops'. He was asking for Singapore to be another Massada. Wavell retired to a separate room and drafted in pencil on the back of a naval message form a similar exhortation which he signed and passed to Percival. The tone was the same: a fight to the death for the sake of the Empire. It is difficult to decide which message was the more discreditable, the Prime Minister's or Wavell's. Churchill's cable certainly deserves the judgement of one diplomat-turned-historian that it was 'militarily unrealistic, an impulsive exercise in self-deception by a national leader who sees his political future threatened by a military disaster'.[6] But it was worse than that; it was grossly immoral: Churchill was demanding the sacrifice of the Indians, the Australians and the citizens of Singapore 'on behalf of the Empire'. *They were the Empire*; fighting now, after the loss of its richest corner because, as one of Churchill's own Secret Circle (generally his most protective commentators) put it, 'The PM has . . . deliberately starved Singapore in favour of home and the Middle East . . .'.[7] Wavell's message loyally echoed the Prime Minister's but had taken the trouble to develop the military comparisons whose inappropriateness should have been as obvious to him as the message's demands were unrealistic, in the light of what he had seen during the day, and knew of the other battlefronts. At this critical juncture in the disastrous campaign, Percival had every right to feel badly let down by commanders above and below him. He nevertheless accepted these wounding admonitions without demur and led his guest into the dining room, where they sat down to a gloomy meal served by the Chinese staff with their customary imperturbability. Percival's own covering note to his commanders which went out with these messages was more realistically framed: '. . . The spirit of aggression and determination to stick it out must be inculcated in all ranks. There must be no further withdrawals without orders. There are too many fighting men in the back areas . . . . Every available man who is not doing essential work must be used to stop the invader.'

The counter-attack did not work; confusion, fatigue, demoralisation and indiscipline had taken their toll. Bennett himself had no stomach for it. The attitude of some of his soldiers who had already absented themselves to the 'back areas' had a blunt logic: 'Chum, to hell with Malaya and Singapore. Navy let us down, airforce let us down. If the bungs (natives) won't fight for their bloody country, why pick on me?'[8] The Japanese did not wait to be attacked. They advanced with tanks and had gained the dominating Bukit Timah feature, their second objective, by midnight. The following day was *Kigensetsu*, the anniversary of the founding of the Japanese Empire; to have taken the island by then would be an unparalleled *coup* for Yamashita.

Percival had a few hours sleep at the Sime Road headquarters on the night of the 10th, but awoke to the sound of machine-gun fire, dangerously close, at the end of the golf course. He transferred his base to the claustrophobic and overcrowded but bomb-proof rear headquarters at Fort Canning and went to see the situation at Bukit Timah where the fresh troops from 18th Division had failed in their counter-attack attempt. To bring maximum resources against the threat in the west, he now made Heath responsible for the whole of the area east of the racecourse. Heath formed a second brigade group-sized force largely from 18th Division and gave it the task of defending the reservoir area and linking up with Tomforce to its south. This force contained the obsolescent light tanks which had recently arrived, as well as some armoured cars and a field battery. This meant that there was now something approaching a continuous line opposing the Japanese in the threatened west and south of the island. But already the north was causing concern.

Brigadier Taylor informed General Key that he was no longer under his command and had received orders to attack south to retake a village on the trunk road. There is no evidence of any such orders having been given. The likeliest explanation is that Maxwell was keen to get back to Bennett's command. Bennett was a personal friend on whose advice he tended to rely. Three days earlier, before the Japanese assault had begun, Maxwell had sought a personal interview with Percival in which he had made it clear that he did not believe that Singapore was worth the fight. He was shown the door.[9] What the GOC thought of Maxwell when he heard of this latest move may be imagined; 27 Brigade's withdrawal forced the realignment of all Heath's troops on the north coast and accelerated their withdrawal to the city perimeter. Their move to positions covering the water supply and linking up with the western and southern forces was agreed with Heath the following day. It all gave a tragi-comical unreality to the 'last man, last round' demands of the Prime Minister and Supreme Commander whose orders Percival was doing his best to follow. His travails were completed by the receipt of an air-dropped surrender demand from Yamashita. Percival ignored it, telling Wavell that he no longer had the means to drop a reply, which would in any case have been 'No'.

Arrangements were now being made for the evacuation from Singapore of the female nursing staff, trained staff officers and all the technicians who could be spared. Percival had given his ADC, Ian Stonor of the Argylls, permission to go. In his place for the last few hectic days of the campaign he appointed George Patterson, a young Colonial Service officer who had led an escape group from Trengganu in the early days of the campaign and, since he was a reservist gunner officer, had then been re-employed in the defences, ultimately in Percival's Headquarters. His command of the local language and skills as a driver got him the job of ADC. He was to see a lot of the General over the next four days.

Percival saw the Governor on the 12th and got his agreement for important civil denial measures. Government House now had a battery of guns in the garden and had taken a heavy shelling during the day; 12 staff had been killed, including the personal servants of the Governor and Lady Thomas. The following day the Governor left the official residence for the relative safety of the Singapore Club. Percival was now desperately tired but managed to preserve his legendary reputation for stamina and imperturbability. 'I saw him daily and nightly during the darkest days of the campaign', wrote one of his staff, 'he was always cheerful and maintained a calm unruffled attitude in the most difficult circumstances'.[10] This was plainly what they were now becoming, for although the remains of 22nd Australian Brigade were holding on grimly at Ulu Pandan, further south the pressure was building against 44th Indian and 1st Malayan brigades along Pasir Panjang Ridge which led directly to the Alexandra Barracks complex and then the harbour.

By dawn on Friday 13th February, Percival's forces were in position along the perimeter around Singapore town, a tight semi-circle backing onto the sea and about four miles from it at the perimeter's broadest point. Inside were crammed the one million Asians and the garrison of over 90,000. So close-packed had they become that the whole town was a legitimate target for the Japanese bombers and the artillery which they were now getting across to the island to supplement the mortars which they were using to good effect. The defenders had food reserves for about a week, petrol was short and ammunition about adequate. The availability of water was now the critical concern. Strict rationing had ensured a basic supply despite the loss of the pipeline from Johore which had been blown up with the Causeway, but great quantities were now running to waste as the bombing and shelling smashed the mains faster than Simson's men could repair them. The last convoy had left the previous day, under the inadequate protection of the cruiser *Durban*, and not without some difficulty since the Governor had withdrawn all the European technical harbour staff a couple of days earlier without telling either Simson or Percival. The Army was now manning the docks as well as everything else. The harbour and town were under continuous bombardment. Growing numbers of deserters, mostly the untrained reinforcements and the majority (though by no means all) Australian, thronged the town and harbour area, searching for drink, loot and more especially a means of leaving the island.

Back home in England, in Hertfordshire, Betty Percival and the general's 86-year-old father anxiously followed the newspapers and wireless broadcasts for news of Arthur. The last letter Betty had received from him had arrived before Christmas. 'Although he is in command in Singapore', she told the Press, 'he is not the type who would burden the overladen cable service at a time like this'. Friday the 13th began for her husband with a conference about the destruction of the naval oil and petrol stocks and the Asiatic Petroleum Company's petrol reserves on Pulau Bukum, a small island off the south coast, behind the defending troops. Spooner had long been arguing for these to be destroyed, but Percival had refused to agree because of the likely effect on civil and military morale. He now relented, since he could no longer guarantee the security of the island. A fresh pall of black smoke soon rose over the doomed city behind the perimeter defences.

Percival then toured all the formations on the front. The main Japanese pressure was still along the Pasir Panjang Ridge in the south-west, where, after heavy shelling and mortaring, it forced back the 1st Malaya Brigade about 2,000 yards during the course of the day. North of them the Australians were gathering in their perimeter around Tanglin. The remnants of 22 Brigade had fought stubbornly and well, but Maxwell's 27th, his battalions out of touch with their commander and with each other and now with conflicting orders, had been a grave disappointment. The GOC had not been told that Bennett intended to surrender if formations flanking his own fell back and allowed the Japanese to enter the city; nor did he know that for some days Bennett had been planning his own escape. North of the Australians, 18th Division at last had its three brigades in line, though 55 Brigade came under pressure and was pushed off Sime and Adam Roads and the cemetery area during the course of the day, leaving it with its back to Mount Pleasant Road and the northern suburbs of Singapore. It was hardly a healthy journey around the front for the GOC as he tried to keep the resistance going. Japanese planes were cruising the skies at will and Percival's car was twice machine-gunned, though he was so weary that he slept right through one attack.[11]

Percival called a command conference at Fort Canning at 2pm. Heath, it appears, was keen for the GOC to hear his commander's views. All the formation commanders and Percival's principal staff officers were present. Heath argued strongly for capitulation, saying that since the Japanese had driven them back down the length of Malaya, he did not see how they could be stopped so near to Singapore city by troops so weary and dispirited. Bennett expressed his entire agreement. Percival emphasised that it was clearly their duty to fight on for as long as they could, as every day gained was important for Wavell's plans. He said that he was considering a counter-attack to recover the Bukit Timah area. Heath replied that they had already tried this without success and there were no longer fresh troops available to make the attempt. He urged immediate surrender. All the formation commanders, including Beckwith Smith of the newly arrived 18th Division, agreed. Percival's response was that there were other factors to take into account: 'I have my honour to consider and there is also the question of what posterity will think of us if we surrender this large Army and valuable fortress.' Heath's retort, cruel, insolent and public, gave the clearest indication of the folly of putting these two lieutenant generals in their respective command positions: 'You need not bother about your honour. You lost that a long time ago up in the North.' This was assuredly a reference to MATADOR which seems to have become an *idée fixe* with Heath and the complete explanation for the failure of his Corps, for which he, quite unfairly, blamed his GOC. Percival took the taunt in silence, and quietly declared, 'I cannot accept your proposal that we should surrender. We will go on fighting as long as we can.'[12] The meeting then turned to the question of the evacuation of the remaining small ships which Admiral Spooner was arranging for that night. Available passages were divided between the military and civilian authorities. Pulford and Spooner were both to leave with this mini-flotilla.

With his senior commanders showing so little enthusiasm for the fight, Percival realised that resistance could not last much longer and cabled the Supreme Commander to apprise him of the state of the siege and get some freedom from the suicidal parameters of the last instructions he had received. He described the tactical situation and then concluded:

In these conditions it is unlikely that resistance can last more than a day or two. My subordinate commanders are unanimously of the opinion that the gain of time will not compensate for extensive damage and heavy casualties which will occur in Singapore town. As Empire overseas is interested I feel bound to represent their views. There must come a stage when in the interests of the troops and civil population further

bloodshed will serve no useful purpose. Your instructions of February
10 are being carried out, but in the circumstances would you consider
giving me wider discretionary powers?[13]

Wavell's response was brief and uncompromising. It accepted the
prospect of house-to-house fighting in the town itself and concluded,
'Fully appreciate your situation, but continued action essential.' The Chief
was not willing to accept personal responsibility for the surrender of
Singapore, though he was privately clear that it could not long be post-
poned. His own cable to the Prime Minister ended, 'Fear however that
resistance not likely to be very prolonged'. From the Prime Minister's
reaction it is difficult to believe that he could have penned the incandes-
cent telegram despatched only four days earlier demanding that
commanders die with their troops with no thought for the civilian population. Now he had become 'sure that it would be wrong to enforce
needless slaughter, and without hope of victory to inflict the horrors of
street fighting on the vast city.' Had there been hope of victory four days
before? His response to Wavell, a 'forlorn little signal', the general's biographer called it, read simply: 'You are of course sole judge of moment
when no further results can be gained in Singapore and should instruct
Percival accordingly. CIGS concurs.'[14]

After the difficult and depressing commander's conference Percival
drove to Government House to explain the situation to Shenton Thomas.
He found the residence had been bombed again and was deserted, but for
a solitary sentry at the door. In the evening he said goodbye to Pulford,
who was actually sailing to his death rather than imagined safety. Percival
and he had become close friends; Pulford was similarly heartbroken at
the way the campaign had gone. His friend recorded Pulford's last words
as they parted, 'I suppose you and I will be held responsible for this, but
God knows we did our best with what little we had been given.'[15] The
majority of the small boats were headed for an area where Japanese ships
were already concentrating prior to the assault on Palembang. Intelligence
reports to this effect were available. Were Pulford and Spooner aware of
them? Or was there some reason why they chose to discount them, as
Percival had the similar report disregarding the threat to his north-eastern
defences? Despite the enormous stress under which Percival was operating, the pressures from commanders above and below, as well as the
Japanese to the front and the joyless knowledge that the city and docks
were thronged with troops who had given up the struggle, the GOC still
managed to set a fine example to those about him. 'The last time I saw
him, at 1915hrs on 13th February', wrote Lieutenant Colonel Ashmore
who had been selected for last-minute evacuation, 'he was leaving Battle
Headquarters for his office in Fort Canning, still the same friendly, cheerful man with a word of encouragement for all. Overburdened as he was

with responsibilities of the greatest magnitude, he remained an inspiration for courage to all about him.'[16]

Percival had received a report that complete failure of the water supply was imminent; burst mains and fractured pipes were allowing half the meagre supply to run to waste. He conferred with Simson and the Municipal Water Engineer on Saturday morning. Their advice was that the supply would last 48 hours at most, perhaps only 24. As it was, only the lower-lying buildings were getting a direct supply; water-carrying parties were already operating from stand-pipes for many buildings, including hospitals. Percival ordered a contingent of Royal Engineers who were fighting as infantry in the south-west of the perimeter to be withdrawn to help with the repairs. Then he motored over to confer with the Governor again. The Singapore Club was now packed with refugees, but the overburdened secretary found a small luggage room where the two were able to talk privately. The Governor was worried about the water shortage and the danger of epidemics among the local population. He cabled the Colonial Office to that effect. Percival sent Wavell another report and then toured the front once more in the afternoon. There was little fresh pressure on 11th or 18th Divisions, both of whose headquarters he visited that day. He discussed the options with General Key, one of the divisional commanders whose views he respected. Key was opposed to the counter-offensive along the whole line which Percival was contemplating as a last effort and urged capitulation whilst the Japanese troops were still under the control of their officers. The enemy pressure was continuing along the Pasir Panjang Ridge in the south where there was heavy fighting before the defenders were forced to surrender Alexandra Hospital and the area around it. Some of these advances were witnessed from the Australian compound further north, but their artillery did not respond, having been ordered by Bennett to fire only against attacks on their own positions.[17] Later in the day, a heavy attack supported by artillery and tanks developed on 18th Division's front and produced a deep dent in the line. The bombing and shelling continued, with heavy casualties in the crowded town area. At one stage, blast lifted Percival's car clean off the ground, but with no damage to vehicle or occupants.

By 5pm he was back at the Municipal Offices for another report on the water situation. The strenuous efforts of the engineers had actually produced a slight improvement. He asked for a further report to be sent to him first thing the following morning and was then driven off to report the situation to the Governor. Most buildings in the town were now closed; the ground floors of some of the larger ones, including the Cathay building which now housed Heath's headquarters, had been taken over as temporary hospitals. Water gushed from broken pipes forming pools around the dead who lay were they had fallen. A pall of smoke hung over the rubble-strewn streets from the many fires, caused by the bombing and the 'denial' burnings. At the Singapore Club Sir Shenton Thomas, the Governor of Britain's richest colony, was now reduced to eating a supper of tinned potato salad and corned beef perched on the edge of his bed. 'Percival told me position is no worse and therefore we would carry on', he wrote in his diary. That night the GOC slept in the 'battle box' at Fort Canning, believing they might hold on a little longer, but knowing that there was only one way the siege was going to end. He had received another message from Wavell ending, 'Your gallant stand is serving purpose and must be continued to limit of endurance.' It was one of the few of the Chief's cables from which he was able to derive the slightest comfort. 'A few words of encouragement in the situation in which we found ourselves have a wonderful effect', he wrote later.

On Sunday morning Percival was again up early and at 6.30am he put a message out calling a conference of his senior commanders for 9.30. He took Holy Communion in his office from the Command Chaplain, George McNeill. It was a quiet, intimate service; just two officers, Percival and his new ADC, the one who had volunteered on the outbreak of the First World War, the other who had joined up at the start of the Second, and two chaplains. 'Percival was absolutely splendid', McNeill later recalled.[18] The morning reports were not good. Simson explained that the water situation was much worse: it would last perhaps for another 24 hours. The news from the front line was no better. The Japanese had renewed their attacks in the south-west and were driving the defenders from the remaining Alexandra depots; 2nd Loyals were bearing the brunt of the fighting and were down to about 130 men.

Percival asked Simson to attend the conference which began with the area commanders giving verbal reports on their sectors of the front. There was little change to what the GOC already knew; but even as they deliberated a late report came in from Beckwith Smith, who had not got to the meeting, to say that there had been widespread infiltration on the 18th Division front during the night which he had been unable to contain. Percival outlined the administrative situation which was that there was sufficient food and small arms ammunition for a few days' further resistance, but that mortar, field and anti-aircraft artillery ammunition was running out; virtually all the petrol left was that in the vehicles' tanks. Simson explained that the water situation was now critical. The GOC then asked for views. Heath was typically outspoken: 'In my opinion there is only one possible course to adopt and that is to do what you ought to have done two days ago, namely to surrender immediately.' Failure to do so would be an act of extreme folly. Do it quickly and get it over today, was his advice. Bennett agreed. The GOC reiterated his instructions from the Supreme Commander to fight on. In his view there were two alternatives: a counter-attack to recapture the food depots at Bukit Timah, or surrender. Heath once again argued that a counter-attack was impractical. Bennett was of the same view; Keith Simmons reluctantly agreed with them.[19]

This was the lowest moment of all for Percival; he concluded that he would have to capitulate, despite Wavell's order for continued resistance.

Thereafter events moved quickly. After discussion Percival decided to request a cease-fire for 4pm, but stressing that resistance should continue until definite cease-fire orders were issued.[20] Major Wild, attending the meeting as a prospective Japanese interpreter for the GOC, recalled that at this late stage in the proceedings, Bennett proposed a counter-attack to capture Bukit Timah, a suggestion which 'came so late, and was by then so irrelevant, that I formed the impression at the time that it was not made as a serious contribution to the discussion but as something to quote afterwards'.[21] Brigadier Newbigging and Mr Ian Fraser, the Colonial Secretary, were chosen as the *parlementaires*, with Major Wild in attendance. They drove to the front line, crossed the wire to the Japanese positions and, after a lengthy delay, handed over to a 25th Army staff officer Percival's invitation for the Japanese commander to visit Singapore to negotiate the surrender. The Japanese response was to require General Percival to meet General Yamashita on their territory, at Bukit Timah at 4pm, a time suggested by Newbigging. A unilateral British cease-fire, to which the British party objected and which Percival chose to ignore, was supposed to apply from then onwards. A large Japanese flag was handed over for display on the top of the Cathay building to indicate the GOC's acceptance of the arrangements.

Meanwhile Percival had informed the Governor of the surrender decision and received from Wavell a fresh signal bearing the injunction to continue fighting, but containing the sentence, 'when you are fully satisfied that this is no longer possible I give you discretion to cease resistance'. The message ended with the words, 'Whatever happens I thank you and all troops for your gallant efforts of the last few days'. With some relief and a clear conscience Percival was able to send his own final signal to Wavell: 'Owing to losses from enemy action water petrol food and ammunition practically finished. Unable therefore to continue the fight any longer. All ranks have done their best and grateful for your help.'

Later, General Percival sat at his desk unmoved, listening to Newbigging's account of the parley with the Japanese, as a blast from a stick of bombs brought down some of the ceiling boards and raised a cloud of dust in the room. He studied the terms of the draft surrender agreement which his envoys had brought back with them and made a note to ensure that the protection of the civilians was agreed with Yamashita. It was now much later than the time which the envoys had agreed. The British party travelled in two cars along the now much quieter Bukit Timah Road, two brigadiers and the interpreter in the first car and Percival in the second with a sergeant holding up the white flag and the new ADC driving. They were met by the same staff officer, Colonel Sugita, at the junction of the Bukit Timah and Adams Road, where the Japanese had stationed a tank. Sugita accompanied the GOC and his party to the Ford factory where the negotiations were to take place. The four Britons walked in line to the historic appointment, Wild carrying the white flag, Newbigging the Union Jack and the Chief of Staff flanking his GOC. It was a necessary piece of military ceremonial with which none of them was familiar and which the Japanese photographers proudly recorded for posterity.

Percival's own account of the campaign gave few details of the 'painful events', as he called them, of that day. 'There was not much chance of bargaining', he recalled, 'but I did what I could to ensure the safety of both troops and civilians'. The British Official History does not give the GOC's statement much support, baldly recording that General Yamashita demanded the unconditional surrender of the British garrison and that 'After a discussion lasting fifty-five minutes Percival agreed, and at 6.10pm signed the terms of surrender'. In fact the negotiations seem to have lasted considerably longer according to Percival's ADC and Japanese recollections.[22] Yamashita was certainly in a hurry. Although the morale of his troops was high and his bombers were still able to pound the almost waterless Singapore, he was running short of ammunition for his ground troops. The meeting of the two commanders later acquired a certain notoriety as Yamashita was said to have bullied Percival into submission, banging the table to emphasise his demands. The painting by war artist Miyamoto Saburo showed the Japanese commander in a heroically threatening pose with arm raised, while the journalists present at the ceremony reported 'General Yamashita in a rage'. However, the press photograph of the occasion shows a more impassive Japanese commander, and whatever impatience he felt at the British general's persistence, the table-thumping episode does have an alternative explanation. Yamashita's official interpreter at the negotiations was Second Lieutenant Hirishikari, a general's son, whose interpreting was particularly hesitant. Yamashita finally lost patience with him, banged his fist on the table and told Sugita, a good English speaker, to take over.[23] However, it was Miyamoto's painting rather than the photograph which was later reproduced in every Japanese soldier's pocket book, giving the story its wider currency.[24] Far from being brow-beaten by Yamashita, Percival's soft-spoken doggedness won him some important concessions from the Japanese and may well have spared Singapore from all manner of mayhem.

The main issue for negotiation was, of course, the timing of the formal cease-fire. It was now much too late for the time suggested at that morning's conference to apply. Percival proposed 10pm, but Yamashita insisted on 8.30pm and the British GOC eventually gave way when Yamashita said that Percival and Shenton Thomas would have to come out as hostages if Percival would not accept his proposal. He later expressed his relief at Percival's agreement, since it gave him sufficient time to call off the night attack for which orders had already been issued.[25]

The most important issue for Percival was maintaining control in Singapore town and keeping the Japanese out of it until the surrender was fully effective and emotions had subsided. The fate of Nanking was no doubt at the back of his mind during the lengthy exchange with the Japanese commander:

Percival: There are disturbances in Singapore City. As there are non-combatants in the city, I should like to keep 1,000 men under arms.

Yamashita: The Japanese Army will be stationed there, and will maintain order. So you need have no worry on that score.

Percival: The British Army is familiar with the situation in Singapore. I should like to keep a thousand armed men.

Yamashita: The Japanese Army will look after that, you need not concern yourself with it.

Percival: Looting is taking place inside the city. And there are non-combatants.

Yamashita: Non-combatants will be protected by the spirit of Bushido. So everything will be all right.

Percival: If there is a vacuum, there will be chaos in the city and looting. Outbreaks of looting and rioting are undesirable, whether from the Japanese or the British point of view. For the purpose of maintaining order, it is desirable that 1,000 men should be permitted to retain their arms.

Yamashita: As the Japanese Army is continuing its assault on the city, an attack is likely to go forward tonight.

Percival: I should like to ask you to postpone any night attack.

Yamashita: The attack will go forward if we cannot come to an agreement.

Percival: I would like you to postpone it.

Yamashita: *(Repeats what he has just said.)*

Percival: Because of the rioting in Singapore, I would like 1,000 men left with their arms.

Yamashita: *(turning to Colonel Ikeya)*: What time is the night attack scheduled for?

Ikeya: Eight o'clock.

Percival: If there is a night attack then you put me in a difficult situation.

Yamashita: Does the British Army intend to surrender or not?

Percival: *(a pause)*: I wish to have a cease-fire.

Yamashita: The time for the night attack is drawing near. Is the British Army going to surrender or not? Answer 'Yes' or 'No'. [*'Yes' or 'No' in English in the text.*]

Percival: Yes. But I would like the retention of 1,000 armed men sanctioned.

Yamashita: *(briefly)*: Very well.[26]

Percival then asked for confirmation that the Japanese Imperial Forces would protect British civilians, men, women and children.[27] Yamashita undertook to ensure this. Lieutenant Colonel Sugita asked Percival to sign the surrender document, and the ceremony was at an end. The two generals rose and shook hands. The 'grievous and shameful blow', as Churchill was to call it, had fallen. Singapore was lost.

19

CAPTIVITY

'When things go wrong the public are naturally inclined to blame the man on the spot. Why was this not done and why was that not done? The answer generally is that the man on the spot was not a free agent.'

Percival, The War in Malaya

When Percival and his officers and men became prisoners of war, Churchill had yet to produce the memorable phrases by which the disastrous campaign just completed would always be remembered. His account of 'the worst disaster and largest capitulation in British history' did not appear in print until 1951;[1] but from the moment Percival signed the surrender document and returned to the Singapore Club for a much-needed whisky and soda with the sympathetic erstwhile Governor of the colony, he was deeply affected by the enormity of the reverse which his forces had suffered. Days later, when the captive Army had been marched to the Changi area, the defeated GOC could be seen sitting, head in hands, outside the married quarter he now shared with seven brigadiers, a colonel, his ADC, cook sergeant and batman. He discussed his personal feelings with few, spent hours walking around the extensive compound, ruminating on the reverse and what might have been, sharing his walks often with his ADC and his reflections occasionally with Brigadier Torrance, his principal staff officer. The scale and speed of the defeat, condemning the large garrison to imprisonment and taking 30 days fewer even than the ambitious Japanese calculations had allotted, came as a great surprise and shock to the embattled British nation and indeed the world at large. 'I realise how the fall of Singapore has affected you and the British people', wrote the American President to the Prime Minister, '. . . and I know you will not hesitate to ask me if there is anything you think I can do'. He also remarked with some prescience that the reverse would give 'the well-known back-seat driver a field day'.[2]

In the public mind, the Army and its GOC bore a direct responsibility for the disaster in a sense which it seemed inappropriate to attribute to the leaders of the other Services. The *Prince of Wales* had had a reputation for invulnerability every bit the equal of 'Fortress Singapore', yet it had been

stormed with even more dramatic ease; Admiral Phillips' belated foray
north had achieved nothing but the loss of his ships and his life. Air
Marshal Pulford's Air Force, the intended bastion of the defences, had
been virtually swept aside in two days; his life also was lost. Yet it could be
readily accepted that the naval and air forces were smaller and technically
inferior to those of the Japanese and therefore were not disgraced and cul-
pable in defeat. Their loss and the death of their chiefs were occasions for
regret rather than blame. But the Army was different, as armies generally
are; theirs is the decisive and enduring act of gaining or giving up territory.
What was remembered about the Army of Malaya (something Churchill
chose particularly to pinpoint) was not its technical and qualitative inferiority, or lack of air and naval support, but its size. The defeat of
Percival's Army, therefore, seemed more a matter of poor tactics, inadequate leadership and absent will-power. The general in command
represented these qualities for his Service more directly than admirals or
air marshals ever could. As one of the GOC's Indian Army officers put it,
'When a great military disaster takes place, there has to be someone to be
a scapegoat. If it is someone who has not hit the headlines by some great
gesture, some last stand heroics, and who is not a great showman, then so
much the better.'[3] In Singapore therefore Percival had to be responsible.
He became the convenient scapegoat.

The pre-war expectations of the average Briton concerning a possible
struggle with Japan had been much the same as those of General Wavell
as quoted in an earlier chapter. The Japanese would present no problem
for a major modern Western army. This confidence was not without its
racial overtones and the accompanying rash of barrack-room jokes about
the military incompetence of the four-eyed, buck-toothed Nip; this fight
was not to be against a Führer and his party henchmen, but an entire
racial group: the old yellow peril of which the Czar had once warned us.
Yet to those in possession of the military facts and in a position professionally to judge them at the time, rather than in hindsight, how
unexpected was Percival's rapid and total defeat? How long did the
military *cognoscenti* of the day expect Malaya and Singapore to last?

When the Japanese first attacked, the CIGS, Dill, returned hurriedly to
London from his pre-retirement farewell visits and conferred with Major
General Kennedy, his DMO. 'We felt there was little hope for Singapore',
Kennedy wrote, 'for the naval and air forces essential for its defence were
lacking, and the army was very short of tanks, and of anti-aircraft and
anti-tank weapons.'[4] That was Kennedy's recollection of their 7 December
judgement. Within a week the new CIGS, Brooke, was writing, 'Far East
situation far from rosy! I doubt whether Hong Kong will hold out for a
fortnight and Malaya a month.'[5] Two days later, before even northern
Malaya had been lost, he had to confess, 'Personally I do not feel that
there is much hope of saving Singapore.'[6] General Ismay, Churchill's

faithful acolyte, was under no illusions about the virtual impossibility of the task facing Percival and his men. His reaction to the Japanese assault was to declare, 'Our eastern possessions, almost undefended, were now open to the Japanese.'[7] The view of Colonel Jacob, another of the War Cabinet Secretariat, was that Singapore was 'hopeless from the very start'. For these military men at the very heart of Britain's strategic affairs, the fall of Malaya and Singapore was a foregone conclusion from the time of the first landings at Singora and Patani.

When Brooke Popham was urging the despatch of reinforcements to Malaya before the Far Eastern war began, the response he generally received from Ismay was of the order that it was 'the old story of a little butter and a vast amount of bread'.[8] Of course this was true in the general sense that Britain was now too weak to fight a major war in the West and in the Far East as well. But the fact of the matter was that Churchill was consciously making choices within the broad parameters of what was possible, choices which effectively determined the fall of Singapore: 'For if there is one pair of shoulders on which blame must be laid', Sir Michael Howard has written, 'it is that of Winston Churchill himself. It was he who in 1941, against the advice of his Chiefs of Staff, gave to the Far East a lower priority in allocation of resources than the Middle East.'[9] The extent of the deliberate choice is best illustrated by the example of the commodity of which the Far East was so grievously starved, fighter aircraft. Between January and October 1941, 1,996 aircraft reached the Middle East, including 857 Hurricanes. Between November 1940 and December 1941 the RAF aircraft strength in Malaya rose by 70, and none was a Hurricane.[10] To be deemed as clearly responsible as Professor Howard suggests, without any consideration of the Russian factor, serves only to heighten the Prime Minister's culpability. From the moment of the German attack on the Soviet Union, the Far East was pushed into third place in the strategic priorities. This occurred despite the knowledge that the US President had pledged American aid for Russia two days after the launching of *Barbarossa* and the rapid realisation by the War Cabinet that some of this aid would be at the expense of planned military allocations to Britain. The decision was again opposed by Churchill's military advisers, as we have noted. General Brooke leaves us in no doubt about his views. 'Personally', he wrote, 'I consider it absolute madness. We have never asked Russia to inform us of the real urgency of these reinforcements.'[11] But the War Cabinet went its own way: 'As they saw it', Ismay explained, 'the collapse of Russia would mean Hitler's hegemony in Europe, while the collapse of Singapore could be retrieved after Hitler had been dealt with.'[12]

Russia's demands for aircraft were also met with fighters, rather than bombers, for the latter would have involved a cut in the planned expansion of Bomber Command, and a diminution of the 'independent role' to which the RAF was so heavily committed. To Russia also went the tanks, half of them light tanks ideal for Malaya, of which Percival had stood so sorely in need. On the day Percival's Army withdrew onto Singapore island, General Brooke was recording resignedly that 'the PM . . . would not stop sending tanks to Russia'.[13] The Prime Minister's decision is all the more inexplicable when one recalls how impressed he had been on hearing that even a dozen tanks might have saved Crete. Moscow did not fall; indeed the Soviet counter-offensive began the day before Malaya was attacked. It is clear that it was Malaya and not the Middle East that was sacrificed for the Russian front, as Sir Maurice Dean reminds us: 'the bulk of the aircraft reinforcements earmarked for Malaya – over 300 aircraft – was diverted to help Britain's newly found and hard pressed ally, Russia'.[14] In the House of Commons debate which followed the fall of Singapore, Sir Archibald Southby's view, a mite optimistic it has to be said, was that, 'One month's supply of the aircraft sent to Russia would have saved Malaya.'[15] That meant saving half the world's tin and rubber, (only a slight debating exaggeration), another member reminded the Prime Minister.

The relative strengths of the opposing forces in Malaya were also a good deal more evenly balanced than Churchill and Percival's critics generally assumed. The 138,708 Commonwealth troops recorded by the official histories is almost certainly an overestimate, the true figure being some-where between the highest 'killed and captured' figure of 120,000 estimated by the Japanese and the slightly larger 125,000 given by Percival in his despatch.[16] The figures quoted for the Japanese strength vary enor-mously between the inexplicably low 35,000 estimate of Louis Allen, and Percival's own figure of 150,000, a by no means gross overestimate, understandable in the circumstances of defeat. In fact the strength of the Japanese 25th Army seems to have been, at 125,408, almost the same as that of their opponents, although the numbers actually taking part in the campaign were somewhat lower.[17] 25th Army also had important help, it will be recalled, from a regiment of 55th Division in capturing the Victoria Point air staging post, preventing speedy reinforcement of Pulford's fighters. For the assault on Singapore, Yamashita had available 27 battalions of infantry and 14 battalions of artillery (168 guns). Also under his command were 78 bombers (roughly half of them heavy), 40 fighters and 14 reconnaissance aircraft were at his disposal.[18] Then there were the Japanese tanks. These were fresh in Percival's memory; 175 took part in the victory parade which processed through Singapore on the morning of 16 February. It was hardly the David and Goliath affair that London had depicted.

That the failure in Singapore and Malaya had a lot to do with Percival's limitations as a commander was a commonly held view, nurtured by such critical descriptions of him as that produced by Ian Morrison in *Malayan*

Postscript which went to press as early as May 1942 and followed much adverse newspaper comment. Morrison was not the first or last journalist to be more impressed by General Bennett than any other commander. Percival's lack of recent operational experience was also emphasised, though this was almost inevitable at the start of a war; no one in the British Army, it has to be remembered, had any experience of fighting the Japanese. Heath had the good fortune to have commanded against the Italians in Ethiopia. Even there, it is instructive to remember, a fully trained British battalion had broken in the face of an enemy air attack, minor in character compared to what the troops faced in Malaya.[19] Few commentators, even post-war and including official historian Kirby, managed to get the details of Percival's early career correct,[20] understating his operational experience and thereby reinforcing the stereotype of the eternal staff officer. 'What was needed in Malaya was a ruthless, brilliant, no-nonsense, hard-driving, operational general', is a common judgement. It was well known at the time of his appointment that Percival, despite his many admirable military qualities, was not this; he did not even look the part. But he cannot be blamed for not being what he was not. His reserved personal manner was shared by other commanders who performed well in less exposed situations and without the odds so heavily stacked against them. The real question is whether that paragon of a commander who might have been appointed in his stead would have saved Malaya and Singapore. The answer is certainly 'no'.

'If we had had our best general out there, it would have made no difference', confessed Jacob.[21] This was a view from the informed detachment of Whitehall, but it was confirmed at the battlefront itself: 'the issue would have been the same whatever general had been in command', reflected General Key.[22] Even the best commanders need sufficient soldiers who are trained and properly equipped, and given the appropriate air and naval support if they are to succeed. They also need time. Percival never had this, either to prepare his forces for the campaign or to ready them for a counter-offensive. He was never allowed the initiative, and was hustled out of Malaya, let us remember, in only a week longer than Montgomery had the luxury of allowing himself for the elaborate and undisturbed preparations for El Alamein. Would that Percival had had the opportunity to observe Montgomery's wise dictum: 'New and untried troops must be introduced to battle carefully. A start should be made with small raids, then big scale raids, leading up gradually to unit and brigade operations.' For Percival the question was rather whether the ships would get them there in time to join the fight at all!

Pownall tells us that Wavell, when he paid his first visit to the Malayan battlefront, was 'not at all happy about Percival who has the knowledge but not the personality to carry through a tough fight'. More interesting than this snap judgement itself is Pownall's concluding thought, 'I hope it doesn't mean that I have to relieve Percival *pro tem.*, . . .'[23] Pownall knew a lost cause when he saw one! Revealing also is his opinion that, 'Percival is not the man to keep Shenton Thomas up to the mark'. Was it his job to? Who else was able to? None of the senior birds of passage, Brooke Popham, Wavell, Pownall himself, or even Duff Cooper, whose main concern it was, were able to do very much about Thomas, as Simson testifies of his time in charge of Civil Defence. 'On many important questions', he wrote, 'the Governor also gave me no "fair wind". I often could get no decisions even when Percival, Duff Cooper, Wavell and others took up important points at my request.'[24] Pownall's criticism also illustrates the incredibly difficult split responsibility which Percival had, part Army Commander responsible for the campaign, and part War Council member being blamed for the colonial government's slowness and slackness in girding itself up for war. Whatever Wavell's immediate impression of Percival when he first visited Malaya Command, he chose not to replace him with the readily available and highly respected Pownall, or anyone else, and subsequently even considered putting the Governor under the GOC, but rejected the idea because he 'did not wish to increase the burden on the GOC at that time.'[25] Nor did the Government at home agree to replace Thomas or appoint a military governor as Admiral Layton suggested (proposing Pownall!). In these circumstances it is difficult to see how Percival could be held responsible for not keeping him 'up to the mark'.

It would have eased that burden immeasurably if Wavell could have given Percival positive encouragement and personal support; he had, after all, little else to offer. Aside from failing to back his GOC, his own performance in Malaya was uninspiring and unsound. His intervention at the operational level in early January, besides misjudging his commanders and the tactical possibilities, was boorishly effected. The fact of the matter was that Wavell acted too impulsively in a situation where he knew neither his own commanders nor his opponent well enough to justify his interference. Colonel Thyer, the able and candid Australian chief staff officer, considered that Wavell's contribution to the operations in Malaya was 'negligible'. Key's view was that Wavell 'hardly uttered and was uninspiring'. His message of 10 February was particularly resented, reflecting as it did on the unit commanders whom he had scarcely seen. General Key issued it reluctantly to his commanders and with a covering note explaining that it did not apply to them.[26]

Key acknowledged that Percival did not have a dynamic style of command, but emphasised that he was 'as straight as a die with a very good brain. And what a situation he had to face!'[27] Considering the inevitability of the outcome of the campaign the question is less whether a more outgoing and inspirational commander (rather than 'one of nature's gentlemen' as Colonel Harrison of 11th Division called Percival) could have saved Malaya, but rather how any GOC could have imposed his personality on such a heterogeneous and polyglot force spread over the great expanses of Malaya and in such a short time, while at the same time attending to his many Singapore-based responsibilities. In common with too many of the Indian Army officers themselves, Percival could not speak the languages of over half his Army and, until the very end of the campaign, had little chance to get close to the soldiers. The 500 miles of Malaya over which his troops were necessarily spread were very different from the 30-mile-wide coastal strip of the other active theatre of the time, the Western Desert. So was the size of the staff through which any dynamism might have been driven; his headquarters numbered 70 (many untrained and locally promoted) as against the 700 in Middle East Command.

The quality which Percival lacked as a commander was ruthlessness, and the one he had to excess was loyalty. There was a good case for him to have had Gordon Bennett removed before the campaign ever started; the problems Bennett posed as a subordinate were recognised by the Australian authorities themselves, but the GOC chose not to act while Bennett was away in the Middle East and had not had the chance to prove himself in combat. The command relationships between the two were something which Brooke Popham should have sorted out more effectively. Equally, Percival should probably have had Heath moved elsewhere at an early stage. 'Piggy' Heath was a popular, respected and impressive figure; but almost from the start of the hostilities his ideas on the conduct of the campaign were at variance with those of his GOC and C-in-C. The presence of the pregnant Lady Heath caused her husband inevitable anxiety and surely gave him divided loyalties; hence Heath's request to leave Malaya at the end of January, which Percival refused, believing the corps commander's place to be with his troops. At that stage he was certainly correct; it would no doubt have been difficult to get any of Percival's superiors to agree to Heath's removal early in the campaign. As Colonel Thyer put it, 'Whoever sanctioned the appointment of Heath, subsequent to the appointment of Percival has much to answer for.' But the nettle should have been grasped. Barstow would have served Percival well as corps commander and got on with Bennett better than most. However, Percival did remove two divisional and numerous subordinate commanders and no amount of opposition from Heath shook either his conviction that his strategy was correct or his determination to apply it.

Percival's loyalty to Brooke Popham, Wavell and the authorities at home led him to get on with the job without 'belly-aching', as Montgomery might have put it. He was perhaps too ready to understand his Chief's reluctance to abandon MATADOR and to accept that the hard-pressed War Cabinet had other operational theatres to supply besides his own. The fact of the matter is that more table-banging would have been unlikely to produce any more resources. An altercation with Wavell might have produced a little more respect for him from the hard-bitten Supreme Commander, but additional friction was the last thing Percival wanted to inflict on an overburdened Supremo. Such actions would have gained him little in practical terms and offended his cooperative instincts. They would, however, have made the 'scapegoat' label more difficult to apply.

The problems of command in Malaya were not really of a character which a ruthless, dynamic extrovert of a general could have solved. Once it had dawned upon the troops that their enemy had mastery of the air and sea and, with tanks, a decisive superiority on land as well, their morale followed a rapid downward spiral which the strategy of controlled withdrawal served only to heighten. This was particularly pronounced in the Indian Corps. The shattering of the belief in Britain's invincibility had an almost palpable effect; from the Slim river disaster onwards the Indians 'exuded a definite feeling of unreliability', in circumstances more testing than the Indian Army had ever met before, where the men were constantly prey to rumour and Japanese propaganda. 'Indian Army officers gave it as their considered opinion that, apart from the Gurkhas and their near kinsmen the Garhwalis, no class in the Indian Army could now be fully relied on to fight . . .', was one considered judgement. As for their officers, 'Determined not to be beaten by an inferior opponent, they failed to take the most elementary precautions against defeat.'[28] The Slim river *débâcle* was replete with examples. The great achievement of the Indian Corps was that it did remain a more or less coherent force until the very end, despite Yamashita's efforts to cut off and smash it. Percival did get withdrawal timings wrong on occasion and, sadly, lost units thereby, but precise judgements were difficult when, lacking aerial reconnaissance, he knew so little about Japanese moves.

The decline in the effectiveness of the Australians was more pronounced, even spectacular, since it occurred after a much shorter period of fighting and was preceded by highly successful prepared ambushes conducted by both brigades. The GOC was even less able to do anything about the Australians given the independence which Bennett insisted on preserving and the 'very false picture', as Percival later realised, which he painted both to his GOC and to Heath, 'of the situation on his front and the state of his troops'. Percival confided to Heath his belief that the weakness lay in the way the Australians selected and trained their higher commanders: 'One finds oneself talking to people who don't even speak the same military language' he confessed.[29] Most observers had recognised before the event that by British and Indian Army standards the Australians were undisciplined to a degree. At that stage it was easy to attribute this to Antipodean individualism, but once the going got tough this state of affairs led to a collapse that is too well documented to be denied. The influx of such a large number of half-trained recruits into the

Australian order of battle at the last minute was an important contributory factor. In his War Diary that was never published, nor even released in full until many years after the event, Admiral Layton wrote of the overwhelming evidence 'that many, I am afraid the majority, threw their hands in as soon as things looked black, and spread the canker of their panic the further by the previous reputation of their country's fighting men'.[30] A report on the behaviour of the Australian troops in Malaya, again withheld from public view for 50 years, led the Whitehall staff officer who reviewed it at the time to conclude, 'It appears that from General Gordon Bennett downwards, the majority of the Australian Div were of the opinion that it was useless to try and defend Singapore island.' It was unsurprising, then, that one of Percival's staff should have recorded that, 'By the morning of 8th February Australian Battalions were reported to be down to 200 other ranks.' The remainder had deserted to Singapore town where, according to another report, this time from a refugee, 'the chief cause of anxiety at that time among the civilian population was not the Japanese but the Australians'.[31]

It had been against this background that Percival had listened to Heath's and Bennett's urgings to surrender on Friday 13 February, but had determined to fight on. It was not craven capitulationism that led him to give up two days later, for he remained, as one of his staff recalled, 'a man of infinite courage, who remained undaunted to the last by overwhelming circumstances',[32] but the knowledge that, water supply and ammunition stocks apart, there was no fight left in much of his Army. The sorry condition to which the Army of Malaya had been reduced on Singapore island was not of Percival's making. It had resulted from it being given a task that was not justifiable on military grounds but was dictated by political factors. As Churchill put it to the Chiefs of Staff, 'the question arises whether we should not at once blow the docks and batteries and workshop [of Singapore] to pieces and concentrate everything on the defence of Burma and keeping open the Burma Road'. For him and them and General Wavell, a 'hesitation to commit ourselves to so grave a step prevailed'.[33]

It was in captivity that the GOC's moral qualities and personal courage shone through most clearly and, in the close confinement of the prison camps, were evident to all ranks. The change in personal circumstances proved a tremendous shock for every soldier and they were particularly pronounced for Percival who bore the additional incubus of local responsibility for the defeat. The appalling treatment of their captives by the Japanese has been too frequently recorded to require repetition here. The camp authorities operated a deliberate policy of humiliating their European prisoners and particularly their officers, including the most senior. At the start of the captivity the POWs were left very much to their own devices, but security and control were soon tightened. The Japanese operated throughout via the prisoners' own chain of command, holding the commanders responsible for the actions of their men. The moral authority and personal example of the GOC in constantly protesting at the Japanese mistreatment of his men and resisting their illegal demands were all-important. He took the simple line of raising no objection to the many irritations and humiliations inflicted by the Japanese, the removal of officers' rank distinctions or the requirement for all prisoners to salute even the lowliest Japanese soldier; but presented an uncompromising opposition on questions of principle or issues connected with the welfare of his soldiers and the conduct of the war. He protested strongly at the inadequacy of the accommodation in Changi camp for the very large numbers housed there, particularly when all the sick and injured prisoners were also moved in from the Singapore hospitals. His representations had no effect. He was asked by the Japanese to provide technicians to repair the British anti-aircraft guns on the island, but declined. 'Then you refuse to obey the orders of the Imperial Nipponese Army?', queried his inquisitor. 'Your orders are illegal but, if you persist in giving them, then I do', replied Percival. At this response the Japanese officer flew into such a rage that Percival 'quite expected him to draw his sword and finish the matter there and then'. The result was three days of solitary confinement without food in Changi jail, followed by a further 14 similarly confined but with food, after a face-saving formula for the Japanese had been arrived at. But they did not get their technicians. General Heath received similar treatment, also believing at the time that he was about to be killed. Both were physically assaulted by the Japanese guards.

Early in the period of captivity there was a full parade of the prisoners, inspected by General Yamashita himself, at which the Japanese commander shook hands with his defeated opponent. Some months later Percival received a personal gift parcel from Yamashita, with an accompanying note:

Syonan
7th July 1942

Lieut General A E Percival

Dear General Percival,

As a small token of my personal interest in your welfare, and a practical contribution to your own comfort, I send you thirty tins of butter, thirty tins of cheese, 150 bottles of beer and two bottles of sherry.

With compliments and best wishes.

Yours sincerely,
Lieut General Yamashita[34]

Ten days later Yamashita had left Singapore, relegated to an inactive area command in Manchukuo and ordered to travel there direct, without the public welcome in Tokyo and audience with the Emperor to which he believed his great victory in Singapore had entitled him. For all its successes on the battlefield, the Japanese Army was still riven by factional politics.

By the end of February the stock of European rations had run out and the low protein, rice-based diet began. From then on there was a steady decline in the health of the prisoners, undernourishment and debilitation laying them open to a variety of tropical diseases. By the end of the first month in Changi the Japanese had surrounded the compound with barbed wire and announced that escape attempts would result in execution. Under such a threat and with the chances of avoiding capture being so pitifully small, Percival issued a directive reaffirming that while it was the prisoners' duty to escape if they could, attempts should only be made after proper planning and providing the chances seemed good. The chief enemy in Changi was boredom and demoralisation after the shock of defeat. In the case of the Australians this was compounded by the last-minute escape of General Bennett, which was a cause of great resentment among the majority of his troops. Percival promoted Brigadier Callaghan to command the AIF and under his leadership and that of some brave and able subordinates, discipline and morale were steadily rebuilt among their troops, a proportion of whom were, of course, the erstwhile deserters.

The internal administration of his old Command kept Percival busy, but all this came to an end in mid-August when the Japanese decided to transfer the senior officers among their prisoners, together with their personal staff, to Formosa. It was one of the typical 'hell ship' journeys which have been so graphically described in many POW accounts. There does not seem to have been any improvement in the conditions for this journey on account of the rank-level of the cargo: 500 prisoners crammed into the converted hold of a cargo boat which might reasonably have carried one tenth of that number. There was a complete absence of privacy for basic latrine functions. Percival's ADC noted that he 'felt terribly sorry for the General', but also added candidly, 'bloody sorry for myself'. They travelled via Saigon and on arrival in Formosa were accommodated in a mosquito-infested transit camp at Heito, a place which Percival noted as having 'no redeeming feature'. At Heito there occurred the confrontation, repeated in similar circumstances throughout the occupied territories, at which the Japanese demanded a 'no escape' declaration from the prisoners. The senior officers' camp was paraded and Percival was asked to step forward to sign the declaration. He refused, and was taken off to a cell in the guard room. The parade remained formed up for three hours and it began to rain in the gathering darkness. Eventually the GOC asked to be released to confer with his senior officers and, as elsewhere in the captured territories, they agreed to sign, the duress involved having rendered the declaration meaningless.

The next move was to Karenko, a small seaside town on the east coast of Formosa, where Percival and his fellow captives joined the American senior officers from the Philippines who were already in residence. Their personal staffs were left behind at Heito. Later their numbers were swelled by the senior British and Dutch officers from the Dutch East Indies and by the Governor of Hong Kong. They were about 400-strong all told, crammed into a Japanese barracks designed for about a company: colonels and brigadiers five to a tiny room and generals and governors not much better off. This was the worst period of the captivity; the food ration fell to a very low level, all officers were made to work, the guards were brutal and all protests – which Percival made frequently – were ignored. They operated, for the Japanese benefit, on a squad system. Percival was appointed a squad leader, but 'very soon got the sack' for not seeing eye to eye with the jailers.

There was a terrible tedium about these days, few responsibilities to occupy the waking hours for most of the officers, a diet which barely sustained the body's metabolism, close confinement with other senior officers, not all of whom provided the most congenial company or took such a principled stand as Percival against the Japanese excesses. He later wrote in confidence that the senior officer prisoners formed two groups, one which he led, which always fought for the prisoners' rights and did its utmost to embarrass the Japanese, and the other which stood for appeasement and 'the line of least resistance'.[35] The relationship between the two groups became quite strained. One of the British brigadiers later wrote of Percival's struggle to secure proper treatment for the prisoners, that 'his efforts in this direction were rendered more difficult by the spineless acceptance and nauseating favour seeking behaviour of other PWs'.[36] According to the Australian, Colonel Thyer, the group of senior POWs in Formosa accepted Percival as the leader, despite the presence of others of the same rank: 'If any problem cropped up the Yanks, the British and the Dutch always referred it to Percival and he tackled the Japs. General Wainwright and the Dutch General Ter Poorten were never accepted in that way.'[37]

Of all the trials of captivity, the worst was the isolation from loved ones and the almost total lack of any news of them. Arthur wrote his permitted monthly letter to Betty, but for an age his words seemed to disappear into the ether; there was never a reply. The opening sentences of his April 1943 letter read, 'Hope you received letter of November. Have not heard from you since November 1941 . . .'. In her turn, Betty Percival was not able to read these despairing words from her husband until the following September. That was what it was like. Arthur's first letter from home finally reached him in October 1943; but it was not until January 1944 that he received his first letter from his wife – he had still been fighting the Japanese when he had last heard from her. Of all the letters sent to him, fewer than half arrived and it took these an average of 17 months to be delivered. Things were a little better at the British end. More letters got through and more quickly; there was the occasional message broadcast via Radio Tokyo and passed on officially or by friendly radio hams: propaganda messages put out by the Japanese allegedly quoting Arthur at least suggested he was alive and well. There was also some information from the International Red Cross. For both Betty and Arthur it was a long and lonely ordeal.

In June 1943 a small party of the most senior prisoners, governors and lieutenant generals of the three main nationalities were moved to a specially built camp at Moksak, near the capital of Formosa. Here the treatment was much better: small individual rooms, a modest library, a gramophone and some records – even the food was better for a time. There was also pressure to take part in Japanese propaganda films which Percival refused to do; they were plainly to be 'staged'. On one occasion each prisoner was given a present prior to a filming session. Percival received a canary in a cage. He let it escape overnight. The furious Japanese commandant demanded to know why. Percival's answer was that he could not bear to see anything in captivity, particularly a bird. However, other prisoners agreed to take part. At Moksak, Percival and Mr C R Smith, the Governor of British North Borneo, spent hours each day trying, with the little Japanese they had picked up, to make sense of the Japanese radio broadcasts they were allowed to listen to. They could recognise a few words and, by dint of continuous effort, after a while they were able to issue a daily communiqué which gave some idea of progress in the war.

Percival spent a good deal of his time in the Taiwan camps producing from memory his account of the campaign. His difficulty was that the records of HQ Malay Command had been buried at Changi, with a view to their recovery after the war. He had given Lieutenant Colonel Cobley, from his Malaya Command staff, the job of putting together a campaign history, using the collective memory of the members of the camp; but of course Cobley was still in Changi. In Formosa Percival had little more than his own memory, and Heath's, to go on. The two generals were not too greatly at variance over the facts, but over their interpretation they had serious disagreements. It is clear that Percival felt badly let down by the performance of the Indian troops, and by Heath personally, especially his behaviour at the final Fort Canning Conference. Heath's words had clearly stung the GOC, as Percival now told him frankly, as being 'not quite worthy of a conference of senior officers gathered together at such a time, when I wanted all the help I could get'.[38] The failure to get an early MATADOR cancellation decision was what still rankled most with Heath. This account of the campaign ran to several hundred handwritten pages, produced and refined over the time on Formosa. Then in October 1944 came the order to prepare for another move, with the inevitable search beforehand. To save the manuscript from the Japanese, Percival burned it. 'The work of eight months was burned in eight seconds', he recalled.[39]

The American Pacific advance was making an attack on Formosa a distinct threat, so the senior prisoners were moved on again, first by air to Japan, then by sea to Korea and finally by train to Manchuria. The journey was a great contrast to their first move from Singapore. In Japan they were treated in a comparatively civilised fashion and in Korea even had a good meal in a large modern hotel; but once at their destination, Seian in Manchuria 200 miles north of Mukden, it was back to the old prison guard regime, though the food was better and supplemented by a large consignment of Red Cross supplies. But there was no longer a radio, letters were few and there was practically no contact with the outside world. Efforts to contact the protecting power, Switzerland, all failed.

When the end finally came it was curiously anticlimactic. After suspiciously large-scale aerial traffic towards Japan, the prisoners were told on Saturday 18 August that an American officer and NCO were expected in their camp the following day. Sure enough, these emissaries arrived the next morning with the news of the atomic bombing of Japan, the Soviet invasion of Manchuria and the Japanese surrender. The American officer left as suddenly as he had arrived to arrange transport for the prisoners. They were then totally isolated again for the next four days: technically free, yet still captive since the Russian invasion had totally disrupted all forms of communication and it was the height of the monsoon flooding. At the end of the week a Russian mechanised detachment arrived at Seian and the reality of the Allied victory became apparent. A Russian captain ordered the Japanese to stack their arms and then handed a rifle to an American prisoner with the words, 'From this day you are free. Now march them round and take them off to the guard house.' Percival and his colleagues were at last able to set off with the Russians through the flooded countryside for Mukden, where they arrived two days later. At the provincial capital two transport aircraft were waiting to return the party to the civilisation from which they had been totally cut off for the last three and a half years. They flew via Sian on the Yellow River to Chungking where the Embassy staff and British military headquarters gave them a warm welcome. At Chungking, Percival and the American General Wainwright left the remainder of the party and flew off to Manila in preparation for the Japanese surrender ceremony in Tokyo Bay which General MacArthur, to Percival's surprise and delight, had invited him and General Wainwright to attend. At MacArthur's insistence, Wainwright and Percival stood immediately behind him at the ceremony at which Shigemitsu and Tojo signed on behalf of the Emperor and the Japanese General Staff. It was a moment of great satisfaction for the British GOC as he stood, underweight but reasonably fit, beside a haggard and emaciated Wainwright, as the Japanese leaders were led in for the signing ceremony. Only one other senior British officer, the Prime Minister's representative with MacArthur' headquarters Lieutenant General Sir Charles Gairdner, was present at the ceremony. 'It was all absorbingly interesting', Percival wrote later, 'and I shall be eternally grateful to MacArthur for inviting me to go there. It was certainly a very fine gesture on his part.'[40] Then it was quickly back to Manila for a repeat performance, infinitely more satisfying for Percival and for Wainwright as well, at which General Yamashita, now commanding the remaining Japanese forces on the Philippines, formally surrendered. 'As Yamashita entered the room I saw one eyebrow lifted and a look of surprise cross his face – but only for a moment', wrote Percival. 'His face quickly resumed that sphinx-like mask common to all Japanese, and he showed no further interest.'[41] It was good to be in at the kill.

PEACEWORK

'Let no one look down on those honourable, well-meaning men whose actions are chronicled in these pages without searching his own heart, reviewing his own discharge of public duty, and applying the lessons of the past to his future conduct.'

Sir Winston Churchill, Preface to The Second World War

The news that Arthur would soon be home reached Betty in a cablegram from him forwarded by the Australian Army Staff in London. It read simply, 'Arrived MANILA thirtieth hope to be home about middle SEPTEMBER best love'. In fact, after the surrender ceremonies things happened more quickly than he had dared hope. On 5 September he said goodbye to the Americans who had been so hospitable and understanding since his release, spent two days at Headquarters SEAC in Ceylon and then flew home. It took only 48 hours to get back, compared with the two weeks he had spent getting out to Singapore at the start of the war. There at the Wiltshire airfield to meet him was Betty, who had borne their separation with such courage and fortitude. On 16 February 1942, after the news of the fall of Singapore and Arthur's imprisonment had reached home, the newspapers had recorded her reaction: 'Even though the battle may take a wrong turning, it is still the one great battle for Britain. The duty of wives at home is to go on showing that they are not second in courage to their fighting husbands. Then we shall win.' Her burden had been all the greater since, after the defeat, the newspapers had been full of stories about the disastrous Malayan campaign conducted under Arthur's leadership. Family and friends had helped, of course, and some contributions to the correspondence columns had suggested that the real reason for the disaster might well lie nearer home. One interesting contribution in the *Daily Telegraph* had quoted a letter which the writer had received from General Sir Ian Hamilton in July 1929 recording the general's opposition to the building of a naval base in the first place where it could not be satisfactorily defended. 'Yes!', the general had written, 'I have done my best in preventing this handsome present being prepared for the Japanese.' The newspaper's contributor had concluded, 'Do not blame the Generals or the forces for the surrender of Singapore.'[1] There had been other similar informed contributions in the papers, and some of Arthur's staff whose evacuation he had ordered before the island fell had been thoughtful enough to write to Betty. One had spoken of how remarkably fit the general had remained considering the amount of work he was getting through. Another letter, from a senior staff officer, spoke of Percival's kindness to his staff and of how he 'seemed to know the answer to every question and remain unruffled however bad the news was. If any man could have saved Malaya he would have done.'[2]

One particular letter, shown to her by her father-in-law Alfred Percival, had given Betty particular comfort. This had been written in the greatest confidence by someone at the heart of Government. It had come from Lord Croft, an old friend of both Alfred and Arthur Percival, who had commanded the local Hertfordshire territorial battalion and then a brigade during the First World War. Henry Croft was Under Secretary of State for War throughout the conflict against Japan. His letter gave some hint of the facts to which the general public were not privy. It explained that Arthur's Indian troops 'were rather a scratch lot' and 'all in and little use to Arthur' by the time they reached Singapore, that 'the Australians were terribly disappointing – I won't [changed from 'can't – Author] say more about them', and that 18th Division had no time whatever to get acclimatised and 'were soft as jelly after three months at sea'. Lord Croft made it clear that only 'far stronger military forces plus adequate air power could have held the Peninsula and Singapore for any length of time'. This was quite a different story from the one the public had been hearing. Lord Croft had passed on these consolatory words in August 1942 after a long private talk with one of Percival's staff who had been ordered out before Singapore fell and had since returned to England. Croft had sworn Alfred Percival to 'absolute confidence' but said he could show the letter to 'Mrs Arthur' but should impress on her that the letter 'must on no account be repeated to anyone'.[3] So that was how it had all happened.

For Arthur Percival himself there were a couple of months of much-needed leave during which he was able to get to know his wife and growing family again, discover what had been said and written about the campaign during his incarceration and get back some of the weight which the years of undernourishment and ill-treatment had caused even his lean frame to shed. He also learnt, with mounting anger, of the appalling treatment to which his men had been subjected in the labour camps throughout the Far East and particularly on the Burma–Siam Railway. There had been but a mild foretaste of this before he had been forced to leave Changi. Letters and telegrams from friends and well-wishers flooded into his Hertfordshire home, many from the United States. But from the Government and the Chiefs of Staff there was what his friend Brigadier Sir John 'Jackie' Smyth called 'an icy silence'. A few months after getting back Percival attended an investiture at Buckingham Palace to receive the CB he had been awarded in the early stages of the war. The King was sensitive and understanding enough to have a private conversation with him after the ceremony, which Arthur much appreciated, but that was the extent of the official recognition. There was no knighthood, the normal reward for the services of an officer of his rank, a slight whose effect was heightened by the fact that fellow-prisoner Air Vice-Marshal Maltby was later awarded one, though he arrived only half-way through the campaign and served for most of the time as Pulford's deputy. Nor was Percival offered another appointment. He was not even confirmed in the rank of lieutenant general, though he had borne its responsibilities in war and imprisonment for four and a half years. 'I am told I am not going to get another job, chiefly on account of my age', he wrote to Heath, 'I suppose there is some justification for that in these days, but I must confess that I should have finished with a better feeling in my mouth if they had done something for me.'[4] Brooke Popham probably had similar feelings; Churchill had promised him a baronetcy when he replaced him in Singapore, but it was never conferred.

On 19 November Percival returned to the War Office where a room had been provided for him, to start clearing up his Malayan affairs. His despatch had to be written and there were the recommendations for awards to be agreed and confirmed with the different national authorities. Curiously enough, a case was already being prepared for an award to Percival himself for his leadership and courage as a prisoner of war, based on the debriefing reports of his fellow officers, by one of the military intelligence departments. The evidence provided by two brigadiers and a colonel was certainly meritorious enough: one spoke of his 'splendid behaviour and leadership', another of his 'dignified courage and exemplary conduct and leadership displayed at all times'. The Military Secretary discussed the case with CIGS Alanbrooke, then in his last months of service and in a position to be magnanimous (if indeed that was what was required), but the 'scapegoat' mantle was too conveniently in place to be removed. Alanbrooke 'felt that in view of all the circumstances of Singapore an award to General Percival would be inappropriate'.[5] This was the same CIGS who in mid-December 1941 had not expected Singapore to hold out for a month.

Percival did not anticipate that the drafting of his despatch would take too much time; he had already produced two versions whilst a prisoner after much discussion with Heath and now had access to documents and Lieutenant Colonel Cobley's comprehensive account to verify the detail. But he did anticipate delay in getting it cleared. 'My chief concern now is to see that the truth of the Malayan business is put across to the public. I feel that many efforts will be made to block it', he wrote to Heath.[6] Before 1945 had ended he was already writing of the likely delay in its publication because of the need for clearance; he was only too aware of the official sensitivity to the full facts of the Malayan campaign becoming known. The draft was finally submitted to the Secretary of State for War on 17 April 1946. A couple of months later Percival was retired as an honorary lieutenant general, but receiving the pension of a major general. However, the despatch did not appear in print until early in 1948.

The official reason for the delay was that the Government wanted to publish all six despatches dealing with the Far East together; but since four of them were already to hand when Percival's was submitted (only Air Vice-Marshal Maltby's came in a little later), the problem was plainly one of clearance. Percival's report was naturally longer than the others since he was the only commander who was there at the start through to the finish. The initial difficulties came from the Air Ministry and from the Colonial Office, essentially representing Sir Shenton Thomas. The RAF were particularly sensitive to what the erstwhile GOC had to say about the way pre-war decisions had been taken over the siting of airfields in Malaya and to Percival's claim that in the late summer of 1941 the RAF had estimated that they would cause 40 per cent casualties to any Japanese invasion force, with the aircraft then available to them; an estimate which they argued had never been made, certainly not on the basis of the existing RAF strength. On both issues they fought hard to get Percival to alter his wording, even enlisting a reluctant Brooke Popham to support their case. Brooke Popham's initial view was that Percival's despatch was 'very fair and broadminded and as you will note I see nothing in it to which to object'. He also made the point that 'There are certain events, which he would have been justified in putting in his despatch, not creditable to the ground staff of the RAF', but which Percival had chosen to leave out.[7] The exchanges continued with Percival providing corroboration for his 40 per cent damage figure from his contemporary tactical appreciation and from a member of his staff, and indicating that the damage figure had been provided by two officers who were joint planners at GHQ Far East. Maltby, significantly, had already agreed Percival's despatch and paid a glowing tribute in his own for the help which the RAF received from the Army in Malaya. Still the Air Ministry pursued their objection. 'This is becoming a *cause célèbre* and I fail to see how it is going to be settled', wrote a despairing Brooke Popham. Ultimately, Percival gave way to the pressure being concerted between the Air Ministry and his old boss ('Better not word the Air Ministry comments on para 20, too like mine', advised Brooke Popham).[8] Keen to get agreement, Percival unwisely removed the 40 per cent figure which had played a significant part in his own calculations at the time. Perhaps respect for the dead Pulford, who had done his damnedest to help the Army, played a part in his decision.

In early April 1947 the Ministry of Information was explaining to Brooke Popham that the length of time taken by other departments to comment on Percival's despatch meant that it was not in such an advanced state of preparation as the others.[9] The Colonial Office had now taken up the cudgels. Percival had been expecting this, as he explained to Brooke Popham: 'I am quite certain there will be screams from the Colonial Office.' He added, 'This is a despatch from a Commander in the Field who has the interests of his own troops to consider, and the Government has no right to dictate what he has to say.'[10] Thomas had many comments to make, and about purely military matters as well as the issues of civil defence and the colonial government's relations with the Army upon which, more justifiably, he had strong views. He complained that Percival had skated over issues of military indiscipline, the half-hearted fighting of the Australians and their behaviour at Kuantan, the mistakes up in Kedah and at the Slim River, Wavell's Order of the Day of 10 February and the absence of northern defences on Singapore. Interestingly, against Percival's comment on the RAF damage falling far below the estimated figure, the ex-Governor had scrawled an emphatic 'Yes'. But his main comments were in defence of the colonial government's actions in the civil defence field and over cooperation with the Services, for example over the 'denial' policy. In defence of his position Thomas explained that 'no one ever gave us a hint before the invasion that we were in danger of defeat'. It was a valid point; however, he did add 'I should like to place it on record that he [General Percival] never joined in these optimistic forecasts.'[11] Percival willingly made some minor changes to his draft, but on the major issues of the difficulties of dealing with the local government, its lukewarm support on several key matters and on the extent of fifth column activity in Malaya and Singapore, he stood firm. In the end, Thomas wrote directly to Percival suggesting a meeting to iron out their differences. Percival was not averse to this, but made it clear that he was not going to back down. 'To be honest', he wrote, 'I am getting a bit fed up with all these delays. We started by expecting the despatch to be published by the end of last year. Now it is August this year and we seem to be very little nearer the goal.'[12] Indeed, in an effort to goad the authorities into action, he had fired off a letter to *The Times* in much the same vein only a couple of days earlier, complaining that, 'It is a great disappointment to me that now, nearly 16 months after it was completed, the despatch still remains unpublished.'[13]

In an attempt to placate Thomas, the Cabinet Office suggested footnotes to the despatch giving the ex-Governor's dissenting views, but Thomas would have none of it, believing that Percival as the responsible senior commander was entitled to have the last word. In any case, perhaps realising his cause was lost, Thomas noted, 'With the meagre resources at his disposal, no commander could have saved Malaya.'[14] Thomas's ultimate defence of his position was to write his own account entitled 'Malaya's War Effort', which was circulated to all concerned, including

Wavell's biographer, but never published by the Colonial Office. At the end of the year Percival was told that the Colonial Office was still object-ing to certain passages and that the Ministry of Information was 'still in the dark about the high level discussions which have been taking place, and which could not, in any case, be mentioned publicly.'[15] There seemed to be more than merely Colonial Office sensitivity to what Percival might say. It seems certain that he had very clear guidance about what he could and could not include, particularly concerning the performance of the Commonwealth troops. Even five years later, when the official historians were gathering the material for their volume on Malaya, they had the firmest instructions 'to say nothing which will cause any rift in Commonwealth relations.'[16] Indeed, publication of their volume was delayed still further so that its account could be harmonised with that in the Australian history.[17] One can imagine how much more constrained Percival must have been by the requirements of Government policy when the memory of the Malayan disaster was all the fresher.

Those who suspected that Percival's despatch had been so long delayed because of the gravity of its disclosures were disappointed. There were no sensational revelations in the long, detailed and restrained narrative; no stories of RAF ground staff in panic evacuations, Indian formations break-ing or Australian deserters crowding the docks. Indeed, when discussing the well-known frequent changes in the higher command in Malaya, *The Times* leader chided Percival with commenting 'in the classic tradition of British understatement'. The *Daily Telegraph* review noted that the erst-while GOC had made the important points: little air support, few tanks, untrained troops. It also explained in the plainest possible language that Singapore was not, and could never have been, the 'fortress' of Churchill's and the popular imagination. The despatch made clear, the review explained, how serious had been the underestimation of Japanese martial prowess. The verdict of *The Times* was that the despatch did not answer all the questions that had been asked about the Malayan campaign, 'but it does answer a number and it also disposes of some extravagances'. The paper's military correspondent commented that the despatch made it clear that 'we were badly caught "on the wrong foot" in Malaya', but added significantly that that conclusion had no necessary connection 'with some of the nonsense written on the subject'.[18]

Others were even less convinced that Percival had been able to tell the whole story. He did admit to the Reuters correspondent that the Government had taken out a couple of sections, though not, so far as he could remember, because of Australian sensibilities. 'I have reason to think that the Australians will be happy with the despatch', he added. He could not, of course, give any hint of the long battles over wording or explain what his 'riding instructions' may have been. The *Sydney Morning Herald* smelled a cover-up. 'The Malayan Commanders' despatches were expected to be a bombshell;' it declared, 'in the event they proved something of a damp squib.' Why had those available in 1942 been held back for six years, it asked, and why had Admiral Layton's not been published at all? Layton was a man 'renowned for his blunt outspokenness'.[19] The *Manchester Guardian* was similarly unconvinced, lecturing Percival that despatches should be 'brief, factual and free of whitewash' and giving its considered view that 'It would have been wiser to hold a formal inquiry into the whole black business instead of publishing these recollections and afterthoughts by senior officers after long years of captivity.'[20]

The delay in the publication of the despatches was of concern to Percival on another score. He had long since contracted with publishers Eyre and Spottiswoode to write his personal account of the campaign and they had been holding his manuscript since May the previous year. Percival had to write and remind them that the book's contents had to be kept secret until the despatch was published. It was an unnecessary precaution; he clearly had not appreciated how long it would take to get a book edited, printed and published in the days of post-war austerity with its rationing of paper and general shortages. *The War in Malaya* was finally published in April 1949 and, as books of this kind go, sold quite well, running to two printings and having a separate publication in India, besides being serialised in Malaya. It was a little more revealing than the despatch, giving rather more background to events, considerably more detail and some information on Percival's time as a prisoner of war. The author's personal opinion obtruded ever so slightly on occasion. What characterised the account more than anything, given the obloquy Percival had suffered for his time as GOC and his growing awareness of the political background to events and the way the needs of his Command had been judged at the time, was that he had written it with such 'restraint and dignity and without rancour'.[21] As another reviewer observed, 'He does not look for scapegoats but writes in the firm intention that these shall not be found in himself or his men.'[22] Not unnatural, one might say, in view of all that both had suffered in the national cause. Percival's Australian friends, those who had fought well and then endured the captivity with him, were again grateful for his restraint and for 'something that the people of Australia . . . can read and derive some comfort from', wrote Jim Thyer, adding that he thought the 'criticisms were very mild and fair'.[23] One of the counsel to the Commissioners who had investigated General Bennett's controversial escape from Singapore wrote 'May I be permitted to say how much I admire the modesty, tolerance and generosity which pervade your book, and to say that 99% of people out here who know the facts realise how scurvily you were treated – in more ways than one.'[24] Percival did not have a copy of his book sent to General Bennett. 'I am afraid he is rather a back number', Thyer confided.

Perhaps most interesting of all was the comment in a letter from Henry

Pownall, Percival's school chum from Rugby and commander-in-chief for a few short days during the campaign. General Pownall, also now retired from the Army, was acting as military consultant to Churchill for the writing of the latter's *Second World War*. He explained that he had ordered a copy of Percy's book 'for WSC and sent it to him with a good deal of sidelining. This doesn't always work with him, but this time it certainly did. He <u>has</u> read it, indeed made a favourable remark to me about the book the other day.' According to Pownall, this accounted for the softening of Churchill's attitude to the events in Singapore as recorded in volume four of his history which was then in draft. Pownall's letter makes clear the extent of Churchill's ignorance of the Singapore situation at the time (and by implication the supine failure of the Chiefs of Staff to enlighten him). 'At least', Pownall confided, 'he does realise that the naval base was on the north shore and that the object was to keep the enemy away from the base, not to fight for the Island amid its ruins.'[25] When Churchill's volume appeared in 1951 it still betrayed, in Percival's view, the Prime Minister's 'complete ignorance of the way the Singapore defences were developed and of the defensive principles which governed them'.[26] It remained, of course, a lacuna in the popular understanding as well: Pownall wrote to Percival on a later occasion 'The letters in the DT [*Daily Telegraph* – Author] about the Singapore defences seem to me remarkably fatuous.'[27] The review of his book which Percival probably enjoyed most, was that written by General 'Boney' Fuller, his old mentor from Staff College days and now a distinguished military critic whose own *The Second World War* had appeared the previous year. Fuller explained Percival's predicament as GOC Malaya as follows: 'When General Percival flew out to Singapore . . . he found himself in command of a naval base without a fleet, a large number of airfields without aircraft and a small army to defend them in an area as large as England, simply *to prevent the enemy using them* – a situation beating anything to be found in *Alice Through the Looking Glass*.'[28] Old 'Boney' hadn't changed; hard-hitting and perceptive as ever!

When General Percival had left Singapore in August 1942 for Formosa, the Japanese had already begun moving parties of prisoners around the region as local labour forces for a range of war-related logistical projects. It was not until he had been released that Percival learnt the full story of the appalling conditions under which they had laboured and of the many who had lost their lives. Among those of his men who returned, some were so sick and debilitated that they never again enjoyed good health; others were mentally scarred by their experiences as prisoners and found their lives ruined by them. Their plight affected General Percival deeply and he spent much of his free time in work for their welfare. The agency through which this work was initially directed was the Returned British Prisoners of War Association, but the experiences and problems of those who had been prisoners of the Japanese were so distinct and special that some 80 separate Far East Prisoners of War (FEPOW) Clubs and Associations were soon established throughout the country. A National Federation came into being and General Percival became its first President.

The welfare work took many forms, a principal one being the effort to get clauses inserted in the Peace Treaty with Japan for a sum of money to be provided to ex-POWs by Japan, by way of compensation for their treatment; the cash to come from frozen Japanese assets in Allied hands. Percival worked in tandem with Jackie Smyth, who was now an MP and better placed to lobby on the issue of compensation for the FEPOWs and their dependants. The proposal was opposed by the Government and Chiefs of Staff of the day, because of the precedent it would set. Some might say it was an excellent precedent. However, the authorities finally gave way in the face of the widespread support which the FEPOWs managed to attract from all parties in Parliament and from the country at large. When the motion was finally put to the House of Commons it was carried unanimously. Ultimately, ten years after Parliament's agreement and the signing of the Peace Treaty with Japan, the money was finally released to the FEPOW leaders. It was by no means a king's ransom, but the £5 million which was initially secured (there was a further smaller sum later) enabled a token per capita grant to be paid to all living FEPOWs and a welfare trust to be established for them and their dependents. General Percival became the first Chairman of the FEPOW Welfare Trust.

Another issue on which Percival fought hard was the matter of back pay and allowances for the Chinese irregulars of Dalforce who had volunteered for service in the campaign. Percival enlisted the aid of Shenton Thomas to right this injustice. The ex-Governor took the matter up with the Colonial Office while Percival badgered the Adjutant General's department. A further matter which provoked his intervention was David Lean's film *Bridge on the River Kwai*, which caused widespread anger and resentment among ex-POWs. It was an early example of the popular but dangerous 'faction' genre which places wholly fictional characters and situations in a realistic historical context (in this case the building of the Tamarkan bridge) and gives them the appearance of fact. Percival took up the cudgels and wrote to the newspapers about the powerful but wholly misleading impression which the film created of people, events and attitudes in the prison camps. He contacted Army public relations, who in turn approached the film company. The result was an agreement to screen an explanation of the totally fictional character of the film at every performance. This hardly satisfied the survivors of the notorious railway, for the film proved immensely popular, but it was better than nothing.[29]

The FEPOW organisations became lively and enduring institutions; the bond of comradeship in extreme adversity whose depths the rest of the nation seemed not to appreciate, was a strong one. The Federation enjoyed the patronage of the Mountbattens and Field Marshal Slim and the enthusiastic support of its President, General Percival, who became a familiar and much-loved figure at its central and regional gatherings, to which Betty sometimes accompanied him. 'He was regarded and respected everywhere as "No. 1 FEPOW"', writes the present Chairman of the Welfare Trust, and he always received a very warm reception for all he was able to achieve on behalf of the Federation and its members. For his part, Percival was proud of the camaraderie of the ex-prisoners. 'The spirit of this FEPOW organisation is really quite remarkable', he wrote to a fellow member, 'Apart from the welfare and other things which it does, I feel that an organisation of this sort with such a real spirit of friendship and desire to help each other must have a good influence generally in the country'.[30]

Aside from his FEPOW work, the correspondence associated with his time as GOC continued to occupy General Percival's attention for many years after the war. All this was in addition to the full-time post he had taken as President of the Hertfordshire Red Cross and which he held for 16 years. In 1950 he was delighted to add another responsibility to the list by becoming Colonel of his old regiment, The 22nd (Cheshire) Regiment. This was a particular pleasure which brought him back just a little into the mainstream of Army affairs from the position of tacit purdah which he had accepted with dignity for so long. He enjoyed his colonelcy enormously and worked devotedly for the regiment's welfare during the five years of his tenure. It was a time of great importance in the Army's affairs, with successive overseas challenges to be confronted and with the Cold War at its height and often with a visible focus in Berlin. The opportunity to visit the regiment, then stationed in the old German capital, was consequently both interesting and exciting. The last time he had been in Europe in uniform had been just prior to the disastrous Dunkirk campaign. It was curious the way that the Dunkirk army had emerged from its ordeal with its men regarded almost as heroes, while the Army of Malaya was so plainly pilloried. The parallels between Dunkirk and Malaya were close. Yet Percival's troops had fought longer, marched further, and operated in much more difficult terrain and without the air cover, the tanks or the naval support that had been available aplenty to the BEF and its allies.

The events of the Malayan campaign itself were never far from Percival's mind for very long. When producing his own despatch and writing *The War in Malaya*, he had been at pains to tell the story of the campaign without criticising his subordinates or his superiors. It had been a remarkable feat of determination and restraint, particularly in the case of the book, over which he naturally had greater freedom. His lips had to remain sealed on so many issues. He and his Army had laboured under so many disadvantages. He was determined to defend himself, his commanders and men against the criticism of others. This applied as much to the official historians, who were now drafting their version of the campaign, as it did to independent authors. If they were critical, he warned the authors, 'I will ask for permission to express my own views on the actions and decisions of my superiors, my subordinates and other leading personalities more freely than I have done'.[31] In fact, he never did 'go public' again, despite feeling very dissatisfied with the line taken in the official volume on the campaign. The authors freely admitted that 'the campaign in Malaya was lost before it began', yet their terms of reference precluded them from a full examination of the vital political dimension in which its loss was effectively determined. 'In our opinion the British Government failed and General Percival and General Bennett failed badly,'[32] was their private and confidential conclusion, as though the generals could have succeeded in the circumstances which the Government had created for them. Since the political aspect was not for close examination, and their particular instructions warned them off criticism of the Commonwealth forces, it seemed inevitable that if there was to be blame, General Percival would be the quarry. 'The general impression one gets after reading your History', he wrote, 'is a very false one because you have concentrated on bringing out everything that might be open to criticism (and quite a bit that really is not) and very little of what was good. Also many of the adverse pictures are heavily overdrawn.'[33]

The choice of General Kirby to write the official volume was interesting in itself. He had served in Malaya in the mid-1930s (when his particular nostrum for the protection of the Naval Base from a landward attack had been a belt of mustard gas across Johore),[34] but had spent the campaign itself on the staff of Army Headquarters in India. General Playfair, who actually worked for Brooke Popham and Wavell throughout the Malayan campaign, was chosen to write the official volumes on the Middle East. Did Playfair know too much about Malaya, or was he merely too close to the events themselves to be trusted to record them dispassionately? His interpretation of the MATADOR decision might have made fascinating reading. The view of one of Percival's senior staff officers was that General Kirby, 'is a very difficult man to tie down. He feels that he has a mission to lay blame on someone; and is prepared to say everyone was wrong all the time – except General Wavell!'[35] Kirby as much as admitted his partiality, declaring to Percival 'I have served under Wavell personally and know that his memory is absolutely infallible.'[36] The power of total recall had not stopped the Supreme Commander from telling Percival on 19 January 1942 that preparations for the northern defences of the island must be *entirely secret*, yet recording in his despatch that on 20 January, 'very little had been done' to prepare them.[37] Percival found Kirby's judgements excessively clinical, taking little account of the turbulent and complex local circumstances in Malaya and Singapore, or the consequences of air and naval inferiority. 'It was not a question of sitting down in a complete void', protested Percival, in defending his Singapore dispositions, 'as one might do at the Staff College, with no outside influences and thinking what the best theoretical allocation of troops would be.'[38] Percival firmly believed that Kirby 'was told to be critical'.

The War Against Japan Volume 1 was finally published in 1957. The *Daily Mail* greeted the publication with the headline 'THE SHAME OF SINGAPORE. GENERALS, ADMIRALS, AIR MARSHALS, GOVERNORS, NONE IS SPARED FROM THE CRITICISM OF MUDDLE AND INEPTITUDE.'[39] Some of the senior commanders concerned were quick to make their reply. Percival's response was 'I have no comment to make on the history. My views are well-known to the panel of officers who have written it and we discussed certain facts and situations.'[40] He and they knew that so much had been left unsaid.

The shock of the fall of Singapore had brought many calls in early 1942 for an official enquiry, or indeed a Royal Commission, to examine the disaster. Churchill had resisted these at the time on the grounds that 'this would not be good for our country, and that it would hamper the prosecution of the war'.[41] Yet in the speech to a secret session of Parliament which argued against such an investigation, he did not forbear from making clear his own dissatisfaction with the conduct of the campaign and the 'premature' fall of Singapore. His account was partial and self-serving, including, for example, the explanation that 'the absence of the Air Force' was accounted for by 'the enemy's domination of our airfields'. How, some members of the House must have wondered, had they managed to dominate them in the first place? 'The generalship is criticised', Churchill also explained, concluding his brief review of the campaign (it occupied only one long, tendentious paragraph in a speech running to 22 pages of printed text) with the recommendation that having 'enough trouble on our hands to cope with', an enquiry should not then be held.

Parliament accepted Churchill's advice, although official enquiries had been ordered into the reverses following Rommel's first offensive in the Western Desert and after the Crete *débâcle* in the spring of the previous year, both less serious matters than the fall of Singapore. Could it be that Churchill remembered the Select Committee's Gallipoli enquiry of the First World War which had tarnished him as a high-risk gambler who tried to do too much with inadequate resources and failed sufficiently to consult his Service advisers? Was the Singapore parallel perhaps too close for comfort? He repeated his arguments against an enquiry when writing his *Second World War*, adding on this occasion, 'I certainly thought that in justice to the officers and men concerned there should be an enquiry into all the circumstances as soon as the fighting stopped. This however has not been instituted by the government of the day. Years have passed and many of the witnesses are dead . . .'[42] Yet of the key figures in the tragedy, only Wavell and Dill had died by the time these words were penned, while their author returned to power himself within months of writing them. Neither then nor later was an enquiry held. Files vital to an explanation of the rapid fall of the 'fortress' remained closed for 50 years. Some still are, including, it is believed, the one considering whether an enquiry should be held.

Much might have been revealed by such an investigation. It could have provided a coherent account of the muddled thinking which had attended the early Naval Base decisions and the failure over many years to plan realistically for its defence. It might even have speculated on the possible outcome of the clash with Japan if all the fighter aircraft and tanks which went to Russia in 1941 had taken the less hazardous route to Singapore; and if the 18th Division had gone to Malaya in the spring of 1941 when it was virtually complete,[43] and trained in the tropics rather than in Scotland in the coldest winter on record. More realistically, the enquiry would certainly have pinpointed the responsibility for giving the defence of Malaya such a low priority and exposed the disagreement between the Prime Minister and his military advisers on this issue. It would certainly have investigated the MATADOR operation and perhaps considered what could have happened if, with a strengthened Army and Air Force in Malaya, MATADOR had been launched on 6 December, as the full tri-service operation it should have been. Of course, it could hardly have speculated on the long-term consequences of the dramatic loss of Malaya and Singapore. Nevertheless, it is difficult to disagree with one historian's judgement, which highlights the significance of Churchill's decisions, that 'The picture of General Percival and his fellow Britons surrendering to an Asiatic race was one which did more to undermine the British Empire than anything except the Americans.'[44]

Arthur Percival died on the last day of January 1966 and was buried in his native Hertfordshire. Three weeks later memorial services were held in Chester Cathedral and at St Martin-in-the-Fields. At the London service a crowded church heard the lesson read by the Colonel of the Cheshire Regiment who had served for a time as a subaltern with Percival's excellent second battalion in the 1930s. The address was delivered by the Bishop of Birmingham, a personal friend of Percival's since the Bishop's time in the diocese of Singapore and, for a short while, as a temporary Army chaplain. There were many Cheshires in the congregation, people from a variety of Hertfordshire organisations and from the British Red Cross Society for which Arthur had worked after the war. Some of his old Malaya Command staff were there with representatives of regiments which had fought in the campaign. Air Vice-Marshal Maltby also attended. The FEPOW headquarters and branches were there in strength, of course, paying a final tribute to the general who had endured the captivity with them. Might any recriminations have troubled old General Percival as, in his final days, he reflected on his crowded life? Probably not. He had never for a moment regretted making that fateful change from temporary citizen-soldier to regular officer when Brigadier General Shoubridge had made the offer to him in the trenches of the Somme. It had given him an absorbing career of adventure and service, danger and responsibility. As for the campaign in Malaya, well that had turned out to be, as he had always suspected it might, 'a pretty sticky business'.

CHRONOLOGY – ARTHUR PERCIVAL

26 December 1887	Born in Aspenden, Herts
1897–1901	Bengeo School, Hertford
1901–1906	Rugby School
1907–1914	Messrs Naylor, Benzon and Co., City of London
5 August 1914	Volunteer – Inns of Court OTC
3 September 1914	Temporary Commission – 7th (Service) Bn Bedfordshire Regt
July 1915	OC A Company 7th Bedfords France
1 July 1916	MC for Pommiers Redoubt Operation, the Somme
July 1916	Regular Commission Essex Regiment, Temporary Majority
October 1916	Wounded, hospital in UK
January 1918	Acting Lieutenant Colonel – Commands 7th (and later 2nd) Bedfords
April 1918	DSO and Croix de Guerre – German March Offensive
May 1918	Acting Brigade Commander, 54th Brigade
January 1919	Brevet Majority
April–October 1919	Second-in-Command 46th Royal Fusiliers, North Russia
August 1919	Bar to DSO – Gorodok Column Operation, Archangel
1920	OC Bandon Detachment 2nd Bn Essex Reg, County Cork
1920–22	Intelligence and Operations Officer 2nd Bn Essex Regt
1923	Student Army Staff College. Majority in 22nd (Cheshire) Regt
1924–28	Staff Officer, Nigeria. Brevet Lieutenant Colonelcy
July 1927	Marries Betty MacGregor Greer
1929	Company Commander 2nd Bn 22nd (Cheshire) Regt

1930	Student Royal Naval Staff College Greenwich
1931–32	Instructor Army Staff College
1932–34	Commands 2nd Bn 22nd (Cheshire) Regt, Malta
1935	Student at Imperial Defence College
1936–37	Promoted Colonel. GSO 1 HQ Malaya Command
1938	Brigadier General Staff Home Command Aldershot
1939	Brigadier General Staff 1st Corps BEF
February 1940	General Officer Commanding 43rd (Wessex) Division UK
May 1940	Assistant Chief of the Imperial General Staff
August 1940	General Officer Commanding 44th (West Midland) Division UK
April 1941	Temporary Lieutenant-General
May 1941	General Officer Commanding Malaya Command
8 December 1941	Japanese 25th Army invades Malaya
15 February 1942	Surrenders Army of Malaya to General Yamashita
1942–1945	POW in Changi, Formosa and Manchuria
1946	Retires from Army with honorary rank of Lieutenant General
1949	Publishes *The War in Malaya*
Post-war	Director Hertfordshire, British Red Cross Society
	Life President Far East Prisoners of War Associations
	Deputy Lieutenant for Hertfordshire
1950–55	Colonel 22nd (Cheshire) Regiment
31 January 1966	Dies in King Edward VIIth Hospital, London
20 February 1966	Memorial Service – St Martin-in-the-Fields, London

BIBLIOGRAPHY

This listing is of the main published works consulted. Unpublished sources are given in the chapter references.

Allen, L, *Singapore 1941–42*, Davis-Poynter, London, 1977.
———, 'The Surrender of Singapore: The Official Japanese Version', *Durham University Journal*, Vol. XXIX, No. 1, Dec. 1967, pp. 1–6.
Attlee, C R, *As It Happened*, Heinemann, London, 1954.
Avon, The Earl of, *The Eden Memoirs: The Reckoning*, Cassell, London, 1965.
Barber, N, *Sinister Twilight*, Collins, London, 1968.
Barry, T, *Guerrilla Days in Ireland*, Irish Press, Dublin, 1949.
Beckett, I W F and Simpson, K (eds), *A Nation in Arms: A Social Study of the British Army in the First World War*, Manchester UP, Manchester, 1985.
Bennett, H G, *Why Singapore Fell*, Angus and Robertson, Sydney, 1944.
Bloom, F, *Dear Philip*, Bodley Head, London, 1980.
Bond, B (ed.), *Chief of Staff: the Diaries of Lieutenant General Sir Henry Pownall*, Volume 2 1940–1944, Leo Cooper, London, 1974.
Bradley, J, *Cyril Wild: The Tall Man Who Never Slept*, Woodfield Publishing, Fontwell, 1991.
Brett-James, A, *Ball of Fire: The Fifth Indian Division in the Second World War*, Gale & Polden, Aldershot, 1951.
Bridges, Lieutenant General Sir Tom, *Alarms and Excursions*, Longmans, London, 1938.
Brooke Popham, Air Chief Marshal Sir Robert, *Operations in the Far East 17 October 1940 to 27 December 1941*, HMSO, London, 1948.
Bryant, A, *The Turn of the Tide 1939–43*, Collins, London, 1957.
Burrows, J W, *The Essex Regiment*, Burrows, Southend, 1931.
Butler, E, *Barry's Flying Column*, Leo Cooper, London, 1971.
Callaghan, R, *The Worst Disaster: The Fall of Singapore*, University of Delaware Press, Newark, 1977.
———, 'The Illusion of Security: Singapore 1919–42', *Journal of Contemporary History*, Vol. IX, No. 2.
Chalfont, A, *Montgomery of Alamein*, Weidenfeld and Nicolson, London, 1976.

Charmley, J, *Churchill: The End of Glory*, Hodder and Stoughton, London, 1993.

———, *Churchill's Grand Alliance*, Hodder and Stoughton, London, 1995.

———, *Duff Cooper*, Weidenfeld and Nicolson, London, 1986.

Churchill, W S, *The World Crisis: The Aftermath*, Thornton Butterworth, London, 1929.

———, *The Gathering Storm*, Cassell, London, 1948.

———, *Their Finest Hour*, Cassell, London, 1949.

———, *The Grand Alliance*, Cassell, London, 1950.

———, *The Hinge of Fate*, Cassell, London, 1951.

———, *Triumph and Tragedy*, Cassell, London, 1954.

Clark, A, *Barbarossa: The Russo-German Conflict 1941–45*, Hutchinson, London, 1965.

Clisby, M, *Guilty or Innocent: The Gordon Bennett Case*, Allen & Unwin, Sydney, 1992.

Cloake, J, *Templer: Tiger of Malaya*, Harrap, London, 1985.

Coates, W P and Z K, *Armed Intervention in Russia 1918–22*, Gollancz, London, 1935.

Connell, J, *Wavell: Supreme Commander*, Collins, London, 1969.

Coogan, T P, *Michael Collins*, Hutchinson, London, 1990.

Cooper, Diana, *Autobiography: Trumpets from the Steep* (one vol. edn.), Michael Russell, Salisbury, 1979.

Cooper, Duff, *Old Men Forget*, Hart-Davis, London, 1953.

Croft, Brigadier General Lord, *My Life of Strife*, Hutchinson, London, 1949.

Danchev, A, *Very Special Relationship*, Brassey's, London, 1986.

———, 'The Central Direction of War 1940–41', in Sweetman J (ed.), *Sword and Mace*, Brassey's, London, 1986.

Dean, Colonel P S W, 'A Guest of Japan – Uninvited and Invited', *Army Quarterly*, Vol. 124, No. 2, April, 1994.

Dixon, N F, *On the Psychology of Military Incompetence*, Cape, London, 1976.

Dobbie, General Sir William, *On Active Service with Christ*.

Elphick, P and Smith, M, *Odd Man Out: The Story of the Singapore Traitor*, Hodder and Stoughton, London, 1993.

Elphick, P, *Singapore: The Pregnable Fortress*, Hodder and Stoughton, London, 1995.

Errington, F L H (ed.), *The Inns of Court Officer Training Corps during the Great War*, Printing Craft, London.

Fergusson, B, *Wavell: Portrait of a Soldier*, Collins, London, 1961.

Fuller, J F C, *Memoirs of an Unconventional Soldier*, Nicholson and Watson, London, 1936.

Gallagher, O D, *Retreat in the East*, Harrap, London, 1942.

General Staff HQ Ireland, *Record of the Rebellion in Ireland 1920–21* (two vols.).

Gilbert, M, *Winston S Churchill*, Volume 4, 1916–22, Heinemann, London, 1975.

Gilchrist, A, *Malaya 1941: Fall of a Fighting Empire*, Robert Hall, London, 1992.

Gillison, D, *The Royal Australian Air Force 1939–42*, Australian War Memorial, Canberra, 1966.

Gough, General Sir Hubert, *The Fifth Army*, Hodder and Stoughton, London, 1931.

Graves, R, *Goodbye To All That*, Cassell, London (rev. edit.), 1957.

Hamilton, N, *Monty: The Making of a General 1887–1942*, Hamish Hamilton, London, 1981.

Hancock, W K and Gowing, M M, *The British War Economy*, HMSO, London, 1949.

Hankey, D, *A Student in Arms*.

Harris, H J, *The Rugby School Corps 1860–1960*, Rugby School, 1962.

Hay, I, *The First Hundred Thousand – K1*, Blackwoods, London, 1915.

HMSO, *Convoys to North Russia 1942*, London Gazette Supplement, 13 Oct. 1950.

Holmes, R, and Kemp, A, *The Bitter End: The Fall of Singapore 1941–2*, Anthony Bird, Chichester, 1982.

Holt, E, *Protest in Arms*, Putnam, London, 1960.

Ironside, Field Marshal Lord, *Archangel 1918–19*, Constable, London, 1953.

Ismay, Lord, *The Memoirs of Lord Ismay*, Heinemann, London, 1960.

Kee, R, *Ourselves Alone*, Penguin edition, Harmondsworth, 1989.

Keegan, J (ed.), *Churchill's Generals*, Weidenfeld & Nicolson, London, 1991.

Kennedy, Major General Sir John, *The Business of War*, Hutchinson, London, 1957.

Kinvig, C, *River Kwai Railway*, Brassey's, London, 1992.

Kirby, Major General S W, *The War Against Japan*, Volume 1, HMSO, London, 1957.

———, *Singapore: The Chain of Disaster*, Cassell, London, 1971.

Labour Party, *Report of the Labour Commission to Ireland*, Labour Party, London, 1921.

Leasor, J, *Singapore: The Battle that Changed the World*, Hodder and Stoughton, London, 1968.

Lee, B, *Marching Orders*, Crown, New York, 1994.

Legg, F, *The Gordon Bennett Story*, Angus and Robertson, 1965.

Leighton, R M, and Coaklet, R W, *Global Logistics and Strategy 1940–43*, Department of the Army, Washington, 1955.

Lewin, R, *The Chief*, Hutchinson, London, 1980.

Liverpool, Lord Russell of, *That Reminds Me*, Cassell, London, 1959.

Lodge, A B, *The Fall of General Gordon Bennett*, Allen and Unwin, London, 1986.

Lowe, T A, 'Some Reflections of a Junior Commander upon "The Campaign" in Ireland 1920 and 1921', *Army Quarterly*, Vol. V, No. 1, Oct., 1922.

Luckett, R, *The White Generals*, Longmans, London, 1971.

Macardle, D, *The Irish Republic*, Gollancz, London, 1937.

Mackenzie, C, *Eastern Epic*, Volume 1, Chatto and Windus, London, 1951.

Macmillan, H, *Winds of Change*, Macmillan, London, 1966.

Maurice, General Sir Frederick, *18th Foot: The History of the Bedfordshire and Hertfordshire Regiment*, Constable, London, 1931.

McDonnell, K K, *There is a Bridge at Bandon*, Mercier, Cork, 1972.

Montgomery, B, *Shenton of Singapore*, Leo Cooper, London, 1984.

Morrison, I, *Malayan Postscript*, Faber and Faber, 1942.

Nichols, Captain G H F, *The 18th Division in the Great War*, Blackwoods, London, 1922.

Niven, Sir Rex, *Nigerian Kaleidoscope*, Hurst, London, 1982.

Owen, F, *The Fall of Singapore*, Michael Joseph, London, 1960.

Parker, P, *The Old Lie: The Great War and the Public School Ethos*, Constable, London, 1987.

Patterson, G, *A Spoonful of Rice with Salt*, Pentland, Durham, 1993.

Percival, Lieutenant General A E, *Operations of Malaya Command 8 Dec 1941–15 Feb 1942*, HMSO, London, 1948.

——, *The War in Malaya*, Eyre and Spottiswoode, London, 1949.

Probert, H, *The Forgotten Air Force: The Royal Air Force in the War Against Japan 1941–1945*, Brassey's, London, 1995.

Quex, 'The Return Push', *Blackwood's Magazine*, Feb. 1919.

Reid, B H, *War Studies and the Staff College 1893–1930*, Strategic and Combat Studies Institute, Camberley, 1992.

Richardson, General Sir Charles, *From Churchill's Secret Circle to the BBC*, Brassey's, London, 1991.

Rigby, B L, *Ever Glorious: The Story of the 22nd (Cheshire) Regiment, Volume 1*, The Cheshire Regt., Chester, 1982.

Risby, M, *Guilty or Innocent: The Gordon Bennett Case*, Allen & Unwin, Sydney, 1992.

Rose, A, *Who Dies Fighting*, Jonathan Cape, London, 1944.

Roskill, S W, *The War at Sea, Volume 1, The Defensive*, HMSO, London, 1954.

Russell of Liverpool, Lord, *That Reminds Me*, Cassell, London, 1959.

Russell Roberts, D, *Spotlight on Singapore*, Anthony Gibbs and Phillips, Douglas, IOM, 1965.

Sassoon, S, *Memoirs of a Fox-Hunting Man*, Faber, London, 1928.

Simkins, P, *Kitchener's Army*, Manchester UP, Manchester, 1988.

Simson, I, *Singapore: Too Little, Too Late*, Leo Cooper, London, 1970.

Singleton-Gates, G R, *Bolos and Barishnyas*, Gale and Polden, Aldershot, 1920.

Smyth, Sir John, *Percival and the Tragedy of Singapore*, Macdonald, London, 1971.

Soutar, A, *With Ironside in North Russia*, Hutchinson, London, 1940.

Spiers, E M, *The Army and Society 1815–1914*, Longman, London, 1980.

Stakhovsky, L I, *Intervention in Archangel*, Princeton UP, Princeton, 1944.

Swinson, A, *Four Samurai*, Hutchinson, London, 1968.

Taylor, A J P, *English History 1914–1945*, Oxford UP, London, 1975.

Townshend, C, *The British Campaign in Ireland 1919–21*, Oxford UP, London, 1975.

Trythall, A J, *'Boney' Fuller: The Intellectual General*, Cassell, London, 1977.

Tuke, Captain R, 'Lawyers in Khaki', *Army Quarterly*, Vol. XXXI, No. 1, Oct. 1935.

Turner, ES, *Gallant Gentlemen*, Michael Joseph, London, 1956.

Tsiji, M, *Singapore: The Japanese Version*, Mayflower, London, 1966.

Vlieland, C A, 'Singapore: The Legend and the Facts', *Daily Telegraph*, 13 Feb. 1967.

Westlake, R, *Kitchener's Army*, Nutshell Publishing, Tunbridge Wells, 1989.

Wigmore, L, *The Japanese Thrust*, Australian War Memorial, Canberra, 1957.

Willmott, H P, *Empires in the Balance*, Orbis, London, 1982.

Ziegler, P, *Diana Cooper*, Hamish Hamilton, London, 1981.

REFERENCES AND NOTES

Abbreviations used: Bedford County Record Office – BCR; Confidential Report – CR; Imperial War Museum – IWM; Liddell Hart Centre for Military Archives, King's College London – LHC; Military Secretary's Department, Ministry of Defence – MOD(MS); National Army Museum – NAM; Percival Papers held in IWM – PP; Percival Private Papers held by the Percival family – PPP; Public Record Office – PRO; Rhodes House Library (Bodleian Library), Oxford – RHL.

Full details of the published works referenced are given in the Bibliography.

Chapter 1 – Beginnings

1. Churchill to Ismay, 12 September 1944, quoted in Churchill, *Triumph and Tragedy*, p. 146.
2. Bridges, *Alarms and Excursions*, p. 78.

Chapter 2 – The Inns of Court OTC

1. Tuke, 'Lawyers in Khaki', *Army Quarterly*, Oct. 1935, pp. 139–144.
2. Based on Errington (ed.), *The Inns of Court Officer Training Corps During the Great War*.
3. Graves, *Goodbye To All That*, pp. 50–61.
4. Simkins, *Kitchener's Army*, pp. 221–222 .
5. Errington, *op. cit.*, p. 14.
6. Simpson, 'The Officers', in Beckett and Simpson (eds.), *A Nation in Arms*, p. 87.
7. Spiers, *The Army and Society 1815–1914*, p. 279.
8. Creedy Papers, IWM, cited in Simkins, *Kitchener's Army*, p. 212.
9. Errington, *op. cit.*, p. 12.
10. Hay, *The First Hundred Thousand: K1*, p. 7.

Chapter 3 – In Kitchener's Army

1. Attlee, *As It Happened*, p. 382.
2. Graves, *Goodbye To All That*, p. 61.
3. Macmillan, *Winds of Change*, p. 63.

  4. Bridges, *Alarms and Excursions*, p. 75.
  5. Turner, *Gallant Gentlemen*, p. 280.
  6. Kelly, *The Ruling Few*, pp. 89–90, cited in Simkins, *op. cit.*, p. 223.
  7. The Maxse Papers 69/53/5, IWM.
  8. Nichols, *The 18th Division in the Great War*, pp. 4–7.
  9. Simkins, *op. cit.*, p. 293.
 10. The Maxse Papers 69/53/5, IWM.
 11. Cited in Simkins, *op. cit.*, p. 252.
 12. The Maxse Papers, 69/53/5, IWM.

Chapter 4 – The Taste of War

The basic references for Chapters 4 and 5 are 7th Bedfords War Diary
and Percival's World War One scrapbook in three volumes, compiled after
the event but clearly based on contemporary notes and supplemented
with maps, reports, photographs and other documents.

  1. Nichols, *op. cit.*, p. 13.
  2. Letter to Alfred Percival, 27 August 1915, PPP.
  3. Hay, *op. cit.*, p. 230.
  4. Nichols, *op. cit.*, p. 17.
  5. Percival, WW1 Scrapbook, February–March 1916, P/16, PP, IWM.
  6. Quoted in 7th Bedfords War Diary, 27 April 1916, BCR.
  7. Report by CO, 7th Bedfords War Diary, 1 July 1916, BCR.
  8. Quoted in 7th Bedfords War Diary, 1 July 1916, BCR.
  9. The Maxse Papers, 69/53/7, IWM.
 10. Letter to Alfred Percival, 4 July 1916, PPP.
 11. Percival, WW1 Scrapbook, 26 September 1916.
 12. Quoted in 7th Bedfords War Diary, BCR.
 13. Percival, WW1 Scrapbook, 3 May 1917.
 14. *Ibid.*, 15 October 1917.
 15. Nichols, *op. cit.*, p. 218–219.

Chapter 5 – The Test of Command

  1. Percival, WW1 Scrapbook, 28 January 1918, PP, IWM.
  2. *Ibid.*, 20 March 1918.
  3. Letter to Alfred Percival, 29 March 1918, PPP.
  4. Quoted in 7th Bedfords War Diary, BCR.
  5. Letter to Alfred Percival, 29 March 1918, PPP.
  6. Percival, WW1 Scrapbook, 2 July 1918.
  7. *Ibid.*, 22 August 1918.
  8. *Ibid.*, 8–23 September 1918.
  9. Maurice, *18th Foot*, p. 220.
 10. Based on Errington, *op. cit.*, Appendix II.
 11. Quex, 'The Return Push', *Blackwood's Magazine*, February 1919.
 12. CR for 1918, MOD (MS).

Chapter 6 – The North Russian Relief Force

1. Ironside, *Archangel 1918–1919*, pp. 11–14.
2. *Ibid.*, p. 55.
3. Churchill, *The World Crisis: The Aftermath*, p. 234.
4. Radcliffe memorandum quoted in Gilbert, *Winston S. Churchill*, Vol. IV. p. 270.
5. Wilson Diary quoted in Gilbert, *op. cit.*, p. 283.
6. Allfrey, *Five Months with 45th Battalion Royal Fusiliers in North Russia*, 86/86/1 IWM, p. 1.
7. Singleton Gates, *Bolos and Barishynas*, p. 2.
8. Letter to Alfred Percival, 10 June 1919, PPP.
9. Ironside, *op. cit.*, p. 147.
10. *Ibid.*, p. 43.
11. Allfrey, *op. cit.*, p. 151.
12. Letter to Alfred Percival, 16 August 1919, PPP.
13. Allfrey, *op. cit.*, p. 120.
14. Operation Report, Gorodok Column, P/19, PP, IWM; Singleton Gates, *op. cit.*, pp. 120–124; Ironside, *op. cit.*, p. 168.
15. Letter to Alfred Percival, 16 August 1919, PPP.
16. Operation Report, No 3 Sector Dwina River, 15 August 1919, P/19, PP, IWM.
17. Singleton Gates, *op. cit.*, p. 120.
18. Rawlinson Diary quoted in Gilbert, *Churchill*, Vol. IV, p. 316.
19. Allfrey, *op. cit.*, p. 158.
20. Quoted in Singleton Gates, *op. cit.*, p. 170–171.
21. *Ibid.*

Chapter 7 – Ireland: The Insurgency Develops

1. Townshend, *The British Campaign in Ireland 1919–21*, p. 1.
2. Taylor, *English History 1914–45*, p. 104.
3. Lowe, 'Some Reflections of a Junior Commander upon "The Campaign" in Ireland 1920 and 1921', *Army Quarterly*, October 1922, p. 51.
4. Barry, *Guerrilla Days in Ireland*, pp. 5–7.
5. Burrows, *The Essex Regiment*, p. 270.
6. Percival, 'Guerrilla Warfare – Ireland 1920–21' (two lectures), P/18, PP, IWM, lecture 1.
7. Wilson Diary quoted in Gilbert, *Churchill*, Companion Volume IV, Part 2, p. 451.
8. Percival, 'Guerrilla Warfare', lecture 1, P/18, PP, IWM.
9. Barry, *op. cit.*, p. 14.
10. Memo of 2 July 1920, cited in Townshend, *op. cit.*, p. 88.
11. Cited in Townshend, *op. cit.*, p. 63. This is a considerably greater total than Barry claims for the whole brigade. The McDonnell account also suggests that Barry underestimates the strength of the local IRA armoury.
12. Percival, 'Guerrilla Warfare', lecture 1, P/18, PP, IWM.

13. McDonnell, *There is a Bridge at Bandon*, p. 157.
14. Percival, 'Guerrilla Warfare', lecture 1; Weekly Sitrep by GOC-in-C Ireland, w.e. 3 August 1920, CAB 27/108, PRO.
15. Percival, 'Guerrilla Warfare', lecture 1, P/18, PP, IWM.
16. Weekly Sitrep by GOC-in-C Ireland, w.e. 3 August 1921, CAB 27/108, PRO.
17. Suggested by a member of an Essex Regiment family.
18. Barry, *op. cit.*, p. 15.
19. General Staff, War Office, *Record of the Rebellion in Ireland*, Vol. 1. p. 21, 72/82/2, Jeudwine Papers, IWM.
20. McDonnell, *op. cit.*, p. 162–163.
21. CR for 1920, MOD (MS).
22. McDonnell, *loc. cit.*
23. Holt, *Protest in Arms*, p. 217.
24. Townshend, *op. cit.*, p. 84.
25. Cuthbert to Alfred Percival, 7 December 1920, PPP.
26. Barry, *op. cit.*, p. 27.
27. Percival, 'Guerrilla Warfare', lecture 2, P/18, PP, IWM.
28. Barry, *op. cit.*, p. 24.
29. McDonnell, *op. cit.*, p. 122–126.
30. *Ibid.*
31. Barry, *op. cit.*, p. 127.

Chapter 8 – Ireland: The Mobile Columns

1. Barry, *op. cit.*, pp. 19–20.
2. Percival, 'Guerrilla Warfare', lecture 1, P/18, PP, IWM.
3. Lowe, *op. cit.*, p. 51.
4. General Staff, War Office, *Record of the Rebellion in Ireland*, Vol. 1, Appx 2, p. 60, 72/82/2, Jeudwine Papers, IWM.
5. Memorandum to General Chetwode, quoted in Gilbert, *Churchill*, companion volume IV, part 2, p. 1,226.
6. Percival, 'Guerrilla Warfare', lecture 1, P/18, PP, IWM.
7. McDonnell, *op. cit.*, p. 120.
8. Lowe, *op. cit.*, p. 52.
9. Barry, *op. cit.*, p. 123.
10. Percival, 'Guerrilla Warfare', lecture 2, P/18, PP, IWM.
11. *Ibid.*
12. Special Order of the Day, 25 February 1921, *Record of the Rebellion in Ireland*, Vol. 1, p. 63, 72/82/2, Jeudwine Papers, IWM.
13. *Irish Times*, 14 March 1921.
14. CR for 1921, MOD (MS).
15. Smyth, *Percival and the Tragedy of Singapore*, p. 36.
16. CR for 1921, MOD (MS).
17. Coogan, *Michael Collins*, p. 147.
18. Hamilton, *Monty: The Making of a General 1887–1942*, p. 158.

19. Barry, *op. cit.*, p. 91.
20. *Ibid.*
21. Russell, *That Reminds Me*, pp. 74–76.
22. Barry, *op. cit.*, pp. 89–93.
23. Barry, *op. cit.*, pp. 195–198.
24. Percival, 'Guerrilla Warfare', lecture 2, P/18, PP, IWM.
25. *Ibid.*
26. Lowe, *op. cit.*, p. 58.
27. Speech to Dail Eireann, 21 December 1921.
28. Quoted in Townshend, *op. cit.*, p 112.
29. Percival, 'Guerrilla Warfare', lecture 2, P/18, PP, IWM.
30. *Ibid.*
31. Montgomery to Percival, 14 October 1923, P/18, PP, IWM.
32. Russell, *op. cit.*, pp. 69–70.
33. Burrows, *op. cit.*, p. 276.

Chapter 9 – From Staff College to Singapore

1. Reid, *War Studies and the Staff College 1890–1930*, p. 13.
2. War Office Press release, 1941.
3. Reid, *op. cit.*, p. 14.
4. Fuller, *Memoirs of an Unconventional Soldier*, pp. 417–418, quoted in Reid, *op. cit.*, p. 18.
5. Trythall, *'Boney' Fuller*, p. 96.
6. Smyth, *op. cit.*, p. 39.
7. CR 1924, MOD (MS).
8. Niven, *Nigerian Kaleidoscope*, p. 78.
9. Report by Director RN Staff College, 1930, MOD (MS).
10. Smyth, *op. cit.*, p. 40.
11. Brigadier B L Rigby to the author.
12. The author is indebted to General Sir Charles Harington, Major General J H Cubbon and Brigadier B L Rigby, all young Cheshires at the time, in developing this pen picture.
13. Rigby, *Ever Glorious*, p. 455.
14. CR 1934, MOD (MS).
15. This contrast was suggested by General Sir Charles Harington.
16. Lecture manuscript, PPP.
17. MOD(MS) to Percival, 16 September, 21 September and 8 October 1935; Percival to MOD (MS), 21 September 1935, PPP.

Chapter 10 – First Round in Malaya

1. Ismay, *The Memoirs of Lord Ismay*, p. 236.
2. Allen, *Singapore 1941–42*, p. 39.
3. Churchill, *The Gathering Storm*, p. 127.
4. The note was by Lieutenant Colonel S W Kirby, later one of the Official Historians of *The War Against Japan*, P/41, PP, IWM.

5. 'Deductions from Japanese appreciation of the attack on the fortress of Singapore 1937', P/39, PP, IWM.
6. Montgomery, *Shenton of Singapore*, p. 32.
7. Memorandum to GOC dated 13 January 1937, P/41, PP, IWM.
8. Percival's handover notes to his successor, P/39, PP, IWM.
9. Comments to GOC on Staff Paper on Local Forces, P/39, PP, IWM.
10. Memorandum on the Defence of the Fortress of Singapore, May 1937, P/41, PP, IWM.
11. Allen, *op. cit.*, citing Japanese source.
12. Comments on Staff Paper on Fortress Security, P/39, PP, IWM.
13. *Ibid.*
14. Kirby, *Singapore: The Chain of Disaster*, p. 30.
15. Percival to Official Historian, 3 November 1954, CAB 101/148, PRO.
16. Memorandum on the Defence of the Fortress of Singapore, May 1937, P/41, PP, IWM.
17. Percival to Brooke Popham, 4 August 1946, Brooke Popham Papers, V/8/40, LHC.
18. Percival, *The War in Malaya*, p. 43.
19. Percival to Official Historian, 23 November 1954, CAB 101/148, PRO.
20. Deductions from the appreciation are given at Annex A to Despatch of GOC Malaya dated 25 April 1946.
21. Clarke to Dobbie, 9 December 1937, P/39, PP, IWM.

Chapter 11 – Frantic Interlude

1. CRs for 1936 and 1937, MOD (MS).
2. CR for 1932, MOD (MS).
3. Percival, *The War in Malaya*, p. 23.
4. P/68-69, PP, IWM.
5. Dill to Percival, 15 February 1940, P/88, PP.
6. Avon, *The Eden Memoirs: The Reckoning*, p. 109.
7. Cloake, *Templer: Tiger of Malaya*, p. 81.
8. Major General J H Cubbon to the author.
9. Churchill, *The Hinge of Fate*, p. 84.
10. Churchill, *Their Finest Hour*, p. 385.
11. *Ibid.*, pp. 592–593.
12. Probert, *The Forgotten Air Force*, pp. 19–20, quoting Air Historical Branch Narrative.
13. Kirby, *The War Against Japan*, Volume 1, p. 55.
14. Kennedy, *The Business of War*, pp. 108–113.
15. Bryant, *The Turn of the Tide*, p. 277.

Chapter 12 – GOC Malaya Command

1. Betty to Arthur Percival 14 September 1939.
2. Brooke Popham to Ismay, 5 December 1940, Brooke Popham Papers, V/1/3, LHC.

3. Brooke Popham to PUS of S (Air), 15 January 1941, Brooke Popham Papers, V/2/3, LHC.
4. Percival, *The War in Malaya*, p. 30.
5. Kirby, *Singapore*, p. 40–41
6. Montgomery, *op. cit.*, p. 38.
7. Brett-James, *Ball of Fire*, p. 16.
8. Wigmore, *The Japanese Thrust*, p. 97.
9. Brooke Popham to Ismay, 19 April 1941, Brooke Popham Papers, V/1/10, LHC.
10. Percival to Dill, 15 October 1941, Dill Papers, 67/274/1, IWM.
11. Diary of Megan Spooner, 27 August 1941, LHC.
12. Kirby, *Singapore*, p. 95.
13. Ashmore, 'Some Personal Observations of the Malayan Campaign 1940–42', P/49, PP, IWM.
14. *Ibid.*
15. Ismay to Brooke Popham, 15 June 1941, Brooke Popham Papers, V/1/13, LHC.
16. Probert, *op. cit.*, p. 28.
17. Percival, *Despatch*, para. 47.
18. This was contested by the Air Ministry after the war, though they admitted they were not '. . . on strong enough ground to press the matter very forcibly', Brooke Popham Papers, V/8/36-45, LHC; Percival to Professor Butler, 7 January 1962, P/88, PP, IWM. See also Chapter 20.
19. Percival, *The War in Malaya*, p. 64.
20. Rose, *Who Dies Fighting*, p. 9.
21. Ashmore, *op. cit.*, PP, IWM.
22. Wigmore, *op. cit.*, p. 103; Churchill, *The Grand Alliance*, p. 418; HMSO, *Convoys to North Russia 1942*; Hancock and Gowing, *The British War Economy*, pp. 362–364.
23. Bryant, *op. cit.*, p. 263.
24. Ismay, *op. cit.*, p. 232.
25. Alanbrooke diary, 30 January 1942, Alanbrooke Papers, LHC.
26. Chiefs of Staff to C-in-C Far East, 17 September 1941, cited in Kirby, *The War Against Japan*, Volume 1, p. 78.
27. Ziegler, *Diana Cooper*, p. 207.
28. Cooper, Diana, *Autobiography: Trumpets from the Steep* (one volume edition), Michael Russell, Salisbury 1979, p. 589.
29. Churchill to Brooke Popham, 6 November 1941, Brooke Popham Papers, V/5/1, LHC.
30. Brooke Popham to Portal, 7 November 1941, Brooke Popham Papers, V/5/5, LHC.
31. Ziegler, *op. cit.*, p. 212; Cooper, *op. cit.*, p. 613.

Chapter 13 – The Japanese Invade

1. See for example Gilchrist, *Malaya 1941: The Fall of a Fighting Empire*, Appendix A.
2. Ashmore, *op. cit.*
3. Percival, *Despatch*, para. 124.
4. Kirby, *The War Against Japan*, Volume 1, p. 182; War Diary HQ Malaya Command, 7 December 1941, WO 172/17, PRO.
5. War Diary HQ Malaya Command, 8 December 1941, WO 172/17, PRO.
6. Heath Papers, LMH 4, IWM.
7. War Diary HQ Far East, WO 172/75, PRO.
8. This possibility was first suggested to me by Mr Peter Elphick and has some corroboration from Major (later General Sir John) Westall RM who was senior intelligence officer on Admiral Layton's staff at the time and in close touch with the Far East Combined Bureau (FECB). He wrote of the intelligence information, 'Further action would have been taken on these reports had it not been for the fact that up-to-date information from "these particular sources" was treated as being so secret that no action on it could be taken.' ADM 233/494, PRO.
9. Heath later claimed not to have known that the MATADOR decision had been delegated to Brooke Popham from London. Heath to Brigadier Blood, CAB 106/190, PRO.
10. 5/14 Punjab did not begin its journey from Penang until 3.30pm on 8 December, having a wakeful night before they reached Kroh in the early hours of 9 December. War Diary of 5/14 Punjab Regiment, 9204-208-1, NAM.
11. Probert, *op. cit.*, p. 30.
12. Kirby, *Singapore*, pp. 113–116.
13. Probert, loc. cit.
14. Kirby, *The War Against Japan*, Volume 1, p. 205.
15. Allen, *op. cit.*, p. 119. This total is from Japanese sources. The squadron concerned estimated much greater Japanese losses. Probert, *op. cit.*, p. 41.
16. Probert, *op. cit.*, p. 42.
17. Allen, loc. cit.
18. Probert, *op. cit.*, p. 44.
19. Lecture to 2nd Argylls, Heath Papers, LMH4, IWM.
20. War Diary HQ Malaya Command, 9 December 1941, WO172/17, PRO.
21. Percival to Brigadier Blood, Cabinet Office, 5 December 1951, CAB106/190, PRO.

Chapter 14 – Jitra and After

1. Allen, *op. cit.*, p. 27.
2. '25 Army Operations in Malaya Nov 41–Mar 42', AL 1066, IWM.
3. *Ibid.* Tsuji, *Singapore: The Japanese Version*, p. 112.

4. Ashmore, *op. cit.*
5. War Diary of 5/14 Punjab Regiment, 11 December 1941, 9204-208-1, NAM.
6. Ashmore, *op. cit.*
7. Brooke Popham, *Despatch*, Appendix M.
8. Probert, *op. cit.*, p. 49. There were six copies of the Court's findings, apparently all destroyed by enemy action.
9. Brooke Popham Papers, V/5/49, LHC.
10. Quoted in Elphick, *Singapore: The Pregnable Fortress*, p. 230.
11. Changi Lecture, Heath Papers, LMH/4, IWM.
12. Kirby, *The War Against Japan*, Volume 1, p. 78.
13. *Daily Mail*, 9 December 1941.
14. Rose, *op. cit.*, p. 11.
15. Changi Lecture, Heath Papers, LMH/4, IWM.
16. HQ Far East War Diary, WO 172/15, PRO.
17. See Elphick and Smith, *The Singapore Traitor*.
18. Cooper, D, *op. cit.*, p. 608.
19. Bryant, *The Turn of the Tide 1934–45*, p. 282.
20. WO 172/15, PRO.
21. 'Notes on My Life', p. 351, Alanbrooke Papers, 3/A/V, LHC.
22. Charmley, *Duff Cooper*, p. 157.

Chapter 15 – Territory versus Time

1. For an outline of the cannibalisation of the Malayan Railways see Kinvig, *River Kwai Railway*, p. 51–52.
2. Morrison, *Malayan Postscript*, p. 70.
3. Montgomery, *Shenton of Singapore*, p. 94.
4. Owen, *The Fall of Singapore*, p. 84.
5. Kirby, *The War Against Japan*, Volume 1, p. 233.
6. Percival, *The War in Malaya*, p. 153.
7. Kirby, *The War Against Japan*, Volume 1, p. 259.
8. Kirby, *Singapore*, pp. 159–160.
9. Maltby, *Despatch*, para. 245.
10. Bond (ed.), *Chief of Staff*, pp. 69–71.
11. Allen, *Singapore 1941–42*, p. 149.

Chapter 16 – Farewell to Malaya

1. Connell, *Wavell: Supreme Commander*, p. 81.
2. Smyth, *op. cit.*, p. 154.
3. Smyth, *op. cit.*, pp. 156–157. No one was in a better position to judge: Smyth commanded 17th Indian Division. It was he who had summoned the DMT to confirm the unpreparedness of his force for action. He later had the Gurkha brigade fighting for him.
4. Bond (ed.), *Chief of Staff*, p. 76.
5. Kirby, *Singapore*, p. 185.

6. Heath to Percival, undated post-war letter, Heath Papers, LMH7, IWM.
7. Kirby, *Singapore*, p. 185.
8. Wavell to Chiefs of Staff, 9 January 1942, quoted in Connell, *op. cit.*, pp. 87–88.
9. WO 172/20, PRO.
10. Quoted in Montgomery, *op. cit.*, p.124.
11. 18 December 1941, CO 967/77, PRO.
12. Kirby, *Singapore*, p. 195.
13. Callaghan, *The Worst Disaster*, p. 191.
14. Thomas, 'War Diary', 9 January 1942, quoted in Montgomery, *op. cit.*, p. 109.
15. Air Historical Branch Narrative, quoted in Probert, *op. cit.*, p. 53.
16. *Despatch*, paras 275–276
17. Wigmore, *op. cit.*, p. 212.
18. In December Percival had issued a paper giving information on Japanese tactics and instructions on countering them. He had emphasised the use of the kind of box ambush Bennett was planning.
19. Quoted in Connell, *op. cit.*, p. 95.
20. Account of Brigadier G G Ballantine, 44th Indian Infantry Brigade, 7309-2-1, NAM.
21. Rose, *op. cit.*, p. 93.
22. See, for example, account of Captain F E Mileham, 4/9 Jats, who wrote of 'signs of potential mutiny' in his battalion after the Muar battle. 9102-302-1, NAM.
23. Maltby, *Despatch*, paras. 347–353.
24. Probert, *op. cit.*
25. Percival, *Despatch*, para. 372.
26. Rose, *op. cit.*, p. 98.
27. Kirby, *The War Against Japan*, Volume 1, p. 340.
28. The fault was that of Brigadier Lay. Even the official historian points an unmistakable finger in his direction. Lay had done well earlier in the campaign and had later been put on extended sick leave by Percival, who subsequently switched him to 8th Brigade. Short of everything else, Percival was also short of experienced brigadiers.
29. Brigadier Painter and Lieutenant Colonel Parkin, correspondence with official historian, CAB 106/190, PRO.

Chapter 17 – The Fantasy Fortress

1. Jacob to Ismay, 24 January 1959, Ismay Papers, I/14/69, LHC.
2. Kennedy, *op. cit.*, p. 196.
3. Note by Lieutenant Colonel Phillips, formerly GSO 1 (O), Malaya Command. Pownall Diaries December 1941–March 1942, Pownall Papers, LHC.
4. Kennedy, *op. cit.*, p. 196.
5. *Ibid.*

6. Churchill, *The Hinge of Fate*, p. 49.
7. Given in full in Churchill, *Their Finest Hour*, p. 591.
8. The issue of defences and the obstructiveness of the civilian bureaucracy in Singapore are the themes of Simson's book, *Singapore: Too Little, Too Late*. This was not published until after Percival's death.
9. Brooke Popham Papers, V/8/10/2, LHC, quoted in Elphick, *op. cit.*, p. 285.
10. Simson, *op. cit.*, pp. 62–63.
11. *Ibid.*
12. *Despatch*, para. 436.
13. Wavell to Percival, 19 January 1942, quoted in Connell, *op. cit.*, p. 111.
14. Diary of Megan Spooner, 26 December 1941, LHC.
15. Kirby, *The War Against Japan*, Volume 1, pp. 318–319; Wavell, *Despatch*, para. 24.
16. Percival, *Despatch*, para. 459; *The War in Malaya*, p. 261.
17. Kirby, *Singapore: The Chain of Disaster*, p. 221.
18. Harrison, *11th Division in Malaya*, quoted in Smyth, *op. cit.*, p. 218.
19. Kirby, *The War Against Japan*, p.319.
20. Ashmore, *op. cit.*, p. 18. This was written in India in July 1942 when the events were still fresh in his mind.
21. Captain A N Grey RN to mother, 27 February 1942, The Grey Papers, IWM.
22. He now had eight Hurricanes and six Buffaloes on the island.
23. Colonels J H Thyer and C H Kappe, 'Operations of 8th Australian Division in Malaya', p. 93, CAB 106/162, PRO.
24. Percival, *Despatch*, p. 134.
25. Ashmore, *op. cit.*
26. Falk, *Seventy Days to Singapore*, pp. 223–224.
27. Colonel Thyer to the official historians, 19 January 1953, CAB 106/151, PRO.
28. Thyer and Kappe, *op. cit.*
29. When Brooke Popham had been in charge, his staff had discounted intelligence reports of Japanese invasion plans as 'alarmist and defeatist'. Captain Grey, 'Fall of Singapore and Dutch East Indies and Defence of Ceylon', Grey Papers, IWM.
30. Ashmore, *op. cit.*, p. 19.
31. War Diary HQ Malaya Command, WO 172/21, PRO.
32. *Ibid.*

Chapter 18 – A Grievous and Shameful Blow

1. Probert, *op. cit.*, p. 61.
2. Captain A N Grey, 'Fall of Singapore and Dutch East Indies and Defence of Ceylon', Grey Papers, IWM.
3. Lieutenant Colonel F G Galleghan to Official Historians, CAB 106/151, PRO.

4. Account of Brigadier G C Ballantine, 7309-2-1, NAM.

5. Grey, *op. cit.*

6. Gilchrist, *Malaya 1941*, p. 161.

7. Jacob, diary entry, 28 December 1941, quoted in Richardson, *From Churchill's Secret Circle to the BBC*, pp. 93–94.

8. James, *Rise and Fall of the Japanese Empire*, quoted in Elphick, *op. cit.*, p. 304.

9. Report of Lieutenant Colonel Phillips, WO 106/2573C, PRO.

10. Ashmore, *op. cit.*, p. 25.

11. G Patterson, *A Spoonful of Rice with Salt*, p. 34.

12. Percival, 'Record of the Fort Canning Conferences', P/31, PP, IWM.

13. Churchill, *The Hinge of Fate*, p. 91.

14. *Ibid.*, p. 92.

15. Percival, *The War in Malaya*, p. 287.

16. Ashmore, *op. cit.*, pp. 25–26.

17. Kirby, *The War Against Japan*, Volume 1, pp. 411–412.

18. McNeill in interview with Sybilla Jane Flower.

19. Percival, 'Record of the Fort Canning Conferences', P/31, PP, IWM.

20. *Ibid.* The timing of the cease-fire was later the subject of misunderstanding. Heath, believing what interpreter Wild merely assumed and told him unofficially, thought the earlier 4pm proposal had been agreed and put out orders to that effect. These were later rescinded on Percival's orders and the correct cease-fire time observed. Heath was 'severely taken to task by General Percival' the following morning, since the misunderstanding resulted in casualties. Another source of acrimony between them.

21. Major C H D Wild, 'Note on the Capitulation of Singapore', Heath Papers, IWM.

22. Kirby, *The War Against Japan*, Volume 1, pp. 414–415; '25th Army Operations in Malaya Nov 41–Mar 42', AL 1066, IWM; Patterson, *op. cit.*, p. 36, and discussions with the author.

23. J B Bradley, *The Tall Man Who Never Slept*, p. 35. This information is from Major Wild who also interrogated Yamashita at the end of the war.

24. L Allen, 'The Surrender of Singapore: The Official Japanese Version', *Durham University Journal*, New Series, Vol. XXIX, No. 1, December 1967, p. 3.

25. L. Allen, *Singapore 1941–1942*, p. 183

26. Japanese Defence Agency, *Mare Shinko Sakusen* (The Campaign in Malaya), pp. 621–622, translated by and quoted in Allen, 'The Surrender of Singapore: The Official Japanese Version', pp. 1–2.

27. This was not an afterthought as the British Official History seems to suggest, but had been stated in writing earlier as a specific item by the British side. Allen, 'The Surrender of Singapore', p. 6.

Chapter 19 – Captivity

1. Churchill, *The Hinge of Fate*, p. 81.
2. *Ibid.*, p. 94.
3. Russell Roberts, D, *Spotlight on Singapore*, p. 294.
4. Kennedy, *op. cit.*, p. 183.
5. Bryant, *op. cit.*, p. 285.
6. Alanbrooke, 'Notes on My Life', p. 332, Alanbrooke Papers, LHC.
7. Ismay, *Memoirs*, p. 241.
8. Ismay to Brooke Popham, 9 February 1941, Brooke Popham Papers, V/1/6, LHC.
9. *Sunday Times*, 27 June 1971.
10. Playfair, *The Mediterranean and the Middle East*, Volume 2, p. 262; Brooke Popham, *Despatch*, paras 573–574.
11. Alanbrooke diary, 25 February 1942, quoted in Bryant, *op. cit.*, p. 376.
12. Ismay to General Sir Henry Jackson, 18 February 1959, Ismay Papers, LHC.
13. Alanbrooke, 'Notes on My Life', p. 351, Alanbrooke Papers, LHC.
14. Dean, *The RAF and Two World Wars*, quoted in Probert, *op. cit.*, p. 35.
15. *Hansard* 378, HC Debates 61, quoted in Allen, *Singapore 1941–42*, p. 17.
16. The Australian, British and Indian Official Histories all use the higher figure. Falk, *op. cit.*, p. 271 and Elphick, *Singapore*, p. 187, both consider the figures for reinforcements were miscalculated and give an estimate close to Percival's total.
17. Allen, *Singapore 1941–42*, p. 271; Percival, *Despatch*, p. 132; Kirby, *The War Against Japan*, Volume 1, p. 543; Interrogation Report AL 902 'Japanese 25th Army Order of Battle', IWM; Colonel Shigemi Mizobe, Institute of Defence Studies, JDA Tokyo to the author, 25 May 1995.
18. '25 Army Operations in Malaya Nov 1941–Mar 1942', AL1066, IWM.
19. Curiously enough it was Percival's old regiment, 1st Essex, in a brigade commanded by Brigadier W Slim, which broke.
20. Compare Kirby, *Singapore*, p. 129 with the military biography at Annex A.
21. Jacob to Callahan, 14 January 1971, quoted in Callahan, *op. cit.*, p. 272.
22. Key to Smyth, 29 December 1969, quoted in Smyth, *op. cit.*, p. 261.
23. Bond, *op. cit.*, p. 76.
24. Brigadier Simson in evidence to Official Historian.
25. 'Report on Operations in Malaya and Singapore', Wavell's secret report to the Prime Minister, PREM 3/168/3, PRO.
26. Colonel A M L Harrison, '11th Indian Division in Malaya', PP, IWM.
27. Key to Smyth, 29 December 1969, quoted in Smyth, *op. cit.*, p. 264.
28. Campaign narrative written by Lieutenant Colonel F R N Cobley on Percival's instructions, Changi 1942, P/75, PP, IWM.
29. Percival to Heath during captivity, P/26, PP, IWM.
30. PREM 3/168/4 (released 1993), PRO.

31. WO 106/2573C (released 1993), PRO. Elphick's ground-breaking study, *Singapore: The Pregnable Fortress*, pp. 299–338, suggests that Australian deserters may have exceeded 8,000.
32. Ashmore, *op. cit.*, pp. 25–26.
33. Churchill, *The Hinge of Fate*, pp. 49–50.
34. PPP.
35. P/26, PP, IWM.
36. Brigadier F H Fraser, Awards/FE 1446/PW2, MOD (MS).
37. Thyer to Smyth 4 February 1970, quoted in Smyth, *op. cit.*, p. 262.
38. P/26, PP, IWM.
39. *Evening Standard*, 14 April 1947.
40. Percival to Smyth, 11 September 1945, Smyth Papers, IWM.
41. Percival, *The War in Malaya*, p. 326.

Chapter 20 – Peacework

1. George Lambert MP to *Daily Telegraph*.
2. Major H C Phillips to Mrs Percival, 7 July 1942, PPP.
3. Lord Croft to Alfred Percival, 6 August 1942, PPP.
4. Percival to Heath, 14 May 1946, Heath Papers, IWM.
5. Awards/FE 1446/PW2, MOD (MS).
6. Percival to Heath, 14 May 1946, Heath Papers, IWM.
7. Brooke Popham to Brockman (Air SD) 27 July 1946, Brooke Popham Papers, V/8/38/3, LHC.
8. *Ibid.*
9. 2 April 1947, Brooke Popham Papers, V/8/41/1, LHC.
10. Percival to Brooke Popham, 4 August 1946, Brooke Popham Papers, V/8/40, LHC.
11. Comments on General Percival's *Despatch*, Shenton Thomas Papers, RHL.
12. Thomas to Percival 15 August 1947, Percival to Thomas 17 August 1947, Shenton Thomas Papers, RHL.
13. *The Times*, 13 August 1947.
14. Thomas to Colonial Office, 22 August 1947, Shenton Thomas Papers, RHL.
15. Ministry of Information to Percival, 2 December 1947.
16. Kirby to Percival, 16 December 1953, P/42 PP, IWM.
17. Kirby to Percival, 14 June 1954, P/42, PP, IWM.
18. *The Times*, 27 February 1948.
19. *Sydney Morning Herald*, 27 February 1948.
20. *Manchester Guardian*, 27 February 1948.
21. *Scotsman*, 27 April 1949.
22. *Time and Tide*, 7 May 1949.
23. Thyer to Percival, 13 July 1949, P/28, PP, IWM.
24. W R Dovey to Percival, P/28, PP, IWM.
25. Pownall to Percival, 21 January 1949, P/28, PP, IWM.

26. Percival to Frank Owen, March 1959, P/44, PP, IWM.
27. Pownall to Percival, 25 October 1951, P/88, PP, IWM.
28. *Truth*, 13 May 1949.
29. For the POWs' (and Japanese) grievances about the film, see Kinvig, *River Kwai Railway*, pp. xii–xiii and 46.
30. Percival to Lieutenant Colonel H S Flower, 15 October 1956, private collection.
31. Percival to Official Historians, CAB 103/340, PRO.
32. Advisory Panel Meeting, 10 April 1953, CAB 103/340, PRO.
33. Percival to Kirby, 22 November 1954.
34. Briefing Note, Kirby to Percival, P/41, PP, IWM.
35. Smyth, *op. cit.*, p. 294.
36. Kirby to Percival, 16 December 1953, P/42, PP, IWM.
37. Wavell, *Despatch*, para. 21.
38. Percival to Kirby, 2 December 1953.
39. *Daily Mail*, 15 November 1957.
40. Quoted in Smyth, *op. cit.*, p. 295.
41. Secret Session Speech, 23 April 1942. Eade, *The War Speeches of Winston Churchill*, Vol. 2, p. 242.
42. Churchill, *The Hinge of Fate*, p. 81.
43. Churchill, *Their Finest Hour*, p. 243.
44. Charmley, *Churchill: The End of Glory*, p. 487.

INDEX